GAME CHANGERS

GAME CHANGERS

What Leaders, Innovators and Mavericks Do to Win at Life

DAVE ASPREY

Thorsons

Thorsons
An imprint of HarperCollins*Publishers*
1 London Bridge Street
London SE1 9GF

www.harpercollins.co.uk

First published in the US by Harper Wave,
an imprint of HarperCollins*Publishers* 2018
This UK edition published 2018

1 3 5 7 9 10 8 6 4 2

A catalogue record of this book is
available from the British Library

ISBN 978-0-00-831863-5

Printed and bound in Great Britain by
CPI Group (UK) Ltd, Croydon

MIX
Paper from
responsible sources
FSC™ C007454

To Bill Harris, one of the most charitable and game-changing brain hackers I've been honored to call a friend, who passed away during the writing of this book.

CONTENTS

INTRODUCTION

What would happen if you sat down, one on one, with 450 successful, unusually impactful people and asked each of them their secrets to performing better as a human being based on their own life experience—and then took the time to statistically analyze their replies and organize what you'd learned?

For one thing, you would be able to use the resulting data to create a word map like the one below. The bigger the word, the more times the experts said it mattered most.

For the past five years, I've been having those conversations with people who are unusually noteworthy in their fields, and this book is based on those interviews and that data.

It all began when I first launched my podcast, *Bulletproof Radio*, with the goal of learning from people who had gained mastery in their respective fields—often in fields they themselves had pioneered. Since then, it has evolved into an award-winning podcast that is consistently rated as one of the top performers in its category on iTunes with about

75 million downloads. My interest in interviewing these experts was originally born out of my now nineteen-year, multimillion-dollar personal crusade to upgrade myself using every tool in existence. This journey took me from antiaging facilities around the world to the offices of neuroscientists to remote monasteries in Tibet to Silicon Valley. I left no stone unturned in my obsessive mission to discover the simplest and most effective things I could do to become better at everything.

Obviously, I needed help.

So I sought advice from maverick scientists, world-class athletes, biochemists, innovative MDs, shamans, Olympic nutritionists, meditation experts, Navy SEALs, leaders in personal development, and anyone else who had an unusual ability or knowledge that I could learn from. Those people changed my life. Using their cumulative wisdom coupled with my own research and endless self-experimentation, I was finally able to lose the hundred pounds of excess weight that had plagued me for decades. My perpetual brain fog lifted, and so did my IQ. I grew a six-pack for the first time in my life—after the age of forty. I learned how to focus. I ditched the fear and shame and anger that had been hiding in plain sight (at least from me) and slowing me down. I got younger. I built a multimillion-dollar company from scratch while simultaneously writing two *New York Times* bestselling books and being a loving and kind husband and father to two young kids.

And I learned to do all of this while exercising less than I had when I was fat, sleeping fewer hours but more effectively, eating tons of butter on my veggies, and, for the first time, enjoying life in a way that had previously been invisible to me. I reached a level of performance I didn't know I was capable of, and doing big, challenging things actually became easier than doing the smaller things I'd once struggled with.

When I set out on this path of self-improvement, I already had a very successful career, but it came with an enormous amount of effort and misery—more than I had the courage to admit to myself. I had no idea how much room there was for improvement until I gradually came to experience what it was like to be in the state of high performance that became the name of my company: Bulletproof. It happens when you take control of your biology and improve your body and your mind so that they work in unison, helping you execute at levels far beyond what you'd expect—without burning out, getting sick, or acting like a stressed-out jerk.

It used to take a lifetime to find fulfillment and realize your passion. But now that we have the knowledge of how to rewire the brain and body, this kind of radical change is available to us all, and new technologies provide us the ability to see results faster than ever. It's freaking awesome—so awesome that I felt obligated to share some of what I've learned.

I started a blog in 2010, written with the idea that if someone had just told me all this stuff when I was sixteen or twenty or even thirty, it would have saved me years of struggle, hundreds of thousands of dollars, and a lot of unnecessary pain. I truly believed that if only five people read it and experienced the kinds of results I did, it was worth the effort. I still believe that. In fact, the desire to offer other people the tools that have changed my life is the guiding force behind my entire company, and especially *Bulletproof Radio*.

On this quest, I have had the unique pleasure of interviewing nearly five hundred people who have impacted humanity with their discoveries and innovations while hundreds of thousands of listeners eavesdropped on our conversations. You may have heard of some of these experts, such as Jack "Chicken Soup for the Soul" Canfield, Tim "4 Hour" Ferriss, Arianna "HuffPo" Huffington, and John "Men Are from Mars" Gray. But the vast majority of my guests are not household names. They are university researchers who have spearheaded new fields of study, maverick scientists who have conducted incredible experiments in their labs, innovators who have created new fields of psychology, doctors who have cured the incurable, authors, artists, and business leaders who have boiled thousands of hours of experience into books that have changed the way we think about what it means to be human.

These experts are not only pushing boundaries in their fields but also often extending them to the cutting edge of what is possible. They are game changers who are rewriting the rules, stretching the limits, and helping to change the world for the rest of us. It has been a rare honor to talk directly with so many of these originators and learn about their ideas and discoveries. As you can imagine, it's incredibly satisfying to get to spend an hour learning about a game changer's life's work. But the real treasure lies at the end of each interview, when I ask them how they have managed to reach the high levels of performance that allowed them to achieve so much. The question is not *what* they achieved, not *how* they achieved it, but what were the *most important* things that powered their achievement.

I posed the same question to each guest: If someone came to you tomorrow wanting to perform better as a human being, what are the three most important pieces of advice you'd offer, based on your own life experience? I was intentional about the phrasing of the question, asking about human performance instead of just "performance" because we are all human, and we all have different goals and definitions of success. You can perform better as a parent, as an artist, as a teacher, as a meditator, as a lover, as a scientist, as a friend, or as an entrepreneur. And I wanted to know what these experts thought mattered most based on *their actual life experience*, not just their areas of study. I had no idea what to expect.

To say that their answers have been illuminating would be a tremendous understatement. Yes, some were shocking. Others were predictable. But the real value came after I had accumulated a large-enough sample size (over 450 interviews) to conduct a statistical analysis. After all, it's easy to ask one successful person what he or she does and to copy it. But the odds of that one person's favorite tool or trick working for you aren't very good, because you aren't that person. You have different DNA. You grew up in a different family. Your struggles aren't the same. Your strengths aren't the same. After asking hundreds of game changers what mattered most to their success, however, there was an incredible amount of data, and I noticed certain patterns emerging. When examined statistically, these patterns reveal a path that offers you a much better chance of getting you what you want.

My analysis revealed that most of the advice fell into one of three categories: things that make you *smarter*, things that make you *faster*, and things that make you *happier*. These innovators were able to grow their success because they also prioritized growing their abilities.

But the things that these top performers *didn't* say were just as revealing as the things they did. Their answers were unanimously far more focused on the things that have allowed them to contribute meaningfully to the world than what may have helped them attain any typical definition of success. My guests include lauded businesspeople, entrepreneurs, and CEOs, but not *one* person mentioned money, power, or physical attractiveness as being key to their success. Yet these three things are what most of us spend our entire lives striving to obtain. So what gives?

If you read my book *Head Strong*, you know that our neurons are made up of energy-producing organelles called *mitochondria*. Mitochondria are unique because, unlike other organelles, they come from ancient bacteria and they number in the billions. Our mitochondria are primitive. Their goal is simple: to keep you alive so you can propagate the species. They therefore hijack your nervous system to keep you unconsciously focused on three behaviors common to all life-forms, intelligent or not. Call them "the three F's": fear (run away, hide from, or fight scary things in case they are threats to your survival), feed (eat everything in sight so you don't starve to death and can quickly serve the first F), and . . . the third F-word, which propagates the species.

After all, a tiger can kill you right away. A lack of food can kill you in a month or two. And not reproducing will kill a species in a generation. Our mitochondria are at the helm of our neurological control panel—they're the ones pushing the buttons when you back down from a challenge, overeat, or spend too much time trying to get attention and admiration from others. We're wired to heed these urges automatically before we can stop to consider what really brings us success or happiness, and they will relentlessly take you off your path if you don't manage them.

When you think about it this way, it's kind of sad that our typical definitions of success represent those three bacteria-level behaviors. Power guarantees some level of safety so you don't have to run away from or fight scary things. Money guarantees that you'll always be able to eat. And physical attractiveness means you're more likely to attract a partner so you can reproduce.

Power, money, and sex. Most of us spend our lives pursuing these three things at the behest of our mitochondria. As a relatively stupid tiny life-form, a single mitochondrion is too small to have a brain, yet it follows those three rules millions of times a second. When a quadrillion mitochondria all follow them at the same time, a complex system with its own consciousness emerges. Throughout history people have given different names to this consciousness. The one you're probably the most familiar with is ego. I'm proposing that your ego is actually a biological phenomenon that stems from your hardwired instincts to keep your meat alive long enough to reproduce. Sad! The good news is that those mitochondria also power all of your higher thoughts and everything you do as you become more successful. They're stupid but useful.

The people who have managed to change the game don't focus on these ego- or mitochondria-driven goals, but they do manage the energy coming from their mitochondria. They have been able to transcend and harness their base instincts so they can show up all the way and focus on moving the needle for themselves and the rest of humanity. This is where true happiness and fulfillment—and success—ultimately come from.

I have experienced this shift in my own life as a result of my journey to become Bulletproof. As a young, secretly fearful, yet smart and successful fat guy, I spent years fighting these instincts—striving to make money, seeking power to be safe, looking for sex, struggling with my weight, and, frankly, being angry and unhappy. Using many of the techniques in this book, I was able to finally stop wasting my energy on those mitochondrial imperatives and start putting it toward the things that really mattered. And I've seen that when you manage to do this, success comes as a side effect of setting your ego aside and pursuing your true purpose.

That purpose is unique to each person. This book is not going to tell you what to do. Rather, it is meant to provide you with a road map to setting your own priorities and then following techniques that will be noticeably effective in helping you kick more ass at whatever it is you love. This order of operations is important. If you try to implement tools and techniques before setting your priorities, you'll do it wrong. But studying the priorities of game changers, identifying your own priorities, and then choosing from the menus of options throughout the book will help you make the biggest difference in the areas that matter most.

To make it simple, you'll find these options broken down into laws summarizing the most important advice from my high-performing guests, concentrated and distilled, along with some things you may want to try if they resonate with you. This style and structure was inspired by that of *The 48 Laws of Power* by Robert Greene, one of the luminaries I interviewed on the show whose books have made an enormous difference to millions of people, myself included. These laws fall into three main categories, which are the areas to focus on when you want to transcend your limits and learn to like your life while performing at your peak: becoming smarter, faster, and happier.

Smarter comes first because everything else is easier when your brain reaches peak performance. Just a decade ago, most people believed that you couldn't actually get smarter. If you'd talked about taking nootropics—aka "smart drugs"—or upgrading your memory, people would have thought you were crazy. Trust me, I know. I included my use of smart drugs in my LinkedIn profile starting in 2000, and people literally laughed at me. But times have changed, and now it's almost mainstream to talk about microdosing LSD for cognitive enhancement. Whether you choose to experiment with pharmaceuticals or upgrade your head by learning visualization techniques, it's okay to want to maximize your brainpower so you can perform at your best. That will free up energy for you to do other things you care about. This part of the book will show you how.

Next up is *faster*, a goal that humans have been striving for since the beginning of time. Hundreds of thousands of years ago, if you could light a fire in your cave faster, you won because you survived, and we haven't stopped working to be faster ever since. The laws in this part of the book will help you make your body more efficient so that you have as much mental and physical energy as possible for the things you want to do. It's difficult to change the game if you're sluggish and weak, but when you maximize your physical output using all of the tools at your disposal, you can do more than you ever imagined you could.

It is only after you gain some control over your mind and body that you can become *happier*, and that's why this section comes last. It was amazing to learn how many game changers had some sort of practice to help them become more aware, centered, and grounded and how those practices led to a higher level of happiness. In huge numbers, they talked about meditating and using breathing techniques to find a state of peace and calm. I didn't draw that answer out of them in the interviews—it's what they actually do.

Remember, these people could have answered the question by saying literally anything. One person said that coffee enemas were one of the most important things! Yet the vast majority credited one of these ancient practices for helping them find true happiness. I have no doubt that these practices have also played a huge role in helping these game changers become so successful in the first place. The people who are moving the needle prioritize their own peace and happiness because they know that at the end of the day it doesn't matter how smart or fast you are; if you're miserable, you will be stuck in mediocrity. This is why happiness plays such a big role in this book.

Of course, all the sections and all the laws in this book are interconnected. If you do one thing to become faster, for example, you will also gain more energy to focus at work, and you will feel happier because life is less of a struggle when you're faster. Likewise, if you practice breathing exercises that increase the amount of oxygen flowing to your brain and muscles, you'll recover from both mental and physical stress more quickly. This will change the way you feel and experience the world and make you happier.

Ultimately, when you change the environment inside of and around you, you can finally gain control of your biology instead of being jerked around by your base instincts. Your biology is everything—your body, mind, and even spirit. This is the core definition of biohacking, and it turns out that professors, scientists, and Buddhist monks were doing it long before I defined the term and created a movement around it. To become the best human you can be, you have a responsibility to design your environment so that you are in control. This book will give you forty-six life-changing "laws" about where to start. Each interview I do takes about eight hours of preparation. That's 3,600 hours of study when you multiply it by 450 interviews distilled into the laws in this book, or about two full years of working full-time.

I wish I'd had access to the information in this book (and that I had been wise enough to listen) twenty years ago, when I was unhappy, fat, and slow and life was a constant struggle because I was chasing the wrong things and wondering why I wasn't happy when I got them. It would have saved me hundreds of thousands of dollars and years of wasted effort. Yet I'm grateful for every bit of struggle, because otherwise I wouldn't be able to share what I've learned along the way with you.

Now you have the opportunity to pay it forward. The wisdom in these pages represents hundreds of thousands of man- and woman-hours of study, experiment, and results. These are the things that no one taught you in school, the real secrets straight from the people who have succeeded in the fields they've mastered. How different would your life be if you were even just a little smarter, faster, and happier? You would gain the power not just to change your own life but to move the needle forward for the rest of humanity. The more of us who do this, the more we can redefine what it means to be human. I invite you to join me in this ultimate game changer.

PART I

SMARTER

FOCUSING ON YOUR WEAKNESSES MAKES YOU WEAKER

When you consider the idea of energy in relation to your biology, you probably think of it as the fuel you use to complete physical tasks. Your legs use energy to run, and your arms use energy to lift weights. But you might be surprised to know that your brain actually uses more energy per pound than almost any other part of your body. Your brain requires a lot of energy to think, focus, make decisions, and generally kick ass at whatever you set your mind to doing.

As I learned from researching my last book, *Head Strong*, there are lots of ways to increase your brain's energy supply. But by far the easiest way is to simply stop wasting the brain energy you already have so you can reserve more of it for the things that matter most to you. This boils down to prioritization: focusing your brain energy on highly impactful things you love and getting rid of the things that drain you, no matter what they are; in other words, removing the things that are making you weak and adding more of the things that will make you strong. Some of these things are biological, but many are based on your choices or beliefs, both conscious and unconscious.

It may seem obvious, but there is a reason that more than one hundred high performers mentioned prioritizing their actions and focusing on their strengths as two of their most potent tools for success. The laws in this chapter are built on the ideas of preserving brain energy and maximizing productivity. Incorporating these principles into my life has made a huge difference and has clearly done the same for many people who are at the forefronts of their fields. When you focus on your strengths and stop wasting energy on things that don't matter, you can spend more time on the things that bring you joy and allow you to contribute meaningfully to the world.

Law 1: Use the Power of No

You have twenty-four hours in a day. You can choose to spend those hours creating things you truly care about, dealing with insignificant matters, or struggling to prove your worth by doing the things that are hardest for you. Master the art of doing what matters most to you—the things that create energy, passion, and quality of life with the lowest investment of energy. Say "no" more often. Make fewer decisions so you have more power for your mission.

Long before I interviewed him, Stewart Friedman was my professor at the University of Pennsylvania Wharton School of Business. He rocked my world by showing me that I was investing my energy in all the wrong places. In addition to being a professor of leadership, Stewart was one of the top one hundred senior executives at Ford Motor Company, responsible for leadership development across the entire company. He also created the Total Leadership Program, which develops top leaders by teaching them how to balance work and life, because he proved that leaders without balance make crappy leaders. *Working Mother* named Friedman one of America's twenty-five most influential men to have made things better for working parents, and his widely cited publications and internationally recognized expertise led Thinkers50 to select him as one of the world's top fifty leadership and management thinkers. There is no doubt that he has changed the game for how tens of thousands of people, including me, work and live every day, both with his teaching and his book *Leading the Life You Want: Skills for Integrating Work and Life.*

In our conversation, Stew explained that when he examined the lives of successful people, he found that at very high levels of performance, they all demonstrated the importance of one key concept: being aware and honest about what was most important to them. It's a simple concept, but it is often a tough one to execute. Stewart says that in the business of everyday life, most of us don't take the time to ask ourselves what we really stand for. This makes it difficult to make decisions that are in line with our goals with any kind of clarity. Knowing what matters to you brings clarity to your decision making and enables you to then do the really important work of saying no to many (maybe even most) things and focusing your attention and energy exclusively on the things that matter most to you.

To gain clarity about your values, Stew recommends thinking about the year 2039, twenty years from when you may be reading this book. What will a day in your life be like in 2039? Whom will you be with? What will you be doing? What impact will you be having? Write all of that down. Keep in mind that you are creating not a contract or an action plan but a compelling image of an achievable future that serves as a window into your true values. Once you have this information, it will be easy to decide where to invest your energy instead of allowing others to focus your priorities for you or getting distracted with drudgery.

Once you know *what* matters most to you, Stewart says, the second step is to determine *who* matters most to you. This is a challenging question for anyone, but Stew suggests that real leaders take the time to ask themselves, "Who matters to me, what do those people want from me, and what do I want from them?" Think about the people in your life who have been influential in shaping your worldview. They should be on the list.

I learned a lot from my time with Stew, and in fact, he made me aware of some uncomfortable truths about where I was spending my energy. One of my core values, I realized, is continual self-improvement, but I had set that aside to focus on my career. So I made a decision to do something *every day* that makes me better. This small commitment helps me invest my time and energy wisely and focus on ways to continually grow and challenge myself.

In order to get better at this, I sought out someone who lives and breathes self-improvement: Tony Stubblebine. Tony is on a mission to make coaching the fastest path to self-improvement in every field, from business to education to fitness. He is the CEO and founder of Coach.me, a company based on the idea that positive reinforcement and community support work in tandem to help people achieve their goals.

Tony sets a decision budget for himself every day. He allows himself only a certain number of decisions, whether they are big or small, and then he "spends" them throughout the day. For this reason, the actions he takes in the morning will largely determine how efficiently he spends the rest of the day. If he wastes a lot of decisions in the morning, he is left avoiding even the simplest of decisions for the rest of the day in order to stay "on budget."

He didn't start out that way, though. He used to check his phone and social media accounts as soon as he woke up each day. Sound familiar? From the moment his alarm went off, his head was filled with all the things he felt he needed to do and people he "had to" respond to. Every subsequent step required him to make a decision. Which email should he respond to first? Should he say yes to that opportunity? Should he "like" someone's post? Should he check out the link a friend sent him? He found that those decisions were wearing down his budget before he even started on the really important tasks he wanted to get to that day.

Over time, Tony learned that as a CEO, his most important daily habits were his decision-making habits, particularly when it came to which opportunities he was going to say yes or no to. And since he began to deplete his decision budget so early in the day, he felt he wasn't able to make the most effective decisions for his company.

This realization led him to set healthier decision-making habits for himself. Now he prioritizes starting his day with a clear mind. He meditates as soon as he wakes up and then writes down his to-do list. To prioritize this list, he asks himself which of the tasks have the potential to significantly change the outcome of his mission. After practicing this habit for a while, he began to realize that many of the items on his to-do lists weren't really critical.

The more clarity he gained about his priorities and which tasks would move the needle in the right direction, the more he found he was able to make quick but informed decisions. Eventually he grew so clear on what was important to him and his company that when opportunities arose it was easy for him to say yes or no without having to negotiate an answer or waste time making a decision. If an opportunity was not going to change the outcome, an automatic no was his habitual response.

This isn't always easy, which is why it's a good idea to work with a coach to help you figure out what habits are hindering you. I hired Jeff Spencer, who cut his teeth as the lead performance coach for top Tour de France teams—including the winners—nine years in a row before turning to coaching entrepreneurs. A good coach will help you see where you're wasting energy in your life without knowing it, predict where you're going to waste energy next as you scale, and hold you accountable for changing it. Jeff made such an impact on me that I interviewed him on *Bulletproof Radio,* too!

Tony's solution of creating a decision budget mirrors the findings of one of my favorite studies of all time. In 2010, researchers in Israel studied how judges make decisions about whether or not convicted criminals are approved for parole.[1] After examining more than a thousand parole hearings over the course of ten months, they uncovered a fascinating and very strong connection between the decisions and the time of day they were issued: If a hearing was held early in the day, the judge gave a favorable ruling about 65 percent of the time. But as the day went on, the likelihood of a favorable ruling steadily declined all the way to zero after a noticeable bump back up to 65 percent right after lunch. This trend was consistent across many variables, including the type of crime committed, the criminal's education, and his or her behavior while in prison.

So what was going on with those judges? It turns out that making all of those decisions about whether or not criminals should be granted parole was using up their decision-making budget, also known as willpower. Willpower seems like an abstract concept. Some of us have a lot of willpower and others don't, right? Wrong! In reality, willpower is like a muscle. You can exercise it to make it stronger, and it gets fatigued when it's worked too much. When your willpower muscle is fatigued, you start making bad decisions. And you do it without noticing.

The idea of a "willpower muscle" is partly based on our understanding of the anterior cingulate cortex (ACC), a little C-shaped part of your brain right by your temple. Scientists believe that the ACC is the seat of willpower. Think of your ACC as maintaining an energetic bank account. When you start your day, it's flush with energy, but every time you make a decision or exert mental effort, you withdraw a little bit of the balance. Choosing what to wear in the morning takes out a little bit. Deciding what to make for breakfast uses a little bit more. Bigger decisions, such as deciding whether or not a criminal will be granted parole or not, empty your account faster. If you overdraw your energetic bank account with trivial decisions, your ACC stops responding well and your willpower runs out. That's when you give in to bad decisions.

This phenomenon is called *decision fatigue*: the more decisions you make, the worse your judgment becomes. Corporations have known about decision fatigue for years. That's why they put brightly packaged candy up front at store registers. As you make decision after decision while shopping, you're depleting your energetic bank account. By the time you're ready to check out, you're more likely to be experiencing decision fatigue—and a craving for a quick hit of sugar to give your brain more energy—so you give in and buy a candy bar.

Judges are not immune to this phenomenon; they use up a lot of willpower throughout the day hearing cases. At the end of the day, when the energy balance in their ACC is running low, it becomes easier to deny parole than to try to negotiate a more complicated decision. This also helps explain why the judges in the study granted more paroles right after lunch than at other times in the afternoon; their ACCs had just received a hit of energy.

One wonders whether the type of lunch they ate was an important variable. It only makes sense that a lunch designed to deliver sustained energy would lead to better decisions. Silicon Valley lore says that many years ago, the once dominant computer company Sun Microsystems banned pasta from the lunch menu used for on-site meetings because its executives noticed that meetings tended to tank after high-carb lunches. The reality is that what you eat *does* impact your willpower—though it is easier to stop making meaningless decisions than it is to change what you eat (I do both).

The good news is, now that you know about decision fatigue, you can be sure to schedule all of your parole hearings for the morning. Even better, you can free up more willpower to start making better decisions so that you don't end up being convicted of a crime in the first place! You can do this in two ways: by building up the amount of energy stored in your ACC and by reducing the number of decisions you make throughout the day to preserve your mental energy.

You can build your "willpower muscle" the same way you strengthen any muscle in your body: by doing hard things you don't want to do. A simple trick I use is to keep a heavy-duty spring-loaded hand-grip trainer on my desk. When I think about it, I squeeze it until it burns and my arm tells me to stop *and then keep squeezing.* Another technique I use is to hold my breath until my lungs scream at me to breathe *and then hold it longer.* When you successfully do the things you don't want to do, everything else seems easier by comparison. Your willpower grows. But consider *not* pushing your willpower on a day when you have other major decisions to make. On those days, don't burn out your willpower reserves before a crucial meeting or presentation.

Some game changers find that simply eliminating as many decisions as possible offers them more mental clarity. Every time you avoid making a choice, you save a little bit of willpower that you can then put toward something that will have a greater impact. Many high performers have developed day-to-day routines that are so dialed in that they don't even think about them. These people simply show up and execute with extreme focus and energy.

Experiment with tracking your decisions for a few days, and then start automating the ones that are a waste of energy. Meal and wardrobe decisions are two common ones that high performers tend to automate. Why do you think Steve Jobs wore a black turtleneck and New Balance sneakers every day, Mark Zuckerberg has ten identical T-shirts in his closet, or most corporate CEOs cycle through three or four suits every week (and I'm usually wearing one of several Bulletproof T-shirts and ugly but massively comfortable toe shoes when you see me online)? When you reach for some version of the same outfit every day, you never have to worry about what to wear. This may seem like a minor decision, but it saves a lot of mental energy that you can then use for something more meaningful.

Admittedly, this is usually easier for men than women, but either gender can opt for a "capsule" wardrobe if you're not ready to go full Steve Jobs. To do this, pick three or four tops, bottoms, jackets, and shoes, all in neutral colors such as gray and navy. Plan so that everything in your closet matches, to the point where you can get dressed in the dark and still look good. Then get rid of all your other clothes so that you have only twenty or so items in your closet. You can find capsule wardrobe guides online for inspiration. Some popular clothing brands now even tag "capsule" pieces in their catalogues. There's nothing wrong with saving a few special pieces for social events and formal occasions. The point is to avoid having to make daily decisions about what to wear when no one will notice whether your outfit is awesome or not.

You can also create a sort of "capsule diet" by cycling through the same few meals. To do this successfully, find five or six different tasty recipes you can cook that your whole family likes. Then you can buy groceries and cook on autopilot without having to make lots of decisions about what to buy and cook each week. When you get tired of one of the meals, swap it out for a new one. One of my most impactful willpower hacks has actually been none other than Bulletproof Coffee. I don't ever have to think about what I'm having for breakfast, and I save the time I would have otherwise spent preparing a meal. You can do the same thing with whatever breakfast gives you the most energy with the fewest decisions and the least amount of work.

When you use these techniques to cut down on decision making, you free up a tremendous amount of mental energy that you can use however you like. I recommend devoting it to your most meaningful life work. Not sure what that is yet? Here's a hint: you decide.

Action Items

- Take a deep breath. Now hold it until you're sure you have to breathe. Hold it for eight more seconds. (Don't do this if you're driving or have health problems.)
- Take note—mentally or on paper—every time you make a

decision for a week. As you notice yourself making a decision, ask yourself two questions:

- Did this decision matter?
- Was there a way to avoid making this decision by ignoring it, automating it, or asking someone else who loves making that kind of decision to make it instead?

- Start now. Name two decisions you make every day that add absolutely no value to your life. Write them down here so you don't have to decide to do it later.

  - Useless daily decision 1:

    _____

  - Useless daily decision 2:

    _____

- Now stop making them.
- Take a look at your breakfast. Can you automate that decision? What's your new "no-thought" default breakfast going to be? Try it for a week.
- Go through your closet and put the most compatible stuff in the front so you can spend a few days making fewer decisions about getting dressed. If you like how you feel, go for a capsule wardrobe!
- Consider working with an experienced performance coach. There are dozens of quality coach training programs. Look for a trainer certified by the International Association of Systemic Teaching (IASC). (I've trained more than a thousand coaches in the Bulletproof-inspired IASC-certified Human Potential Coach program who would be pleased to help you, too!)

Recommended Listening
- Stew Friedman, "Be Real, Be Whole, Be Innovative," *Bulletproof Radio*, episode 83

- Stew Friedman, "Success, Leadership & Less Work," *Bulletproof Radio*, episode 196
- Jeff Spencer, "Success Intoxication & the Champions Blueprint," *Bulletproof Radio*, episode 213
- Tony Stubblebine, "Getting Out of Your Robot Mindset," *Bulletproof Radio*, episode 296

Recommended Reading

- Stewart D. Friedman, *Leading the Life You Want: Skills for Integrating Work and Life*

Law 2: Never Discover Who You Are

To change the world, tap into your strengths, but do not passively discover who you are. Actively *decide and create* who you are. If you abdicate this duty by allowing others to tell you who to be, you will struggle greatly in life and likely fail to achieve greatness. So discover your passion and follow it, but do it as the person you create. The difference is a life of mediocrity and creeping misery compared to a life of freedom and passion.

Brendon Burchard is the founder of the High Performance Academy, the host of *The Charged Life* podcast, and the author of the number one *New York Times* bestsellers *The Motivation Manifesto: 9 Declarations to Claim Your Personal Power*, *The Charge: Activating the 10 Human Drives That Make You Feel Alive*, and *The Millionaire Messenger: Make a Difference and a Fortune Sharing Your Advice*. Brendon has the number one–rated personal development show on YouTube and is one of the one hundred most followed public figures on Facebook. His educational work has helped millions of people around the globe achieve the results they are looking for in the areas of business, marketing, and personal development, and his programs, such as Experts Academy and World's Greatest Speaker Training, have helped thousands of people—including me. So of course I had to interview him!

Getting time on Brendon's calendar to meet him in Portland was surprisingly easy because he manages his time like a boss. Of course, it helps that we're friends, but he genuinely has more free time than anyone else I've met at his level of achievement because he has consciously built his life that way. The man truly practices what he preaches at every level.

Brendon believes that humankind's main motivation is to seek personal freedom, which he defines as the ability to fully express who we are and pursue the things that are meaningful and important to us. But we have two enemies that get in our way every single time. One of them is self-oppression, our tendency to put ourselves down. The other is social oppression, the people who judge us and fail to be supportive of who we are or what we want. Brendon suggests that we can overcome these two barriers by developing what he terms a "competence-confidence loop." The more you understand something, the more confidence you will have to pursue it further, despite what anyone else may say. And of course, the more you pursue a subject and learn about it, the closer you'll get to true mastery.

This strategy is similar to Stewart Friedman's advice in the sense that both require knowing what matters most to you. But Brendon believes that we should be intentional about our aspirations rather than focusing on what may feel the most practically achievable. He recommends recording three words on your phone that describe your highest, best self. These are the words you would most want someone to use when describing you, and they should apply to both personal and professional settings. Some of the words I've heard from game changers are: engaged, grateful, energized, warm, loving, devoted, and impactful. Choose three that resonate with you, then set an alarm to go off three times a day and remind you of this aspirational sense of self.

When you act without intention, you will experience self-doubt. But when you are reminded of who you want to be throughout the day, you are more likely to act in accordance with your highest goals. This process serves as an endless feedback loop that leads you to find more confidence in yourself and thus to become more competent. You can actively generate the emotions that you most want to feel by doing things that are in line with your vision of the person you want to be. Brendon believes that the most important skills to master are setting intentions and taking the necessary steps to become that person. In other words, instead of *discovering* who you are, you become powerful when you *decide* who you are.

No conversation about acting with intention would be complete without input from Robert Greene, the author of the *New York Times* bestsellers *The 48 Laws of Power, The Art of Seduction, The 33 Strategies of War, The 50th Law* (coauthored with 50 Cent), and *Mastery.* In addition to having a strong fan base within the business world and a deep following in Washington, DC, Greene's books are hailed by everyone from war historians to the biggest names in the music industry (including Jay-Z and 50 Cent) because he has relentlessly studied the world's best to see what makes them tick.

I sought out Robert because long before I interviewed him, he transformed my career. Twenty years ago, I helped to start part of the company that held Google's very first servers, eventually attending board meetings with people who were twice my age and about a hundred times more experienced. (Of course, I was the most junior person in the room, so I wasn't allowed to speak at those board meetings, but I got to witness what went on in them.) As a rational engineering kind of guy, I simply did not understand the powerful executives around me. Their choices and the way they conducted themselves often made no sense to me. They looked irrational, if not downright crazy.

Then I picked up a book that changed that dynamic. It was called *The 48 Laws of Power.* This incredibly well-researched book included stories from throughout history examining how people in power had gotten there and stayed there and elegantly distilled lessons from those stories into actionable "laws." A week after I read it, I sat in the next executive staff meeting and realized: These people are not crazy. They're powerful! The rules they are following are entirely rational, but they're not engineering rules. They're power rules.

That taught me how to function at a new level in Silicon Valley, how to work in a venture capital firm, how to raise money, how to work with powerful people, and how to do what I now do at Bulletproof every day. If I hadn't known those rules that enabled me to start thinking like a chess player, I wouldn't be where I am now. *The 48 Laws of Power* not only changed the course of my career, but it also inspired the structure of this book.

When I sat down with Robert and asked him about his views on becoming the person you want to be, he said that most of us have always known who we wanted to be—we've just forgotten. When you were a kid, it was probably pretty obvious. He refers to the subjects you were inclined to pursue, even when you were as young as three years old, as your primal inclinations. These are your basic strengths, and they should not be taken lightly, because you are a completely unique person. No one else has ever had or ever will have your exact set of molecules or your DNA. And your unique brain learns at a much faster rate when you are learning about something that excites you. When you *want* to learn, you do. Robert says that if you're forced to learn something that you're not interested in, you will absorb only one-tenth of the information that you would if you were deeply engaged in the subject.

Yet when most people choose a career, they heed the well-meaning advice of their parents and friends or chase money instead of pursuing the things they truly care about. You can get pretty far this way, but you'll never develop true mastery in something you don't love because you won't be learning at your optimum rate. Robert says that if everyone discovered the one thing they really loved and spent all of his or her time and energy on it, mastery would develop organically. I can attest to the fact that it does.

It really comes down to playing to your strengths, something I wish I had learned to do sooner. When I was starting out in my career, I sucked at project management. I didn't like the way it felt to be bad at something, so I decided to get better at it. I put all of my energy into becoming a certified project manager and ended up just barely average at something that drained my energy and went against my natural strengths. I realized that I could have better used the energy I'd wasted becoming a less than halfway decent project manager to really move the needle in other areas. So I deleted Microsoft Project and worked with experienced project managers who seemed to have magical unicorn project management powers but in reality were simply good at their jobs because they loved what they did and had mastered the necessary skill set.

Later, I was able to put this lesson into practice when I went to Wharton, where people worked really hard to get straight A's. I decided ahead of time to get base knowledge and just barely pass the classes that actively drained me in order to free up energy to dive deep into areas that fascinated me. I ended up intentionally getting a D in several classes, but I got the same MBA that my straight-A friends did without feeling like a failure. Focusing on the areas I loved did more for my career than spending extra time on areas of study that didn't light me up.

With coaching from the legendary entrepreneur coach Dan Sullivan of Strategic Coach, I have learned to prioritize my actions into three buckets: things that drain my energy, things I don't mind and are important and useful, and things that give me energy and bring me joy. My goal is to break my daily actions down so that I spend none of my time on tasks that fall into the first category, 10 percent of my time on the second category, and 90 percent of my time in the final category, the one that Robert Greene calls *primal inclinations*. When I find myself drifting too far from the goal, I reset my actions.

This may feel impossible to you right now. Most people spend the majority of their time on tasks that fall into the first category, but it truly doesn't have to be that way if you use the competence-confidence loop to create the motivation to become the person you want to be and focus your energy on your primal inclinations.

Action Items

- Find three words that describe your highest, best self and write them down where you'll see them throughout the day. Or do what Brendon does and set a phone alert to go off three times a day to remind you of these words. Write them down here. Do it now.

- Word 1: _____

- Word 2: _____

- Word 3: _____

- Identify your primal inclinations—the things you love that you just can't help learning about.

  - _____

- Write down what percentage of your time you spend doing things you hate, things you don't mind, and things that light your fire. Write them down here.

  - Percentage of time spent on things that drain me:

    _____

  - Percentage of time spent on things I don't mind:

    _____

  - Percentage of time spent on things that give me joy, including my primal inclination: _____

- Now do what it takes to shift your ratio to 0:10:90.

Recommended Listening
- Brendon Burchard, "Confidence, Drive & Power," *Bulletproof Radio*, episode 190
- Brendon Burchard, "Hacking High Performers & Productivity Tricks," *Bulletproof Radio*, episode 262
- Robert Greene, "The 48 Laws of Power," *Bulletproof Radio*, episode 380
- Dan Sullivan, "Think About Your Thinking: Lessons in Entrepreneurship," *Bulletproof Radio*, episode 485

Recommended Reading
- Brendon Burchard, *High Performance Habits: How Extraordinary People Become That Way*
- Robert Greene, *The 48 Laws of Power*

Law 3: When You Say You'll Try, You Are Lying

The words you choose matter more than you think, not just to the people you speak to but also to your own nervous system. Your language sets your limits and to a great extent shapes your destiny. When you unconsciously use words that make you weak, you stop trusting yourself and lead others to question your integrity. Game changers deliberately choose truthful words to build trust and break free from self-imposed limitations. So stop trying and start doing.

My dear friend JJ Virgin is a well-known health and wellness expert and a four-time *New York Times* bestselling author who has benefited hundreds of thousands of people with her work in nutrition. On top of that, she teaches some of the most innovative experts in medicine how to use their knowledge to reach the people who need it. A few years ago, JJ's teenage son, Grant, was out walking to a friend's house when a hit-and-run driver left him for dead on the side of the road. Doctors told JJ that it wasn't worth airlifting Grant to the only hospital that could perform the risky surgery he needed to save his heart because it would cause his brain to bleed out. She could have his heart or his brain, they said, but not both.

JJ, being the dedicated mother and unstoppable badass that she is, overruled the doctors in charge of Grant's care time and time again as Grant went on to defeat the odds with her help. He survived the surgery, he woke up from his coma (which doctors had said would never happen), and he began to read, walk, and then run. JJ attributes Grant's survival against the odds to many things, from cutting-edge therapies and good nutrition to skilled surgeons. But there was one action she took that she believes played a critical role in her son's recovery: she was intentional about the words that she and others used around him.

Even when Grant was in a coma and doctors believed he couldn't hear her, JJ never expressed any doubts about Grant's recovery in front of him, and she didn't allow the doctors or nurses to, either. This is because JJ knows that our bodies listen to our words at a subtle level. At his bedside, JJ told Grant over and over that this was going to be the best thing that had ever happened to him and he was going to come out of it at 110 percent. When a doctor told her, "We're doing our best to get him to the point where he'll be able to walk again if he ever wakes up," JJ quickly ushered the doctor out of Grant's earshot. She didn't want him to hear that not waking up and never walking again were even distant possibilities.

Sure enough, when Grant woke up, he already had the intention of recovering to 110 percent. He never considered the possibility of not being able to walk again. And I have no doubt that the words JJ so carefully chose played a huge role in Grant's incredible recovery. Words are powerful. They set expectations and limits and send messages to our brains and even our bodies about how much we are capable of. Language is a part of your mental software. Use it consciously and with precision, and you will achieve things you probably never thought you could.

Perhaps no one knows the power of words better than Jack Canfield, the man behind *Chicken Soup for the Soul,* who has sold several hundred million copies of his books and broke a world record when he had seven books on the *New York Times* bestseller list *at one time.* Jack's focus is on distilling what makes people successful, culminating in his book *The Success Principles: How to Get from Where You Are to Where You Want to Be.* In my interview with him, we talked about how language impacts success, and I was surprised to hear that he keeps a list of limiting words that he guides successful people to avoid.

I do this, too. As I used biohacking to upgrade my abilities to focus on and pay attention to my words as they came out of my mouth, I discovered that I often used self-limiting words without even realizing it. Even when I was in a deep state of consciousness using neurofeedback, I was unknowingly setting intentions by using those limiting words. My subconscious was choosing safe words that made unimportant things feel huge and other words that allowed me wiggle room to avoid doing the big things I wanted to do.

I call such limiting words "weasel words." People who work at Bulletproof know that I'll call out someone in a meeting who uses weak language in a subconscious attempt to avoid responsibility. Similarly, Jack says that he keeps empty fishbowls in his offices, and if one of his team members uses a weasel word, he or she has to put two dollars into the bowl. This is meant not as punishment but to show that there is a cost to using such words. Clear speech means clear thinking and clear execution. By listening to and analyzing the words you use on a regular basis, you can learn to stop unconsciously programming yourself to have limited performance.

There are four particularly insidious weasel words that you likely use many times a day without even noticing it. Use them in front of me, and I'll make sure you start to notice it (at least, if I like you!).

WEASEL WORD 1: CAN'T

This word is first on Jack's list and mine, too. It is perhaps the most destructive word you use every day. The word "can't" means there is absolutely no possible way you can do something. It robs you of power and crushes innovative thinking. When you say, "I can't do that," what you actually mean is one of four things: you could use some help doing it; you don't currently have the tools to do it; you simply don't know how to do it; or you just don't want to do it. Or heck, maybe no one in history has figured out how to do "it" yet. Given enough resources and enough problem-solving creativity, you *can* do whatever it is. It may or may not be worth the time and effort to figure out, or maybe it's just a stupid idea, but it's not impossible.

The true meaning of "can't" is obvious to your conscious brain, but it isn't so obvious to your unconscious brain because that part of your brain doesn't understand context. Yet it is still listening to the words you use. This miscommunication between the two parts of your brain creates confusion and subtle stress. If you start to use words that mean the same thing to both your conscious brain and your unconscious brain, you will be a calmer and more empowered person. And because other people also hear your words on both a conscious and unconscious level, when you choose your words more intentionally, other people will tend to trust you more.

This lesson came into action for me as I was writing this book. I was catching a flight to New York to be on *The Dr. Oz Show*, but I arrived at the airport fifty-nine minutes before takeoff instead of one hour. Even though I had checked in online for the flight, I couldn't get through the security line without a printed boarding pass. The United gate agent was adamant that she would not print one for me. She even said, "You can't make this flight." Because I am programmed to hear "can't" as a lie, it caused me to think about the problem differently. So I asked another, more helpful airline for the cheapest ticket to anywhere and bought it, which provided me with a precious printed boarding pass to get through security and board my original flight. It felt good to walk up to the United gate and see the look of disbelief on the face of the agent who had said I couldn't get past security without a boarding pass for her flight. It felt even better to make the flight so that I didn't fail to show up for a commitment.

"Can't" is always a lie. Learn to see it that way, and you'll solve problems differently. Go one week without using the word "can't." Normally, I would say, "I bet you can't do it," but it would be more honest for me to say, "I bet it will be very difficult until you have practiced."

WEASEL WORD 2: NEED

Parents use the word "need" with kids all the time: "We *need* to go, so you *need* to wear a coat." The truth is, you didn't *need* to go, and you didn't *need* to wear a coat. Your parents might have *wanted* to leave, and you would simply have been cold without a coat. By telling your primitive systems that you need something, you end up turning a desire for something into a straight-up survival issue. On a deep level your primitive brain believes that you'll die if you don't get the things you say you "need," even though your conscious brain knows better.

Of course, you probably use this word in all sorts of other ways, too. "I need a snack" or "I need a new coat" are two good examples. You do not need those things, and lying to your brain about what you need is making you weak. The harsh reality is that there are few things you actually need: oxygen every minute, water every five days, and food before you starve after a couple *months* of hunger. You need shelter, and you need a way to stay warm. The rest are wants, not needs. Be honest by choosing the word "need" only when it is 100 percent truthful; the rest of the time replace it with the truth. You want. You choose. You decide.

This matters even more if you're in a leadership position. Our systems aren't good at distinguishing between real and perceived threats. Imagine the panic and bad decisions you can initiate if your team believes at some level that they will die if they don't do something you suggest they "need" to do. In a physical state of stress, they would be unable to perform and make wise decisions. You can motivate people to run away from something scary, or you can motivate them to run toward something amazing. So instead of telling my team at Bulletproof that we need to hit a deadline, I say, "This is mission critical, and we're going to do it. What obstacles can I remove for you? What will help us do this?" That truthful language means we can have an honest conversation if we're really not going to be able to hit the deadline. People who believe the "need" lie will run like maniacs toward a deadline they know isn't going to happen because that's what you do when your life is at stake. So stop needing, and start wanting. You're not going to die.

Challenge yourself to go a week without using the word "need" unless it's true. You will be tempted to use the word as long as you qualify it, but even in those cases it is unlikely to actually be true. For example, you might say, "We need to leave now if we want to get to the store before it closes." Even with this qualifier in place, this is still a limited way of thinking. What if you were to simply call the store and asked the people there to stay open a few minutes late? Or simply asked a friend to go? By using the word "need," you put an unconscious box around the solution set, create subconscious stress, and limit your creativity.

WEASEL WORD 3: BAD

In reality, very few things are inherently "bad"; bad is a value judgment you assign to something. The problem with labeling things as "bad" is that your subconscious listens and prepares you psychologically and biochemically for impending doom. The vast majority of the time, when you say something is bad, you actually mean that you don't like it or don't want it. For instance, you might say, "I was planning a picnic, but now it's raining, and that's bad." The truth is that you can have lunch somewhere else, probably without ants. And you're damned lucky to be able to have lunch at all today. So is it really bad that it's raining? Nope.

People tend to use the word "bad" a lot in relation to food, which also creates problems. Some foods work better for certain people than others. Those foods aren't good or bad—and neither are the people who eat them! Even eating something obviously "bad," such as an MSG-filled vegan pseudoburger, is better than starving to death. The word "bad" creates a false binary. The world doesn't naturally fall into two camps. Sure, there are things that are truly tragic, such as violence and natural disasters, but when it comes to our everyday lives, judging things through a filter of either good or bad is limiting and creates unnecessary obstacles and black-and-white thinking. When you label something "bad," you miss out on an opportunity to figure out how it can be good.

WEASEL WORD 4: TRY

"Try" *always* presupposes a likelihood of failure. Think about it. If someone says he's going to *try* to pick you up at the airport when you land, are you going to count on him to do it? No way. You know that there is a good chance he won't show up. However, if someone says he *is* going to pick you up, you can believe it. If you tell yourself that you're going to *try* to stay on a diet or *try* to read a book, you've subconsciously already planned to fail. You won't do it.

Jack illustrates the power of "try" during his powerful keynote presentations when he asks audience members to put something (a notebook, a pen, or whatever else they have handy) on their laps and lift it up. After they do it and put it back down, he says, "Now this time just try to pick it up." That confuses everyone, and they don't move for a moment. Then a few people start to pick up the item, but suddenly they're struggling with the same item they lifted effortlessly a moment ago, as if it had gained several pounds. This is because as soon as you hear the word "try," you assume that whatever you are going to "try" to do might not be possible. It gives your brain an out.

The point is that in order to become a better human, you want to push your brain to perform at its full potential instead of giving yourself an excuse to fail. This doesn't mean that you have to do everything that is asked of you. If you don't think that something is the best use of your time and mental energy, you can honestly and clearly (and kindly) say no. But if you choose to take something on, commit to it with all your might. As Yoda said, "There is no try. Only do." Do you think he developed Jedi powers merely by trying? No way, and the point is that neither will you.

Action Items

- Ask someone at work and someone at home to call you out when you use weasel words and to fine you a dollar to put into a jar for charity (or the office coffee fund) when you do.
- Set your computer's autocorrect to automatically capitalize or highlight weasel words so you'll have to change them to more truthful words. It's amazing how frequent reminders drive behavior change!

Recommended Listening

- JJ Virgin, "Fighting for Miracles," *Bulletproof Radio*, episode 386
- Jack Canfield, "Go Beyond Chicken Soup & Confront Your Fears," *Bulletproof Radio*, episode 471

Recommended Reading

- JJ Virgin, *Miracle Mindset: A Mother, Her Son, and Life's Hardest Lessons*
- Jack Canfield with Janet Switzer, *The Success Principles: How to Get from Where You Are to Where You Want to Be*

GET INTO THE HABIT OF GETTING SMARTER

Doctors and other scientists used to believe that we were born with a brain that was either high functioning or not. Either you were inherently wired to be smart, focused, and able to learn easily—or you weren't. It wasn't until around the end of the twentieth century that scientists began to understand the concept of neuroplasticity, the brain's ability to grow new cells and forge new neural connections throughout your life.

You can use these new cells and newly formed connections to develop new habits and beliefs, learn faster, and remember more effectively. These are dramatic upgrades that can have an enormous impact on your performance in every aspect of life. It also means that if you think you're not smart enough or not good enough, it doesn't matter. You can change it.

An overwhelming number of my podcast guests believe that creating good habits and discipline is one of the most important things you can do to perform better as a human being. In fact, this answer came in *third* out of anything in the world to improve performance, even ahead of education. These innovators know that your habits, the things you do every day without even thinking about them, to a great extent determine who you are and what you are capable of.

Yet creating new habits is not as simple as making resolutions. To transform your actions into automatic habits that you can use without conscious effort, your mind must create new neural networks. It follows that anything you can do to maximize your ability to create these pathways will help you actually wire in the habits that will benefit your performance. Habits work because they free up mental space for doing big things. The new habits and strategies highlighted in this chapter's laws will help you transform your false beliefs and allow you to learn faster, remember more easily, and ultimately make space in your head and your life so you can more quickly and easily achieve your goals.

Law 4: Even Your False Beliefs Are True

The beliefs you hold and the stories you tell yourself shape your internal model of reality. When your model is wrong, you build broken habits and make decisions that don't create what you want. You suffer. A flexible mind changes itself and builds a better model as it gathers more data about reality. Build a flexible mind with the built-in habit of questioning your assumptions about reality so you can grow.

Vishen Lakhiani has been a meditation teacher for more than twenty years and runs the world's largest meditation training program online. His two-hundred-person company, Mindvalley, has enabled him to become a substantial philanthropist, and his bestselling book, *The Code of the Extraordinary Mind: 10 Unconventional Laws to Redefine Your Life and Succeed on Your Own Terms*, teaches you how to optimize your brain for prime happiness and performance.

In his interview, Vishen shared with me how he came to believe a false story about himself. He is of South Asian descent, but he grew up in Asia, where he looked different from the other kids. He had a larger nose than most of his classmates and more hair on his arms and legs. The other boys called him Gorilla Legs and Hook Nose, and Vishen internalized those messages. As his mind, which he calls a "meaning-matching machine," tried to make sense of the world around it, as all young minds do, it created the meaning that he was ugly, and he held on to that belief for many years.

Vishen refers to these types of stories and beliefs as our hardware, because they are instilled in us, usually before the age of seven, much as hardware is installed in a computer. We do not deliberately choose them. Authority figures, our society and culture, our education systems, and the observations we make as children indoctrinate such beliefs into us at a very young age. If we allow them to go unquestioned, they can have a hugely detrimental impact on our lives. Our beliefs tell us how important we are, what we are capable of, our role in society, and so on. If our beliefs are limited, they can drastically diminish our human potential. The problem is that our beliefs *feel* like reality because they *are* reality until you realize they are false.

The good news is that just as you can upgrade the hardware on your computer, you can upgrade your beliefs once you become aware of them. In Vishen's book, he teaches a codified form of learning and human development that he calls *consciousness engineering*. The first step of consciousness engineering is to recognize that your beliefs are not who you are. They are simply hardware that was installed in you long ago and can be upgraded or replaced.

Neuroplasticity teaches us that we can swap out a negative or limiting belief for a belief that will serve us better. Vishen says that when people change their beliefs, their lives completely transform because those beliefs inform how they experience the world. For instance, when Vishen got rid of the false belief that his differences made him ugly, it changed his confidence and his entire perspective, and his life and relationships quickly shifted in a positive way.

Swapping out your limiting beliefs is crucial if you want to go from Human 1.0 to Human 2.0, but it isn't easy. Humans hold on to limiting beliefs without even realizing it. They seem so real to us that we don't always realize they even exist. To us, they are simply the way things are. Vishen recommends modalities such as hypnotherapy or meditation (more on this later), which can lead to awakening moments that make you conscious of your beliefs. Then you can begin to change them intentionally.

High performers focus on recognizing and changing limiting beliefs because they know that their beliefs will become true whether or not they are based in reality. In fact, helping people discover and correct self-limiting beliefs is one of the primary roles of a life coach or a business coach. For example, if you believe that you are having a lucky day before a presentation, it doesn't matter whether or not there is any such thing as luck. Your belief in your own luck will lead you to have more confidence and to actually perform better in that presentation. It's like the placebo effect on steroids.

When I meditate, I tell my nervous system I'm grateful that things happen the way they're supposed to happen, that there is a conspiracy to help me succeed, and that the universe has my back. (Gabby Bernstein, the author of a great book by that title, inspires that last part. Her interview on *Bulletproof Radio* was amazing.) It doesn't matter if any of those beliefs are actually true or even if my rational brain thinks they're true. I want the simple-minded systems in my body to believe that they are true so they will automatically help me to make things happen with less resistance.

Your positive beliefs can literally bring you success. You can tell yourself the story that you're successful, and your brain will believe it and act on it. The opposite is also true. Based on thirty years of research on more than a million participants, Dr. Martin Seligman and his colleagues at the University of Pennsylvania found that optimistic expectations were a significant predictor of achievement.[1] When salespeople believed that they would make a particular sale, they were 55 percent more successful than their pessimistic counterparts. Your beliefs directly impact the outcome of your efforts, so it is essential to swap out your negative beliefs so you can reach your potential or surpass what you presently believe is your potential. I spend a substantial amount of energy and time with people who think bigger than I do because it edits my own stories about my potential, and doing so has expanded my life and my company more than I ever expected. (Of course I didn't expect it; I had a limiting story!)

The second aspect of consciousness engineering is upgrading your systems for living, also known as your habits. Vishen says that your habits are like the apps on your phone. They consist of things such as your diet, your exercise routine, and your sleep hygiene—the patterns that shape your days. He recommends learning new systems through studying the greats and finding out what habits made a difference for the most impactful people . . . kind of like what you're doing by reading this book!

To learn more about how to easily create new habits, I sought out Robert Cooper, a neuroscientist and *New York Times* bestselling author who has positively impacted the 4 million people who have bought his books. Robert effectively combines two fields that seem completely unrelated—neuroscience and business strategy—to help elite performers and top leaders get the most out of their brains, their time, and their performance.

I asked Robert to deliver the keynote address at the third annual Bulletproof Biohacking Conference and sat down with him afterward to talk about how to hack the hardwired habits that can limit performance and build new habits that will burn better programs into the structure of the brain. Robert says that the brain has an embedded performance code for the world of two thousand years ago. You can ignore this outdated programming and hope for the best, or you can upgrade and reprogram (or rewire, in neuroscientific terms) the brain to become compatible with the reality of today's world.

First, you have to become aware of the brain's default settings. Our instinct is to do things the same way we've always done them. This is helpful on a day-to-day basis, such as when you drive to work using the same route as always without even thinking about it, but constantly reverting to automatic behaviors can shut down innovative thinking. Robert calls this your "hard wiring." Your "live wiring," on the other hand, represents your ability to grow and change—the "plastic" part of neuroplasticity.

Robert says that even when you are relying on your hard wiring, your brain is constantly changing. The question then becomes: In which direction are you changing? When you settle in to your default mode and rigidify like a grumpy creature of habit that gets mad if someone takes his or her favorite seat at the table, you are "downwiring." Many people downwire as they age, but it doesn't have to be that way. When you lean into possibilities and become different with the intention to get better, you are "upwiring."

The key to upgrading your performance is to spend the majority of your time upwiring rather than downwiring. Yet, to conserve energy, your brain's instinct is to downwire. It likes repeating the same things it's done before and keeping you the same person you've always been.

This is why for many people it is more comfortable and less scary to stay the same. In many ways, your brain is a scared, dumb organ that fears change. (No offense.) Upwiring requires more effort and more risk. You have to aim your brain away from its comfortable default mode and instead steer it toward intentional choices that support the kind of growth you want to achieve.

To do this, Robert encourages you to identify moments when you can prevent an automatic response and instead guide yourself in a better direction. Many mindfulness experts refer to such a moment as a "meta moment"—a sliver of time between a trigger and a response. For example, when someone says something that bothers you, instead of reacting with anger as you normally would (downwiring), pause to consider why the comment upset you so much and then choose with intention how you want to respond (upwiring). With practice, finding meta moments will eventually become a habit like any other.

It's exciting to know that your brain, your beliefs, and your reality are incredibly changeable. You decide who you are, and you can also choose your own truth. That is a powerful game changer.

Action Items

- Chose one of the methods from this law to figure out which of your beliefs about yourself are actually true. Be extra suspicious about any belief that suggests you "should" be some way or do something, any belief that says you "have to" or "need to," and any belief that paints people or the world in terms of good and bad. Write down the first three that come to mind:

  - Belief 1: _____

  - Belief 2: _____

  - Belief 3: _____

    - Meditate on things you believe to be true about yourself and the world around you. Do it either in the morning or at night.

- Journal about the things you believe to be true for a half hour once a week. Start today.
- Schedule a recurring monthly or weekly appointment with a coach or a therapist who can point out when you believe your own story.

- For one week, as you meditate or when you wake up, experiment with repeating and focusing on this phrase and actually summoning the feeling of gratitude: "I'm grateful that there is a conspiracy to make things happen the way they're supposed to. The universe has my back." You don't have to believe it, but do your best to feel it—you're tricking your nervous system.
- Build the habit of listening. The programming most of us have is to think about what we're going to say next instead of listening to what the other person is saying. The story that drives this habit is one you learn as a child—that when adults are talking, no one will hear you unless you talk right away. The reality we live in now is that if you listen and then speak, *everyone* will hear you. Choose a friend or colleague who usually has something good to say and commit to consciously *not* planning what you're going to say the next time you chat with them. You'll be surprised by what you learn and what you do end up saying when you don't plan ahead. Who is the person near you most worth listening to?

Recommended Listening
- Vishen Lakhiani, "10 Laws & Four-Letter Words," *Bulletproof Radio*, episode 309
- Robert Cooper, "Rewiring Your Brain & Creating New Habits," *Bulletproof Radio*, episode 261
- Gabrielle Bernstein, "Detox Your Thoughts to Supercharge Your Life," *Bulletproof Radio*, episode 455

Recommended Reading

- Vishen Lakhiani, *The Code of the Extraordinary Mind: 10 Unconventional Laws to Redefine Your Life and Succeed on Your Own Terms*
- Robert K. Cooper, *Get Out of Your Own Way: The 5 Keys to Surpassing Everyone's Expectations*
- Gabrielle Bernstein, *The Universe Has Your Back: Transform Fear to Faith*

Law 5: A High IQ Doesn't Make You Intelligent, but Learning Does

Your IQ score measures your crystallized intelligence, the sum of your learning and experience. You can raise it, but it doesn't matter as much as fluid memory, your ability to learn and synthesize new information. Most scientists still believe that fluid intelligence is fixed, but it's not. So hack it. There are specific techniques to drastically increase your fluid memory that are waiting for you to use them. You can waste your time learning slowly or set yourself free by changing your brain and upgrading how you learn.

Jim Kwik is a superhero. He is a widely recognized world expert in speed-reading, memory improvement, brain performance, and accelerated learning. He's humble about it, but he's trained countless Fortune 500 CEOs and dozens of A-list actors and actresses, including the cast of the *X-Men* movies. He actually trained Professor X! Jim often appears onstage doing speed-reading demonstrations and memorizing hundreds of people's names. But he doesn't do this to impress or show off. He does it to show what is possible not just for him but for anyone. When we have dinner, Jim memorizes the name of every restaurant employee who comes to the table because it makes people feel good when you refer to them by name.

Jim was not born with these abilities. In fact, when he was in kindergarten, he had a very bad accident that resulted in brain trauma. He was left with learning challenges and poor focus, and he constantly struggled to keep up with his classmates. When Jim got to college, he was sick of always lagging behind. He wanted to start fresh and make his family proud, so he began working so hard that he neglected things such as sleeping, eating, exercising, and spending time with friends. Instead of fueling his performance, this left him passed out in the library from sheer exhaustion. He fell down a flight of stairs and hit his head again. When he woke up in the hospital two days later, he was down to 117 pounds, hooked up to a bunch of IVs, and deeply malnourished. He thought to himself, "There has to be a better way."

A moment later, a nurse came in with a mug of tea. The mug had a picture of Albert Einstein on it with the famous quote "The same level of thinking that's created the problem won't solve the problem." The universe had Jim's back that day, because the mug helped him realize he had always thought the problem was that he was a slow learner, so he had tried to solve the problem by spending all of his time learning. Now he asked himself if he could think about the problem differently: Instead of spending more time learning, could he find a way to learn faster?

Jim thought back over his education. In school, his teachers had taught him *what* to learn, but he'd never taken a class on *how* to learn—on creativity, problem solving, or how to think, concentrate, read faster, and, most important, improve his memory. Socrates said, "Without remembering, there is no learning." Jim realized that he could learn faster if he could remember more. So he began to study the mind and how it remembers to see if he could come up with shortcuts.

The memory techniques that Jim developed worked immediately. He went from struggling in his courses to getting straight A's, and he soon started using his techniques to help other people. He didn't want anyone to suffer or struggle the way he had.

One of Jim's very first students more than two decades ago was a freshman who wanted to read thirty books in thirty days and was able to do so successfully using Jim's techniques. He asked her why she wanted to do so and found out that her mother had been diagnosed with terminal cancer and was told she had sixty days to live. The books the student was reading were all about health, wellness, medicine, psychology, self-help, and spirituality—anything that she thought might be able to help save her mother's life.

Six months later, Jim got a call. At first he couldn't even make out the voice on the other end. All he heard was crying. Finally, he realized it was the same young woman. She was crying tears of joy because her mother not only had survived but was starting to get better and really thrive. The doctors didn't know how or why that had happened, but her mother attributed it to the great advice her daughter had gotten so quickly from all of those books.

That was when Jim realized that his ideas could change lives and in some cases even save lives. Ever since, he's been on a mission to help change the way people learn, help them fall in love with learning, and allow them to realize the genius they're capable of. He focuses a lot of his work on reading, because reading is a fundamental way people learn. If an author possesses decades of experience and knowledge that he or she has put into a book and you can sit down and read that book in a day or two and directly download all of that information, that's a powerful hack.

Unlike traditional speed-reading, which is more about skimming and getting the gist of what you read, Jim teaches how to read with greater focus and concentration so that you don't just read faster but you also learn and remember what you read more efficiently. His method aptly breaks down into the acronym F-A-S-T:

F: FORGET

It may seem kind of weird, when talking about learning, reading, and memory, to start with forgetting, but Jim found that a lot of people fail to learn anything new when they feel as though they know the subject already. Let's say you're an expert in nutrition and you attend a seminar on the subject. You should be absorbing all of the latest information, but most people fail to do that because when they consider themselves experts they close themselves off to learning anything new. You have to temporarily forget what you already know about a subject so you can learn something new. It may be a cliché, but it's true: Your mind is like a parachute; it works only when it's open. To open yours, forget about what you already know.

You also want to forget about limitations. A lot of people have self-limiting beliefs about how good their memory is or how smart they are. As Vishen suggests, these beliefs can hold you back. Jim explains that your mind is always eavesdropping on your self-talk. If you tell yourself that you are not good at remembering people's names, your mind won't be open to learning at its full potential. This is exactly how your false beliefs become true.

The last thing that you need to forget is everything else that's going on around you so that you can focus on what you are learning. Jim says that we can focus on only about seven bits of information at once. So if you're reading a book and thinking about the kids and worrying about work and wondering if you should take the garbage out, you are left with only four bits of new information that you can focus on. Set all that aside so you can focus on the book and learn as much as possible.

A: ACTIVE

Twentieth-century education was based on the model of rote learning and repetition. A teacher stood in front of a class and stated facts for the students to repeat over and over again. The students did learn that way, but the problem with this type of learning is that it takes a lot of time. Jim compares it to working out: You can go to the gym and lift five-pound weights for an hour every day, or you can go far less frequently but dramatically increase the weight you lift. Intense learning, like intense exercise, gives you results in less time.

Jim says that in the twenty-first century, education should be based on creation, not consumption. That requires us to be active partic-ipants in our learning, grabbing for knowledge instead of letting it be spooned into our mouths. That means taking notes actively and sharing what you learn. These techniques not only help you learn, they enable you to remember what you've learned.

Jim recommends taking notes the old-fashioned way: with pen and paper. Put a line down the middle of the page. The left side is for "capture notes," where you write down the thoughts and ideas you are learning; and the right side is for "creating notes," where you write your impressions, thoughts, and questions about what you are learning. This strategy engages your whole brain so that you can learn faster and remember more.

S: STATE

All learning is state dependent. Jim defines your state as the current condition or mood of your brain *and your body*. A lot of people don't realize that this is something that's fully within their control. Most people think that if they're bored, it's because of their environment. If they're down, it's because something bad happened to them. But Jim says that we're not thermometers, we're thermostats, meaning that we don't have to merely react to the environment around us. Instead, we can set a high standard for ourselves and then create and modify our environment to meet that setting.

T: TEACH

If you had to watch a video or read a book and then present it to someone else the next day, would you pay a different level of attention than you would otherwise? Would you organize or capture the information differently? If you ever have to learn a new subject or a new skill really fast, put on your professor's cap. Ask yourself, "How would I teach this to someone else?" All of a sudden you'll find that your retention of the information is doubled because you're taking it in with the intention of being able to explain it to someone else.

This last point about teaching is more powerful than you might imagine. At the start of my career in Silicon Valley, I sought out a side job at the University of California teaching working engineers how to build the internet. I ended up running the Web and internet engineering program at UCSC's Silicon Valley campus during the birth of the modern internet! That put me into a situation where I delivered a two-hour lecture several nights a week to a room of smart, experienced engineers. I had to absorb the material well enough to teach it, and I did. The result was that within two years, at the ripe age of twenty-seven, I was promoted to the head of technology-strategic planning for a billion-dollar company. There is simply no way I could have assimilated the knowledge required for that job had I not taught it first. So find an excuse to teach people what you want to learn, and you'll master it more quickly than you think. If you're not actually teaching something, pretend that you will be!

A conversation about fluid intelligence wouldn't be complete without talking with Dan Hurley, an award-winning science journalist who has developed a niche writing about the science of increasing intelligence. Dan is someone who has fundamentally changed the way we think about learning and intelligence. He says that when people talk about being smart, they're often referring to the knowledge and information they already possess. But they fail to look at where they got that knowledge and information in the first place. If a group of people were to sit in a class for the exact same amount of time and then study the information presented there for the exact same amount of time, they wouldn't all end up getting the same grades on a test. That's because they don't all learn as well—they have varying levels of fluid intelligence.

Your IQ is different from your fluid intelligence. Most IQ tests assess all sorts of factors, including crystallized knowledge, which speaks more to a person's experience than their abilities. As such, most intelligence studies don't bother with IQ tests. Scientists have known about fluid intelligence for a long time, but until recently, psychologists who study intelligence all agreed that you could not increase your fluid intelligence. They had been trying for a hundred years; they had done study after study after study. Then, in 2008, a group of scientists decided to focus on boosting working memory, a part of short-term memory.

Working memory is critical to fluid intelligence, and those scientists wanted to see if improving someone's working memory would also boost their fluid intelligence. They asked people to practice a simple two-minute test called the Dual N-Back to improve their working memory. After five weeks of practicing for half an hour a day, the people's fluid intelligence increased on average by 40 percent.[2] That was an incredible finding.

There's one downside, though. The Dual N-Back test is so irritating that it makes you want to throw your computer across the room. Think of it as CrossFit for your brain—you just have to keep pushing. When you take the test, you see something like a tic-tac-toe board on a screen. One square lights up, then another, then another. You are first asked to press a button every time a square that lit up two times ago lights up again. That's a two-back. Then, if you master that skill, which is pretty easy, you move on to a three-back. Throughout the test you are also listening to a voice reciting letters in a specific order that you also have to remember. So you have to remember which squares lit up three times ago *and* which letter you heard. It forces you to narrow your focus and really concentrate.

Though the test isn't much fun, it definitely produces results. Since that groundbreaking study in 2008, dozens of other studies have confirmed that performing working memory tasks increases not only your working memory but also all kinds of other intelligence-based skills, from reading comprehension to math ability. And this is just the tip of the iceberg; the field of intelligence research is really catching fire, and I'm excited to see what the future will hold.

I used a clunky open-source n-back training app when I started the Bulletproof blog in 2011, and when I had my IQ tested afterward, it had increased by 12 points. When I wrote about that result on my blog and shared the software I had used, it was surprising how many people insisted that my results were impossible. It's the standard science troll argument: "That can't be, therefore it isn't." All I can say is that the training worked for me then, and there is a lot more science supporting its efficacy now.

According to Dan, even though IQ tests don't measure fluid intelligence, IQ scores commonly increase when people improve their fluid memory. Despite my results, I found that the training was so exhausting and discouraging that many people wouldn't complete it. In the early days of Bulletproof, I flew around the world teaching hedge fund managers how to hack their brains. Even among this highly motivated crowd, very few people completed the n-back training because it makes you feel like a failure over and over before you see results.

If you're interested in trying it, my suggestion is to first use the other tools in this book to help strengthen your brain and your willpower. The n-back is a lot less triggering when your brain is running at full power, and if you're exercising your willpower muscle on a regular basis, you're a lot more likely to stick with it. Then I recommend doing the training for about a month. Your brain won't like it at first—you will get bored and frustrated and probably have strange dreams. As you get better, you may find that you have more verbal fluency (Dual N-Back radically improved my live presentation skills to the point that I regularly speak in front of millions of people with confidence and ease), better listening ability, better reading recall, and more. When you've completed it, you won't know how you functioned with only half of the working memory you just gained. It's that strong, like a RAM upgrade for your brain.

The best part about n-back training is that the effects seem to be permanent. After completing twenty sessions I did no training at all for a full eight months to see if I'd forget the skills I'd learned and have to start over. Astoundingly, the results were the exact opposite of what I had expected. After the break, I did better than ever, as if my brain had further optimized itself during those eight months off.

Action Items

- Try one of Jim Kwik's courses (https://kwiklearning.com) or another speed-reading course so you can literally learn faster.
- Teach a summary of this book to a friend, colleagues, your spouse, or your kids, so you'll remember it all!
- Improve your fluid intelligence by doing Dual N-Back training. I recommend the Dual N-Back app by Mikko Tyrskeranta on the iTunes and Android stores.

- Hints:
  - Do it for at least twenty days, but forty is best.
  - Do it at least five days a week, when you're not tired.
  - You may get stuck for a couple of weeks, but do it anyway.
  - Do not subvocalize (mutter to yourself) when you're training so that you're only activating the right side of your brain.
  - Push yourself to failure every time—move up a level even if you're only at 70 to 80 percent at an existing level. The software I recommend does this for you automatically.
  - Tell a friend or coach you're going to do Dual N-Back so they can make fun of you when you tell them how annoying it is. It's like going to the gym every day for a month—accountability helps.

Recommended Listening
- Jim Kwik, "Speed Reading, Memory & Superlearning," *Bulletproof Radio*, episode 189
- Jim Kwik, "Boost Brain Power, Upgrade Your Memory," *Bulletproof Radio*, episode 267
- Dan Hurley, "The Science of Smart," *Bulletproof Radio*, episode 104

Recommended Reading
- Dan Hurley, *Smarter: The New Science of Building Brain Power*

Law 6: Remember Images, Not Words

Your brain evolved in a world of sense, sound, and images, not a world of words. Train yourself to build images from what you read and hear so you can make full use of your brain's deeply rooted on-board visual hardware. Remembering in words will slow you down and waste energy you can put to better use.

Mattias Ribbing has a title you've probably never heard of: he is the leading brain trainer in Sweden and a three-time Swedish memory champion who is ranked number seventy-five in the world. Mattias has actually been awarded the title Grand Master of Memory by the World Memory Sports Council, which only 154 people have ever achieved. Mattias started hacking his memory in 2008. Before that, he says, he had an average memory; he could remember only ten or so digits at a time, while now he can memorize up to a thousand.

Mattias always loved learning, and when he discovered that his memory could be improved dramatically, he set out to train his brain. Just a few months later, he won his first Swedish memory championship. He compares brain training to learning to drive a car. It takes a few months, and then you have a new ability for the rest of your life. Even better, the skill can increase and become stronger over the years, just like (hopefully) your driving skills.

Mattias says that the basic way to hack your memory is to teach your brain how to think in *images* rather than words. This requires training your visualization skills. When you visualize images, information takes a shortcut in the memory-storage part of the brain, skipping over short-term memory and heading straight to long-term memory. Out of our five senses, our sight is the most important to the brain, because it is the most closely tied to our survival. Three-quarters of the neurons that work with our senses are connected to sight. (This is also why poor-quality light sources drain so much of your brain energy and why we use TrueDark glasses when brain training at the 40 Years of Zen neurofeedback program.) Some people think that they learn better through sound or through touch, but Mattias says the experts know that we learn best through visualization. Learning through doing or teaching is an even more powerful way to remember new information, but that's because both of those approaches engage your visual senses.

When you learn through sound by repeating information out loud over and over again, the brain can take in only a tiny amount of data at once. When we learn in images, our brains absorb more information more quickly. How does this work on an everyday, practical level? Let's say you're reading the newspaper. As you read, see if you can visualize the contents of a particular article as if it were a movie in your mind. Start off with something that's relatively easy to visualize. For example, instead of using an article about the economy or international politics for this purpose, look at the local police blotter and imagine a story about a robbery.

Picture the robber fleeing, coming out from a bank, and running down the pavement. What does he look like? Picture his black hat, green jacket, and yellow pants. Imagine him running, being chased by two cops with their guns drawn. Can you really see it? Train your mind to hold that image for a little bit. Then make it bigger. Notice the robber's eyes, his hair. What does his face look like? Start to see the pavement in greater detail.

You've probably done this before without even thinking about it, most likely when reading a novel. When you intentionally create such images, though, you can better remember the details because the images create a lasting imprint in our brains. The more often you do this, the more it will start to happen naturally. Images will start to pop up automatically, and learning through visualizations will become your new habit.

If you think you're "not a visual person," you simply need to become better at visualization. To do so, start with something simple. Close your eyes and visualize a dog. Choose a specific type of dog, the first one that comes to your mind. When visualizing, you should always use the first image that comes to your mind. See the dog in front of you. Now make that image bigger. See it in more detail, as clearly as possible. It's important to make sure that your visualizations are in 3-D. Those images last longer in the brain than one-dimensional images do.

You can start with a dog or a newspaper article, but Mattias says that after a while you will begin to habitually translate all kinds of information into images, even numbers and crazy math formulas. He suggests practicing this skill every time you hear someone speak. As you listen, see what images pop up in your mind and hold them there. Really focus on the details so you remember them well. The images will function like clues that your brain can follow to find its way back to the original information. Eventually, with practice, your brain will work almost like a magnet, attracting new information and holding on to it.

Of course, the technique of visualization is nothing groundbreaking— it's an ancient concept that has been practiced for millennia. When I went to Tibet to learn meditation, the monks directed me to sit for hours in a temple with my eyes closed performing incredibly detailed visualizations. Not "Visualize the Buddha." More like, "Visualize the Buddha sitting on a throne. The throne has three steps. Each step has a painting of three flowers with six petals." By the time they got to describing what the Buddha was wearing and in what position he was sitting, there was no possible way to remember it all without crafting the image. I didn't realize at the time that visualizing was training my brain to paint images instead of remember words, but that was exactly the outcome.

At his level of expertise, Mattias says that he can store information indefinitely by scrolling through the images he's created, as if he were browsing through pictures on his smartphone. He never has to reference the original information again, just the images in his mind. He practices visualizations during quiet times, such as when he's waiting for someone or brushing his teeth. He scrolls through a few images at a time to keep them stored in his memory.

Images are useful for more than remembering lists. In fact, I still suck at remembering long lists, and memorizing things has always made my eyes cross. Yet I'm grateful for the tool of visualization, because it allows me to harness the power of images to upgrade my performance. It allows me to understand and interact with a wide variety of experts from all sorts of backgrounds as diverse as functional neuroscience, business leadership, hormone replacement, athletic performance, and antiaging without being clueless. I couldn't keep all of the information about each of these people and their areas of expertise straight in my head to conduct a good interview if my brain were simply full of words. In fact, I wrote my last book by first drawing pictures of mitochondrial pathways for each chapter and *then* crafting the words. It's all about the image: when you visualize a detailed picture of something, you gain a kind of knowledge that simply isn't possible through rote memorization.

After all, as Mattias explained to me, language is limited. There are only so many words in any language, but there are endless images. And just like those images, if you train your brain and upgrade your hardware, your software, and your wiring, you, too, can become limitless.

Action Items

- The next time you listen to a podcast or an audiobook, *close your eyes* and see if you can imagine the pictures that the speaker is trying to draw in your head. Closing your eyes puts you into an alpha brain state, which is conducive to creativity and frees up your visual hardware. (Obviously, do this only when you're not driving or otherwise engaged!)
- Try mind mapping—drawing notes on paper using very few words but illustrating the connections between them.
- Consider taking Jim Kwik's courses on memory at www .jimkwik.com.
- Especially if memorizing things is a goal, consider Mattias Ribbing's online courses (including a free training) at www.grandmasterofmemory.com.

Recommended Listening

- Mattias Ribbing, "Mastering Memory," *Bulletproof Radio*, episode 140
- Jim Kwik, "Speed Reading, Memory & Superlearning," *Bulletproof Radio*, episode 189
- Jim Kwik, "Boost Brain Power, Upgrade Your Memory," *Bulletproof Radio*, episode 267

GET OUTSIDE YOUR HEAD SO YOU CAN SEE INSIDE IT

Time and time again, the world-changers I've interviewed have brought up the importance of finding self-awareness in order to achieve success and happiness. In the data analysis, self-awareness ranked as the sixth most important thing for performing better. But what is self-awareness, really? You could define it as an intimate understanding of the normally subconscious factors that motivate you. These factors include not only your passions and your fears but also your limiting beliefs and all of the ways your past traumas—big and small—are affecting your daily life. It is only when you make these normally subconscious pieces of yourself conscious that you can start doing the necessary work to change them and finally get out of your own way.

There are many ways to become more self-aware, from meditation (which we will discuss in chapter 13) to creating intimate connections with others (which we will explore in chapter 5). But there is another powerfully effective—albeit less conventional—method for tapping into an enhanced state that can lead to self-awareness:

Drugs.

More specifically, nootropics—compounds that enhance brain function, also known as "smart drugs," as well as strategically used (usually) legally regulated substances. Although none of the guests on the show said outright that using mind-altering drugs (psychedelics or hallucinogens such as ayahuasca, DMT, mushrooms, MDMA, or LSD) was one of their most important pieces of advice for someone wanting to perform better, looking at the data and judging from our behind-the-scenes conversations, it became clear that many of my guests have used these tools *occasionally* as a mechanism to find that all-important self-awareness. Game changers honor and seek the transcendent parts of life because that is where the boundaries of high performance are found. One reason you don't hear guests talk about it on the air is because microdosing—the practice of taking small, controlled doses of these substances—is still illegal in most places. It does carry real risks, but this book would be incomplete if it ignored this increasingly common and effective technology. Dozens of guests have asked me about it or shared stories—just not when the microphone is live.

It's important to note that all of the guests who mentioned hallucinogens *also* have a meditation practice and other means of finding self-awareness that they use in conjunction with natural or pharmaceutical drugs. They're not taking drugs recklessly or with the goal of getting high. Though there is a vocal minority out there that insists you can simply take a bunch of hallucinogens to find enlightenment or inner peace, that's not what I'm talking about here, and it doesn't work. The whole concept of biohacking is about doing everything you can to achieve your biological goals, and it's up to each of us to define his or her own risk/reward ratio.

For years, I've been open about my goals—to live to at least 180 years old, maximize my potential, and literally radiate energy—and my occasional use of carefully chosen plant medicines and pharmaceuticals to help me reach those goals. For some reason, taking brain-enhancing drugs is seen as controversial. Some people view it as "cheating," but chemicals are just tools: you can use them for good or harm. In my mind, taking a drug to help me become more self-aware or to sharpen my focus is no different from drinking coffee to help me become less tired, using reading glasses to see the words on a page more clearly, or popping a Tylenol to quell a headache that is preventing me from getting my work done. There is risk involved in each—coffee can harm sleep, reading glasses make your eyes weaker, and Tylenol is bad for your liver. Yet we regularly use these tools when the benefit is greater than the risk *based on our own goals.*

It's about time that we consider all available options to help people better understand themselves. Face it: spending your whole life slowly struggling to get out of your own way is simply disrespectful of the life you're lucky to have and all the people you may not treat with compassion or respect because of what's going on in your head. In my opinion, if an occasional pharmaceutical dosage of a hallucinogenic drug in a legal, safe setting can help, it's worth considering. It's helped me.

Few people know that one of the founding fathers of our country was a physician named Dr. Benjamin Rush. He lobbied to include medical freedom as a basic right and warned the other founding fathers of the risk of "medical tyranny" if they did not protect our right to choose what medicines we wanted. Dr. Rush was one of the original biohackers. Two hundred years ago, he believed in organizing all medical knowledge around explaining why people got sick instead of how to treat them and the importance of the environment and the brain on health, and he was a founder of the field of American psychiatry. His science was way off base (inducing vomiting, bleeding, and blistering aren't really good for you, although they were common tactics two hundred years ago, before we knew about microbes). Still, he'd be at the top of my list of people to interview if he were alive today, based on the change he caused. (I hope Lin-Manuel Miranda, who created *Hamilton*, is reading this!)

I side with Dr. Rush when it comes to medical freedom. Whether or not you approve of others using cognition-enhancing drugs—including psychedelics—it is a basic human right to choose what we put into our own bodies. My body, my biochemistry, my decision. So let's talk about it.

Law 7: Smart Drugs Are Here to Stay

When your brain is working at its full capacity, everything you want to do requires less effort, including the work it takes to become more self-aware. Nootropics, or smart drugs, do just that: they make you smarter. Lots of them are legal, but some are not. If you're not actively supporting your cognitive function in every way, you're simply less likely to perform well at whatever matters most to you.

There are literally hundreds of compounds documented to increase cognitive function in one way or another, and more of them come from plants than from pharmaceutical manufacturers. Over the last twenty years, I've tried every one I could find. Some had relatively no impact on me (other than causing headaches and nausea); others have had a tremendous impact. My feedback from those experiences has resulted in the development of multiple plant-based nootropic formulas at Bulletproof. But what I want to discuss here are the potent nootropics you *aren't* going to find made by a supplement company.

A Swiss chemist named Albert Hofmann first discovered high-dose LSD's effects in 1943 when he accidentally ingested some in his lab. At first he was terrified that he had poisoned himself, but when his lab assistant checked his vital signs and assured him that he was fine, he settled down and found that LSD opened his mind to perspective-altering insights and intensified his emotions. He recognized that LSD had therapeutic benefits.

A few years later, Dr. Stanislav Grof, the father of transpersonal psychology, legally, as a licensed psychiatrist, treated thousands of patients with LSD with great success in what was then Czechoslovakia. Today, LSD is probably the most famous psychedelic, but over the last several years the conversation has shifted from dropping acid at Burning Man to taking a controlled microdose as a nootropic. Among Silicon Valley tech employees and other high performers, including ultraendurance athletes, microdosing LSD has become pretty commonplace (and at least one elite athlete disclosed to me that he thought *most* people running 100-mile races were microdosing LSD).

This idea is not as crazy as it may sound. LSD is certainly a mind-expanding drug. The key to using it as a nootropic is taking a tiny dose—one-twentieth to one-tenth of a full dose. For some people, this leads to increased positivity, creativity, focus, and empathy without creating any psychedelic effects. A few creative leaders have been using drugs such as LSD for years but very infrequently. Steve Jobs credited LSD with contributing to his success with Apple. He said that taking a full dose of LSD was a profound experience and one of the most important things he'd done in his life.[1]

LSD causes the region in the brain that is involved in introspection (thinking about yourself) to communicate more intensely than usual with the part of the brain that perceives the outside world.[2] This could explain why many people feel at one with the universe and others and set their egos aside when using LSD. It also interacts with the brain's neural circuits that use the "feel-good" neurotransmitter seratonin, mimicking seratonin in the brain.[3] Though some people worry that this could potentially cause addiction (when a drug mimics a chemical, the body can begin to rely on that drug instead of producing the chemical itself), studies suggest that LSD is far less risky than its reputation suggests.

Even at a full dose (ten to twenty times a microdose), researchers ranked LSD as the fourth least dangerous recreational drug—far below alcohol and nicotine[4]—and historically not a single person has died from an LSD overdose.[5] But lots of people *have* died from doing stupid things while tripping on LSD, and some people who take it end up worse off psychologically than when they started. Long-term usage is also probably a bad idea. In one study, researchers administered full doses to rats every other day for ninety days and found hyperactivity, decreased social interaction, and changes to the genes for energy metabolism.[6] It is not risk free, especially if you use it for fun instead of for personal growth with assistance from trained and experienced experts, or if you use it before your brain is done growing (in your early twenties).

The benefits of LSD are real, however. In two double-blind studies, participants with life-threatening illnesses showed a significant decrease in anxiety after LSD-assisted therapy with no negative side effects or safety issues.[7] A meta-analysis of 536 participants taken from studies in the 1950s and 1960s (before the drug became illegal) found that a single dose of LSD significantly decreased alcoholism.[8] The effect lasted for many months after the single dose. More recently, a 2006 study found that LSD decreased the intensity and frequency of cluster headaches.[9]

More relevant to this book, LSD can actually power up your brain. It increases the production of brain-derived neurotrophic factor (BDNF), a powerful protein that stimulates your production of brain cells and strengthens existing ones.[10] Studies have found that psyche-delics help rabbits learn a new task more quickly.[11] We don't know for sure if this translates to human learning, but it's promising and may be one reason why psychedelic-assisted therapy helps patients combat depression and post-traumatic stress disorder (PTSD) more effectively than standard therapy does. Other psychedelics, such as mushrooms and ayahuasca (a shamanic brew from South America containing dimethyltryptamine [DMT], which we will discuss later), also raise BDNF. Exercise also increases BDNF; I like to stack my BDNF stimulators for the greatest possible benefit.

Steve Jobs was not the only game changer to have used psyche-delics on the quest for self-awareness. Tim Ferriss, the author of *The 4-Hour Workweek, The 4-Hour Body,* and *Tools for Titans,* appeared on *Bulletproof Radio* twice. Tim talked about his experience using ibogaine, an African psychedelic, in a microdosing protocol.

Ibogaine is used by some people as a very mild stimulant. In fact, it was sold in France many years ago for precisely that purpose. Ibo-gaine has a poor safety record compared to other psychedelics, mostly related to cardiac events. Tim estimates that somewhere between one in a hundred and one in three hundred people who use ibogaine will experience a fatal cardiac event and recommends doing so only un-der proper medical supervision while hooked up to machines that track your pulse and heart rate. Tim microdosed ibogaine at very low dosages—a range of 2 to 4 milligrams, which is about one-hundredth of a full dose. He experienced a mild prefrontal headache and had a slightly buzzy, very mildly anxious feeling for the first three to four hours. But in that period of time, he did experience heightened at-tention.

What was most interesting, though, was not what happened on that first day but what happened subsequently. For the next two to three days, Tim reports, his happiness set point was about 15 to 20 percent higher than usual. He also felt highly nonreactive: He was cool and dispassionate and didn't react emotionally. This is a state he says would normally take him two to three weeks of daily meditation to reach.

Am I suggesting that you microdose ibogaine to increase your performance? Absolutely not. I haven't tried it and am not planning to because the risk isn't worth the reward for me. I have young kids. My happiness set point is consistently higher than it ever has been. My flow state comes from service to others, public speaking, EEG neuro-feedback, and writing. But again, I believe everyone should have the right to weigh the risks and choose for themselves.

Tim made sure to have medical personnel in attendance when he tried ibogaine, in part because he has witnessed the negative effects of hallucinogens firsthand. When he was much younger, he experi-mented with LSD, decided to go for a walk, and stepped right into the street. He "came to" standing in the middle of the road at night with headlights bearing down on him. He also knew someone with a family history of schizophrenia who had gone from super-high-functioning to barely communicative after they'd used LSD. Some medical ex-perts believe that psychedelics can exacerbate or even trigger mental illnesses such as schizophrenia. Yet there are many applications for these drugs, and Tim and I are both glad that many game changers are initiating a responsible conversation about them.

In service of my own growth, I traveled to Amsterdam nineteen years ago to try medical mushrooms, which were legal there. That sin-gle experience profoundly changed my brain, drawing my attention to hard-to-find patterns. It taught me to look at the world more closely, and I believe it helped me process some of my own fears that were holding me back and to see the stories I was telling myself so I could start editing them. That's the real value of this type of medicine. Did taking mushrooms help in my success, and would I do it again? Abso-lutely, and without reservation.

Note that I was in a country where I could legally use mushrooms. As a biohacker, I make it a point to try everything that might help me raise my limits, but I don't want to go to jail, either. In 2013, I micro-dosed LSD for thirty days straight and found the effect to be simi-lar to that of other entirely legal nootropics you'll read about later in the chapter. I found it's not worth the legal risk because the rewards weren't that high *for me*. If it were free of legal risk, I'd add it to my nootropic stack some of the time.

Even microdosing isn't without career risk. During my thirty-day experiment, I accidentally took a slightly higher dose than planned one morning. I felt mild elation right before I went onstage in front of a room of about 150 influential executives in Los Angeles to be interviewed about biohacking. Not good. I made it through the interview mostly unscathed, although I cracked a couple jokes that weren't funny to anyone except me. If the dose had been even a little bit higher, who knows what else I would have said? Even when you're far from high, your judgment may be altered when microdosing, and you won't know it until later.

And yes, I go to Burning Man and greatly value my experiences there, some of which may include full-dose psychedelics. When they do, it's always with people who are there to make it safe (including medical professionals), and I walk away better off. More on full-dose experiences later. The bottom line is that microdosing psychedelics is neither a panacea for personal growth and performance nor entirely useless and dangerous. Psychedelics can heal. They can harm. At very low doses, they can increase your performance. If you decide to use them, start slowly, do so with a trusted person, do so for the first time when you're not planning a big day at work, and do so in a legal jurisdiction. These aren't party drugs.

You also can't expect to pop a pill and suddenly possess new levels of self-awareness. When used appropriately, these drugs can activate an elevated consciousness that triggers new insights, but to truly cultivate self-awareness, you still have to do the work. In other words, drugs in and of themselves won't make you more aware, but they can give you the opportunity to see the things you need to work on. It's up to you to then take action and work on them!

But microdosing psychedelics is far from the only way to benefit from certain drugs. I have actively benefited from another class of drugs, nootropics, since 1997, when I was grappling with a steep decline in my cognitive performance at work. When my doctor was ill equipped to help, I took matters into my own hands and ordered almost $1,000 worth of smart drugs from Europe (the only place where you could get them at the time). I remember opening the unmarked brown package and wondering whether the contents would actually improve my brain. They did, and I've been a big fan of certain cognitive enhancers ever since.

Like psychedelics, smart drugs won't automatically blanket you in self-awareness. Finding self-awareness takes energy. Anytime you can give yourself better cellular function, more energy, increased neuroplasticity, and improved learning abilities (which many of these drugs do), it makes gaining self-awareness easier. You can progress more quickly if you're running on high power.

The trouble with using a blanket term such as *nootropics* is that it lumps all kinds of substances together. Technically, you could argue that caffeine and cocaine are both nootropics, but they're hardly equal. With so many ways to enhance your brain function, many of which have significant risks, it's most valuable to look at nootropics on a case-by-case basis. Below are just a few of the nootropics I've had the most success with over the years.

RACETAMS

Perhaps the biggest supporter of the racetam family is Steve Fowkes, a biochemist who wrote and edited a newsletter called *Smart Drug News* starting in the 1980s. It was his early work that brought nootropics to my attention and inspired me to order that umarked brown package of smart drugs. Imagine my delight when he ended up becoming a guest on *Bulletproof Radio* twenty years later! Steve explains that the racetam family of pharmaceuticals contains dozens of related compounds, including a few well-known nootropics. The best studied one is piracetam, but the most effective racetam nootropics I've found are aniracetam and phenylpiracetam. I like aniracetam more than piracetam because it is fast acting, reduces stress, and increases your ability to get things into and out of your memory. Phenylpiracetam is highly energizing and stimulating, which helps with some tasks but hinders some others. It is also a banned substance in some sports.

When I take 800 milligrams of aniracetam, I find I speak more fluently and don't ever grasp for words. This effect is likely due to the fact that the racetam family improves mitochondrial function and sends extra oxygen to the brain. Most of the research has been done on people with neurological problems (with amazing results), but there is plenty of good evidence to support its use in healthy individuals. In studies, 400 milligrams of phenylpiracetam taken daily for a year significantly improved brain function and cognition in people recovering from a stroke;[12] 200 milligrams of phenylpiracetam taken for thirty days improved neurological function by 7 percent in people with brain damage[13] and by 12 percent in people with epilepsy.[14] In studies on rats, aniracitam improved memory and countered depression.[15] A single small study of piracetam in healthy adults found that after fourteen days it significantly improved verbal learning.[16]

The side effects are minor—mostly racetams can amplify the effects of caffeine or use up a nutrient called choline, which you can easily replenish by eating egg yolks or supplementing with CDP choline or sunflower lecithin. The risk/reward ratio of this family is very good. They're legal in the United States and widely available online. Do not start with a "stack" of multiple racetams. Try each one separately and note how you feel; the effects of each are highly variable. You're as likely to get angry, develop a headache, or feel nothing from a stack as you are to get what you're looking for because of cross reactions.

MODAFINIL (PROVIGIL)

Have you ever seen the movie *Limitless* with Bradley Cooper? It's loosely based on modafinil. This stuff gives you superhuman mental processing powers with few to no downsides. Studies show that in healthy adults, modafinil improves fatigue levels, motivation, reaction time, and vigilance.

I used modafinil for eight years—it helped me with everything from studying at Wharton to working on a start-up that sold for $600 million. I wouldn't have an MBA without it. I've recommended it to countless friends with great results, and you may have seen me on ABC's *Nightline* or CNN talking about using it for executive performance.

Nightline sent a crew to my house for two days because I was the only executive they could find who would publicly admit I was using it to get ahead at work and school. I was public about it because I wanted to drive a national conversation about smart drugs and remove the stigma. It worked, and smart drugs are much better known now.

Modafinil improves memory and mood, reduces impulsive decision making, increases your resistance to fatigue, and even improves your brain function when you are suffering from lack of sleep. A recent peer-reviewed analysis from Oxford and Harvard of twenty-four studies of modafinil since 1990 found the same things I've been writing about based on what it did for me: it significantly enhanced attention, executive function, and learning in healthy people who were not deprived of sleep while they were performing complex tasks—with just about zero side effects. The authors concluded that "modafinil may well deserve the title of the first well-validated pharmaceutical nootropic agent."[17] Bam!

Unlike many other smart drugs, modafinil is not a stimulant; it is actually a eugeroic—a wakefulness-promoting agent. That means it doesn't make you speedy or jittery like most classical stimulants do, and it doesn't cause you to crash or go through withdrawal because it is not addictive.[18] I found that I could actually decrease my dose as my health improved and I needed less of it to function optimally. At this point, it's been four years since I've had a use for it. When I apply all the other hacks, there is no meaningful measurable difference between my brain on modafinil and off it. But I keep it in my travel bag in case I want to pull out all the stops in an emergency. I don't think I'll ever need it again because I have built energy reserves beyond my wildest expectations, but I'm glad it's in my bag of tricks if I ever do.

Actually, screw that. After rereading all the research that went into writing this section, I just decided to take 50 milligrams in case it makes the rest of the book better. I'm kind of excited to see what happens.

If you deal with jet lag or intense fatigue or occasionally really want to get something done, this can be a powerful nootropic and a life changer. It's not risk free—some people develop headaches when using it, and about five in 1 million people can develop a life-threatening autoimmune condition—a risk similar to that of taking ibuprofen. If you know your genetic sequence (from 23andMe or a similar service), you can check to see if you have the genes that put you at risk. They are listed on the Bulletproof blog. Modafinil does not mix well with alcohol.

You can buy modafinil online from India without a prescription from a US doctor, and most of it is real. However, to get a prescription in the United States, it really helps if you can claim to have symptoms of shift worker sleep disorder, which most insurance companies will reimburse. Since this is a medical drug, it's best to get a prescription. Your doctor may recommend a more expensive, sometimes more potent, form, called Nuvigil.

Holy crap, the modafinil from two paragraphs ago just kicked in. Why have I been writing this book without it?

NICOTINE

I have never been a smoker, and smoking is gross and bad for you. But nicotine, separately from tobacco, is just one of the thousands of chemicals in cigarette smoke. And when you use it orally at low doses in its pure form—without toxins and carcinogens wrapped around it and rolled into a cigarette—nicotine can be a formidable nootropic. It's reportedly the most widely studied cognition-enhancing substance on Earth, even more than coffee.

When you take the right amount, nicotine can do a lot for your performance. For starters, it gives you faster, more precise motor function. People show more controlled and fluent handwriting after taking nicotine, and they're also able to tap their fingers faster without sacrificing accuracy.[19] Nicotine makes you more vigilant and sharpens your short-term memory. In a study, people who were given nicotine via patches and gum better recalled a list of words they'd just read and also repeated a story word for word making fewer mistakes than people who took a placebo.[20] You can even speed up your reaction time with nicotine. Both smokers and nonsmokers reacted more quickly to visual cues after a nicotine injection,[21] although I'll save my injections for vitamins, thanks.

Of course, there are some real downsides to nicotine, the most infamous of which is its addictive potential. Nicotine activates your mesolimbic dopamine system, which scientists have aptly nicknamed the brain's "pleasure pathway." The pleasure pathway is a double-edged sword. Food, sex, love, and rewarding drugs all cause this part of your brain to light up, sending a euphoric rush of dopamine through your system and leaving you in bliss. If you indulge on a regular basis, though, the constant stimulation dulls the pathway. Your receptors start to pull back into your neurons, where they are very hard to activate, and you start to feel physically ill unless you get more of whatever you were enjoying or something else equally stimulating. That's how dependence starts. The good news is that the physical symptoms of nicotine withdrawal peak three to five days after quitting. It's the psychological withdrawal from smoking (not just nicotine) that is famously hard to resist. So don't smoke or vape. Lozenges, gum, spray, and patches work better and are less habit forming.

Nicotine by itself (separate from tobacco) also promotes cancer in rats and mice. This cancer link has never shown up in human studies, even after lots of tries. What is known is that nicotine promotes angiogenesis, the formation of new blood vessels.[22] If you have heart disease or are exercising or training your brain, angiogenesis is a good thing because your body is supposed to be growing new blood vessels as part of its self-repair. If you have existing tumors, this is a very bad thing.

If you don't have cancer, nicotine, taken orally, is kidney protective, and it mimics the effect of exercise on the body through a protein called PGC-1 alpha. Researchers believe this compound may have played a key role in differentiating humans from apes,[23] and it is the master regulator of mitochondrial biogenesis.[24] In other words, it makes your cells (including brain cells) build new power plants. It's also a key regulator of energy metabolism and upregulates thyroid hormone receptor genes and mitochondrial function. If you read *Head Strong*, you know that almost anything you do to make your mitochondria function well is going to help your brain. Nicotine fills the bill!

(Pardon me while I take a writing break to enjoy an unreleased early version of a "clean" nicotine product. It seems that a great many works of literature have been written under the influence of caffeine and nicotine, including this one.)

You can get addicted to nicotine, so it is good for occasional use unless you decide that it's okay to be addicted to something that grows new blood vessels and increases mitochondrial function. It is profoundly helpful for writing, and the test product I mentioned earlier contained 1 milligram of oral nicotine, compared to the 6 to 12 milligrams you would find in a nasty cigarette. Gums, patches, and oral lozenges or sprays are the best forms because oral (not smoked or vaped) nicotine provides different benefits. Most oral nicotine products have bad artificial sweeteners and chemicals in them. If you're using nicotine for your brain, why add in crap that moves the needle in the wrong direction? I'm a fan of start-ups such as Lucy gum (www .lucynicotine.com) that are working to release nicotine products with clean ingredients. Gum chewing never makes you look cool, so it's a good thing that you use nicotine gum by tucking it into your cheek instead of smacking it.

I'm so glad nicotine is in my brain. And smoking is gross.

CAFFEINE

Few people know this, but the first commercial product ever sold over the internet was a T-shirt that read, CAFFEINE: MY DRUG OF CHOICE. I know this because in 1993 I sold it out of my dorm room, resulting in a photo of my three-hundred-pound round-faced self appearing in *Entrepreneur* magazine wearing the shirt in size XXL. So of course, caffeine is my favorite nootropic of all time. Actually, coffee is. Coffee is made up of thousands of compounds, and caffeine is just one of them.

By itself (not just in coffee), caffeine is an energy booster and cognitive enhancer. Caffeine may even help ease cognitive decline and lower your risk of developing Alzheimer's disease by blocking inflammation in the brain.[25] You already know that this book is powered by coffee (and just a few additional nootropics).

One reason caffeine is in this book is to give you pause. If you think cognition-enhancing substances are something too crazy to try, put down that coffee cup and pick up a glass of nice, bitter kale juice. See how long that change lasts! If you're like most people, you've been taking one of Mother Nature's greatest nootropics for years, without knowing that you were on nootropics. The truth is that mankind has sought out cognitive enhancement since the beginning of civilization, and the technologies in this chapter are just a continuation of that long and noble tradition.

The bottom line is that all cognitive enhancers carry some risks, but top performers decide whether those risks are worth the rewards. It's up to you to weigh the benefits against the potential downsides and determine if it's worth it to you. If you do decide to experiment with any nootropics, please be safe, know your local laws, and follow the recommendations of a medical professional.

Smart drugs make you more of what you are, and they can be important tools in your self-awareness arsenal. They won't make you an enlightened, loving human overnight. If you're an asshole generally, you'll be a bigger one on smart drugs. But the experience of taking these drugs can help you to see your asshole tendencies when you would ordinarily be blind to them. The goal is to observe yourself and use your newfound smarts to do important personal development work if you haven't done so already.

Action Items

- Use psychedelic drugs only with intention, supervision, and solid legal advice to make sure you're not breaking the law. These are powerful tools, not toys. And do it after age twenty-four, after your brain's prefrontal cortex is fully formed.
- If you're going to microdose anything—from nicotine to LSD or anywhere in between—do your research first and know what you're getting. Start slow. Don't break the law. And don't do it for the first time before you go onstage, into a big meeting, or even behind the wheel of a car.
- Consider trying aniracetam or phenylpiracetam, the entry-level, very safe, quasi-pharmaceutical smart drugs.
- Consider a plant-based nootropic to see how it makes you perform. There is real science behind plant-based compounds

for cognitive enhancement, but it would take a whole book to write about them all. (I recommend Bulletproof's Smart Mode because I formulated it, but there are many.)

- Ask three people you trust to give you honest feedback about how you behave when you start using any nootropic—one family member, one close friend, and one colleague. Sometimes when you get a lot faster all at once, everyone else seems stupidly slow. You can act like a jerk or get depressed and not know it. These people will be your feedback system. Who will they be?
  - Family _____
  - Friend _____
  - Colleague _____

Recommended Listening

- "Mashup of the Titans" with Tim Ferriss, Parts 1 and 2, *Bulletproof Radio,* episodes 370 and 371
- Tim Ferriss, "Smart Drugs, Performance & Biohacking," *Bulletproof Radio,* episode 127
- "The Birth of LSD" with Stanislav Grof, Father of Transpersonal Psychology, *Bulletproof Radio,* episode 428
- Steven Fowkes, "Increase Your IQ & Your Lifespan for a Dime a Day," *Bulletproof Radio,* episode 456
- Steve Fowkes, "Hacking Your pH, LED Lighting & Smart Drugs," Parts 1 and 2, *Bulletproof Radio,* episodes 94 and 95

Recommended Reading

- Michael Pollan, *How to Change Your Mind: What the New Science of Psychedelics Teaches Us About Consciousness, Dying, Addiction, and Transcendence*

Law 8: Get Out of Your Head

There is incredible value in accessing altered states where you face your inner demons. This is where magic and healing happen. Ancient cultures have always known this, and today's game changers do, too. So go to the jungle and try ayahuasca. Do a ten-day silent meditation Vipassana retreat. Fast in a cave on a vision quest. Stick EEG electrodes on your head to access altered states. Do advanced breathing exercises until you leave your body. Go to Burning Man. Or consider consciously and carefully using full-dose psychedelics in a spiritual or therapeutic setting. Do whatever it takes to occasionally get out of your own head so you can more powerfully own what you do once you're back. And do it with help from experts.

Not long ago, when I was visiting New York City, my friend Andrew invited me to a dinner party hosted at his hip $20 million SoHo penthouse. Given that I didn't know he owned a place like that, I was blown away when I stepped through the door into what looked like a palace. He obviously likes surprising people, because I had no idea that the "dinner with a few friends" would turn out to be a gathering of incredibly powerful, successful, and influential people from across New York's industries, ranging in age from twenty-five to seventy-five. The dinner was structured as a Jeffersonian dialogue. Only one guest spoke at a time, so the entire table stayed on topic. When I had an opportunity to ask a question of all the guests, I asked, "How many of you have used psychedelics for personal development at least once?"

Every hand at the table went up, from hedge fund managers to artists, from CEOs to professors. We talked about it for the next half hour in one of the most fascinating conversations I've had in a long time.

Though psychedelics have been lumped in with other illicit drugs and labeled "bad" by the government, when used therapeutically, they can be extremely powerful tools for finding self-awareness and (debatably) getting into a state of flow. High performance is an altered state. When you're willing to go to an even more extremely altered state at times, you can learn things that will make you stronger in your regular living and working states.

This is a topic that has come up with many of the people I've interviewed, from award-winning journalists to doctors and lots of people who are changing the world in between. One of them is Dr. Alberto Villoldo, who spent more than twenty-five years studying the healing practices of the Amazon and Incan shamans. He is a psychologist and a medical anthropologist, a bestselling author, and the founder of the well-respected Institute of Energy Medicine of the Four Winds Society. Back when Dr. Villoldo was twenty-seven years old, he was a broke grad student. A big pharmaceutical company gave him a grant to go to the Amazon and help it discover the next big drug. He went to remote areas and learned from native healers.

Three months later, the pharma executives asked him what he had found. "Nothing," he said. "I didn't find anything because the people I visited had no Alzheimer's, no heart disease, and no cancer." There were no diseases to cure, so they had no need for pharmaceutical drugs. But he went back anyway and trained to become a shaman.

Dr. Villoldo credits the differences between the health of the people in the Amazon and in Western culture to stress. When you live in a state of fight or flight, the brain secretes two steroid hormones, cortisol and adrenaline. This leads you to always being hyped up and prevents you from accessing the ecstatic, blissful state where you can actually be creative and dream the future into being, which is called a state of flow. When your brain is riddled with stress hormones, it activates the hypothalamic-pituitary-adrenal (HPA) axis. When the HPA axis is turned on, it is dedicated to the fear hormones and triggers the pituitary gland to keep manufacturing more and more stress hormones. When you are not in a state of fight or flight, however, under the right circumstances the pituitary gland can help you get into a state of flow by transforming neurotransmitters such as serotonin into dimethyltryptamine (DMT), a molecule that occurs naturally in many plants and animals.

DMT is one of the most powerful psychoactive substances on the planet. It is prepared by various cultures for healing and ritual purposes. It triggers visionary ecstatic states. And we can produce it ourselves. We do so naturally after giving birth and at the end of life, but Dr. Villoldo says that we can do it other times, too, when we are in the right mental state.

Yet, according to Dr. Villoldo, 99 percent of us have brains that are broken from stress and cannot create their own hallucinogenic substances. This is why we cannot hold or entertain the idea that we can manifest our dreams into reality. When Dr. Villoldo was in the jungle in the Amazon as a medical anthropologist and eventually as a student of the shamans, the shamans told him, "You have to eat the bark of that tree and those roots over there." When Dr. Villoldo asked why, they simply said, "Because the plants told us." That wasn't good enough for him. He wanted to learn the science behind it, but he went ahead and ate them.

Twenty years later, when he took these things to the lab, he found that the shamans had been repairing his brain. The barks and roots they had told him to eat had turned on the Sir2 longevity genes, and there are very few substances that do that.

Dr. Villoldo says that we can also repair our brains by healing the gut and by consuming omega-3 fatty acids, which are essential building blocks of the brain. When we do all these things, the mystical abilities that we associate with voodoo priests, shamans, and psychics have the potential to become the natural abilities of us all. Now, we find these abilities in such a small number of the population that we consider them abnormal or even silly or laughable. But Dr. Villoldo says that they are ordinary, and so do other ancient traditions from other parts of the world, including the yoga sutras of Patanjali. When you repair the brain, heal the gut, feed the brain with high-mitochondrial foods, and trigger mitochondrial repair, these abilities can begin to appear on their own. You just have to do the basics, and then your human potential will begin to reveal itself to you.

For thousands of years, the shamans in the Amazon have been using ayahuasca, a psychedelic that is known to induce these kinds of spiritual experiences. The ayahuasca vine contains DMT, but you can use it only when it is brewed with other plants containing chemicals called monoamine oxidase (MAO) inhibitors. Yes, the same DMT that your body can produce is the active ingredient in the powerful psychedelic ayahuasca. Without the right combination of plants, your gut would destroy the DMT and you would feel no effects from it at all.

Studies on ayahuasca have shown that it does more than just provide a spiritual experience. In a 2015 pilot study by the University of

São Paulo, researchers gave ayahuasca to six patients with treatment-resistant depression. Their symptoms of depression decreased significantly within an hour of ingesting ayahuasca, and they showed an approximately 70 percent decrease in their depressive symptoms twenty-one days after taking that single dose. They reported no significant side effects except vomiting shortly after taking it, which the shamans consider cleansing and essential to the experience.[26]

There is also evidence that ayahuasca can help alleviate addiction. In a 2013 study, twelve participants who went through therapy sessions while on ayahuasca reported significant decreases in alcohol and cocaine abuse even six months after the therapy ended.[27] Many scientists believe that ayahuasca is so effective because it increases serotonin receptor sensitivity in the brain.[28] Popular drugs that fight depression, such as Prozac, push your brain to release more serotonin, a neurotransmitter that contributes to feelings of well-being and happiness. But those medications take about six weeks to kick in and actually deplete the brain of serotonin in the long run,[29] while ayahuasca seems to better enable the brain to utilize the serotonin you already have.

That compelling science led me to seek out the world's top experts in plant hallucinogens. Dennis McKenna's work focuses on ethnopharmacology and plant hallucinogens. When he received his doctorate in 1984, his doctoral research was actually on ethnopharmacological investigations of the botany, chemistry, and pharmacology of ayahuasca and oo-koo-he, two orally active tryptamine-based hallucinogens used by indigenous peoples in the northwest Amazon. (Who knew you could get a PhD in hallucinogens?)

Dennis credits (or blames) his famous brother Terence for his interest in the topic. Terry was four years older than Dennis, who always wanted to do whatever his big brother was doing. It was the 1960s and Terry was living in Berkeley, where everyone was taking LSD. When Terry discovered DMT and shared it with Dennis, they both thought it was amazing and decided to throw everything else away and focus on what they believed was the most important discovery that man had ever made.

Forty-five years later, Dennis hasn't really changed his mind much about that. He believes in the therapeutic potential of psychedelics, which was pretty thoroughly explored in the 1960s as a treatment for alcoholism and depression. It's taken forty years or so to get back to where that research left off. But Dennis says that the therapeutic potential is clear. The challenge is how to take these substances, which have long been reviled and prohibited, and reintegrate them into medicine, particularly when drug companies rely on profits from consumers who take their drugs every day instead of the three or four times it takes to get the same or better benefits from a psychedelic.

Yet we must find a way, because, as Dennis puts it, not only are psychedelics therapeutic for individuals, but used in the right context they would also be therapeutic for societies and ultimately for the whole planet because they tend to make us more compassionate. He believes that this was one of the reasons the government wanted to suppress the use of LSD in the 1960s; people were taking LSD and saying, "You want me to go to Vietnam and kill those people? Why would I want to do that?" That is particularly ironic because there is compelling evidence that the CIA actually did introduce psychedelics into the United States, although I believe the outcome today is not what it anticipated.

Dennis and I agree that a society of people who are less interested in killing others is a good thing. So does Rick Doblin, the founder and executive director of the Multidisciplinary Association for Psychedelic Studies (MAPS), a nonprofit research and educational group that he started in 1986 to do the important work of developing medical, legal, and cultural contexts for people to benefit from the use of psychedelics and marijuana. You might not expect someone with that job description to have a PhD in public policy from the John F. Kennedy School of Government at Harvard University. Rick works to progress the research and education behind the benefits of psychedelics and marijuana primarily as prescription medicines, but also for personal growth for otherwise healthy people.

Like Dennis, Rick grew up in the 1960s, but he believed the propaganda that one dose of LSD would make him permanently crazy. Yet he was studying the psychological mechanisms of what was going on in the world and the dehumanization of the "other"—the core belief that can cause people to fear and then work against and kill other people. It started him thinking that if people could be helped to experience their sense of connection with others, it would lead to more peaceful discussions and negotiations. Of course, that led him to LSD, which made him feel connected, as if he were going beyond his ego. He realized that psychedelics were incredible tools with major therapeutic and political implications, and when the government cracked down on those drugs and criminalized the people who sold and used them, Rick became an underground psychedelic therapist. Then he began to work on bringing psychedelics back up from the underground.

Today, MAPS is a nonprofit pharmaceutical company working to develop psychedelics and marijuana into FDA-approved prescription medicines. It is making an effort to work within a very rigorous scientific context to make the drugs available as prescription medicines to be taken only a few times and only under supervision. They often work with veterans through a three-and-a-half-month-long treatment program. During that time, patients take the drug once a month combined with weekly nondrug psychotherapy for about three weeks before their first dose and then again after each dose to help with the integration. It's essentially an intensive psychotherapeutic process that's punctuated occasionally by powerful experiences with hallucinogens that bring traumas and experiences to the surface, where they can be fully explored and worked through so that healing can begin.

Another guest I spoke with on *Bulletproof Radio* is the three-time Emmy Award–winning journalist Amber Lyon. Amber is a former CNN investigative correspondent who used psychedelics to treat her own PTSD. Amber is a filmmaker, photographer, founder of the news site Reset.me, and host of the podcast *Reset with Amber Lyon*, both of which cover potential natural therapies and psychedelic medicines. As a journalist who covered war zones and child sex trafficking, she began experiencing many of the same symptoms of PTSD as soldiers facing combat. She had absorbed the trauma she had witnessed, was having trouble sleeping, and was hyperaroused. If she heard a loud noise, she'd start to panic. That began affecting her career and her entire life.

Amber knew that she needed help, but she didn't want to go the prescription drug route after having reported on the negative side effects of prescription medications throughout her career. She started researching natural medicines, and a friend suggested psychedelics. At first she was suspicious. She had always thought that psychedelics were dangerous drugs. But when she began reading anecdote after anecdote of people who had been healed of mental health disorders, including PTSD, by psychedelics, she began to believe that they could help her. She went down to Iquitos in Peru and attended a ceremony with about fourteen other people led by a shaman. In a yurtlike structure, they all consumed ayahuasca at the same time and then stayed together and discussed their experiences the next day to integrate what they'd learned.

Amber found it to be a beautiful and profoundly healing process. Within twenty seconds of consuming the ayahuasca, she realized that there was so much more to the universe than she had been experiencing. It also allowed her to process a lot of the trauma that she'd stored in her body. She felt a presence in front of her sucking dark forms of energy out of her body. One took the shape of a thirteen-year-old sex-trafficking victim she'd interviewed for a documentary. Another was in the shape of an animal she'd seen covered in oil during an oil spill. Those forms departed from her until all of the trauma she'd been carrying had left her body.

Then she was able to go back in her mind and watch a movie of her life to see where her own trauma had started, which was in childhood during her parents' tumultuous divorce. She relived and reprocessed those experiences, moving them from the "fear and anxiety" memory folder in her mind to the "safe" folder. That was tremendously healing.

Like Amber, I tried ayahuasca in Peru. That was back in 2003, when I was fat, burned out from working in Silicon Valley, and slowed by mold poisoning I didn't know I had. The traditional medical approach had failed me, so I began looking into alternative ways to improve my mood and cognitive performance. I ended up in a guesthouse in the Peruvian Andes, asking the owners in horrifically broken Spanish to connect me to an ayahuasca shaman. Back then it was hard to find someone who would agree to do so with me, a gringo. Now I notice a huge difference in Peru, where locals are lined up offering "ayahuasca tours." It's more important than ever to be careful about whom you trust with this experience. I knew the shaman I found was good when he asked me whether I was taking MAO inhibitors or other antidepressants that interact with *Banisteriopsis caapi*, one of the plants used to brew ayahuasca. You could die if you try ayahuasca while on certain antidepressants.

At dawn the next morning, the shaman led me to a hill overlooking the Sacsayhuamán ruins, just outside the capital of the ancient Incan Empire. He set up a tent and pulled out a little bag of stones, which he set around us in a circle while he chanted. I was skeptical of the stones and the chanting, but I was willing to suspend my disbelief and enjoy the experience. The first cup, to my surprise, he poured into his dog's mouth, explaining that his dog always journeyed with him. He drank the next dose and then gave a double dose to me. (I'm six feet four and weighed around 260 pounds at the time.)

I don't remember much about the few hours that followed, just fleeting images and a feeling of freedom I had never experienced. I did come away from the experience with enormous, bounding energy. For my whole life up until that point, I'd had to push so hard to do everything because I was always tired. All of a sudden that was gone, and that feeling lasted for several months. On a deep level, it helped me understand that we are more than just meat robots. There's more in there, and what we think, feel, and do must be in alignment. That made me focus on creating alignment in my life. Then again, so did many other things that weren't drugs. In my case, the things I experienced helped me to understand that I needed to work on my physical body as well as the emotional side and that the two were inseparable.

It comes as no surprise to me that more and more people, especially high-powered executives, are "coming out of the closet" about their use of therapeutic psychedelics. If you have a mission in life and you're stuck spending two-thirds of your time dealing with childhood trauma that instilled a pattern into the way you interact with the world, why would you spend all of your time and energy using low-powered techniques to heal when you can choose from an array of faster techniques that can get you to the point where you can see your programming? Yes, they are certainly scarier and even more risk prone, but for many the risks are worth it to gain access to that programming more quickly. Then you can rewrite the code so that you are in charge of your biology and how you interact with the world instead of letting your primitive systems choose for you.

Don't get me wrong, psychedelics are powerful. But they are not a panacea, they are often not fun to do, and they are often illegal. You don't have to do them to get outside your own experience, and they are not the right choice for many people. I have done them very few times, but they mattered in my evolution as a human being, and I'm not alone by a long shot. And they are not always safe.

There are many other things you can do with similar effects. Many executives attend ten-day Vipassana silent meditation retreats that force them into an altered state. I experienced this during a Tibetan meditation retreat in Nepal. But as a formerly obese person with massive cravings who always felt lonely no matter who I was with, I wanted to push my fear buttons all the way, so I went on a version of a vision quest. In many cultures, when someone is stuck or reaches a certain age, he goes off into the wilderness and doesn't return until he has a vision. I did it alone in the middle of the desert in a cave with no food, led by a shaman who drove me there and picked me up when it was done. It was a profoundly transformative experience to sit for days in a fasted state, feeling my loneliness and wondering if animals were going to eat me at night.

The key is that all such experiences involve altered states. But amazingly, another way of getting into an altered state, breathing, has had a deeper and even more profound effect on me than any plant medicine.

Action Items

- Figure out how you're going to get into an altered state in an intense experience. Here is a checklist of things I've done. Rank the list from what appeals to you most to what appeals least. Then research your top pick and schedule it. Or pick something else entirely.
  - Attend a medicine ceremony with hallucinogens.
  - Attend a Vipassana ten-day silent meditation retreat.
  - Go on a vision quest in the wilderness.

- Finally go to Burning Man.
- Try holotropic breathing (see the next law).
- Attend an intense, five-day 40 Years of Zen neurofeedback retreat (I founded this, so I'm biased).
- Consider finding a certified psychedelic-assisted therapist who has 180 hours of training from the California Institute of Integral Studies (www.ciis.edu) or a traditional shamanic practitioner with an authentic training lineage and lots of experience if you decide to try plant medicines.

Recommended Listening
- Alberto Villoldo, "Shamanic Biohacker," *Bulletproof Radio*, episode 79
- "Adventures in Ayahuasca and Psychedelic Medicine" with Dennis McKenna, *Bulletproof Radio*, episode 329
- Rick Doblin, "Healing with Marijuana, MDMA, Psilocybin & Ayahuasca," *Bulletproof Radio*, episode 200
- Amber Lyon, "Psychedelic Healing & Reset.me," *Bulletproof Radio*, episode 143

Recommended Reading
- Alberto Villoldo, *One Spirit Medicine: Ancient Ways to Ultimate Wellness*
- Terence McKenna and Dennis McKenna, *The Invisible Landscape: Mind, Hallucinogens, and the I Ching*

Law 9: The Breath Is the World's Most Powerful Drug

The simple act of breathing is so powerful that the godfather of LSD replaced his psychedelic therapy with a profound breath control practice. Taking a deep breath is simple, but you can go far deeper into your own head by learning how to really breathe.

You read earlier about Dr. Stanislav Grof, one of the great leaders in the field of psychedelic research. He holds both an MD and a PhD, and the research he conducted with his wife in the 1960s and '70s led to the creation of the field of transpersonal psychology, which recognizes the spiritual and transcendent aspects of the human experience and marries them to a framework of modern psychotherapy and psychology.

Dr. Grof literally wrote the book on LSD psychotherapy. His clinical research started in the 1960s in Moscow and at Johns Hopkins University, focusing on the types of therapeutic experiences that become available to the average person who uses these powerful psychedelic substances. Dr. Grof was later a scholar-in-residence at the Esalen Institute in Big Sur, California. He's the author of more than twenty books and hundreds of articles and still teaches despite being eighty-six years old. He lectures and leads workshops all over the world and is one of the great masters of this school of therapy. He is so energetic that he recorded his fantastic interview onstage with me at a Bulletproof event at night after the attendees spent the day doing his breathing exercises.

Yet Dr. Grof started out as a traditional psychologist. Early in his career he grew increasingly disappointed by the limits of traditional psychoanalysis. At the time, the field of psychiatry was medieval. Psychiatrists were still using barbaric treatments such as electroshock therapy, insulin shock therapy, insulin coma therapy, and even prefrontal lobotomies.

Dr. Grof was working at the psychiatric clinic in Prague when it received a box from Sandoz Pharmaceuticals in Switzerland full of ampules, mysteriously labeled LSD-25. A letter enclosed described it as a new investigational substance. It seemed, on the basis of a pilot study, that it would be something interesting for psychiatrists and psychologists. Dr. Grof was excited about the possibility of a whole new approach, so he volunteered to try the LSD and had an experience that transformed him completely. Within six hours it sent his entire life in a completely different direction.

Committed to studying the therapeutic uses of LSD, Dr. Grof came to the United States in 1967 on a scholarship. But it wasn't long until

LSD was made illegal in the United States. Dr. Grof was devastated. He believed that the field of psychiatry had lost a valuable tool with a great potential for healing. He began searching for an alternative that could help his patients experience the same benefits they got from LSD. Amazingly, he found it in the breath.

For thousands of years, ancient cultures and wisdom traditions have recognized the breath as more than simply a function that keeps us alive but as a vital force that can be manipulated to effect great change. Dr. Grof found that when breathing is accelerated, people experience something akin to a psychedelic state. In fact, any doctor will be able to share a story with you about someone who was admitted to the emergency room with a "psychiatric condition" but was actually just hyperventilating. That's how powerful the breath is.

Of course, if someone is hyperventilating, most doctors slow the breath. But not Dr. Grof. He developed a breathing technique called holotropic breathing. It is a profound practice that can help you tap into a nonordinary (or holotropic) mental state. The process itself is very simple, combining accelerated breathing with evocative music in a peaceful setting. With the eyes closed and lying on a mat, each person uses his or her own breath and the music in the room to enter a nonordinary state of consciousness. This state activates the natural inner healing process of the individual's psyche, leading to a particular set of internal experiences. With the inner healing intelligence guiding the process, the quality and content brought forth is unique to each person and for that particular time and place. Though recurring themes are common, no two sessions are ever alike.

I've done holotropic breathing several times, two of those times with Dr. Grof, and I found it personally even more beneficial than ayahuasca. Holotropic breathing was the very first transcendent or spiritual experience I ever had, and it took me from my focus on smart drugs to understanding that in order to upgrade yourself, you have to pay attention to the spiritual, emotional, cognitive, and physical parts of life all at the same time.

When I did holotropic breathing in combination with hypnosis in the same week at a nonprofit called the Star Foundation, I went right back to the moment I was born. I'd had no idea that that would happen. I already knew that I had come into the world with the umbilical cord wrapped around my neck. But I'd had no idea that that meant my infant brain had interpreted the experience as trauma, predisposing me, as an adult, to a quickly aroused fight-or-flight response. Holotropic breathing allowed me to feel the terror I'd experienced as a baby and remember more details of my birth that I was later able to confirm with my parents. Frankly, as a rational engineer, it scared the hell out of me.

As was the practice in hospitals at the time, doctors put me into a warming chamber, which meant I was immediately taken away from my mother. During the altered state induced by holotropic breathing, I reexperienced the sensation of lying there defenseless, realizing that I was alone, and making the decision as a five-minute-old baby that since I had come into the world alone, I would have to remain alone forever. For thirty years after that moment, I didn't make healthy connections to other people. Mind blown. No LSD required.

It pains me to say this, but separating a baby from its mother right after birth is seriously bad for babies. Yet this practice is par for the course in the United States, especially after a cesarean birth. If you were born or gave birth via cesarean, don't stress or feel guilty about it. Knowledge is power. Now that you know that birth trauma can cause stress later in life, you can use one of many healing modalities to reset the stress response. Holotropic breathing helped me find an impossibly hidden trauma that had been holding me back on so many levels. Once I knew what it was, I embarked on a path to heal it, and I did. Now I have real friends. I have love in my life. I'm equipped to be a good parent. And I stopped running from failure, which let me embrace the big, badass mission that fires me up every day.

If you'd told me that any of that was likely or even possible one minute before I started the facilitated breathing session, I would have laughed at you. I'm sharing it here with the sincere hope that it will open your mind to the possibility that there are things you're not aware of that are holding you back no matter how successful you are. At the time I did it, I had the material markers of success. But all the money and recognition in the world doesn't mean that all is right in your life.

If you experienced birth trauma or another type of trauma, or are experiencing a troubling pattern of behavior, you can finally do something about it. Drugs are one way to access a state that leads to personal breakthroughs. Holotropic breathing is another. Neurofeedback and a form of rapid eye movement therapy called eye movement desensitization and reprocessing (EMDR) can work, too, as can tapping, a technique that uses the body's energy fields to release anxiety and trauma. No matter which you choose to use (if any), finding a safe practice to identify hidden patterns in your life—almost always caused by past trauma—is one of the most powerful ways to become a game changer. Getting out of your own way is so much easier when you know what's holding you back. The happiest, most successful, most impactful people in the world universally find a way to do it.

Holotropic breathing is just one aspect of breathing for high performance. Yogis have been practicing pranayama, the yogic side of breathing, for thousands of years (this is the foundation of the popular Art of Living breathing techniques, which I practiced every morning for five years). Biohackers such as Patrick McKeown modify their oxygen levels with special breaths. At a minimum, learn the Ujjayi breath, which Brandon Routh discussed on *Bulletproof Radio*. Brandon played Superman in *Superman Returns* and today plays the Atom on *Legends of Tomorrow*. If it works for a superhero, it's worth trying! Master your breathing, master yourself.

Action Items
- Consider holotropic breathing—there are local groups or therapists offering it in most cities.
- Learn the Ujjayi breath—instructions are at www.bulletproof .com/ujjayi.
- Try an Art of Living course or a pranayama course.

Recommended Listening
- "The Birth of LSD" with Stanislav Grof, Father of Transpersonal Psychology, *Bulletproof Radio*, episode 428
- "How to Breathe Less to Do More" with Patrick McKeown, King of Oxygen, *Bulletproof Radio*, episode 434

- Brandon Routh, "Hacking Hollywood & Avoiding Kryptonite," *Bulletproof Radio*, episode 162

Recommended Reading
- Stanislav Grof, *LSD Psychotherapy (The Healing Potential of Psychedelic Medicine)*
- Stanislav Grof and Christina Grof, *Holotropic Breathwork: A New Approach to Self-Exploration and Therapy*
- David Perlmutter and Alberto Villoldo, *Power Up Your Brain: The Neuroscience of Enlightenment*

DISRUPT FEAR

If there's one key aspect of success that all game changers agree on, it is this: You must be fearless.

That's not to say that innovators don't experience fear—everyone does—but unlike most people, game changers refuse to allow this instinct to keep them from stepping into the unknown. Of course, the unknown is usually scary. Remember, your mind is a creature of habit, and it operates based on fear—it is always scanning your environment looking for things to be afraid of, and it makes decisions for you in the interest of keeping you "safe." But in reality, giving in to fear doesn't make you safe. And not taking risks makes you weaker, not stronger.

Game changers know this. To borrow a phrase from the legendary self-help author Susan Jeffers, they feel the fear and do it anyway. They educate themselves, keep learning, take action, and stay curious. They create a sense of mission and develop habits that prevent their bodies from hijacking their creativity so they can spend their lives constantly innovating. This is how they end up changing the game for the rest of us.

They also reject the comfort that comes with hiding behind rules and authority. There is no great mystery here: authority figures are created to protect the status quo. Becoming an innovator requires that you think differently. Stagnation is the enemy of innovation. With apologies (and sincere gratitude) to all of my former teachers, innovation doesn't happen unless you're willing to break the rules that other people have written. It's as simple as that.

Law 10: Fear Is the Mind Killer

Failure is scary because as humans evolved, failure meant a tiger would eat you, you'd run out of food, your tribe would banish you, or you'd never find a mate, so you'd die, and so would your entire species. None of those are true today, but the biological fear of failure remains in the automated parts of your nervous system. Learn to face your irrational fear of criticism and failure and do big things anyway. When you learn to make your body less afraid of failure, it liberates enormous energy that you can use to do what you choose. Fear of failure causes failure. Don't give in to it. Hack it instead.

Ravé Mehta is a game-changing engineer, entrepreneur, and professor, as well as an award-winning pianist and composer. He is changing the way we educate kids through his company, Helios Entertainment, which creates games, music, and books that teach adults and kids to overcome fear while learning complex science, technology, engineering, and math (STEM) subjects. I asked him to join me on *Bulletproof Radio* to talk about fear.

He told me a story about being on a safari in South Africa, where he and a group of others observed a pride of lions from an open-air Jeep. Suddenly one of the lions walked right up to the vehicle and approached him. Ravé was in the front seat, closest to the ground, and as the lion got closer and closer he heard the ranger sitting by his side say quietly, "Stop moving. Stop breathing. Pretend you don't exist." Ravé could feel the lion's breath on his forearm. He was afraid that he was about to die, and he needed to keep himself from making a sound or moving an inch. He began to practice a breathing technique to calm down his parasympathetic nervous system and pull himself into the present moment. Even though he didn't quite believe it, he told himself that everything was going to be fine. And within moments, the lion turned around and walked away.

At the time that happened, Ravé had spent years studying, hacking, and chasing fear to find out how it worked. But that moment really put his knowledge and skills to the test. If he hadn't been able to tap into a place of trust and stay connected in the present moment, who knows what could have happened?

Throughout his study of fear, Ravé discovered that all negative emotions—anger, jealousy, insecurity, guilt, shame, and greed—are rooted in fear, while all positive emotions—confidence, grace, humility, courage, gratitude—are rooted in trust. When he broke it down into just those two fundamental states, fear and trust, it became easy for him to see how he could transform fear-based emotions into ones that are rooted in trust.

Ravé believes that there is one life force underpinning all feelings and emotions, which he calls love. This is the force that binds everything together and through which everything is created. George Lucas called it the Force. In China they refer to it as *chi*. In India it's called *prana*. Ravé just refers to it as love. He envisions our ability to access love as a pipe. Fear constrains the pipe so that love can't flow in, while trust opens up the pipe.

According to Ravé, trust and fear exist on a spectrum. Fear starts with doubt, which leads to skepticism and ultimately ends with paralyzing fear. Trust starts with hope and moves up the scale until you have full trust in the universe, your place in it, and all of the events happening around you. Even though you may or may not know why something is happening, you have a sense of comfort that everything is working in your favor and life is flowing as it should be. When you're in a state of ultimate trust, you are able to tap into that flow.

In this state, you can allow yourself to become vulnerable because you trust that you will not get hurt, either physically or emotionally. Vulnerability, Ravé says, increases your ability to achieve a state of flow. He says that allowing ourselves to be vulnerable and trusting strengthens our "emotional immune system"—our ability to protect ourselves from painful experiences. This system can become weak when we are constantly inoculating ourselves from getting hurt by blocking our true feelings. When we practice being vulnerable, we become more resilient to life's inevitable blows. It's the knowledge that vulnerability creates resilience that inspired me to share the hard parts of my own story throughout this book.

Ravé breaks fear down into three pillars:

TIME

When you are fully trusting, you are present and receptive in the moment. It's when you move away from being present that you allow fear to come in. This normally takes the shape of "what if" questions. What if that lion attacks me? What if I die? Fear will always take you out of the present moment, because fear is based on what *might* happen in the future, not what is happening now. When you allow fear to enter, it disrupts the present moment. However, when you're completely present, there is no room for fear and you have access to unlimited love, or flow.

ATTACHMENTS

The idea of being attached to ideas and material objects has a bit of a bad reputation, and at first Ravé believed that we shouldn't have these attachments at all. Over time he realized that there was nothing wrong with attachments themselves. It's the nature of those attachments that can become problematic.

According to Ravé, there are two main types of attachments. The first is a rigid attachment, which is like a steel beam that connects you to the object of your attachment and creates stress. The other type is a gravitational attachment. In this case, there is a secure connection between you and the other person or object, but it is more flexible than a rigid attachment. As Ravé says, nothing is holding you in place other than your own gravity and the gravity of the object of your attachment. You rotate around each other without any stress on the system. As dynamics change, you can naturally gravitate either away from each other or closer together. For example, if you have a rigid attachment to another person, you will try to control him or her. In the case of a gravitational attachment, however, you are more confident in your connection and focused on yourself and becoming a better person. This will attract the right things into your space and push the wrong things away. This requires a slight shift in mind-set: instead of focusing on something else, focus on yourself, and everything will correct itself.

EXPECTATION

The third pillar of fear is expectation. Ravé defines expectation as being attached to a specific outcome—wanting to see a certain result of your efforts. Having expectations is a lose-lose scenario: if you achieve your expectation, there's no joy in it because it's merely what you expected to happen. But if you don't achieve the outcome you'd expected, you feel disappointed or possibly even angry, guilty, or ashamed. All of these negative emotions inhibit your flow state.

This doesn't mean that you shouldn't ever desire an outcome or goal. Ravé encourages us simply to shift our expectations to preferences. This way, if you achieve your desired outcome, you will feel elated, but you won't be dismayed if you don't. You've left the door open for other outcomes. The one you wanted was merely a preference.

Ravé says that all three pillars—time, attachment, and expectation—have to be active for fear to exist. If you knock down even one of them, fear will get up as that lion did and quietly walk away.

This is incredibly important because fear can hijack more than just your creativity; it can also hijack your cells. When I interviewed the cell biologist Dr. Bruce Lipton, who is one of the fathers of epigenetics—the study of how the environment affects our genes—we had a fascinating conversation about the ways in which fear impacts our biology. That was not the topic that had brought him to *Bulletproof Radio*—I had actually sought him out to discuss cellular function—but we ended up talking about how emotions impact our health at the cellular level.

Dr. Lipton's groundbreaking work began in 1967, when he was cloning stem cells in his lab. At the time, he was one of a handful of scientists in the entire world who even knew what a stem cell was.

Stem cells are embryonic cells that remain in your body after you are born. They have the potential to give rise to multiple other cells. Dr. Lipton was fascinated by stem cells because he knew that no matter how old we are, every day we lose hundreds of billions of cells due to normal attrition. Old cells die, and the body has to replace them. For example, the entire lining of the digestive tract, from your mouth to your anus, is replaced every three days. So where do all those new cells come from? Stem cells.

Dr. Lipton put one cell into a petri dish by itself and saw that it divided every ten or twelve hours. After a week, he had fifty thousand cells, and his most important observation was that every cell was genetically identical. They came from the same parent stem cell. Then he split those genetically identical cells into three different petri dishes and altered the chemistry of the culture medium a little bit in each of the dishes, effectively placing the genetically identical cells into three slightly different environments. In one dish, the cells formed muscle, in another dish, they formed bone, and in a third culture medium, they formed fat cells.

At the time, Dr. Lipton was a professor at a medical school. He taught his students the well-established belief that our genes control our lives, but he was seeing in his laboratory that that wasn't true. The genes did not control the cells' fate; the environment did. That led him to look at how cells are altered by their environment inside the body, our blood. He found that as we change the composition of our blood, we change the fate of our cells. So what controls the composition of our blood? The brain is the chemist. What the mind perceives, the brain will break down into complementary chemistry.

For example, if when you look at the world you see joy and happiness, the brain will translate that joy and happiness into chemistry, such as a dopamine release from feeling pleasure. This chemistry enhances growth. If you look at the world through a lens of fear, it will cause the brain to release stress hormones and inflammatory agents that will put you into a state of self-protection, which halts growth. It became very clear to Dr. Lipton that the chemistry of the blood, the cell's culture medium, changes based on our view of the world. This greatly impacts the fate of our cells.

As Dr. Lipton explained on the podcast, when you are in a state of fear, driven by your ancient survival mechanisms, your body focuses on survival rather than growth. This would be a good thing if a saber-toothed tiger were chasing you, but if you are in a chronic state of fear, you are continuously inhibiting your growth and potential. To make matters worse, the stress hormones that halt growth also shut down the immune system in order to save energy. Then you have two strikes against you. Dr. Lipton believes that this is the root of over 90 percent of disease. He ended up leaving his position at the university because he no longer believed in what he was teaching. The medical community claims that our genes control our lives and that we are the victims of our heredity. But Dr. Lipton saw that we are not powerless; we are responsible for our own lives and our own destinies. That is a profound insight, and I'm so grateful that he rejected authority and stayed curious enough to keep asking the hard questions that led to such game-changing answers.

In my quest to hack my own fear, I've tried a lot of crazy things, but nothing quite as extreme as Jia Jiang, an entrepreneur, speaker, blogger and author, has done. You may be familiar with Jia from his Ted Talk about rejection, which went viral and has now been viewed more than 4 million times. I reached out to interview him when I heard about his unconventional fear-hacking approach, which he calls "rejection therapy." He figured that if his body got used to experiencing rejection, it would no longer shift into a fear state when faced with the possibility of being rejected.

Jia set a goal of being rejected once a day for a hundred days by asking strangers for outlandish things. He went to a fast-food restaurant and asked for a "burger refill" after he'd finished eating his burger. He knocked on a stranger's door and asked if he could play soccer in his yard. He asked strangers for money. And so on. His goal was to get to "no" every day.

The funny thing is that even though Jia set out to get rejected (which he was many times), people said yes to him far more often than he'd expected. On the third day of his experiment, he went to Krispy Kreme and asked an employee to make doughnuts that were interlinked to look like the symbol of the Olympics. When the woman in charge said yes and proudly presented one to Jia, he almost cried. He was blown away by her kindness.

Even when people couldn't give Jia what he wanted, they often tried to give him something else instead. That made him wonder how many things he'd previously missed out on because he'd been so afraid of being rejected that he hadn't bothered to ask for what he wanted. He realized that by doing so he had been saying no to himself.

To hack your own fear, Jia recommends celebrating failure. When you play it safe, you won't be rejected. If you are willing to try something audacious enough that it fails, celebrate that. It is an accomplishment in and of itself.

Everything that Ravé, Dr. Lipton, and Jia said about fear deeply resonated with me, particularly Ravé's ideas about the spectrum of fear. When I work with executive clients over the course of five days of neurofeedback at 40 Years of Zen, I teach them about what we call the "emotional stack." Apathy and shame lie at the bottom of the stack. This is the least conscious state you can be in. Above apathy and shame is sadness, above sadness are anger and pride, above anger and pride is fear, and above that fear sit happiness and freedom. Here is a diagram to help you remember.

Happiness and Freedom
Fear
Anger and Pride
Sadness
Apathy and Shame

To prioritize your survival, your body will always try to steer you toward the lower emotions. The stack is useful because it is *always* right. If you're feeling shame about something, ask yourself what you're really feeling sad about. Then look for anger or pride. When you figure that out, look for the fear, because when you feel fear, happiness is right around the corner. And when the stack has hacked your negative emotions enough times, you start to learn that it always leads to your hidden fears.

The sad truth is that your body believes that if you are happy, you will fail to focus on external threats and you won't be safe. It wants you to remain vigilant, ready to run away from, kill, or hide from threats (and eat doughnuts or reproduce if there are no threats nearby). To trick you, your body sets up this hierarchy to keep you from experiencing happiness and instead focus on threats. This would all be well and good, except that fear inhibits growth and creativity. Plus, you probably want to be happy. So you have to reset your programming.

At 40 Years of Zen there is a process called "Neurofeedback Augmented Reset Process" that is designed to help clients stop automatically responding to things that aren't actually threats. You use neurofeedback to help find a situation that triggers a negative emotion, re-create the sensation as accurately as you can, and then find one thing, however small, that you can be grateful for in the given situation. Gratitude turns off the fear. Then you summon a feeling of profound forgiveness toward whatever or whoever caused the situation.

With the help of neurofeedback technology, this is easier than it sounds, but it's still challenging work to actually feel a negative emotion on purpose, find something good in it, and then let go of your hard feelings. Yet when you do it, you are liberated from the fear, and it doesn't come back. I've spent four months of my life doing this work, and as a result, I have very few buttons that get pushed without my permission. Still, I'm grateful to assist others on the rare occasions when I get to lead a session with clients at 40 Years of Zen. Watching someone relentlessly reset his or her fears always teaches me something about my own path.

You can derive similar benefits (though it may take longer) from any meditation practice that teaches forgiveness, gratitude, or compassion, as long as you apply those tools both to whatever caused your fear *and to yourself*. The most important thing is to be aware that the critical voice in your head is not you; it's your ancient survival instinct, and it is working desperately to keep you from turning off the fear it thinks will keep you alive. When you know what it is, guilt and shame melt away, and you can work your way up the stack to happiness. It's real—the only thing you have to fear is fear itself.

Action Items

- Remember that fear requires time, attachments, and expectations.
- Work to stay in the moment by eliminating distractions. (Turn off alerts on your phone, already!)
- Rephrase expectations to become preferences. Say "I want" instead of "I need."
- Consider doing a nightly practice, such as the one I do with my kids. At the end of each day, I ask them to list three things they're grateful for. Then I ask them one thing they failed at today. Failure means "something I worked hard on but didn't achieve." Then, if they failed at something that day, I praise them for having worked hard enough to fail. If they had no failures that day, I put on a sad face and tell them that I hope tomorrow will be a better day, one where they push themselves hard enough to fail. If you have kids, try it. If you don't, try journaling. Write down a failure, not just a misfortune, and recognize that it means you pushed yourself. Congratulate yourself in the journal for taking the risk. It's amazing how much weight comes off your psyche when you do this even a few times.
- Get rejected on purpose! Try a week of rejection therapy—ask for things you think you won't get every single day until you hear "no." You'll quickly learn that people desperately want to help others when given the chance. People are awesome.

Recommended Listening

- Ravé Mehta, "Fear & Vulnerability Hacks," *Bulletproof Radio*, episode 303
- "The World Is Your Petri Dish" with Bruce Lipton, *Bulletproof Radio*, episode 336

- Jia Jiang, "Seeking Rejection, Overcoming Fear, & Entrepreneurship," *Bulletproof Radio*, episode 237

Recommended Reading
- Bruce H. Lipton, *The Biology of Belief: Unleashing the Power of Consciousness, Matter & Miracles*
- Jia Jiang, *Rejection Proof: How I Beat Fear and Became Invincible Through 100 Days of Rejection*

Law 11: Average Is the Enemy

The people who create the most positive change most quickly are by definition disrupting the way things are. The world will push back at them, which leads to fear or uncertainty in even the strongest innovators. Throughout history, people with new ideas have consistently been criticized, disparaged, or worse. Manage your emotional response to critics and forge ahead despite encountering obstacles. Learn to face criticism and follow your path with joy. The last thing you want to be is average.

Today, Dr. Daniel Amen is widely regarded as one of the world's foremost brain specialists. He's a ten-time *New York Times* bestselling author, the founder and CEO of Amen Clinics, and someone who to a great extent was responsible for my decision to become a biohacker.

In 1991, Dr. Amen was a practicing psychiatrist when he attended a lecture on single-photon emission computed tomography (SPECT) medical imaging that radically changed the course of his career. SPECT is a nuclear medicine technique. Whereas CT scans and MRIs are anatomical techniques that show what brain structures look like physically, SPECT reveals what's happening in your brain by mapping your blood flow and activity, revealing the areas of your brain that "light up" when performing certain tasks or experiencing particular emotions.

Dr. Amen was fascinated by SPECT scans and began using them in his clinical practice to help diagnose and treat patients, many of whom quickly saw vast improvements. Yet he received no end of grief from his colleagues, who complained that such a technique was not the proper standard of care and called him a charlatan. No one enjoys being diminished and belittled when he is working to help people. It took a lot of courage for him to keep going despite those accusations, but he was curious. If he couldn't look at the brain, he argued, how could he understand how well it was working? How could he help his patients feel their best? He wanted to see what he was treating, so he persevered despite facing backlash.

Then his sister-in-law called him late one night and said that out of the blue, his nine-year-old nephew had attacked a little girl on the baseball field. Dr. Amen asked his sister-in-law, "What else is going on with him?" She said, "Danny, he's different. He's mean. He doesn't smile anymore." Dr. Amen went to their house and found two pictures his nephew had drawn. In one of them he was hanging from a tree, and in the other he was shooting other children. He turned to his sister-in-law and told her, "You have to bring him to my office tomorrow."

When Dr. Amen sat with his nephew, he asked, "What's the matter?" The boy said, "Uncle Danny, I don't know. I'm mad all the time." Dr. Amen asked if anyone was hurting him or teasing him or touching him inappropriately, and he said no. So Dr. Amen scanned his nephew's brain and found a cyst the size of a golf ball occupying his left temporal lobe. His nephew was actually missing the space in his scan where his left temporal lobe should have been. It was the first time Dr. Amen had seen that, but he's seen it many, many times since. Back then, a normal psychiatrist would likely have focused on the emotional symptoms without examining the function of the brain with a scan.

The left temporal lobe is an area of the brain that studies show is linked to violence.[1] When Dr. Amen found a surgeon to take out the cyst, his nephew's behavior returned to normal. The surgeon said the cyst had been putting so much pressure on Dr. Amen's nephew's brain that it had actually thinned the bone over his left temporal lobe. If he had been hit in the head with a basketball, it would've killed him instantly.

At that moment, Dr. Amen stopped caring if people thought he was a charlatan. He thought about all of the people who are in jail or who have died because their doctors didn't know they had problems with their brains that could have been identified with the help of a SPECT scan, and he made it his mission to use the tool to help as many people as possible.

I am one of those people. When I first learned about Dr. Amen in 2002, he was the target of huge criticism, but his science was incredibly solid. I was getting my MBA at Wharton while working full-time at a start-up, and I was desperate. I was pushing as hard as I could, but I was becoming less successful in my career, barely passing my classes, and absolutely not successful in my relationships. I was floored when one of Dr. Amen's scans told me that my brain looked toxic. When Dr. Amen saw the results, he said, "If I didn't know you and I saw your brain scan, I'd guess it was the brain of an addict living under a bridge." Compared to a healthy brain, my brain had really low activity in a pattern that he says he often sees in drug addicts or people who have been exposed to environmental toxins such as toxic mold. He says the scans showed that I actually had chemical-induced brain damage. There was clearly something wrong with my brain.

This may sound odd, but I was thrilled to hear that news. I finally had some hope because I had something concrete that I could work on. My whole life I had thought I was just weak and not trying hard enough, even though I was outwardly successful. But the SPECT scan showed me that it wasn't a character issue, it was a hardware issue. I had been exposed to toxic mold as a child and again before I started business school. With Dr. Amen's help and lots and lots of biohacking, I was able to rehabilitate my brain, which then allowed me to take it to levels beyond what I'd expected. I'm so grateful that he persevered and stayed curious enough to use SPECT when others were content to mock him while they treated patients without the benefit of fully knowing what was happening inside their brains. If I hadn't looked at mine, I would never have known how to fix it, and I certainly wouldn't be where I am today.

Even when they haven't directly changed the course of my life, I constantly seek out experts who have rejected authority with great results. When I read one of Dr. Gerald Pollack's books, *Cells, Gels and the Engines of Life*, I was fascinated by his discovery of a fourth state of water. The guy told every biochemist on the planet that they'd missed a huge fact about the nature of something as simple as water, which turned the field of cellular biology on its head. Of course he has critics, but he also had the data from his research. I wanted to hear more about his work and what had led him to study something as seemingly mundane as water.

Dr. Pollack is a distinguished professor of bioengineering at the University of Washington, the executive director of the Institute for Venture Science, and the founding editor in chief of the journal *Water*. He is also a founding fellow of the American Institute for Medical and Biological Engineering and a fellow of the American Heart Association and the Biomedical Engineering Society. In other words, he is a biohacking badass, although I'm pretty sure this is the first time he's been called that.

Dr. Pollack became interested in water when he was studying muscles and how they contract. It struck him that when we think of muscles at the molecular level, we typically consider only how the proteins interact to produce force. But muscles contain not only proteins but also water. In fact, two-thirds of our muscles, by volume, are water, even more than that if you consider the number of water molecules. More than 99 out of every 100 molecules in our muscles are water molecules.

It struck Dr. Pollack that other scientists had discounted 99 out of 100 molecules when trying to figure out how muscles work. How could they be insignificant? The prevailing theory about how muscles contract dated back over sixty years. But in his lab, Dr. Pollack found that the evidence didn't fit the theory. He realized that the missing element was none other than water. All of those tiny water molecules did in fact play a significant role in how our muscles function compared to the dominant theories.

That led Dr. Pollack to set aside the research of muscles and begin to study water itself, and what he found was disruptive. Most of us have learned that there are three states of water: solid, liquid, and vapor. But Dr. Pollack discovered that there is actually a biologically important fourth state of water that is between a solid and a liquid. This fourth state of water is highly viscous, kind of like honey. It's called exclusion zone (EZ) water.

Dr. Pollack may have been the first to discover this fourth state of water, but there were others more than a hundred years ago who predicted this discovery. It seems that all those years ago, a group of scientists was close to discovering the fourth state of water, but they faced a great deal of criticism. So they gave up. The detailed study of water molecules in biology lost respect in the scientific community, and more and more people then became reluctant to pursue it. It wasn't until Dr. Pollack and his colleagues allowed their curiosity about water to take over their studies of muscle contractions that they were able to make their discovery and change the study of water.

The implications of this fourth state, EZ water, are limitless. This is the type of water we have in our cells that supports our mitochondrial function. The more EZ water we have in our bodies, the better our cells are able to function. Dr. Pollack has found that infrared light, natural sunlight, and vibration all create more of this type of water. Since speaking to him, I have made increasing EZ water in my cells a priority, and I can feel the results in my performance. In fact, I'm so convinced of its health-conferring and performance-enhancing benefits that I funded additional research at his laboratory. And guess what he discovered? When you mix butterfat (ghee) into water, it creates a *huge* amount of EZ water.

That solved the mystery of Bulletproof Coffee. I've always been annoyed by the fact that if I try to eat butter and then drink black coffee, I don't feel the burst of clarity that I get when I take the time to blend them together, and now we know why. Blending butter into coffee creates EZ water. Dr. Pollack's groundbreaking discovery solved another mystery!

Along the way to discovering EZ water, Dr. Pollack faced his fair share of doubters, but he stayed on his path and ended up having the last laugh. That's what game changers do: they stick to their guns when they believe they are right, even if it takes years for them to prove it.

And speaking of outliers, when I created the special-process, anti-jitter, lab-tested, mold-free coffee beans that are part of Bulletproof Coffee, the market for it was exactly zero. It was a crazy idea that attracted critics right away (not even counting the idea of adding butter). I was obsessed with the idea after I had to give up drinking normal coffee because it kept giving me anxiety, jitters, and a crash. I created a special process for roasting the beans and put them on the market anyway. Six years later, in 2018, people have drunk more than 100 million cups of Bulletproof Coffee made with those special beans, and thousands of people who had problems with standard types of coffee have thanked me for enabling them to drink coffee again.

Along the way, more critics popped up. Most were trolls looking for a reaction, and the best-known critic was clearly financially motivated, but my favorite was a coffee magazine writer who said that it simply wasn't possible for a computer hacker like me to change the process of making coffee because I wasn't a coffee industry veteran. My success came from curiosity followed by doing what I believed in even when that success drew critics.

That's why having a mission is so important—it gives you the power to stand your ground. It's also why gratitude is so important (see chapter 15 for more on this). The voice in your head will worry that other people might believe the critics. You can change your story by reminding yourself that every time a critic talks about your work, he or she is drawing more attention to it no matter what he or she says. In today's world of social media, no one believes what critics say without verifying the facts on Google first. At Bulletproof, no matter what annoying or worrying story was running in my head, sales actually rose every time a critic with a powerful online presence attacked the science, and I was energized when I realized that people who shared my mission would happily step up to its defense. So I still say a silent "thank-you" every time I see baseless criticism online. Remember, offering gratitude to the people who challenge you is part of overcoming fear. And being able to thank your critics feels pretty awesome.

We all owe a huge debt of gratitude to scientists such as Dr. Amen and Dr. Pollack, who were willing to speak up and keep digging when they discovered something contrary to conventional knowledge. Both overcame tremendous obstacles in order to change their fields and pushed through the fear that came with being maligned by their peers. Without that level of curiosity and courage, there would be no innovation, and the game would remain forever the same.

Action Items

- Ban useless critics on social media so they don't take you off your mental game. It takes you only one second to do so, but it takes them a lot more time to make up stuff about you. When you do the math that way, you always win.
- Before banning them, say a silent "thank-you" first because at least they are talking about your work.
- Engage with useful critics both online and offline who genuinely question your work, but don't add personal insults to the conversation. They have much to teach you. Be sure to thank them, too.
- If criticism gets to you, use the emotional stack on page 83. Criticism always touches on either shame or pride. Shame hides sadness, which hides anger or pride, which hides fear, which hides happiness. So figure out what you're really afraid of, face it, and watch as the criticism loses its power.

Recommended Listening

- Daniel Amen, "Alzheimer's, Brain Food & SPECT Scans," *Bulletproof Radio*, episode 227
- Daniel Amen, "Reverse the Age of Your Brain," *Bulletproof Radio*, episode 444
- Gerald Pollack, "It's Not Liquid, It's Water," *Bulletproof Radio*, episode 304

Recommended Reading

- Daniel G. Amen, *Change Your Brain, Change Your Life: The Breakthrough Program for Conquering Anxiety, Depression, Obsessiveness, Lack of Focus, Anger, and Memory Problems*

- Gerald H. Pollack, *The Fourth Phase of Water: Beyond Solid, Liquid, and Vapor*

Law 12: Don't Lead a Horse to Water; Make It Thirsty

Game changers don't get bored. They seek out the things that fascinate them, and that make them want to leap out of bed in the morning. Without passion and purpose, there is no happiness, so find the things you care about and devote your life to their pursuit. Put passion before money, and success will follow—but don't ignore the money, either.

Naveen Jain is a classic American success story. He came to the United States as a student from India with five dollars in his pocket and rose to become the billionaire founder of seven companies. His work has changed the game for information (his company Infospace was a major internet company), the solar system (he started Moon Express, which is sending the first robot miners to the moon this year), and he is now bringing his visionary approach to uncover the mysteries of the human body with his company Viome.

Naveen wants more hours in a day. He sleeps for only four hours a night because he loves what he does and that's all the sleep he requires. At almost sixty, he's as energetic as I am at forty-five. He wakes up in the morning and jumps out of bed because he's so excited about what he might learn that day. He says that the day you stop learning is the day you die and that most people who are bored are actually already dead. Where is there room for boredom with everything there is to see and learn in the world? Naveen believes that the minute your brain is no longer growing, you become a parasite on society because you are no longer contributing. The day you stop dreaming and being intellectually curious, you become a zombie.

Naveen believes that remaining intellectually curious is one of the most important things you can do. He does not understand how people can talk about playing golf—to him, if you have so much spare time in your life that you can spend eight hours on a golf course, your life is not worth living anymore. (Unless, of course, golf excites you and creates real joy. Naveen's idea is that you should focus on what you care about and what actually moves the needle, and golf doesn't move the needle for many people.) Though people talk about being passionate about something, Naveen says you should be obsessed instead: find the one thing you are so obsessed with that you can't sleep and will pursue that subject with all of your being.

To find out what you are obsessed with, imagine having everything you want in life. You have billions of dollars, a wonderful family, and everything else you want and need. Now what are you going to do? Your true obsessions are the things you would pursue if you already had what you want in life, when it's not about making money or reaching a goal. Naveen says that making money should never be the goal. Instead, making money is a by-product of pursuing the things you care about. Naveen says that making money is like having an orgasm: If you focus on it, you're never going to get it. But if you enjoy the process, you will eventually get there.

Naveen encourages you to dream so big that the people around you will think you're crazy. And then, when people start to tell you that you're crazy, take it to mean that you're *still* not thinking big enough! This requires never being afraid to fail. Naveen says that you fail only when you give up. Everything else is just a pivot. If the things you're doing are not working, you change, adapt, and pivot, and then, unless you give up, you still have not failed. Every idea that doesn't work is simply a stepping-stone to a bigger success. Success comes when you are still curious and still learning.

As a parent, Naveen believes his job is to encourage and nurture intellectual curiosity in his children. People often say that you can lead a horse to water but you can't make it drink. Naveen believes that you should never lead a horse to water, just make it thirsty. If a horse is passionate, thirsty, and obsessed with finding water, it is going to go out and find its own water, and it's going to drink.

I wish this were the goal of all education systems—to make children so intellectually curious that they enter the workplace fired up and passionate about making a difference. To learn more about how we can encourage as many people as possible to make the greatest potential impact, I sought out Subir Chowdhury, a management consultant who works with top Fortune 500 CEOs to improve their performance. If you want to improve your performance, there's probably no better way than to pay attention to what he has to say, particularly about the link between passion and action. Subir came on *Bulletproof Radio* to talk about what he does to help the most powerful CEOs in the world, but he also shared much more. His most recent work is focused on how to develop a caring mind-set as a path to personal performance and how to make entire corporations start caring.

Subir told me about a young woman named Trisha Prabhu. One day, Trisha, who was thirteen at the time, found out that an eleven-year-old girl had committed suicide after suffering the abuse of cyberbullying. Trisha was devastated to learn that a girl who was so young had taken her own life. She began to research cyberbullying and found that there were many other adolescents who had taken their own lives for the same reason. And she found that social media sites weren't doing enough to stop the problem.

This became an issue about which Trisha cared deeply, and she decided to take action. She created an app called ReThink, which uses patented technology to pick up on potentially offensive messages and then asks a user to stop and consider the damage he or she might cause before posting something that might be hurtful or offensive. She found that when teens were asked to stop and reconsider their decision, they changed their minds about posting something harmful a whopping 93 percent of the time.

The thing that impressed Subir the most about Trisha was that she didn't ask adults or any sort of authority figures to help her. She saw a problem, and she took action to solve it. Trisha embodies the four human attributes that Subir says make up a caring mind-set: straightforward, thoughtful, accountable, and results driven.

To become a more caring person, Subir says, ask yourself how you can apply these four attributes to every aspect of your life. Can you be more straightforward in the way you communicate? Do you think about your actions before you take them, even the little ones? Do you own both your failures and your successes? Do you care enough to do things that create results? We're all stronger in some areas than others. He finds that accountability is a common weakness. When something happens, many of us assume that it's someone else's problem. How easy would it have been for Trisha to leave the solution to cyberbullying to social media sites or other authority figures? Instead she took matters into her own hands and accepted responsibility.

Mother Teresa said, "Do not wait for leaders, do it alone." Game changers don't let fear get into the way of doing the things they care about. When you care enough, are passionate, and have no fear, your actions can truly make a difference.

Action Items

- Find a problem you are obsessed with and devote as much time and energy as possible to pursuing it because it will make you happy.
- Develop a caring mind-set—straightforward, thoughtful, accountable, and results driven.

Recommended Listening

- Naveen Jain, "Listen to Your Gut & Decide Your Own Destiny," *Bulletproof Radio*, episode 452
- Subir Chowdhury, "The Most Powerful Business Success Strategies That Make All the Difference," *Bulletproof Radio*, episode 419

Recommended Reading

- Subir Chowdhury, *The Difference: When Good Enough Isn't Enough*

EVEN BATMAN HAS A BAT CAVE

At this point in the book, some of the wisdom from these game changers may be clicking for you. You've already been able to identify the things you're most passionate about and have set aside some of the fear that holds you back from pursuing those things. If so, you're *on fire*. It's an amazing feeling, and if you experience it only a few times in your life, you're lucky. But when you turn it on all the time, there's a hidden downside. Passion for work that makes a meaningful difference often takes over your entire life, leaving little time to recover and enjoy the fruits of your labor. It can be no less addictive than drugs, and more than a few people have willingly died for their passion.

Yet more than one hundred of the game changers I interviewed said that downtime was critical to their success and their well-being. How can this be? How is it that the people who are working so hard to change the world and loving every minute of it believe that it's essential to take time to relax, recharge, and play?

Society teaches us that we'll be most successful if we push ourselves to the brink of exhaustion, but the people making a difference prove that the opposite is true. These people are able to operate at such high levels of performance precisely because they make time for play. They prioritize recovery and schedule it into their days because they know that if they leave it up to chance, it will never happen. Some of them learned this the hard way. Many of my most impressive guests have experienced burnout before learning to prioritize downtime. So have I.

I spent the first half of my career burning the candle at both ends, driven by my own unacknowledged deep-seated fear of failure, and I was profoundly successful. The story in my head was that if only I worked harder, if only I had more money, I'd be happy. So I put my head down and skipped vacation, skipped sleep, and never stopped.

There was no way to know that I wasn't as productive, happy, or effective as I could have been until I really focused on self-care and began investing energy, time, and a good percentage of my money into my mental and physical health. That strategy worked well enough while I was building Bulletproof, but when I started to pursue other passions, such as creating a podcast and writing books, I hit a wall. Following my passion for what was essentially three full-time jobs, not to mention my job as husband and father, made it far too tempting to cut corners on self-care.

I decided to make some changes, including blocking off time on my calendar to recharge and making it nonnegotiable. Now, whenever I'm not traveling, I take time to drop my kids off at school and then have "upgrade time." I've made a commitment to myself to spend that time doing something that makes me a better human being. Sometimes it's doing biohacking exercises on the crazy equipment in my labs. Other times it's meditating or listening to Dr. Barry Morguelan's energy meditations while doing his unusual stretches. Sometimes it's running an electric current over my head or taking a morning walk in the sun with my shirt off to catch some rays and set my circadian rhythm.

The point is that I do something, and I do it before I work. It's taken some hard conversations with my amazing executive assistants to explain exactly how nonnegotiable this time is, but since they got it, they've held the line . . . because, frankly, I won't. I care too much about what I do, so I'll whittle away at that time if it's up to me. There is no doubt that taking this time for myself—and taking it out of my own control—has helped me scale up as an author, a broadcaster, a CEO, and a dad at the same time.

I also created an order of operations for organizing my time, one that belongs in your tool kit. I share it with Bulletproof employees and, most important, those who help set my calendar. It's straightforward: Your health always comes first, because it drives your performance at everything else; your family (and friends who are as close as family) comes second; and work is a close third. Most people live according to the exact opposite order: they put work first, family and relationships second, and themselves dead last.

The fact is that you will never be the worker, partner, parent, or friend that you want to be if you don't prioritize your own health and happiness. When you build downtime into your schedule, right there on your calendar for everyone to see, you'll be better at taking care of your family, more effective at work, and able to make the impact you most desire.

Law 13: Don't Push Your Limits for Too Long

The only time an animal pushes itself until it drops is when it's starving or being hunted. When you push yourself without recovery, your body believes you must be under threat. An automatic system kicks in and shuts down the less necessary systems in your body. The ones that keep you young. The ones that keep you happy. The ones that help you think. You must learn to be a professional recovery artist. Screw running a marathon every day. Sprint, rest, sprint instead. Massively create and then massively rest to keep your passion—and your meat—alive for the whole race.

Dr. Izabella Wentz has completely changed the game for hundreds of thousands of people with thyroid disease. She is the brilliant author of the blockbuster book *Hashimoto's Protocol: A 90-Day Plan for Reversing Thyroid Symptoms and Getting Your Life Back*, which distills her years of research into all of the things that took a deep toll on her own body. Her series of protocols, which focuses on hormone optimization, overcoming traumatic stress, eradicating chronic infections, improving nutrition, and clearing toxins, has helped countless people beat an incredibly common autoimmune disease and live a rich and healthy life. It's worth mentioning that I once had Hashimoto's disease, too, although I've tested negative for antibodies, and I don't have symptoms anymore. I invited her onto the show because she is a master of untangling our complex biology, and her book was so popular that it was the top-selling nonfiction hardcover on the *New York Times* list for weeks.

Dr. Wentz had been struggling with chronic fatigue for almost a decade by the time she found out that she in fact had Hashimoto's. When she was little, everyone called her the Energizer Bunny. She was a bright-eyed, bushy-tailed kid who was always full of energy, a type-A straight-A student who obsessed over having the best grades. (She's like that again now.) But during her first year in college, her energy disappeared. She started missing classes because she was so exhausted that she couldn't get up in the morning. One day, she was preparing for a final exam when she fell asleep at two in the afternoon and slept until nine the next morning. The exam had started at seven thirty a.m.

That continued for years. Dr. Wentz slept for fourteen hours at a time and woke up still feeling exhausted. While her friends were out enjoying their twenties and achieving their goals, Dr. Wentz was sleeping. Soon she started experiencing additional symptoms. She developed brain fog, carpal tunnel syndrome, acid reflux, and irritable bowel disease. Eventually she started having panic attacks and experiencing memory loss. She couldn't remember the simplest things and had to write everything down. She knew that she had the potential to be a game changer, but no matter how hard she pushed, she wasn't getting results.

It took nine years for Dr. Wentz to be diagnosed with Hashimoto's disease, a condition in which the immune system attacks the thyroid, and then several more years for her to get her health back. She went on to become a pharmacist and then a leading expert in the disease, over time developing protocols that give her patients results in as little as two weeks.

What does this have to do with prioritizing downtime? Well, after treating, interviewing, and surveying thousands of people with Hashimoto's, Dr. Wentz has come to the conclusion that stress is the number one factor that triggers patients to go from stage one, when they simply have the right genes for it, to stage two, when they begin to develop symptoms. About 70 percent of her patients reported that they were going through a significant stressful period in their lives when they progressed to stage two.

This happens because when you are severely stressed, without the opportunity to recover, your body thinks it is under threat. This triggers inflammation and causes white blood cells to attack the thyroid gland or other systems in the body. This is known as an autoimmune response, because the body is using its own defense system to attack itself. Dr. Wentz says that one of the most important considerations for preventing Hashimoto's (or any other autoimmune disease) is minimizing the things you do every day that make your body feel as though it is under threat. This matters more than you might think—up to 20 percent of the population suffers from an autoimmune disease, the rate of increase is up to 20 percent annually,[1] and the percentage is probably higher for higher-stress personalities.

What are these everyday things that increase your risk, and how can you avoid them? They include getting stressed out by traffic, being in an unhealthy relationship, not getting enough sleep, holding on to anger, and depriving your body of nutrition due to ongoing calorie restriction. Analyze your life, and eliminate everything you can that would freak out your inner caveman or -woman. This will send your nervous system a clear signal that you are safe.

It is no coincidence that Dr. Wentz notes that a large percentage of patients with Hashimoto's are people who, like her (and me), are type-A high achievers who push themselves to their limits and then keep on pushing. She asks her patients to commit to eliminating stress from their lives for one month. In addition, she helps them learn to cope with any remaining stressors by practicing mindfulness exercises that allow them to pause before reacting and let go of stress and anxiety. So when their boss says something inflammatory or offensive, they can pause and find compassion for the other person instead of immediately setting off a stress response in the body. But Dr. Wentz says that you must find compassion for yourself before you can find it for others. She's right.

Many type-A people think of self-care as frivolous, but the reality is that it is essential to nurture your mind and body as you would your child or pet, even though children and pets are far smarter than the

systems running your body are. You can do this by not only eliminating stress but also adding things you enjoy to your day. Very simply, minimize the things in your life that don't give you pleasure, and
maximize the ones that do. That is how you change the game for your
genes, your performance, and the lives of those around you. It's not as
hard as it sounds.

As Mark Bell, a self-made entrepreneur and extremely fit inventor
who could pop my head in his bicep if he cared to, puts it, the most
important person in the room is always you. Mark is ranked as one of
the top ten power lifters of all time and leveraged his career as a professional athlete to kick-start his businesses, including the renowned
Super Training Gym and Super Training Products. He knows that no
matter what your goals are, you must take care of yourself first and
foremost. Sitting across from me on Vancouver Island, he reminded
listeners that flight attendants always instruct passengers, in case of
emergency, to put their own oxygen mask on first before they assist a
child with his or hers because you can't help anyone else if you're debilitated. And if you don't prioritize downtime and self-care, you will
inevitably become debilitated.

Mark is on a mission to help other people, which leads him to devote a great deal of time to his own personal development. He spends
an enormous amount of time reading books, listening to music and
podcasts, going for walks, and even sometimes just sitting in silence
and doing absolutely nothing. It may seem counterintuitive, but when
you stop pushing yourself and respect your body's limits, you can ac-
complish more than you would if you just kept pushing.

It is not only type-A folks who fall prey to burnout. As I've learned
from my discussions with some of the world's foremost healers and
spiritual leaders, they, too, have suffered the consequences of giving
all of their energy to their craft and putting other people's needs above
their own.

In fact, it's such a problem that years ago, Jack Canfield created an
invitation-only group of personal development leaders who meet twice
a year at resorts just to focus on taking care of themselves and one another. I have been honored to join those retreats and have frankly been
blown away to see so many legends of personal development talking

about how their passion for helping others had nearly burned them out. During those retreats, they focus on self-care as though their lives depend on it, and, given that these healers help to serve millions—or tens of millions—of people, that's no exaggeration.

One such healer is Genpo Roshi, whom I interviewed at the Be Unlimited event sponsored by the Bulletproof Training Institute. Genpo is a Zen priest in both the Soto and Rinzai schools of Zen Buddhism. He has distilled what he's learned over the course of decades of study into a series of teachings that he calls Big Mind and has been a game changer for thousands of people.

In 2011, Genpo had been teaching Zen Buddhism for almost thirty years when he was on his way to Europe to host a ten-day event with four hundred students. After he landed, his wife called him. She had found messages on his BlackBerry, which he had forgotten at home, about an affair he was having with another woman. It was hard to hear the story in the interview, but Genpo told it like it is, without fear.

Genpo initially couldn't own up to his mistakes, so he lashed out at his wife, but he later came clean with his students about being dishonest and cheating on his wife. His life and his reputation soon crumbled. Sixty-six other Zen teachers signed a petition stating that he shouldn't be able to teach for at least a year.

Genpo needed to hold himself accountable. After working with a therapist and his mentors, he came to realize that because he had felt drained from giving so much in service to others for so many years, he'd felt entitled to have a little fun and had acted out impulsively and recklessly. As we talked, he made it clear that that explanation wasn't meant to justify his actions, but it had helped him understand why he had done something he regretted deeply. He was resolved to learn from his mistake and, as he began to investigate the importance of boundaries, honesty, and integrity, he underwent quite a transformation.

Genpo compares this phase of his life to going through cancer, which he also experienced in 2003. Now he can see that it was one of the best things that ever happened to him, but he wouldn't wish it on anybody or want to ever go through it again. His work today is an effort to help people avoid making similar kinds of mistakes.

To understand where he went wrong, Genpo studied the five stages of development according to Chinese Zen philosophy (this is not so much an organized religion as it is a study of human behavior and the mind). The first stage is when someone has his or her first glimpse of something bigger, higher, and greater. This is called a Buddha awakening. Once someone has this awakening, he or she can begin a devotional practice where he or she begins to actualize the wisdom of the Buddha. This eventually leads to what Buddhists refer to as the Great Doubt. This occurs because even when someone is doing everything he or she is supposed to be doing, he or she is still not completely happy.

During the first year of Genpo's awakening, he was incredibly happy. But his Great Doubt led him to question everything, including his own happiness and even reality. He found himself questioning what he had really experienced, what he had really gained, and what he had really learned. Putting everything up for question, going through it, and ultimately owning his doubt led him to another great awakening, which is the third level of development. At this stage, the individual becomes the absolute reality. There is no relative existence, no fear, no suffering, no self, and no other.

Genpo says that many spiritual teachers get stuck here because when they get to this stage, they believe they have no ego. Yet this is actually the most egotistical place a person can be in. This is where Genpo himself got caught because, he says, when he was in this place he was not open to feedback, for the simple reason that he was greatly enlightened and he knew it. Yet no matter how enlightened a person is, the ego is always present. (I believe that this is because the ego is the operating system that keeps the meat in your body alive.) When it's aware, your ego can become your final authority. It tells you right from wrong. And without it, there are no rules.

This leads you to the fourth stage, which is the fall. It is impossible to avoid this stage, but Genpo says it's best to hurry through it as quickly as possible. Here you let go of being enlightened and begin the process of integrating the fears and shadows and angers—all of the things that we believe are poisons—into the self. Then, when you think you have fallen completely, the fifth stage is an even more complete descent, during which everything is shattered. Light and dark are fully integrated into the self, and you are able to fluctuate back and forth between the two.

That was an incredibly enlightening conversation, although I have quite a few stages left to go through, apparently. What Genpo said about how all of the time he spent serving others made him feel entitled particularly intrigued me. It says a lot about our cultural attitudes to self-sacrifice. We glorify it in a way that sets people up to become self-anointed saints, whether they are Buddhist priests, workaholics, or parents. The culture of self-sacrifice and the value we attribute to it hinders our performance.

This shows yet again how important it is to prioritize self-care even when caring for others is your spiritual or professional practice—and what can happen if you don't.

For practical guidance on how to do this, I sought out Dr. Pedram Shojai, the *New York Times* bestselling author of *The Urban Monk: Eastern Wisdom and Modern Hacks to Stop Time and Find Success, Happiness, and Peace* and *The Art of Stopping Time: Practical Mindfulness for Busy People*. Dr. Shojai is a doctor of Oriental medicine, the founder of Well.Org, an ordained monk, and an acclaimed qigong master who applies knowledge from Eastern traditions to help people overcome the challenges in their very Western lives. If anyone could tell me how to create habits that prioritize downtime, I knew it would be the man who rightfully calls himself the Urban Monk. Plus, I know he walks the talk because I see him do it. He's a friend.

When he was starting out as a young acupuncturist working with high-profile patients in a private setting, Dr. Shojai had the opportunity to learn firsthand what kept top performers up at night. He saw that they were often miserable because they had prioritized money and financial success over their families and emotional health. He realized that his definition of prosperity, which was tied to financial success, needed an upgrade.

Once you have figured out the things that are most important to you, Dr. Shojai's advice is to write down your thirty-, sixty-, and ninety-day goals and then weigh all requests for your time against those goals. If an opportunity comes up that is not in service of your goals, you owe it to yourself to say no because saying yes to something new typically necessitates saying no to something you've already agreed to do. This creates the kind of overscheduling and overwork that leads to more stress. Most people are stressed because they are living in compressed time—they have too much to do in too little time because they've overcommitted themselves. There is no amount of yoga or meditation that you can do to help with setting time boundaries. A lot of us are careless with our time, but small changes, which Dr. Shojai calls microhabits, can help change that.

To start, look at what five things are most important to you and ask yourself how much time you need to allocate to them. Then compare that with how much time you have available. Commitments that are not aligned with your goals are unimportant. Dr. Shojai compares them to weeds in a garden. When you cut the weeds and nurture the plants (your priorities), your garden will flourish.

To help himself focus on his priorities, Dr. Shojai intentionally resets his mind and attention several times a day using the Pomodoro Technique, a time-management technique developed in the 1980s by Francesco Cirillo. Dr. Shojai sets a timer for twenty-five minutes to tackle a specific task and then takes a five-minute break. During those five minutes, he moves his body and drinks some water. I sometimes do the same type of sprint, but you're more likely to find me doing stretches on a whole-body vibration plate and drinking coffee, at least in the morning. Different strokes for different folks.

When he first started doing this, Dr. Shojai feared that taking so many breaks would be a waste of time, but after working with hundreds of companies on their corporate wellness he has seen the profound differences it makes when employees give themselves permission to rejuvenate throughout the day. Absenteeism declines, while productivity, happiness, and performance increase. Instead of feeling as though they can't afford to take breaks, workers, as well as Dr. Shojai himself, realize that they can't afford not to.

What works for Dr. Shojai may or may not work for you, but you owe it to yourself to experiment with different strategies, including radical self-care and creating better time-management habits to help you avoid stress and burnout so that you can succeed beyond your limits without pushing yourself too far.

Action Items

- Think about the things you are doing on a regular basis that makes your body think it is under threat. Stop doing them.
- Write down the top three things that suck the most energy from your life:

_____

- Write down the top three things that give the most energy to your life:

_____

- What percentage of your time do you spend on the things that suck energy?

_____

- What percentage of your time do you spend on the things that generate energy?

_____

- What are the things that suck your energy and feel like threats to your nervous system? Which of these things that suck your energy can you simply stop doing?

_____

- What is the easiest thing you can do to convince someone else to do one of the energy-suckers that make you weak? Whom will you ask to do it?

_____

- Prioritize daily self-care even (or especially) if you spend much of your time caring for others. (Yes, this means you, moms.) Schedule it the same way you would a dentist appointment or a job interview.
  - How much time every day will you allocate to self-care?

    _____

  - What time of day will you do it?

    _____

- Write down a weekly and a monthly recovery task that takes more time, and schedule them for the next six months. Open your calendar. Do it now.
  - Weekly recovery task:

    _____

  - Monthly recovery task:

    _____

- Write down your thirty-, sixty-, and ninety-day goals, and then weigh all new requests for your time against those goals. Say no to anything that isn't aligned with your goals, or get someone else to do it. You're going to need a journal to do this one.
  - When will you write them down?

    _____

  - Where will you write them down?

    _____

  - Have you put time on your calendar to write them down?

    _____

Recommended Listening
- Dr. Izabella Wentz, "Hashimoto's Thyroiditis & the Root Cause," *Bulletproof Radio*, episode 256
- Mark Bell and Chris Bell, "Bigger, Stronger, Faster," *Bulletproof Radio*, episode 432
- Genpo Roshi, "Learn How to Meditate from a Zen Buddhist Priest," *Bulletproof Radio*, episode 425
- Pedram Shojai, "The Urban Monk," *Bulletproof Radio*, episode 283

Recommended Reading
- Izabella Wentz, *Hashimoto's Protocol: A 90-Day Plan for Reversing Thyroid Symptoms and Getting Your Life Back*
- Dennis Genpo Merzel, *Spitting Out the Bones: A Zen Master's 45 Year Journey*
- Pedram Shojai, *The Art of Stopping Time: Practical Mindfulness for Busy People*

Law 14: Miracles Are Possible Only in the Morning

How you start the day sets the tone for how you will spend the rest of your day. No matter when you awaken, do not begin your day by reacting to the world around you. That is the path to stress, burnout, and a failed agenda. Put yourself first in the morning, prepare your mind and body for the day, and prioritize the things you will do. Then face the day.

If you are going to listen to what anyone has to say about miracles, it should be Hal Elrod, a motivational speaker, success coach, and author of the number one bestseller *The Miracle Morning: The Not-So-Obvious Secret Guaranteed to Transform Your Life (Before 8AM)*.

(You will benefit from his advice even if your morning naturally starts later, as mine does!) Hal cheated death not once but twice.

When he was twenty years old, Hal was hit by a drunk driver going seventy miles per hour and was declared clinically dead for six minutes before he recovered consciousness. He overcame medical opinion by bouncing back not only to walk again but to complete a fifty-two-mile ultramarathon fueled by passion and willpower. He subsequently went on to become a record-breaking sales rep and national-champion sales manager for the famous knife company Cutco and eventually a sought-after keynote speaker before becoming a multiple-time best-selling author.

At Cutco, Hal says, his mentor taught him a technique called the Five-Minute Rule that changed his life. According to this rule, it's okay to be negative when things go wrong, but not for more than five minutes at a time. To practice this, set a timer and allow yourself up to five minutes to bitch, moan, complain, and vent about something that is annoying you. When the five minutes are up, it's time to stop putting your energy into something that you can't change and start focusing on where you want to go and what is within your control to get there.

Hal put this rule into practice after his accident. A week after he came out of his coma, the doctors called his parents in and said, "We're worried about Hal. Physically he's doing well, but we believe your son is in denial." They did not understand why Hal was always laughing and joking with the nurses and therapists. That was not the normal behavior of a young man who'd been told he would never walk again. The doctors believed that the reality was so scary and painful for Hal that he had checked out of reality and was living in a state of delusion.

But Hal was not in a state of delusion; he was living by the Five-Minute Rule. He could not go back in time, so he saw no point in sitting around wishing the accident hadn't happened. Instead, he felt that he had two options: if the doctors were right and he would never walk again, he would accept it, but there was also a chance that they were wrong, in which case he would not accept it.

As it turned out, they were wrong. Within three weeks of being found in a coma with his femur broken in half and his pelvis shattered into three pieces, Hal took his first steps. He left the hospital a month later, went back to work against doctors' orders, and ended up breaking sales records. But it wasn't just thinking he would walk again that allowed him to do so. Positive thinking doesn't magically solve all of your problems. Hal believes that the key to creating miracles is putting yourself into the best possible mental, physical, and emotional state possible to create optimum results in your life.

Hal says that you can most easily access this state in the morning. Most people wake up because they have to. They set an alarm based on what time they need to be somewhere, do something, or answer to someone else. But this sets the tone for spending the day serving the needs of others before their own and reacting to whatever is in front of them in the moment instead of choosing deliberate, intentional actions that are aligned with their values and goals. Hal uses his mornings to focus on himself and become a better person than he was the night before. He spends an hour each day doing an extraordinary personal development routine that he credits with saving his life. He breaks it down into the acronym S-A-V-E-R-S: silence, affirmations, visualizations, exercise, reading, and scribing. This is his miracle morning, the oxygen mask that allowed him to thrive despite all of the odds stacked against him. Hal's process is rather lengthy, but he has condensed it into a five-minute program that anyone can make time to complete.

Hal claims that if you do these practices at other times of the day, you miss out on experiencing their benefits throughout the day. In particular, meditating and practicing affirmations and visualizations impact your subconscious and change the way you think, act, and react all day, which in turn affects your quality of life. He recommends different practices in the evening, particularly asking yourself what you could have done better that day. This is a simple way of striving to improve while gradually becoming numb to the idea of being imperfect so that it doesn't hurt your ego.

Hal credits his miracle morning and the mental, physical, and emotional state it evokes with saving his life yet again in 2016 after he was diagnosed with acute lymphoblastic leukemia only two weeks after we shared a ride to an airport together. Although developing cancer wasn't his conscious choice, he believed that he was responsible for choosing how he would respond to it. By accepting what he couldn't change, remaining grateful for all that he had, and finding and creating meaning and purpose from what might otherwise have been a negative experience, he found once again that every adversity holds within it a profound, life-transforming advantage. In fact, I believe that Hal instinctively followed almost every law in this book as he recovered from cancer. People like Hal have already figured out the importance of these habits!

We all face adversity, and it's up to us to decide what meaning we give to it and what purpose it serves for ourselves, our loved ones, and the greater good. As I write this, Hal's cancer is in remission, and I have no doubt that he will continue to use his mornings to create many more miracles.

Action Items

- Begin a daily practice of doing something meaningful right after you wake up. Try journaling, meditating, doing visualizations, or writing down goals. Find out what works best for you.
- Put your phone into airplane mode before you go to bed, and keep it on airplane mode until you're done with your morning practice.
- When you feel an urge to vent, complain, or think negative thoughts, seek forgiveness right away. If you don't find it, set a timer for five minutes and let loose. When the time is up, go back to being productive.

Recommended Listening

Hal Elrod, "Be Happier, Healthier & More Productive," *Bulletproof Radio*, episode 176

Recommended Reading

- Hal Elrod, *The Miracle Morning: The Not-So-Obvious Secret Guaranteed to Transform Your Life (Before 8AM)*

PART II

FASTER

SEX IS AN ALTERED STATE

This section of the book starts with a bang (get it?). The truth is that sex was not actually one of the game changers' top recommendations for performing better. Though many guests did bring up the topic of sex over the course of our interviews, few spoke frankly about how much it matters. Maybe they were afraid that people would judge them as hedonistic or shallow. It's certainly true that many people carry shame and embarrassment about sex. Some people are taught at a young age that it's dirty or "bad" and certainly not something that they should talk about in public.

So sex is missing from the data, but there are enough echoes of it throughout my hundreds of interviews that I would be remiss to ignore it. Certainly it's one of the three most important things you do, and whether you are a man or a woman it directly impacts your performance in ways you may not realize. Sex affects your hormone levels, your neurotransmitters, your brain waves, and your overall happiness levels, each of which in turn has a direct impact on your ability to perform as a parent, partner, friend, employee, and any other roles you may have or aspire to fill.

As you read earlier, we are hardwired to do three things in order of importance: fight (or flee), feed, and . . . the F-word that this chapter is about. These are the behaviors that keep you alive and ensure that you will help propagate the species, so your body prioritizes them above all else. That means your body produces the most energy to support these instincts. The entire point of being Bulletproof is to master these motivations so that you can redirect the energy behind them as you see fit. Sex is one of the three reasons your body thinks it is alive, so it is a powerful motivating force that can either suck up a ton of your energy or, if you follow the advice in this chapter, super-charge your performance.

Law 15: Stop Thinking with What's in Your Pants

If you're a man, you need to learn to redirect your sexual energy into being a better human being. Your body uses huge amounts of energy to make sure you help the species reproduce. Instead, put that energy to better uses. Doing so will help you to be happier, live longer, and kick more ass. Your stress will go down and your energy will go up when you teach your body that the world won't end if you don't have an orgasm, just as it won't end if you skip a meal. A craving is a craving, and any craving will take you off your game until you master it.

In 2011, researchers at New York University learned some inter-esting things about sex and violence. They injected light-sensitive proteins into the brains of male mice and then used fiber-optic tech-nology to stimulate the proteins. Specifically, the proteins were in-jected into the hypothalamus, a region of the brain involved in certain metabolic processes, including hunger, body temperature, and hor-mone regulation. When they put male mice together in a cage and triggered this part of the hypothalamus with a flash of light, the mice suddenly turned violent. Out of nowhere, the mice that had previ-ously been completely docile attacked other mice or whatever objects were nearby.

There was only one activity that prevented these violent urges: sex. When the researchers lit up the same part of the brain while the mice were having sex, nothing happened. But interestingly, once the male mice ejaculated, they went back to being easily provoked. The researchers looked at the mice's individual neurons and found an overlap between the neurons that were active during fighting and dur-ing sex.[1]

This may have been the first time scientists were able to see on a neuron-by-neuron basis that the same part of the brain is involved in violence and sex. When you think about it, it makes sense that the same part of the brain controls two behaviors that keep the species alive. Being able to fight off predators obviously keeps you alive. And having sex ensures that the species will continue to live. But that's no excuse for any behavioral overlap between sex and violence, and it's why it's so powerful to channel your sexual energy to positive ends. Psychologists and spiritual masters call this "sublimation"—the act of consciously transforming sexual or any other urge into creativity or physical action. Boxers and other professional athletes have long been known to forgo sex before a competition. Muhammad Ali reportedly refused to have sex for six weeks before a boxing match, and some teams at the World Cup even institute sex bans for players before competition.[2]

I first came across this idea in the seminal book *Think and Grow Rich*, published by Napoleon Hill in 1938. This classic book, which was perhaps one of the first business and personal development books ever to be published to acclaim and success, includes an entire chapter on transforming male sexual energy into productivity. Hill's book was based on observations because he didn't have access to neuroscience, but his ideas and techniques have been really helpful to me. He claims that a man's sex drive is the most powerful force he possesses, and several of the high performers I've interviewed agree.

John Gray, for example, is the author of perhaps the best-known relationship book of all time, *Men Are from Mars, Women Are from Venus*. Over the last several decades, he has researched the impact of hormones on sex and relationships. In fact, the first time I met him, I was shocked to discover that he's almost as much of a biohacker as he is a relationship hacker.

According to John, a relationship is a system between two people, and a lot of relationship problems stem from hormone imbalances between the men and women in that system. He insists that we can dramatically improve both our sex lives and our relationships if we start paying more attention to and honoring those differences.

Women's sex hormones naturally ebb and flow over the course of a month much more than men's do. Most premenopausal women ovulate around day 12 of their cycle. There is a surge of estrogen at that time because of the evolutionary imperative to procreate. So from day 6 to day 12, a woman is more hormonally inclined to want to have sex. John calls this period around ovulation the "love window."

How can estrogen be stimulated, if not through a woman's natural hormonal cycle? Gray suggests that one way is through pair bonding. When a woman feels that her partner is meeting her needs (outside of sex), her body is wired to release estrogen. The idea isn't that women are needy and incapable; it's that they can kick ass *and* still benefit from extra nurturing during hormonal shifts. According to John, a woman's biological operating system needs to know that there is a dependable mate in order to want to have sex and potentially make a baby; it is an evolutionary imperative. The same is true of all mammals: they won't reproduce if the circumstances aren't safe.

John explains that during the beginning of this "love window," a woman will often feel that her husband is ignoring her. Maybe he's just a jerk, or maybe her shifting hormones are influencing her perception of his behavior. (Or maybe he really is ignoring her!) John says that as her hormones surge and her body releases an egg for fertilization, she is wired to want to feel a sense of connection and support. John suggests that a male partner plan a special date right at the beginning of the "love window." If a woman feels cared for, her body will release estrogen; if a male partner feels good about meeting her needs, his body will release testosterone. It's important to note that age and hormonal health play an important role here; postmenopausal women and men with a low testosterone level (like I had in my twenties) won't experience hormone fluctuations in the same ways.

If everything goes well during the love window, there is a higher likelihood of the couple having sex. This is when, biologically, a woman is likely to find her mate the most desirable and when she has the potential to have her best possible orgasm. If she has a mind-blowing orgasm, the man's testosterone levels can double because he'll feel like a hero. (We guys are pretty predictable.) But after his ejaculation, his testosterone level will decline. It will then build back up over the course of a week, when it will again reach its highest point.

John recommends having sex once every seven days to optimize both men's and women's hormone levels. That means no masturbation, no porn, none of that—just abstinence all week and then sex on the seventh day. This is especially important for men who have a low testosterone level, which unfortunately includes more and more men these days. We now know that around a quarter of all men over the age of thirty have a low testosterone level.[3] Just as you may have obeyed the voice in your head that tells you to eat too much, too often, is it possible that there is another voice in your head telling you to have sex too often? Maybe.

John says that many couples experience problems immediately after sharing an intimate connection. They have a wonderful time together and feel so close and bonded, but all of that connecting makes a man's estrogen level soar and his testosterone level plummet. Remember how feeling independent stimulates testosterone production? Well, unfortunately that means that the man retreats to rebuild his testosterone level. He sequesters himself and becomes consumed with an activity that has nothing to do with his partner. According to John, this behavior is fairly predictable from a biological point of view. When a man pulls away, he's rebuilding his testosterone level. (Although sometimes he might just be a jerk.)

It's important to understand how your sex hormones push your biology, even if you have no desire to follow any of this advice. They drive a major source of your urges. Christopher Ryan, a coauthor of the bestselling book *Sex at Dawn: How We Mate, Why We Stray, and What It Means for Modern Relationships,* has changed the way thousands of people view relationships. He says that the idea of monogamy is more cultural than genetic and that human sexuality looks more like the sexuality of our primate relatives the chimps than we'd like to admit. Yet Chris doesn't suggest that we should necessarily avoid monogamy. Instead, he says, monogamy is a decision, not an instinct. He draws a corollary to one of our other hardwired imperatives: eating. Being a vegetarian is not an instinct; it's a choice. For most people, it doesn't necessarily come naturally, and it doesn't mean that bacon won't smell good anymore. (As a former raw vegan, I can tell you that he's right about that. I can also tell you that the heritage-breed piglets on my farm absolutely love to eat the kale I dutifully choked down when I was a vegan.)

If you are monogamous, no matter how much you love your partner, you're still going to be attracted to other people. That's part of being human. And just because you're attracted to other people or fantasize about other people, that doesn't mean that there's a problem with your relationship or with you; it simply means that you're a *Homo sapiens* with hormones.

You may be surprised to hear that Chris's beliefs intersect with John Gray's. Chris says that when monogamous men have sex with a new partner, their testosterone levels increase. So cheating actually makes men feel good about themselves on a hormonal level. If you choose to be in a monogamous relationship, using John's techniques to intentionally keep your testosterone level high might keep you from feeling tempted to stray and preserve your relationship. How many top executives are taken down by inappropriate relationships or destructive behaviors? Not the best way to change your game.

As a biohacker, I had to test some of those theories on myself. My lovely wife, Dr. Lana, wasn't a fan of testing out Chris's beliefs, but we did experiment with some Taoist sex practices. As my journey into biohacking led me to explore Eastern philosophies, I found that ancient Chinese Taoists—some of the world's original biohackers—recommended transforming sexual energy into immortality. They even had a formula for how often men should ejaculate to maintain youthfulness:

$$(\text{Your age} - 7) / 4$$

That yields your ideal number of days between ejaculations. Who said that algebra wasn't sexy? A man who wants to live forever, they say, should ejaculate only once every thirty days and keep his orgasms to less than an hour each (?!). Then again, I haven't met an immortal Taoist that I know of.

I tested this out a few years ago, when I was thirty-nine years old. According to the Taoist equation, my ideal number of days between ejaculations was eight, remarkably close to John Gray's recommendation. I followed this equation for almost a year and tracked how often

I had sex (or masturbated), how often I ejaculated, and my perceived quality of life using a scale of 1 to 10 (1 = everything sucks, 5 = everything is normal, 10 = everything rocks). I incorporated everything into the score—how satisfied I felt with my career, my energy, my relationships, and my health.

Yes, this is a little bit embarrassing, but I'm going all in and sharing the results here to show the importance of mastering your lust to power your performance. If the idea of seeing data about my sex life (free of juicy details) turns you green, feel free to skip ahead to the next section. I promise I won't be offended, but you will be missing out on some really interesting and at times surprising results that will probably apply to you. The whole point of this is that your body is funneling huge amounts of energy into sex, and you could use that energy elsewhere.

For the first phase of the experiment, I followed the magic Taoist equation and went eight days between ejaculations, which is very similar to John Gray's every-seven-days philosophy. That doesn't mean that I turned into a monk. I did still have an active sex life; I just didn't ejaculate. After an initial few days of frustration, that energy had to go somewhere, and with a little effort it overflowed into the other parts of my life. Soon I noticed my life satisfaction levels going up as I tracked them each day. And as time went on, the frequency at which I was having sex increased even though I ejaculated less. The less I ejaculated, the more I wanted to have sex. Duh. My perceived quality of life went up even more when I had more sex, too. Those Taoists were definitely onto something.

Graph of my daily life satisfaction, showing drops after orgasm in 8-day cycles

For the next phase of the experiment, I decided to go all in on the immortality thing and try thirty days between ejaculations. That was difficult and required starting over a few times after some . . . accidents. (Hey, I'm human.) But the results were amazing. I saw a huge increase in my life satisfaction levels, my sex drive went through the roof (again, duh), and I was phenomenally productive and full of energy. The biggest surprise to me was that I got a lot more attention from women, both my wife and others, though of course I acted on it only with my beautiful and brilliant (and incredibly patient) wife, Dr. Lana. Surprisingly, my satisfaction with life was higher on this regime.

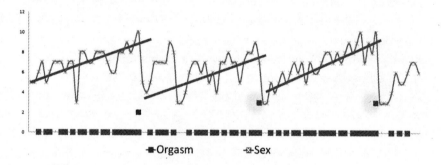

—■-Orgasm   -☒-Sex

Graph of my daily life satisfaction, showing that it continues to grow when I only ejaculate every 30 days, but drops after orgasm

The final phase of the experiment was to go thirty days with no sex at all. I call this one "Monk Mode." That was more challenging, and I don't really recommend it unless you're looking for a remarkable test of willpower. After a few false starts, I did become happier and more productive as the month went on, but the results were less significant than during the previous thirty-day challenge. I also saw some pretty terrifying shrinkage after thirty days—about 20 percent. Use it or lose it, I guess. Thankfully, everything returned to normal after a few weeks of Taoist exercises designed to counteract shrinkage (and lots more sex). Phew!

That experiment certainly didn't make me want to go into Monk

Mode all the time, but it did make me far more conscious of how I felt after ejaculating. I found that I had a two- or three-day "ejaculation hangover," during which I was less energetic and engaged in whatever I was doing and my satisfaction with life was lower. When I had fewer ejaculations, I was having a lot more sex, and I liked everything about my life better, which is not what I had been expecting at all. Over the course of the experiment, I experienced my highest levels of satisfaction when I was having a lot of sex but ejaculating only once every thirty days.

That really surprised me, but there is plenty of science to explain those findings. After ejaculating, men experience a sharp increase in the hormone prolactin, which extinguishes their sex drive and makes them want to take a nap.[4] Women also produce prolactin after having an orgasm, but not at the same levels as men. Prolactin counteracts dopamine, the "feel-good" hormone, which explains why a lot of us guys feel a little bit depressed hours after completing the act.

Elevated prolactin levels decrease men's testosterone levels, which is one of the reasons studies show that abstinence for three weeks increases testosterone levels in healthy men.[5] Meanwhile, having sex without ejaculating also increases testosterone levels, in this case by up to 72 percent.[6] That might explain why women seemed so interested in me during my experiment—they could sense my elevated testosterone levels and off-the-charts desire for sex even though I wasn't consciously doing anything to attract them. Or perhaps it was because of changes in my pheromones. If only I'd known back in school that my lack of a sex life could actually be a source of power and even a turn-on for women!

It's important to note that the Taoist teaching is that a woman finishes orgasm "undiminished," so this is an experiment for men only, and women who have tried this universally report a bad experience, as their oxytocin levels plummet. (See the next law for more on this.) For men, it's much easier to follow the program with the support of a loving partner who will back off at the right time to help you stick to the rules. I have no data to show whether the rules are different for gay couples, but I suspect this stuff applies to anyone with a penis.

When I first reported on this research, many *Bulletproof Radio* listeners privately told me that they had tried it with astounding success. Several couples said that it had radically improved their relationship. One guy in his late twenties reported receiving a $30,000 raise sixty days after starting. Another guy finally got enough energy to launch a company he'd wanted to start forever and grow it quickly. And not so strangely, the year I ran those experiments, I was a new father working full-time as a tech executive while moonlighting to start Bulletproof. All that energy had to come from somewhere, and harnessing my body's desire to propagate the species helped.

Later on, you'll read about how porn and masturbation are sure ways to wreck these results. Sure, they're fun, but they're not frequent habits of people who change the world. If you can't go at least thirty days without either one, you're not in charge, and you're wasting energy.

Action Items

- If you are a woman, identify your love window and see if John's findings are apparent in your life. Share the dates with your partner, and ask your partner to set up a date.
- If you are a man, see if John's testosterone comments ring true for you. If you are with a woman, ask her when her love window starts, and set up a date!
- Chart your sexual activity along with your overall life satisfaction to see how your orgasms affect your energy, happiness, and productivity.
- If you are a man, boost your testosterone level by having less frequent orgasms, doing high-intensity exercise, reducing your sugar intake, increasing your intake of healthy fats, and even (nicely) retreating from your partner when necessary.

Recommended Listening

- John Gray, "Addiction, Sexuality, & ADD," *Bulletproof Radio*, episode 222
- John Gray, "Beyond Mars & Venus: Tips That Truly Bring Men and Women Together," *Bulletproof Radio*, episode 414
- Christopher Ryan, "Sex, Sex Culture & Sex at Dawn," *Bulletproof Radio*, episode 52

- Neil Strauss, "Relationship Hacks for Dealing with Conflicts, Monogamy, Sex & Communication with the Opposite Sex," *Bulletproof Radio*, episode 406

Recommended Reading
- John Gray, *Beyond Mars and Venus: Relationship Skills for Today's Complex World*
- Christopher Ryan and Cacilda Jetha, *Sex at Dawn: How We Mate, Why We Stray, and What It Means for Modern Relationships*

Law 16: Never Underestimate the Power of a Female Orgasm

If you're a woman, regular orgasms are one of the keys to showing up fully in your world. When you orgasm, every hormone tied to happiness and performance goes up, your immune system improves, and you get younger. Having orgasms is a skill that can unlock new levels of happiness and even altered states. Changing your game is easier to do when you learn to master your orgasms.

After spending all that time thinking about my own orgasms, it seemed only fair to interview some of the top experts on women's orgasms, so I sought some out. The first was Emily Morse, a doctor of human sexuality and the host of the wildly popular podcast *Sex with Emily*. Dr. Morse's show is mission driven: she started it to get the word out about the power of female orgasms and to help everyone have the best sex of their lives.

As Dr. Morse shares in her interview, she comes from a very liberal family, so you might not expect her to have any hang-ups about sex. Her mom even told her, "Talk to me about sex if you have any questions," but Dr. Morse didn't have any questions because no one in her family talked about sex! When she got to college and started having sex, she didn't think it was all that exciting. Then she heard some of her friends talking about something called an "orgasm" and asked, "What's that?" This is all too common, and it is one of the reasons this chapter exists.

Now Dr. Morse travels around the world to sex conferences to learn about the latest and greatest developments in the world of sex and helps women incorporate those developments into their own sex lives. The issue she sees more than any other is low sexual desire in women. Many of the women she meets feel frustrated and hopeless, but Dr. Morse has found that a great way to boost female libido is through something as simple as increasing blood flow.

To feel desire and have an orgasm, women (and men) need their blood to flow down to their genitals. "Big gun" erectile dysfunction drugs such as Viagra can solve this problem in both men and women, but there are also safe and natural solutions for women without drugs. Dr. Morse recommends mindful masturbation to stimulate arousal, CBD-infused clitoral massage oils that relax and stimulate arousal, or any other clitoral-stimulating pleasure products.

Kegel exercises are another simple solution. They exercise the pelvic floor muscles—the ones you would use to stop the flow of urine. Both men and women experience benefits from tensing and holding those muscles for ten seconds at a time for a few minutes a day. Men experience better ejaculatory control and stronger orgasms. Who doesn't want that? Women also experience stronger orgasms, urinary continence (no more peeing when you sneeze), and greater sexual desire.

Next I sought out Dr. Jolene Brighten, a functional medicine naturopathic doctor specializing in women's health. Dr. Brighten told me that when women have at least one or two orgasms a week, they feel better and live longer. According to her research, women who have regular orgasms have better overall immune system modulation and lower inflammatory markers. This makes sense since the stress hormone cortisol, which decreases in women after they orgasm, causes inflammation. This means that more orgasms lead to less stress, less disease, and less aging—but only for women. Almost all the advice in this book applies equally to men and women, but definitely not when it comes to orgasm frequency. (Yes, it's technically possible for men to orgasm without ejaculating . . . it's just very rare without advanced practice.)

Women's orgasms support healthy hormone levels, relieve stress, and can unlock altered states of consciousness.[7] While frequent orgasms tend to lower testosterone levels in men, they flood the female body with estrogen[8] and oxytocin.[9] Oxytocin has earned the nickname "the love molecule" because it fosters social bonding, trust, relaxation, and generosity. That buzzy, warm afterglow a woman feels with her partner after having sex is thanks to oxytocin. Estrogen enhances the effects of oxytocin, too.[10] The two work in synergy when a woman orgasms, creating a cocktail of feel-good bonding and relaxation.

On top of that, women get a postorgasm increase in the neurotransmitter serotonin that boosts mood even more.[11] Basically, *more frequent* orgasms do the exact same things for women that *less frequent* ejaculation does for men. If that's not an argument for the idea that there's a *Mother* Nature out there controlling things, I don't know what is.

Action Items
- If you are a woman, your orgasms are the key to a healthier and longer life and a not entirely unpleasant way of achieving those goals.
- If you are suffering from low libido, make sure to do Kegel exercises regularly to boost sexual desire.
- If you are a woman's partner, pay attention to her pleasure so you can grow old together.

Recommended Listening
- Emily Morse (Sex with Emily), "Orgasms, Kegels & Sexology," *Bulletproof Radio*, episode 233

- Emily Morse, "Hack Your Way to a Better Sex Life," *Bulletproof Radio*, episode 373
- Jolene Brighten, "On Women's Health, Post–Birth Control Syndrome, and Brain Injuries," *Bulletproof Radio*, episode 415
- "Hugs from Dr. Love" with Paul Zak, *Bulletproof Radio*, episode 334

Law 17: Go Off Script During Fairy-Tale Sex

Sex is a gateway to flow states and the altered states of high perfor-mance. To access these states, you must have the courage to seek experiences that push your boundaries. When you get sex out of your head in order to allow your body to seek what it wants, you can tap into deep levels of freedom, healing, and creativity.

Okay, so orgasms do different things for each sex. But there's a spir-itual side to sex that goes deeper than just orgasms, so I set out to find guests who have studied how to use our sexual potential to reach al-tered states of flow in which your body and mind can do more than you might think. The first stop was to call "Mistress Natalie," a New York dominatrix who works with high-powered executives. Fortunately, she works out with a sports trainer friend of mine, so it was easy to find her. (Apparently spanking can cause repetitive stress injury and mus-cle imbalance unless you practice functional movement exercises!)

This was definitely an interview I could not predict. Mistress Na-talie uses a lot of varied bondage, discipline, submission, and masoch-ism (BDSM) practices to help willing participants access a state of flow. Though it's easy to write off BDSM as some weird fetish, Natalie says that her clients find their work with her therapeutic and at times transformative. In fact, she was so inspired by the therapeutic value of BDSM that she went back to school to become a life coach. Her unique "Kinky Coaching" uses BDSM along with several biohacking principles as tools to elevate a person's mental and physical state.

The key is that Natalie's work takes sex into the unknown. We all know how most fairy tales begin ("Once upon a time") and end ("They all lived happily ever after"), and the same is true for most sex. The standard expectation is that sex begins with foreplay, proceeds to penetration (in most cases), and then (ideally) ends in climax. This formula generally works, but it does have some shortcomings.

According to Natalie and her clients, it makes sex repetitive. You're doing the same thing every time, which can become less and less rewarding. The second issue is setting climax as a goal. When you focus on getting to the end of something, you tend to miss out on the buildup and fail to fully let go and allow things to unfold naturally. It also sets up an expectation that both partners will climax, which means you can "fail" at sex if you or your partner doesn't have an orgasm. That's a fast track to shame, performance anxiety, and lots of other problems. No one wants to feel as though they've failed at sex.

When you remove the goal and go off script, however, you become liberated to get out of your head and focus on the connection between you and your partner. It also allows you to ask for whatever it is you really want, even if you haven't asked for it before. That matters because from your nervous system's perspective, sex is a matter of life and death. If you're not getting what truly fulfills you sexually, a subconscious part of you can feel starved. Going off script and having the courage to ask for what you want enables each time to become unique, so you can also start to enjoy the very idea of sex as much as the climax, just as you enjoy the experience of a fine meal, not just the fullness you feel when you're done eating. In the case of Natalie's clients, this experience happens in the mind as much as in the body. Natalie never has sex with her clients. A lot of them wear a chastity belt (yes, that's a thing) the entire time she's with them. The power dynamic of their interplay forces them to see themselves in a different light and is ultimately therapeutic. As I said, there was no way to predict where that interview would go.

It's the psychological work necessary to push limits that most often puts Natalie's clients into a state of flow. Natalie explains that in her line of work a state of flow is known as the "sub space." After a session her clients feel the effects for days. They are relaxed and have more focus and clarity. To Natalie, BDSM and all the other unusual parts of her practice are just another way for someone to push his or her boundaries to access a flow state.

There is still a lot of judgment of consensual practices like BDSM, but Natalie compares it to activities such as skydiving and ultramarathons— anything that physically forces you out of your comfort zone and pushes your limits can flip a switch in your head, releasing a powerful neurochemical cascade. What helps someone get into this state is completely individualized. Who's to say that it's any more of an aberration to choose humiliation or bondage over jumping off a bridge with a cable attached to your back? Different strokes for different folks.

Just thinking about sex is a powerful way to get into a state of flow. During weeklong intensive executive neurofeedback training sessions at 40 Years of Zen, we teach clients one surefire method to use if they get "stuck" trying to create a self-induced flow state during neurofeedback sessions. The easiest and most reliable way to get unstuck and move back into a flow state is to imagine a brief sexual fantasy. As soon as clients start to think about what really turns them on, their brain waves skyrocket, and they get unstuck.

The thing is, this works only if you think about what you really like, no matter what it is. Fairy-tale sex doesn't do it for most people, but visualizing what really pushes your buttons always works, especially if you don't judge yourself for it. I've had some of my highest recorded EEG levels at 40 Years of Zen while using this technique to break myself out of a plateau. And I'm not going to tell you the details of what I fantasized about!

Acknowledging the things that work best for you in the bedroom to yourself (and your partner) can help you tap into some of the altered states that unleash your best performance, even days later. If you are focused on a goal, however, you remain in an analytical state, which studies show blocks emotion and empathy.[12] That is not a recipe for good sex. When you shut off your analytic mind and tap into your intuition, you feel more empathy, joy, creativity, and calm and a sense of oneness with those around you. Now, *that's* sexy.

The fact that sex can unleash flow states, creativity, and even spiritual states led me to look for experts on precisely how to unlock them.

So I found a leader in orgasmic mediation, a "consciousness practice" during which one partner (who is usually but not necessarily male) strokes a female partner's clitoris for fifteen minutes with no expectation other than experiencing sensation and a sense of connection between the two partners. This may seem out-there, but hey, I just shared a graph of all my ejaculations for a year with you. If you're still reading at this point, you can handle this.

Eli Block, a lead orgasmic meditation instructor at OneTaste, a somewhat controversial company that teaches orgasmic meditation, says that one reason people come to this practice is that they want a sexual experience that's completely outside of their heads. In his interview, he shared the (PG-rated) techniques he teaches. As people use the body as a mechanism to access flow states between themselves and their partners, they tune into each other's sensations and become completely absorbed in the moment. This liberates them from a typical sex story line, and they report that being fully present with a partner is a powerful, transcendent experience.

Action Items
- If (and only if) it appeals to you, try orgasmic meditation, BDSM, or anything else safe and consensual that your body truly desires to see if it helps you access a flow state.
- Ask yourself what you really want in the bedroom and ask your partner for it, even if it's scary.
- Think about how you can stop making sex routine and introduce an element of the unknown to your lovemaking. The result is likely to be a more powerful connection with your partner and perhaps an otherworldly experience.

Recommended Listening
- "50 Shades of Dave" with Mistress Natalie, *Bulletproof Radio*, episode 341
- Eli Block, "One Taste, Orgasmic Meditation & Flow State," *Bulletproof Radio*, episode 254
- Geoffrey Miller, "Sex, Power, and Domination," *Bulletproof Radio*, episode 138

Law 18: Use Sex to Get the Best Drugs

Having conscious sex with the right people creates neurochemicals that set you free and create a state of flow. Viewing pornography creates neurochemicals that make you an addict and block the flow state. Porn is the high-fructose corn syrup of sex. Choose wisely.

If orgasm can release feel-good hormones and neurotransmitters and sex can lead to altered states of creativity and high performance, what's the downside? Answering this question led me to interview one of the original experts in hacking the brain, Bill Harris, who sadly passed away as I was in the final editing stages of this book. As the founder of the Centerpointe Research Institute, Bill is well known for creating brain upgrade programs for hundreds of thousands of people, and for donating tens of millions of dollars to charity. Thanks to my work with neurofeedback, I've had a chance to see Bill's brain waves, and they're truly advanced.

During a powerful interview, Bill explained that right before the economy crashed in 2008, he went through an awful divorce. He was under a lot of stress, and without even realizing it he found himself in a chronic state of fight or flight, making bad decisions. Within a short time frame, he got six speeding tickets and his license was temporarily suspended. After having a brain scan done by Dr. Daniel Amen, the game-changing psychiatrist and brain specialist you read about in chapter 4, Bill found that chronic stress had caused his limbic system, the emotional house of the brain, to become overactive.

Bill explained that when your limbic system is overactive, you are more likely to make dopamine-driven decisions. This means you are motivated to do things that cause your brain to release dopamine, a neurotransmitter that triggers the reward center of the brain. Dopamine is the neurotransmitter of immediate gratification. When you are driven to get a hit of dopamine, you are more likely to seek things that feel good in the moment but are bad for you in the long run, such as sugar, processed foods, and even drugs.

What does this have to do with sex? Well, having sex is one thing that causes your brain to release feel-good hormones; watching porn leads it to release different amounts of each chemical than having sex with a partner does. Specifically, watching porn causes you to release more dopamine, while having sex with a partner causes you to release more oxytocin.

There is such a thing as too much dopamine. Our brains aren't equipped to handle the kind of stimulation that online porn viewers now have constant and unlimited access to. Your brain responds to porn much as it does to cocaine, alcohol, or sugar, with a big rush of pleasure and diminishing returns over time.[13] And just as with addictive drugs, porn seems to cause a tolerance to dopamine, meaning you require more and more of it to feel the same effects.[14]

As a result, it seems that the more you watch porn, the more stimulation you will eventually require to get turned on. A 2014 study out of Germany showed that regular porn viewers have smaller, less responsive reward pathways in their brains.[15] A French study from that same year showed that 60 percent of men who regularly watched porn could not get erect with a human partner, though they continued to be able to get an erection while watching porn.[16]

Still think that porn isn't addictive? A Cambridge University neuroscientist looked at brain scans of men who believed they were addicted to porn and saw significant changes to their brains' gray matter that paralleled changes in the brains of drug addicts.[17] This is pretty scary stuff, and I highly recommend ditching porn for a month to see if you notice any changes to your sexual desires and performance. It might be more difficult than you expect. If it is, it's time to do it anyway.

The antidote to this problem came in the form of a profound interview with Dr. Pooja Lakshmin, an orgasm researcher at Rutgers University (pretty cool job). She credits the neuropharmacological effects she identified while studying orgasmic meditation with turning her entire life around. After growing up in a traditional Indian family and feeling constant pressure to be successful, she became a doctor and married a man who met her parents' approval. But she was miserable. Throughout her entire life, she had lived inside her head, unable to really feel or experience positive or negative sensations.

It wasn't until she discovered orgasmic meditation that she began to really go into her body and feel pain and pleasure, which she found terrifying at first. Over time, she grew more comfortable with herself and became able to fully receive pleasure and connect more deeply with others. That led her to her life's work studying orgasms and helping other people experience oxytocin-based connection.

According to Dr. Lakshmin, yet another problem with porn is that unlike other forms of sex, it does not allow you to access a state of flow. Just as the brain responds to different types of sex by releasing varying amount of chemicals, it responds differently to partnered orgasms and solo orgasms. Namely, when you masturbate you don't go into an involuntary state. It's sort of like how you can't tickle yourself no matter how hard you try. You need to have a partner to surrender fully.

Dr. Lakshmin claims that when you do access a flow state through conscious sex with a partner or the orgasmic meditation practice she researches, you can feel sensations more deeply, eventually getting the same effects from lighter and lighter pressure if you're on the receiving end of an orgasmic meditation session. This increased sensitivity can even act as an antidote to the dopamine resistance caused by watching too much porn, and the person providing the stimulation can benefit from it, too. The nervous systems of both people attune to each other during the practice.

This connection has a direct impact on the brain. Dr. Lakshmin says that it actually calms the limbic system. Whereas Bill Harris opted for meditation to calm his limbic system and take himself out of a chronic state of fight or flight so that he could start making better decisions, Dr. Lakshmin calls orgasmic meditation "meditation on speed" because, she says, it works faster to train the limbic system to help you tap into your intuition and feel deeper and more powerful sensations.

Action Items

- Try quitting porn for a month; if it's difficult to do, quit it for another month.

- Prioritize calming your limbic system through regular meditation, orgasmic meditation, or regular orgasms with a partner.

Recommended Listening
- Bill Harris, "Make Bad Decisions? Blame Dopamine," *Bulletproof Radio*, episode 362
- Pooja Lakshmin, "Orgasmic Meditation & Sex Life Hacking," *Bulletproof Radio*, episode 60
- "Sleep, Sex & Tech at the Bulletproof Conference," *Bulletproof Radio*, episode 327

FIND YOUR NIGHTTIME SPIRIT ANIMAL

Game changers may be known for crushing barriers and pushing themselves to the limits, but real innovation is not born from an exhausted mind and body. That's why more than a third of my podcast guests named good sleep as highly critical to their performance. In fact, getting high-quality sleep was the fifth most commonly cited piece of advice for improving performance.

This chapter is personal for me because as I've learned to become a higher-performance individual, I've had to reexamine my attitude toward sleep. I still don't like it that a meaningful amount of my time each day is spent unconscious, but I've resolved that as long as I have to do it, I'm going to find a way to kick ass and get the most amazing sleep I can in as little time as possible.

When I set off to hack sleep, I did what I always do: I interviewed some of the world's top experts and began my own investigation of the available research. I found a groundbreaking study that analyzed the sleep habits of 1.2 million people over the course of several years—the first and only study to gather enough data to correlate longevity with small changes in sleep duration. This study was so comprehensive that statisticians couldn't begin to crunch the numbers—it took modern computing to fully analyze the data. But in the end, researchers found that the study participants who slept only six and a half hours per night lived longer than those who slept eight hours a night.[1]

It's tempting to draw the conclusion that you'll live longer if you sleep for six and a half hours a night, but the truth is that it's a little bit more complicated than that. It's likely that the healthiest people simply require less sleep. Likewise, when you get good-quality sleep, you probably need less of it. I've been tracking my sleep for years. The data from the past 1,726 nights show I've had an average of six hours and five minutes of sleep a night, and I wake up feeling more refreshed than I used to when I slept for eight or nine hours at a time. I won't do you the disservice of repeating my favorite sleep hacks here from *The Bulletproof Diet* and *Head Strong* or the Bulletproof blog. Instead, we will focus on the new science of sleep straight from top sleep and wellness experts and physicians, because sleep quality drives happiness, and as we've seen, happiness drives success. After what I learned from these interviews, I've become militant about getting the best sleep I possibly can—and I hope you will, too.

Law 19: Waking Up Early Does Not Make You a Good Person

There is no morality in waking up early or staying up late. There is a huge amount of power in finding out when you sleep best and then building your life so that you can sleep.

To learn as much as possible about every nuance of sleep, I began by interviewing Dr. Michael Breus, a clinical psychologist, best-selling author, and well-known sleep expert who has spent his entire career treating sleep disorders. When he was starting out, Dr. Breus wanted to stay away from pharmaceuticals as much as possible, so he experimented with many different techniques to treat his insomnia patients, including natural supplements and cognitive behavioral therapy. Those treatments worked for some patients, but many others saw little or no improvement. So he got to hacking.

Dr. Breus was determined to figure out what was preventing those people from sleeping, and after studying their sleep patterns and hormone levels, he realized that they were often sleeping well, but they were going to sleep and waking up at the wrong times. It turned out that they weren't insomniacs at all. Their bodies were able to naturally sleep for a full six-and-a-half- to seven-and-a-half-hour sleep cycle, but they were going to bed either too early or too late and their bodies weren't able to sync with their schedules.

It's not as if those people were purposefully or carelessly messing up their sleep. They created their sleep schedules based on logistics— they had to get up early to go to work, take care of their kids, or go to school, just as most people do. But Dr. Breus felt confident that they would be more alert and productive if they were able to go to sleep and wake up in accordance with their bodies' natural circadian rhythm, which is the brain's sleep/wake cycle. Inside our brains is an internal clock called the suprachiasmatic nucleus (SCN), which determines when we're sleepy and when we're awake. It does this by stimulating the release of certain hormones such as melatonin (the "sleep hormone") at particular times of the day.[2] This is an area of science (chronobiology) that is rapidly developing, and we're gaining new insights virtually every day into just how much our circadian rhythm affects our health. In fact, in 2017 the Nobel Prize in Medicine was awarded to researchers who discovered a new protein that sets our body's clock. We're just figuring out *how* all this stuff works, but clinical physicians like Dr. Breus can see *what* works.

Dr. Breus was so sure that a simple shift in his patients' schedules would help them sleep better that he actually called their bosses and asked if they would allow their employees to begin their workdays later if it meant they would be more productive. The bosses agreed and were thrilled when their employees' levels of productivity did increase with their new schedules that allowed them to get more sleep.

That was the beginning of Dr. Breus's fascination with *The Power of When*, which happens to be the title of his bestselling book about how to schedule your day around your natural patterns to maximize your productivity. He looked at his patients' hormonal distribution throughout the day and helped them create customized schedules that allowed them to take advantage of their biology by doing things when their bodies were primed for those specific actions.

Dr. Breus found that some of his patients were skeptical. The value we attribute to being an "early riser" is so ingrained in our culture that we often fear changing our sleeping patterns. The early bird catches the worm, right? That is what we learn from a very young age—that if you get up early you'll catch the worm and go about your day productively, and when the lazy, no-good bums who sleep late finally wake up, the worms will all be gone. Seems pretty bleak, and it is. We got that idea because when we switched to growing food instead of hunting it, if you didn't get up early to work on your farm, you could starve to death. It's insane that we never rethought the schedule, given the fact that today not nearly as many people work in fields.

But Dr. Breus explains to his patients that they won't win by fighting Mother Nature. Your circadian rhythm is not just a preference; it is genetically predetermined. Scientists have known about this since 1998, when they isolated the mPer3 gene and found that the first step of this gene's expression showed a clear circadian rhythm in the SCN.[3] Signals from the SCN synchronize miniature circadian clocks throughout the body. In other words, the mPer3 gene determines your sleep drive, and the SCN sets your circadian rhythm. When you work with those genetic factors instead of against them, everything becomes less of a struggle. This is one of the core principles of biohacking—working with your biology to make performance effortless.

Through this work, Dr. Breus identified four chronotypes, or behavioral manifestations of natural circadian rhythms. Instead of labeling them "early birds" or "night owls," he matched these chronotypes with the circadian rhythms of other mammals. Indeed, only mammals have the mPer3 gene, and when it comes to our biological drives we have a lot more in common with other mammals than we do with birds. These four chronotypes are:

BEAR

This is by far the most popular chronotype. A full 50 percent of people are bears. Their sleep-wake patterns follow the sun, and they generally have no difficulty sleeping. Bears are most ready for intense tasks smack in the middle of the morning, and they feel a slight dip in energy in the midafternoon. Overall, bears have steady energy and are good at getting things done. They work well within society and help things flow, and they can maintain their productivity all day as long as they use a midafternoon energy slump to recharge and don't push past their natural energy limits.

LION

Lions are the classic "early birds." These are the go-getters who fly out of bed before the sun is up. They might not reach for a cup of coffee until a little before lunch, after their most productive hours have already passed. Because of their action-packed mornings, they tend to fizzle out in the evening and turn in early. They make up about 15 percent of the population.

WOLF

Wolves are on the nocturnal end of the spectrum. They are the "night owls" who get a later start to their day and ride the productivity wave while the rest of the world is winding down. Interestingly, wolves have two peak periods of productivity: from noon to two in the afternoon and then again later, just as most of the working world is clocking out. Wolves tend to be creators—writers, artists, and coders. The creative areas of the wolf's brain light up when the sun goes down. More often than not, wolf types tend toward introversion and crave their alone time. Sometimes they don't feel like being the life of the party. Instead, they want to sit back and observe what's going on around them.

Wolves also make up about 15 percent of the population, the 15 percent best suited to hiring early birds to hunt for worms and bring them home in time for a late breakfast. (Okay, I'm a wolf. I'm writing this at 3 a.m., and it makes me happy. But I'll sleep well tonight and get my six hours.)

DOLPHIN

Dolphins are the insomnia patients. They may or may not have a regular sleep routine, but they're type A and often don't get as much done as they want to during the day. Then they stay up tossing and turning as they ruminate over the day's perceived failures. They're also light sleepers who wake frequently throughout the night and struggle to fall back asleep. Dolphins' high intelligence and tendency toward perfectionism probably explain why they spend so much time chewing over their days. They do their best work from midmorning through early afternoon. Dr. Breus found that if his dolphin patients set up parameters around their sleep schedules, it helps them get back on track and start getting the sleep they need to be more productive.

You can take a quiz at www.thepowerofwhenquiz.com to find out your chronotype, but there are other ways to figure it out yourself. Another guest on *Bulletproof Radio*, Dr. Jonathan Wisor, is one of the world's foremost researchers on sleep and nervous system function. The Department of Defense and the National Institute of Neurological Disorders and Stroke funded his laboratory to apply molecular genetic and biochemical techniques to the study of sleep. Yet, somewhat ironically, he recommends an extremely low-tech method for determining your chronotype—simply taking a week off from work and going to sleep and waking up whenever you feel like it. Dr. Wisor believes that your circadian rhythm is such a strong biological drive that it will make itself obvious even within this short time frame.

I bought into the "early bird" myth for a long time. Before I became a biohacker I spent my whole life working against my natural circadian rhythm and pushing myself to be an early riser. For two years, I forced myself to wake up at five in the morning and meditate for an hour. I truly believed that that was what it would take to be successful. But guess what? It didn't make me more productive. It didn't make me any happier. And it didn't make me a better person. It just made me feel more tired and foggy and less creative.

It took years of tracking and hacking my sleep for me to realize that I'd been wasting a ton of energy trying to be a morning person. Instead of fighting my body by forcing it to sleep when it was naturally alert and wake up when it was naturally tired, I eventually learned to work with my natural rhythms, and guess what? I became more productive, happier, and more likely to outperform someone who was fighting his or her own rhythms to get that proverbial worm.

It was incredibly validating to talk to Dr. Wisor because it explained why I am stronger at night than I am in the morning. I am most definitely a wolf. I am at my most creative and productive late at night and perform better when I sleep until about 8:45 in the morning. In fact, I wrote most of this book (and my previous ones) between midnight and five in the morning, when everyone else was asleep, *and I loved it.*

I am hopeful that with these scientists at the forefront of the current research on sleep, our society will finally begin to shift away from the old-fashioned "early bird" mentality and start allowing people to follow their body's natural rhythms. I know that as a CEO I would much rather see my staff start working a couple of hours later and be more productive throughout the day than start early but without the energy to really bring their A-game. I believe that others would feel the same way if only they had this information, so I am grateful to Dr. Breus and Dr. Wisor for helping to get the word out about the importance of chronotypes.

Yet there is one variable that both doctors warn can disrupt your natural rhythms and make it difficult to stay true to your chronotype: light. Your chronotype is genetically based, but it is sensitive to light exposure. To learn more about this, I visited the lab of Dr. Satchin Panda at the Salk Institute for Biological Studies in San Diego. Before I interviewed him for the podcast, his grad students used an electron microscope to show special light sensor cells in the eye (called melanopsin sensors) that help set circadian rhythm. These light sensors pick up on light frequencies and send messages to the body to emit hormones based on the time of day. Interestingly, light triggers these reactions even in blind people.[4] Dr. Panda has identified a single gene that controls the central timing system in the body and found a pair of genes that help keep eating and sleep in sync. That research helps to explain why the intermittent fasting recommendations in the Bulletproof Diet actually work. His book *The Circadian Code: Lose Weight, Supercharge Your Energy, and Transform Your Health from Morning to Midnight* is a treasure trove of information about what to eat when.

According to Dr. Panda, when the sensors in your eyes are exposed to full-spectrum light (such as the sun as it comes up in the morning), they send signals that prime your body to wake up, and when it is dark they signal your body that it's time to sleep. This is one reason it is so important to make sure that your bedroom is *completely* dark at night. If the light sensors in your eyes pick up on even small amounts of artificial light at night, it can disrupt your sleep patterns by slowing down melanin production. In other words, your body won't get the signal that it's time to sleep. One signal your body expects before bed is red light, because that spectrum arises at sunset. When I'm home, I often use the Joovv light, a high-powered red and infrared LED light therapy device, before bed, which amplifies the "sunset signal" my body expects. The side effects of exposing oneself to those spectrums include better skin, faster healing, and deeper sleep.

It's even more important to make sure you avoid blue light—the frequency that your smartphone, laptop, and tablet emit—in the evening. The light sensors in your eyes are particularly sensitive to this light frequency, and exposure before bed can ruin your quality of sleep even if you use an LED light therapy device. A simple hack is to use black tape (or special dots designed to look better) to cover all the lights in your bedroom so it is completely dark. I also recommend wearing TrueDark glasses before bed; these use layered optical filters to block every known spectrum of light that interferes with sleep, far beyond "blue blocker" glasses. (Full disclosure: I believe so strongly in this science that I backed the creation of the company. I have experienced a doubling of my deep sleep when I use them, and I'm wearing them as I type this sentence.)

It's also crucial to make sure that you are exposed to adequate sunlight during the day. When you're exposed to daylight, your body produces serotonin, the "feel-good" neurotransmitter. Your body breaks serotonin down into melatonin, the hormone that helps you sleep. If you're not exposed to enough natural sunlight during the day, you won't develop enough melatonin to sleep well at night. This can mess with your circadian rhythm even if you follow the ideal schedule for your chronotype. Office windows, automobile glass, contact lenses, and sunglasses block vital spectrums of light that your body needs in order to regulate your internal clock, so it's vital to get outside for at least a few minutes at a time several times every day!

Action Items

- Figure out your chronotype by going to sleep and waking up when you feel like it for a week or by taking Dr. Breus's quiz at www.thepowerofwhenquiz.com.

- Consider red-light LED therapy such as Joovv before bed and in the morning—it works!
- Consider using TrueDark glasses or light therapy devices that go beyond red.
- Do everything you can to shift your daily schedule so you are stacking the deck in your favor and doing things when you are biologically primed to do them.
- Make sure you get adequate sunlight during the day, and block all artificial light at night to start experiencing dramatically better quality, more efficient sleep.
- Don't eat after dark!

Recommended Listening
- "Lions, Dolphins and Bears, Oh My!" with Dr. Michael Breus, *Bulletproof Radio*, episode 344
- Jonathan Wisor, "Hack Your Sleep," *Bulletproof Radio*, episode 31
- "Owning Your Testosterone" with John Romaniello, *Bulletproof Radio*, episode 340
- Satchin Panda, "Light, Dark, and Your Belly," Parts 1 and 2, *Bulletproof Radio*, episodes 466 and 477

Recommended Reading
- Michael Breus, *The Power of When: Discover Your Chronotype—and the Best Time to Eat Lunch, Ask for a Raise, Have Sex, Write a Novel, Take Your Meds, and More*
- Satchin Panda, *The Circadian Code: Lose Weight, Supercharge Your Energy, and Transform Your Health from Morning to Midnight*

Law 20: High-Quality Sleep Is Better than More Sleep

Laying your head on a pillow means nothing if you suck at sleeping. You are wasting your life if you need more sleep because you haven't treated your sleep performance the same way you treat your athletic or job performance. Change how and where you sleep and track your sleep until you're a world-class sleeper, or face the consequences at work tomorrow and in the hospital years from tomorrow.

It was fascinating to interview Dr. Phillip Westbrook, a leading sleep expert and clinical professor of medicine at UCLA, who first became interested in the science of sleep when he read a report about people who repeatedly stopped breathing in their sleep. Dr. Westbrook, who is a pulmonologist, wanted to understand how and why that could happen.

In what was a primitive experiment at the time, he found a patient who stopped breathing when he was asleep and performed a rudimentary sleep study: the patient lay on a gurney outside Dr. Westbrook's office at the Mayo Clinic while hooked up to all kinds of monitors until he fell asleep. Sure enough, as soon as sleep set in, he stopped breathing. It became one of the first documented cases of what was at the time a very rare condition: sleep apnea, a sleep disorder in which breathing repeatedly stops and starts throughout the night. That simple study changed the trajectory of Dr. Westbrook's career.

He began looking at what happens to the airway when we sleep and found that when the brain is asleep it does not signal the muscles that control the upper airway opening to keep it open so we can breathe. Those muscles relax during sleep, as all muscles do, and under certain circumstances the airway can collapse or nearly collapse and interfere with our ability to breathe. If we don't breathe, obviously we die, so the body wakes itself up whenever we momentarily stop breathing.

Even with a minor sleep disorder, you can have many unremembered awakenings each night. This interferes with the continuity and quality of sleep, often making you unable to perform during the day. It is also a significant risk factor for high blood pressure, cardiovascular disease, type 2 diabetes, and decreased cognitive capacities, including executive function (decision-making skills).[5]

Unremembered awakenings are a real thing. When I experimented with a near-zero-carb deep-ketosis diet as part of the research for *The Bulletproof Diet*, my sleep monitor notified me that I was waking up at least a dozen times a night without any knowledge or memory of it. I just knew I felt like crap when I woke up in the morning. My sleep monitor helped me discover the power of cyclical ketosis as opposed to never-ending ketosis. By adding in carbs a couple times a week, I fixed my sleep and ultimately improved the diet recommendations. I found it shocking that I didn't know I was waking up so often, even though I didn't have apnea. But it does illustrate how easy it would be to have sleep apnea without even knowing it. Dr. Westbrook estimates that about 10 percent of people who read this book have some degree of sleep apnea that is affecting their health and daily performance. Do you?

When the entrepreneur and serial inventor Dan Levendowski, who has spearheaded the development of several disruptive medical technologies, met Dr. Westbrook, he already knew he had a sleep problem. Dan had been a loud snorer from a very young age. By the time he was in his early forties, his snoring had evolved to full-blown sleep apnea. Around the year 2000, he and Dr. Westbrook began talking about what type of technology they could use to help raise public awareness of sleep apnea and enable patients to be diagnosed in their own homes. Together, they developed a device called the ARES (Apnea Risk Evaluation System) that can diagnose sleep apnea if patients wear it on their foreheads during sleep. (Sadly, Victoria's Secret would never approve of any of the sleep-monitoring gear I've tried, and this is no exception.)

When Dan used the ARES device, it showed that he stopped breathing a whopping seventy times an hour when he slept on his back, causing his blood oxygen levels to dip dangerously low. Yet he slept almost completely normally when he was on his side. The number of times he woke up each hour was shocking, but the importance of his sleep position was not. Sleep experts have long known about the importance of avoiding the "supine" sleep position—lying flat on your back.

In this position, gravity contributes to the collapse of the airway.

Almost everyone, whether they have a sleep disorder or not, is more susceptible to airway collapse and deeper oxygen desaturation when they sleep on their backs. People who don't have sleep apnea will simply snore more when they're on their backs, while those with sleep apnea are more likely to stop breathing in this position.

Doctors had known this for years, but they didn't have any real solutions. Sleep medicine physicians often recommended that patients sew tennis balls onto the backs of their pajama tops so they would be uncomfortable sleeping on their backs and naturally avoid the supine position. Patient compliance was understandably low, although today you can buy shirts on Amazon with tennis balls stitched in. Dr. Westbrook and Dan wanted to find effective alternatives that patients would be more willing to use.

They developed a product called Night Shift that patients wear around their necks. Night Shift senses when you are sleeping on your back and vibrates gently so that you change positions. The key is that it doesn't wake you up or disturb your sleep patterns. The gentle vibration gradually increases in intensity if you do not respond. Another advantage of Night Shift is that it records information during the night on how well you're sleeping, including how many times you shift onto your back and how quickly you respond to feedback from the device.

In my own quest for better sleep I also discovered the importance of proper jaw alignment in preventing the airway from collapsing. Over ten years ago, I got a custom splint made that positions my lower jaw forward and has really helped improve my sleep quality and eliminate snoring. It was created by Dr. Dwight Jennings, who has changed the lives of thousands of people—including me—by fixing their jaw alignment with oral appliances. In his interview, Dr. Jennings explained that the benefits of jaw alignment go way beyond just fixing apnea to include shocking improvements in neurological function, stress management, tinnitus, and even chronic diseases. My brain works better because he fixed my bite.

The National Institutes of Health gave Dan and Dr. Westbrook a grant to research how they could improve sleep apnea outcomes with oral appliance therapy. They developed a product that serves as a temporary oral appliance and allows patients to try it out and see if they get a good outcome before they spend the money on a custom appliance. They have made this product available for dentists and in hospitals for patients who are recovering from general anesthesia and have the greatest risk of complications from undiagnosed sleep apnea.

How do you know if you could have sleep apnea? One of the most common symptoms is snoring. Snoring is a sign that your airway is collapsing somewhat during sleep and your airflow is being limited when you try to inhale. If you snore really loudly, you have an increased risk for sleep apnea. If your spouse or other bed partner notices that you appear to stop breathing during sleep, that's an even bigger risk factor. But most important, if you are sleepy during the daytime, meaning that you're not just tired but actually fall asleep when you don't intend to, such as when you're watching TV or reading a boring book, you're at even greater risk. If you are experiencing these symptoms, I think you owe it to yourself to get it checked out so you can go back to sleeping well at night and kicking ass during the day.

Whether or not you snore, it's also worth considering investing in a bite guard, because nighttime teeth grinding causes chronic headaches and oral health issues in addition to poor sleep. I wouldn't dream (ha!) of sleeping without one. Whether it's an off-the-shelf bite guard or a custom-made one to precisely align your jaw and keep your airway open, it's an easy sleep hack.

Dr. Günther W. Amann-Jennson, the creator of the SAMINA mattress (most easily described as the Bentley of mattresses), believes he has found another solution to sleep apnea and other health problems in a surprising place: nature. All two hundred species of primates, including humans, experience musculoskeletal problems.[6] But of all the species, we suffer from more of these issues than forest dwellers and folks who sleep on the ground. It turns out that when you sleep on the ground instead of on a mattress, you intuitively find positions that can correct the musculoskeletal imbalances that cause lower back pain, knee pain, bunions, and more.

The forest floor is "nature's chiropractor." It keeps your chest immobile, aligns your vertebrae, and lubricates your joints. Does this mean that you have to ditch your bed and start sleeping on the ground? No, but it *does* mean that you should pay attention to how your body is positioned when you sleep. This affects not only the quality of your sleep at night but your mental state and productivity throughout the day, as well.

When I learned this, I started sleeping on the floor on a very hard one-inch-thick foam pad and found that after a few stiff weeks of adjusting, I slept fantastically well and woke up with zero aches and pains. I sleep on that pad at least four nights a week, which keeps my body working better. (The other nights I'm on a SAMINA mattress.) On long business trips, I will sleep on the floor in hotels that have overly soft mattresses for the simple reason that it helps me get higher-quality sleep in less time. The only hotel mattress I've ever found that was as hard as my mat was a traditional Japanese buckwheat mattress in Tokyo, Japan.

But there are other hacks for sleep besides an amazing mattress or a hard floor. Dr. Amann-Jennson noted that wild animals and domestic livestock all have a natural preference for sleeping on the ground with their heads slightly uphill. That led him to study the role that gravity plays in our sleep processes. When we are awake and standing upright, our heads are above our hearts and our blood flows against gravity from the heart up to the brain. But when we go to sleep, we lie horizontally; our hearts and heads are at the same level, which eliminates the effects of gravity on brain circulation and increases the pressure inside the skull, or intracranial pressure. Dr. Amann-Jennson believes that this pressure increases throughout the night, causing extra fluid to accumulate in the brain chambers, ventricles, and neurons. He says this causes cerebral edema, which is a swelling of the brain due to excess fluid. In addition to causing the brain to swell, sleeping horizontally creates sustained pressure on the eyes, ears, face, sinuses, and even gums. The entire head becomes overtaxed due to the increased pressure in our skull.

There is actually a field of medicine that has already done a tremendous amount of study regarding the effects of gravity on human physiology: space medicine. Indeed, astronauts are often at the forefront of biohacking. When they are in space, they experience excess fluids in the head and thus the brain, causing increased intracranial pressure with accompanying symptoms such as migraine headaches, glaucoma, Ménière's disease, and many others. This suggests that we need the benefits of gravity to get healthy sleep, and that, like animals in the wild, we should be sleeping with our heads above our hearts.

The medical anthropologist Dr. Sydney Ross Singer has studied the effects of inclined sleeping on patients who suffer from migraine headaches. He had a hundred migraine patients sleep with their heads elevated 10 to 30 degrees. The majority of them felt an improvement in their symptoms within just a few nights, and many experienced additional benefits: they reported feeling more rested and experiencing less sinus congestion.[7]

Dr. Amann-Jennson has observed that in addition to helping relieve migraines and congestion, inclined sleeping lowers blood pressure, reduces water retention and therefore varicose veins, and even has the potential to help prevent Alzheimer's disease. Some researchers believe that Alzheimer's disease is partially caused by brain congestion and excessive pressure in the head. The ventricles of Alzheimer's-afflicted brains are often expanded, suggesting that there is a correlation between chronic ventricular pressure and lesions along the ventricles in the brain tissue of Alzheimer's patients.

This is certainly an area deserving of further study and your consideration if you are suffering from headaches, chronic congestion, or sleep apnea. It's cheap and easy to put wooden blocks under the head of your bed! I have been sleeping on an incline for several years in addition to using my custom bite guard, a variety of sleep trackers, absolute darkness, and other sleep hacks. You owe it to yourself and the people you serve to find sleep upgrades that work for you. I have certainly seen a huge difference in the overall quality of my sleep, which hopefully means I'll live longer and perform better along the way. The best part is that most of these changes don't require ongoing effort—they're just simple onetime changes.

Action Items

- Start tracking your sleep to find out if you're waking up at night without realizing it.

- Adjust the incline of your bed so that your head is elevated 10 to 30 degrees.
- Get an awesome mattress (without flame retardants or formaldehyde).
- Try sleeping on a thin, hard foam pad for a month (I recommend 1-inch-thick high-quality neoprene in 80-by-48-inch sheets, which cost about $150).
- Experiment with a bite guard that helps position your jaw properly.
- Try Night Shift if you believe you are suffering from sleep apnea.
- At the very least, stop sleeping on your back!

Recommended Listening
- Phillip Westbrook and Dan Levendowski, "Sleep for Performance," *Bulletproof Radio*, episode 129
- Dwight Jennings, "A Live Look at Bite Realignment & How TMJ Impedes Performance," *Bulletproof Radio*, episode 182

Law 21: Go to Sleep Before Your Wake-up Call

The highest-performing people who are under the most pressure are the most likely to avoid sleeping, and they pay the highest cost. You can't kick ass when you're tired. Sleep isn't optional.

It was really fun to interview Arianna Huffington, the bestselling author, high-powered entrepreneur, and founder of *Huffington Post*, twice. The first time, she kindly hosted me in her studio at *Huffington Post*, and we hit it off right away. Arianna is a certified badass. In 2011, *Time* magazine named her one of its "100 Most Influential People in the World." Getting there took hard work, and Arianna ended up paying the price after sacrificing sleep to move her career forward.

In 2007, Arianna was working in her home office when she passed out. On the way down, she hit the corner of her head on her desk, broke her cheekbone, and cut her eye. She woke up in a pool of blood. After going from doctor to doctor to find out if there was an underlying medical problem that had caused her collapse, she learned that there wasn't; she had collapsed from exhaustion and lack of sleep.

That was a classic wake-up call that led Arianna to examine the type of life she was living and how she was defining success. She had founded *Huffington Post* two years earlier, and since then it had been growing at an incredible pace. Building her business required eighteen-hour workdays, seven days a week, and it was paying off. From the outside, Arianna looked extremely successful. She was on the covers of magazines, her company was booming, and she looked as though she were firing on all cylinders.

But after her fall, she started to ask herself if this was really what success looked like. She found that most people define success as wealth and power, but those are only the first two metrics, and relying on them to define a successful life is like trying to sit on a two-legged stool: you'll fall over every time. The third metric, according to Arianna, is well-being. And well-being includes taking the time to rest properly and renew yourself as well as connecting with your sense of purpose and inner wisdom.

Since then, Arianna has made many changes to the way she lives, particularly when it comes to her sleep habits. The results have surprised even her. Instead of slowing down her career, being rejuvenated led her to reach new levels of success. AOL acquired *Huffington Post* in 2011, and in 2016 she launched a new start-up called Thrive Global to provide content and training on health and wellness, then joined the board of directors of Uber to help it improve its culture. She found that the more she prioritized connecting with and caring for herself, the more productive and successful she became. Arianna believes that she is accomplishing more now because she gets between seven and nine hours of sleep each night and makes time to meditate, take walks, and do yoga each day.

It wasn't until she tapped into this third metric of well-being that she realized how far away she had been from it. She says that if you had asked her on the morning of her collapse how she was doing, she would have said she was doing great—and she would have meant it. She believed, as so many people do, that the sacrifices she was making for the sake of her business were necessary and worthwhile. Now she sees that that was a delusion. We don't have to sacrifice our well-being in the name of success. In fact, the more we prioritize our well-being, the more successful we will become.

Arianna compares the assumption that we have to work hard and burn out in order to succeed to other false beliefs people have held on to throughout history, such as believing that the earth was flat or that the sun revolved around the earth. Her goal with Thrive Global is to shatter this false belief, and it is working. In a recent partnership with J.P. Morgan, senior executives saw a positive impact on the bottom line when employees were challenged to focus on sleep, recharging, gratitude, and mindfulness.

So many of us have experienced a wake-up call like Arianna's. We push and push ourselves to the point of exhaustion as if we'll win some sort of award for trying the hardest. But that is the opposite of what it means to be Bulletproof. Before I figured this out, I once flew from San Francisco to China to give a keynote presentation. The next day, I hopped on a plane to Florida to give another keynote at some other tech conference that seemed important at the time. The morning after, I boarded a 5 a.m. flight out of Florida before having my Bulletproof Coffee or even drinking water (because I'd had to dump it at security) and literally passed out in the airplane aisle sometime after takeoff. I don't remember passing out, but I do remember being shaken awake from what felt like the most blissful sleep I'd ever experienced.

I was exhausted and probably dehydrated, and honestly, I should have known better. As I came to, the flight attendant on the intercom was frantically asking if there was a doctor on board and another flight attendant was trying to get me to drink a cup of orange juice. "No," I insisted in my half-awake state, "I'm in ketosis!" Luckily, I hadn't hit my head on the way down or experienced any other medical problems as a result of my fall. It served as a good reminder to always go to sleep before being forced to have a wake-up call.

Though our approaches are slightly different—I've hacked my sleep so that I can get better-quality sleep in less time, while Arianna focuses on the number of hours of sleep she gets each night—our experiences are remarkably similar. I know that I'm a better husband, father, and CEO when I am recharged and well rested. Neither Arianna nor I was able to get anything done when we were passed out! Arianna says that such stories are common, and she wants you to learn from our mistakes and focus on your well-being now so that you, too, can truly begin to thrive.

Today I work with my assistant to set up my calendar so that I get enough sleep, and every day has at least a half hour of "upgrade time" built into the calendar *during the workday*. If you don't schedule that time for yourself, someone or something else less important will fill that time, and you'll pay the price.

Action Items

- For one week, force yourself to go to sleep an hour earlier than normal and see how much better you feel the next day.
- Go through your calendar and cancel meetings and events that are not critical to your mission and at which your attendance isn't mandatory.
- Replace those appointments with personal time to recharge, recover, and refuel.

Recommended Listening

- "Arianna Huffington Is Thriving," *Bulletproof Radio*, episode 133
- Arianna Huffington, "Preventing Burnout & Recharging Your Batteries," *Bulletproof Radio*, episode 384

Recommended Reading

- Arianna Huffington, *Thrive: The Third Metric to Redefining Success and Creating a Life of Well-Being, Wisdom, and Wonder*

THROW A ROCK AT THE RABBIT, DON'T CHASE IT

When we think of being successful and performing at the highest levels, we tend to think about pushing ourselves beyond our limits. As we've seen, pushing past the point of exhaustion is a losing strategy. Getting adequate rest is a critical component of high achievement. So, too, are some of the other strategies we've talked about: carving out time in your schedule to meditate, do yoga, practice breathing techniques, or just go for a long walk.

Notice that in the list in chapter 7 I didn't include doing boot camp, spin classes, or marathon training. Not that there is anything wrong with those pursuits—exercise can be good for your health, it makes some people feel great, and it was the game changers' fourth most cited strategy for kicking more ass. The problem is that a lot of us are so focused on "exercise" that we forget about movement. There's no question that the human body was designed to move and that most of us don't move nearly enough. Sure, exercise is technically a form of movement, but it is a short, intense burst of movement. Sustained, functional movement is not the same thing as exercise.

So even though many of my guests identified exercise as one of the most important things they do, I'm going to slightly modify that piece of advice and focus on movement. In my experience, when people focus too much on the idea of exercise, they often waste a lot of time and effort. When I weighed 300 pounds, I resolved to exercise my way out of it. I worked out for ninety minutes a day six days a week for eighteen months. No matter how much it hurt or how tired I was, every day I did forty-five minutes of cardio and forty-five minutes of weight training. The demotivating (and demoralizing) result was that I ended up a very strong obese person. The truth is that the highest-performing people I've coached—including CEOs and hedge fund managers—are also the type to overexercise or train for Ironman triathlons while running companies. The result is predictable: reductions in libido, sex hormones, and sleep quality, and injuries and inflammation that often result in chronic pain that, ironically, leads to less overall movement. A few do pull it off, but it's unusual for it to be sustainable.

Once you free your muscles and joints to function as they're intended to, you'll look healthier and feel better. You'll be able to pick up your kids without cringing in pain. You'll be able to stand tall throughout the day without slumping into a hunched position by noon. And you'll finally be able to exercise effectively and do so for years without getting injured. Being able to move correctly is the foundation of any type of exercise or athletic pursuit. There is no type of exercise on Earth that does not require functional movement. So this chapter will focus on the importance of movement and what the experts say about how to exercise for the most game-changing results.

Law 22: Don't Run Until You Can Walk

High-risk sports—including running—don't make you a better person, but the injuries that come with them are a tax on everything you do as a human being. When you rewire your nervous system to move well, high-risk exercise becomes low risk. And all the energy you waste moving wrong becomes available for you to put to better uses. Exercising for the sake of exercising is not only a waste of time, it's also bad for you if you do it wrong.

Remember that scene in *The Matrix* where Neo looks at the world and sees ones and zeroes the way only a hacker can? There are experts who can take a look at the way you stand, the way you walk, and the way you move and know more about you than you'd ever expect. Kelly Starrett is one of those guys. He's a famous figure in the world of CrossFit and has taught some of the world's top athletes and executives to move well. He is also a coach and physical therapist and the author of an unusual but awesome fitness book, *Becoming a Supple Leopard: The Ultimate Guide to Resolving Pain, Preventing Injury, and Optimizing Athletic Performance.*

Kelly wants to change the way you think about running and moving. Running enthusiasts believe that running is a healthy, smart way to exercise, even perhaps something that makes us uniquely human. But is that true? Are humans really meant to run? In our interview, Kelly explained that he was always athletic, but while playing football in high school he developed knee pain that ended up plaguing him for years. He later discovered that his pain was stemming from his incorrect running form. His feet were weak, he didn't have the range of motion necessary to run properly, and his knees were paying the price.

This is not a unique problem. According to Kelly, 80 percent of people who run at least three times a week are injured over the course of a year. That number may be shocking, but it isn't because running is inherently dangerous. It's because most people don't have the motor control and range of motion they need to run safely. In order to perform any sort of exercise, whether it's yoga, Pilates, CrossFit, or running, you have to make sure that you are asking your body to complete only movements that it is capable of performing properly. This often requires going back to basics and learning the right form for simple movements that our current sedentary lifestyles prevent us from doing correctly. In other words, you need to master a *movement* practice before you can begin an *exercise* practice.

Where should a movement practice begin? In 1995, two physical therapists, Gray Cook and Lee Burton, started working together to gather statistical data to help prevent injuries. Their research on human movement patterns evolved into what is now called Functional Movement Systems, which assesses people's ability to move properly. It's hard to know where to start any project unless you establish a baseline. Though some problems are obvious, other limitations to your range of movement may be less so. Functional Movement Systems has created a standardized program that measures your mobility and provides techniques to address your limitations. Once you have the mechanics to be able to exercise correctly, you will be able to run or do any other form of exercise without risk of being injured.

According to Kelly, the good news is that the body is able to self-correct once it learns how to move correctly. The wiring for proper alignment is already there, and when you practice putting your body into a better position, it turns back on. Kelly and other therapists work with their patients to practice proper patterning, which he describes as pulling the wires through the conduit that has already been laid. You weren't born with stiff muscles and inflexibility; years of bad habits have caused these problems, but they are fixable.

The number one cause of the problems Kelly sees in his patients is sitting too much. This surprisingly goes for athletes as well as people with more sedentary lifestyles. This is another problem with the whole idea of "exercise": people tend to check it off their list in the morning or at night and then spend the rest of the day sitting in a chair. So essentially they are sedentary people who move for forty-five minutes a day but think they're superhealthy and virtuous. Kelly asked the members of a professional football team he was working with to track their daily movement patterns and found that they were sitting for fourteen to sixteen hours a day. Those were professional athletes! Sure enough, many of them were experiencing chronic knee pain and low back pain that were negatively impacting their performance. Kelly found that their problems weren't stemming from athletic injuries; they were caused by lack of movement.

Another leader in the world of movement is BJ Baker, the first strength and conditioning trainer for the Boston Red Sox, who has been involved in the training, preparation, nutritional counseling, and rehabilitation of professional athletes in virtually every sport. He agrees with Kelly's assessment and says that sitting for six or eight hours a day can undo the effects of a one- or two-hour workout.

BJ conducts functional movement assessments with his patients to quantify which movements they can and can't perform. When he evaluates kids as young as eight years old, he often sees that they can't perform a simple squat. The kids themselves are sometimes shocked to discover that they're unable to perform fairly basic movements that don't require a lot of strength. But it's not strength that's required to complete these movements; it's stability and mobility of the joints, which little kids who spend most of the day seated are lacking. However, by sitting lesss and practicing correct movement, these abilities can be regained.

Many of BJ's patients experience tremendous healing just from learning to move properly. For example, in his interview, BJ told me about a client named Bill who was on statins for high cholesterol and medication to lower his blood pressure. He was forty pounds overweight and had atrocious posture. In fact, he had lost a full two inches from his height because of rounding of his spine. BJ corrected his movements, addressed his posture, and made small changes to his diet. After eight months, Bill was able to stop taking both of his medications, he'd lost forty pounds, and he'd gained back an inch and a half in height. All it took was improving his posture and core strength and reestablishing muscle tissue length, and Bill was able to undo twenty years' worth of bad habits!

I grew up thinking it was normal to be in pain when I moved. It didn't stop me from playing competitive soccer for thirteen years, in agony the whole time. Much of the pain—and the constant injuries—went away when I learned to make small tweaks to the way I moved after practicing yoga with experienced teachers several times a week for five years. Yoga is awesome for flexibility and learning how to activate certain muscles in the body, but it's not the best way to learn how to walk, sit, or move most effectively. Even after all that work, learning proper functional movement by working with experts who assessed the way I moved and made small tweaks to the ways I sat, moved, and walked gave me another level of freedom in how I moved with results that reflected themselves in the way I showed up in the rest of my life.

The same results are possible for you when you learn to move your body the right way. Whether or not you choose to run, swim, lift, put your feet behind your head, or dance, doing it with the right form will improve your ability to change your game. But choosing a form of exercise that will provide the most benefits in less time matters, too, which leads us to the next law . . .

Action Items

- Work with a functional movement coach to undo incorrect movement patterns. Functional Movement Systems (www .functionalmovement.com) is a good place to start.
- Get an adjustable standing desk so you can both sit and stand every day (I use www.standdesk.co).
- Try the Egoscue method of exercise (www.egoscue.com) to improve your posture, minimize pain, and enhance your performance.

Recommended Listening

- Kelly Starrett, "Bulletproof Your Mobility & Performance," *Bulletproof Radio*, episode 43
- Kelly Starrett, "Systems Thinking, Movement, and Running," *Bulletproof Radio*, episode 156
- BJ Baker, "Primal Movements," *Bulletproof Radio*, episode 93
- Doug McGuff, "Body by Science," *Bulletproof Radio*, episode 364
- "Mastering Posture, Pain & Performance in 4 Minutes a Day with Egoscue," *Bulletproof Radio*, episode 429
- John Amaral, "Listen to the Force: Upgrade Your Life," *Bulletproof Radio*, episode 462

Recommended Reading

- Kelly Starrett with Glen Cordoza, *Becoming a Supple Leopard: The Ultimate Guide to Resolving Pain, Preventing Injury, and Optimizing Athletic Performance*
- Doug McGiff and John Little, *Body by Science: A Research-Based Program for Strength Training, Body Building, and Complete Fitness in 12 Minutes a Week*

Law 23: Strong Muscles Make You Smarter and Younger

It's tempting to believe that running a marathon will make you a better human being, and it might the first time you do it because it will increase your willpower. The bigger truth is that too much cardio stresses the body and takes too long to achieve results. High performers exercise efficiently, which means stimulating the right hormones using the right protocols at the right times.

Charles Poliquin was one of the first biohackers out there, long before I wrote the definition of the term. He's a world-renowned strength and conditioning educator and coach who has helped many of the world's most elite athletes kick ass to achieve hundreds of medals, wins, and personal bests in seventeen different sports. For decades, Charles has been investigating how the signals you send to your muscles create changes in your body, and he really doesn't care whether you or I or anyone else likes what he's learned. He's a visionary who tends to know things years before everyone else catches on, and that's exactly why so many pros work with him. It's also why I like to hang out with him and invited him to be on the show.

Charles has come to the conclusion that strength training is better for your brain health and overall performance than long-distance aerobic exercise, which he claims ages the brain. That view has really pissed off some people (namely endurance athletes), but it has been verified by some of the latest medical research. If you're one of those pissed-off people who love endurance exercise, stay with me. I'm not saying you should quit your favorite exercise altogether, but I would suggest you make sure you're working on your muscle strength, too. (That's true whether you're a woman or a man.)

In 2013, scientists looked at what types of exercise were most beneficial for patients who were suffering from Parkinson's disease.[1] In a clinical trial, they tested three forms of exercise: low-intensity treadmill exercise (walking), high-intensity treadmill exercise (running), and a combination of stretching and resistance (weight) training. I was already familiar with the study when I spoke to Charles, but I did not know that he had actually consulted on the protocols used by the scientists. He told them before the study started that the aerobic work would worsen the patients' condition, and it turned out that he was right. Charles calls this a "no-shit-Sherlock" study. As he expected, the patients who did a combination of stretching and weight training had the best results, while some patients also benefited from low-resistance walking on a treadmill.

Do those results translate to those of us who do not have Parkinson's disease? Charles believes that the answer is yes. Though he says there are some legitimate benefits of aerobic exercise, especially for people with high blood pressure or who are obese or sedentary or have significant visceral belly fat (fat stored around major organs), long-term aerobic training has substantial negative effects that many people fail to realize.

First of all, aerobic training raises the cortisol (stress hormone) level, which causes inflammation and accelerates aging. A high cortisol level elevates the amount of oxidative substances in the body. These oxidative substances increase inflammation in the brain, heart, gastrointestinal tract, and other organs. To be clear, resistance training elevates the cortisol level, too, but this elevation is offset by a release of other beneficial hormones that does not occur after aerobic exercise.

A 2010 study tested cortisol levels in more than three hundred endurance athletes (long-distance runners, triathletes, and cyclists) and compared their measurements with a control group of nonathletes. The results showed that the aerobic athletes had significantly higher cortisol levels than the control group, and there was a positive correlation between higher cortisol levels and greater training volume. The researchers concluded, "These data suggest that repeated physical stress of intensive training and competitive races among endurance athletes is associated with elevated cortisol exposure over prolonged periods of time."[2]

Another study in 2011 looked at the effects of cycling on healthy, active young men, and found that it significantly increased cortisol levels and inflammatory markers.[3] This is a big deal, since chronic inflammation is at the root of many life-threatening diseases including cardiovascular disease, cancer, diabetes, and Alzheimer's disease.[4] It also has a more immediately noticeable link to decreased mental clarity and energy.

In addition, your body produces harmful free radicals in response to the oxygen-rich environment generated by increased respiration during aerobic training. These free radicals create oxidative stress, meaning that they overwhelm the number of antioxidants in your body that can counteract their damage. Oxidative stress is a major contributor to the aging process, and it is well established that excessive aerobic exercise can cause oxidative stress.[5]

Charles and I recommend supplementing with antioxidants and/ or probiotics to counter these aging effects of aerobic exercise, but he believes that it's even more effective to simply add resistance training to your routine. Strength training triggers the release of anabolic hormones that help counter oxidative stress and build muscle, bone, and connective tissue, which also lets you do more cardio without the damage. We know, for example, that to prevent osteopenia, which is loss of bone, strength training is very valuable, while aerobic sports decrease bone mineral density, which can lead to osteopenia.[6]

Charles told me about a group of studies conducted at Tufts University back in the 1980s that looked at factors that could predict aging. The studies revealed that the most important parameter was muscle mass, and number two was strength. Those markers outranked cholesterol level, high blood pressure, resting heart rate, maximum heart rate, and all other factors as predictors of healthy aging. The reality is that starting at age thirty, we begin to lose as much as 3 to 5 percent of our muscle mass per decade.[7] This degenerative loss of muscle mass is called *sarcopenia*. But although the loss is pretty much inevitable, it is also wholly reversible. By stimulating the muscles and nervous system together through a combination of movement and weight training, you can rebuild lost muscle and experience less inflammation, reduced oxidative stress, greater strength, and better bone health, all while slowing down the aging process. Sounds like a pretty good deal to me!

Mark Sisson, a health and fitness expert and the author of the best-selling book *The Primal Blueprint: Reprogram Your Genes for Effortless Weight Loss, Vibrant Health, and Boundless Energy,* coined the term "chronic cardio" over a decade ago to describe the way so many endurance athletes were training: at about 75 to 80 percent of their maximum heart rates for long periods of time. Mark himself used to train the same way. A former long-distance runner, triathlete, and Ironman competitor, Mark used to take in a lot of carbohydrates to support his endurance sports. The combination of that lifestyle of inflammatory food and overtraining had left him with osteoarthritis, irritable bowel syndrome, and a career that had basically evaporated.

Mark became a coach and saw the same problems manifest themselves in the athletes he was coaching—they were training too hard and too long and not getting the results they wanted. He started researching how to improve endurance without overtraining and found a formula that worked: moving around a lot at a low level of activity, lifting heavy things only once in a while, and sprinting once a week. The key to endurance training, he says, is low-level training combined with occasional all-out, really hard training. That was how our ancestors moved. They didn't run for an hour or more at a time. Instead, they consistently worked at low levels of exertion, which burned stored body fat, and then exerted themselves fully once in a while, when they were in danger or chasing animals for food.

It's not easy for most of us to replicate this pattern today, so Mark suggests doing anywhere from thirty minutes to an hour of low- to moderate-level aerobic movement, such as walking briskly, hiking, cycling, etc. It doesn't need to be every day, but doing it at least a few times a week is important. The goal during these sessions is to maintain the heart rate that burns mostly fat. For very fit people, this could be as high as 70 to 80 percent of your maximum heart rate, but it is more like 60 to 70 percent for most people. This is the ideal level of activity for decreasing body fat, increasing the capillary network, and lowering blood pressure and reducing the risk of developing degenerative diseases, including heart disease. Many of the benefits start at much lower levels of intensity—as little as a twenty-minute brisk walk daily.

Mark also recommends adding a few anaerobic interval workouts once or twice a week to this routine. He says that weight-bearing, anaerobic bursts are the best type of training for building muscle, and lean muscle mass is essential to lowering inflammation and gaining overall health. This type of training also increases your aerobic capacity, boosts the production of natural growth hormones, and increases insulin sensitivity.

Though they have very different backgrounds, it's interesting to note that Charles and Mark recommend remarkably similar protocols for almost identical reasons. So does someone you might be surprised to learn is an expert in this area, the seventy-eight-year-old, world-renowned Dr. Bill Sears, who has written more than thirty books on neurological development and parenting.

Dr. Sears was in Singapore for a lecture when he visited a beautiful greenhouse where the trees and the plants were dying off at alarming rates despite receiving the best possible care. Finally, the caretakers noticed that the trees were not moving and put fans in the greenhouse. When the trees were able to move a bit, they began to flourish. Dr. Sears uses that observation as a metaphor for understanding human health at its most basic level: like plants, humans need more than just food, water, and sunlight to thrive. We also need an environment that stimulates movement.

All forms of conscious movement lead to a cascade of effects that stimulate neurogenesis (the birth of new neurons), neuroprotection, neuroregeneration, cell survival, synaptic plasticity, and the formation and retention of new memories. Moving also makes you happier, most likely because it stimulates the release of endorphins. The Gallup-Sharecare Well-Being Index shows that people who exercise at least two days per week experience more happiness and less stress than those who do not.

Though they are a generation apart and come from dramatically different backgrounds, Kelly Starrett and Dr. Sears are in full agreement. As Kelly puts it, cognition is bootstrapped onto the nervous system. If you want to upregulate cognition, you have to upregulate movement. The only thing that's debatable is how often you have to do so.

Action Items

- Take a lesson from the leaves: if you are still too much, sit too much, and don't move, you will wither and die; but if you move naturally and freely, you will flourish.
- Lift heavy things once a week.
- Stretch twice a week.
- Sprint once a week.
- Walk or do slow cardio for twenty to sixty minutes three to six times a week.

Recommended Listening

- Charles Poliquin, "Aerobic Exercise May Be Destroying Your Body, Weightlifting Can Save It," *Bulletproof Radio*, episode 378
- Mark Sisson, "Get Primal on Your Cardio," *Bulletproof Radio*, episode 314
- Bill Sears, "How to Avoid & Fix the Damaging Effects of Diet-Induced Inflammation," *Bulletproof Radio*, episode 397

Recommended Reading:

- Mark Sisson, *The Primal Blueprint: Reprogram Your Genes for Effortless Weight Loss, Vibrant Health, and Boundless Energy*

Law 24: Flexible People Kick More Ass

Though stretching doesn't always lead to visible results, it can change the way you move and perform. A key ingredient of high performance is resilience, and aligning the mind and body through stretching, yoga, or another type of movement is a powerful way of developing that.

When you picture elite performers, it's hard not to think of Navy SEALs. That's why I invited Mark Divine, a retired Navy SEAL, onto *Bulletproof Radio* to share how he became one of the best in the world at what he does. Today, instead of leading teams of elite warriors, he teaches teams of executives how to maintain the intensity, focus, toughness, and calm that were the hallmarks of his distinguished military career. Mark is so calm and good-natured, in fact, that he laughed instead of laying me out on the floor when I mentioned that he had a name better suited for a career as a stripper.

Mark explained that one of the things that most helped him change his game was practicing Ashtanga yoga, in part because it reminded him of his martial arts training. He memorized each series of movements and went through them progressively, graduating from one series to the next as he had when he'd earned each of his belts doing martial arts. It felt achievement-oriented and militant, which is an accurate description of that school of yoga. (There are gentler forms of yoga that work, too.)

But because Mark was doing the same set of sequences over and over, he began to develop overuse injuries similar to what people experience when they perform the same military calisthenics or CrossFit moves every day. The repetition causes dysfunctional movement patterns that can result in an injury. Mark loved the benefits he was gaining from his yoga practice—including mental clarity and flexibility—but he was getting injured and burnt out.

At the time, Mark was a reserve officer, and then, in 2004, it was his turn to go to Iraq. Not long before, a friend of his, Stephen "Scott" Helvenston, had been one of four Blackwater military contractors who were in a convoy ambushed by insurgents in Fallujah. Scott and the others were killed cruelly. The graphic imagery of the killings rattled Mark, and he knew that he would soon be stepping into the same area where his friend had met a violent end. Then, just days before his deployment, a terrorist group posted a video of the decapitation of Nick Berg, an American radio tower repairman from Pennsylvania.

As Mark traveled to Baghdad, he had never been more nervous in his life. Keenly aware that anything could happen, he felt on high alert. Unable to sit still, he went to the back of the plane and began doing yoga, which calmed his mind and helped him regain control of his emotions. He felt much better as the plane turned its nose toward the Iraqi desert. By the time it landed in Baghdad, he wasn't in a perfect Zen state by any means—it was in a combat zone, after all—but he was far more calm, present, and centered and ready for what would come next.

That turned out to be a very good thing. Mark hadn't been on the ground for more than fifteen minutes when he heard someone shout, "Incoming!" followed by the unmistakable whistle of a mortar flying toward him. It exploded about a quarter of a mile away. Okay, he said to himself. Welcome to combat.

Later, a couple of SEAL team guys drove up to retrieve Mark and took him to the SEAL compound at one of Saddam Hussein's former palace grounds. There, it was hard to find a place to exercise. Yet, he says, SEALs will always improvise to find a way to train, even when operating on combat missions that go late into the night. The nearest gym was located at Camp Victory, and getting there required a combat drive in an armored Humvee. It was not worth the risk or the time. So Mark began running around the compound in a three-mile loop and doing body-weight training. Soon he felt the itch to do yoga, but he was not aware of any yoga classes being held in Baghdad or Iraq. So he decided to follow his intuition and just go it alone, based upon what he had learned from hot yoga, power yoga, and Ashtanga yoga.

Finding a small patch of ground next to a lake in the compound, he set up shop. It wasn't as picturesque as it might sound—for starters, the house was pitted with pockmarks from a firefight—but there were some trees to provide shade from the desert heat, and the spot was removed enough that he wouldn't get awkward stares from the other warriors on base. Mark skipped breakfast every morning and found a refuge in his new training spot, where he started playing around with different combinations of yoga poses, functional interval workouts, self-defense moves, and breathing and visualization exercises. He found that when he was finished with the practice, he felt amazingly clear and calm.

By that time, he had enough knowledge of movement and breathing practices to be able to combine them sensibly. If he needed to recover, he chose the poses, breathing techniques, and visualizations that he knew would help him recover and ward off combat stress. If he wanted a workout, he would choose more aggressive poses to warm up and then complete a body-weight routine before doing some seated poses and concentration training. That practice became Mark's center post in the storm of combat. At the height of the Iraq War, he was able to start each day feeling calm, present, energized, in control of his emotions, and ready for the mission at hand. We could all use a dose of that.

Over time, Mark worked to evolve his routine into a practice that was customizable for anyone who wished to take it on, and he began using it to train other Navy SEALs. What he found along the way is that yoga is the perfect complement to a solid functional fitness program, not a replacement. Paired with some form of weight training, yoga provides a well-rounded workout that balances hormones, increases strength and flexibility, and is phenomenal for stimulating the release of growth hormones, which are essential to cell reproduction and regeneration.

Mark's practice integrates a breathing exercise, mental training (concentration, visualization, or meditation), and functional movement. Those movements can consist of traditional yoga poses, Cross-Fit, swinging a kettlebell, or anything else that forces you to become aware of your body in space and time and that connects your breathing with movement. Through a consistent practice, Mark found that he was cultivating his inner domain, curating his thoughts and emotions, and really connecting with a warrior spirit. He named his practice Kokoro yoga, after the Japanese concept of the warrior spirit.

Working inward like this has helped Mark recover better from his workouts and allowed him to progressively build his fitness skills without degrading his performance through plateaus, burnouts, or injuries. He considers the primary physical benefit of this practice to be spinal health. It keeps the space open between the vertebrae, allowing blood and energy to flow. If your spine is healthy, he says, your nervous system will be healthier, and that will radiate out to the rest of your body.

Another benefit of Kokoro yoga is detoxification. Twisting poses detoxify your internal organs, and the mental training detoxifies your mind and emotions, allowing for greater focus and concentration. A third physical benefit is flexibility in both joint articulation and muscular flexibility. This does not mean that you have to be able to put your feet behind your head or twist yourself into a pretzel in order to do Kokoro yoga—quite the contrary. Mark calls these types of show-off moves "stupid human tricks" that are ultimately irrelevant.

That said, after a few years of learning proper movement through my own yoga practice, I'm pleased to be a forty-five-year-old, six-foot-four, almost muscular guy who can perform the stupid human trick of putting my foot behind my head—something I couldn't do when I was sixteen. (Yes, sometimes people stare when I do it in an airport before boarding a long flight . . .)

So do you need to learn yoga to change your game? Not really. But it's one of the most effective ways to gain physical strength and flexibility at the same time as mental calm and clarity. You can make some progress with online training, but nothing replaces the subtle movement tweaks a great teacher can make in person.

Action Items

Try a few types of yoga (tight pants optional) to see what works and what teachers resonate with you. Ashtanga, Vinyasa, or "flow," yoga, and Iyengar are common forms to try.

Recommended Listening

- Mark Divine, "Becoming a Bulletproof Warrior," *Bulletproof Radio*, episode 38
- Mark Divine, "Downward Dog like a Real Life Warrior One," *Bulletproof Radio*, episode 319

Recommended Reading

- Mark Divine with Catherine Divine, *Kokoro Yoga: Maximize Your Human Potential and Develop the Spirit of a Warrior*

YOU GET OUT WHAT YOU PUT IN

By now you might be wondering what the number one piece of advice from the game changers would be. And you're probably hoping that whatever it is, it doesn't require any more brain training or developing secret ninja powers. Well, I have good news for you. The most critical aspect of performance for more than 75 percent of the high performers I interviewed is something you encounter every day, hopefully with pleasure:

Food.

That's right—three-quarters of game changers said that what they ate (or didn't eat) was the most important thing that helped them kick more ass. More than meditation. More than exercise. More than literally anything else. Of course, you could say that this might have something to do with the fact that I've interviewed some of the top experts in medicine and nutrition in the world. That's in part because my path to becoming better as a human being has led me to realize that what I eat impacts everything I do, which of course naturally draws me to interview people who know and care a lot about food. This includes experts who are leading the way toward a major shift in how we think about food.

But none of this accounts for the strength of the data. So many of my guests who have nothing to do with the wellness space have told me that the energy, focus, and brainpower they relied upon to become leaders in their fields was a direct result of intentionally fueling their bodies and brains with high-quality food.

Of course, there is plenty of debate about what exactly qualifies as high-quality fuel for humans. If you want to know what I think and why, take a look at *The Bulletproof Diet*. The point of this chapter is not to tell you what to eat but to focus on why it matters so much to people who lead their fields and why it belongs near the top of your list, too. I promise, none of these laws will tell you to put butter in your coffee!

Law 25: Make Sure You're Really Hungry for Food

People eat when they feel a lack. Sometimes it's a lack of food. Sometimes it's a lack of energy. Sometimes it's a lack of sleep. But too often, it's a lack of love, connection, or even a feeling of safety. Do whatever it takes to find out when your hunger is for food and when it is for something deeper, and work relentlessly until you are free of whatever makes you feel empty.

Cynthia Pasquella-Garcia is a celebrity nutritionist, spiritual leader, model, media personality, and bestselling author. Oh, and before that, she was a computer engineer. She is now the founder and director of the Institute of Transformational Nutrition, a nutrition certification program that combines nutritional science, psychology, and spirituality. She also hosts *What You're REALLY Hungry For*, a web series that goes beyond food to examine the things that keep people from having the body, health, and life they want.

Several years ago, Cynthia was working in the entertainment industry as a model and television host and living the typical Hollywood lifestyle. She worked long hours, neglected her sleep, went to too many parties, and drank more alcohol than she should have. It all caught up with her, and she ended up twenty-five pounds overweight with cystic acne, hair that was breaking and falling out, and cellulite in places where she hadn't known she could get cellulite. But it wasn't just her physical body that was suffering. Cynthia has openly discussed her struggle with depression for pretty much her whole life, and her lifestyle had triggered another episode. She was also diagnosed with chronic fatigue syndrome. It didn't matter how much sleep she got; she was exhausted from the time she woke up to the time she went to bed. Then she started struggling with short-term memory loss.

Cynthia knew she needed help. She went to doctors, nutritionists, and trainers. She tried all kinds of spiritual ceremonies and energy healing, popped pills, drank shakes, and nothing changed. She woke up one morning in her tiny studio apartment in Los Angeles and found a lump in one of her breasts. Then she found a lump in the other one. She sank to the floor—feeling numb and as though she was ready to check out—as she asked herself how that could be happening.

It wasn't the first time she had faced major obstacles. While she was growing up, her family had struggled to get by, and there had been very little money for food and basic necessities. She had experienced domestic abuse and been sexually abused as a young girl, something that leaves deep unconscious emotional blocks that often persist into adulthood. The morning she found the lumps, she said, she was sick of fighting. She felt as though she'd been fighting her whole life and couldn't do it anymore. She was angry that so many terrible things had happened to her and kept happening. I admired her openness and courage during our interview.

Then, she said, she got quiet and heard an inner voice telling her to find gratitude and that, *These things happened for you, not to you.* She realized that she had taken on the identity of "victim" and that there were plenty of people who had gone through similar struggles and had once felt hopeless and defeated and worthless just as she did. And she realized it was her mission to help those people.

But first she would have to help herself. Cynthia started researching her symptoms and dug into every facet of nutrition. She attended schools and training programs where she learned about holistic health and psychology. She also learned about meditation and herbs, became aware of food intolerances and weight loss resistance, and discovered how to detox and cleanse her body the right way. She tested spiritual practices and experienced how they really brought everything else together, and she started implementing what she was learning into her lifestyle. She saw slow results at first, but she kept at it, and over time her symptoms went away completely. Her body and heart were healing, and she wanted to share what she had learned.

Cynthia started working with people who were going through similar struggles using a combination of science, psychology, and spiritual practices. And she saw those people transform. They didn't just lose weight, clear up their skin, and gain lots of energy, they also got out of relationships that weren't serving them, quit jobs that weren't letting them live their passions, and remembered who they were and that they were meant for greatness. Food was just a part of it.

She realized that for so many people who struggled with their weight, the problem wasn't the food at all. It was about a bigger hunger that they couldn't fill without combining dietary changes with psychological and spiritual work. She called her method Transformational Nutrition because it is about a whole-life transformation rather than a simple dietary shift, and she founded the Institute of Transformational Nutrition to teach coaches how to devise a personal protocol based on each person's individual needs.

I love the idea of this type of personalized nutrition because it helps you see when the problem is food and when it's not (and why you sometimes find a half-eaten cookie in your hand without knowing how it got there). It's been clear to me for a long time that the same things don't work equally well for everyone. That's why I included an entire category of "suspect foods" in the *Bulletproof Diet*. These are foods that work well for some people but not for others. Cynthia takes this one step further by creating a completely personalized protocol that works with your psychological and spiritual needs as well. This, she says, is the magic that helps the people she works with transform.

Cynthia's story may sound extreme, but the truth is that most of us eat for emotional reasons at least some of the time—out of joy, anger, boredom, sadness, you name it. Emotional eating is so ingrained in our culture that it's hard for many people to identify when they're doing it. But Cynthia suggests that it's easy to know when you're eating for emotional reasons—it's simply when you're eating for any reason besides being physically hungry. That doesn't mean that you should *never* celebrate with a favorite meal. Eating for emotional reasons is a problem only when you start doing it to excess. To spot this habit quickly, Cynthia offers the following telltale signs:

- If you go back for seconds even though you aren't hungry

- If you receive exciting news and your first thought is to eat something to celebrate

- If you are feeling bored and eating sounds like the perfect solution to that feeling

- If eating makes you feel safe

- If a friend or loved one makes you upset and you decide that eating a comfort food is the best way to feel better fast

- If you are feeling stressed and overwhelmed and seek solace in food

- If you are feeling disappointed that you slipped up on your diet and decide to indulge in your favorite foods to feel better

- If you finish eating and can't remember how your food tasted

The following behaviors are also on Cynthia's list, but in my experience they can either be signs of emotional eating *or* come from eating the wrong foods for your biology, toxins in food or your environment, or chemical additives such as MSG. If these are your only symptoms, the problem is probably biological and not emotional. If they are paired with the above, look at both causes.

- If your "hunger" hits suddenly and involves intense cravings

- If you still feel hungry after eating

- If you are hungry only for a specific food

Based on these lists, if you determine that you are not overeating but rather eating the wrong foods, the next law is for you.

Action Items
- Pay attention to what you eat and drink when you're uncomfortable.

- Try logging what you eat using an app that doesn't track calories (calorie tracking in apps is largely fictional). Rise Up + Recover is a good app if you already know you are an emotional eater because it lets you track emotions when you eat. YouAte is an app that lets you take photos of food so you can look back and see if you're actually eating what you tell yourself you are.
- Consider following Cynthia Pasquella-Garcia's program or another personal development program that appeals to you.
- Think about seeing a therapist if you don't know what you're hungry for.

Recommended Listening

- Cynthia Pasquella-Garcia, "Transformational Nutrition: Why Food Isn't the Only Source of Nourishment," *Bulletproof Radio*, episode 433
- "Dinner and a Side of Spirituality" with Cynthia Pasquella-Garcia, *Bulletproof Radio*, episode 328
- Marc David, "The Psychology of Eating," *Bulletproof Radio*, episode 114

Law 26: Don't Eat like a Caveman, Eat like Your Grandma

Ancient wisdom told your ancestors what to eat and how and when to eat it. The Big Food industry replaced that innate knowledge with cheap fast food. Go back to your roots, and pay careful attention to what "your people" ate generations ago. Your genetic background may in part determine the best food for you, and there are food habits that were nearly universal one hundred–plus years ago. Use them.

Dr. Barry Sears is a leading authority on nutrition as it relates to hormonal response, genetic expression, and inflammation. You've probably heard of The Zone Diet, his hugely popular series of books that first brought attention to the field of anti-inflammatory medicine back in 1995. Dr. Sears is incredibly accomplished; he has published forty scientific articles and holds fourteen US patents in the areas of intravenous drug delivery systems for cancer treatment and hormonal regulation for the treatment of cardiovascular disease. He's also the founder and president of the nonprofit Inflammation Research Foundation, where he continues his work in the development of new dietary approaches for the treatment of diabetes and cardiovascular and neurological diseases.

According to Dr. Sears, your grandmother was at the cutting edge of twenty-first-century biotechnology. Through her ancestors she had accumulated a millennium's worth of observations about what worked and what didn't. But after World War II, we started to disregard the wisdom of those observations. Food morphed into a big business. Gone were the "direct from the source," small-batch days of buying from your local grocer or farmer; after the war, companies mechanized and industrialized the production of food and promised consumers that the "food" they made was not only good for us but also incredibly tasty and cheap. And in the decades since then, we've largely pursued those goals without considering the possible downside. Today that downside includes not only record levels of obesity and disease but also alterations to the structure of our genes. These genetic changes are passed from generation to generation; what you eat now will impact your kids' genes years from now. So eat like your grandmother—or maybe even her mother. It's not just your health that's on the line; the next generation is counting on you.

In my quest to learn from the brightest minds in nutrition, I sought out Dr. Cate Shanahan, a powerful researcher and influential voice in the world of nutrition who has worked extensively with the LA Lakers (Kobe Bryant says that he trusts her implicitly!). Dr. Shanahan is also a board-certified family physician trained in biochemistry and genetics at Cornell. Her research led her to agree with Dr. Sears on this point and to author *Deep Nutrition: Why Your Genes Need Traditional Food*, a book that is worth your time to read.

In our interview, Dr. Shanahan explained that when we get sick, it's because our genes have expectations that have gone unmet one too many times. To understand our health from a genetic perspective, we have to go back to not just what we ate yesterday or even last week but to our food and lifestyle choices for the past years and decades if we're old enough, as well as the choices our parents and grandparents made.

Dr. Shanahan has worked with star athletes who have perfect bodies and experience what they think is peak performance, yet they eat dozens of candy bars a day. She says that such habits do come with a cost, even if it's not immediately obvious. People like these athletes have genes that were well nourished generation after generation and serve as a fortress of health to protect them from their own poor eating habits. On the other hand, if your ancestors were malnourished or suffered from famines, those experiences have damaged your genes a little, making you more susceptible to health problems. In other words, maybe all of your problems really *are* your parents' fault.

Dr. Shanahan says that if you follow the "Domino's and Doritos diet," it's going to catch up with you eventually—or more precisely, it's going to catch up with your grandchildren. My first book, *The Better Baby Book*, dug into this problem, too, and I like to think that my kids (and grandkids) will benefit as a result. Yours can, too.

No conversation about nutrition is complete without input from Dr. Mark Hyman, an eleven-time *New York Times* bestselling author and the director of functional medicine at the famous Cleveland Clinic. He wisely says that food is not just calories; it's information. It actually contains messages that communicate to every cell in your body and your genes and affect gene expression in real time. This is why it's so important to focus on the quality of the food you eat. In other words, it's time to get back to the wisdom of our grandmothers. You don't have to eat like a caveman, but you do have to eat real food.

Pulling from my conversations with Dr. Sears, Dr. Shanahan, and Dr. Hyman, it's clear that Grandma said four things that were particularly cutting edge:

1. Grandma said to eat small meals infrequently throughout the day. She did so because food used to be very expensive.

Dr. Sears says that the best way to test whether your diet is working for you is to pay attention to how soon you are hungry again after eating a meal. If you are not hungry again for *five hours* after eating, that is a sign that your metabolism is working properly and that your last meal was hormonally correct for your biochemistry and your genetics. Of course, Grandma wasn't able to eat more than once every five hours because she was busy working and didn't have access to today's convenience foods. Plus, she ate wholesome, satisfying meals that did not leave her blood sugar crashing an hour or two later.

It's healthy to go for extended periods of time without eating, as humans have done for eons. This teaches your body to dip into its fat storage, which helps you burn fat and produce ketones, water-soluble molecules your liver creates from fatty acids to use as fuel. Then you do truly appreciate food when you get it because you don't have all these weird chemicals and artificial cravings driving your hunger.

It was only after becoming Bulletproof that I felt what it was like not to be starving all the time. For the first time in my life, I could spend six hours kicking ass before thinking, "I could eat," instead of, "I need to eat right now or else I'm going to die!!" According to Dr. Sears, that was a sign that my metabolism was healed and I was eating the right foods for my genes and my body. I learned what I was capable of when I got hunger out of the way.

2. Grandma said to eat adequate protein, and in particular protein that is rich in the amino acid leucine. (Of course, she probably didn't say it that way!) Of the twenty different amino acids, only leucine can activate a gene transcription factor called mammalian target of rapamycin (mTOR), which increases protein synthesis in your muscles and therefore helps build muscle and prevent loss of muscle as you age. Food sources of leucine include dairy, beef, chicken, pork, fish, seafood, nuts, and seeds. As you read in the previous chapter, it's important to prevent muscle loss as we age, so Grandma was right about this

one. But Grandma never went on a high-protein diet, because protein was expensive. Too much protein (from plants or animals) is harmful, as is too little.

3. Grandma said that you couldn't leave the table until you ate all of your vegetables. Why not? They contain polyphenols, compounds found in herbs, spices, coffee, chocolate, tea, and veggies, that are necessary for your cells to run at full power. We now know that when taken even at low levels, polyphenols activate antioxidant genes, which create antioxidant enzymes. This is important because most antioxidants are one and done. They knock out one free radical, and then they're done for the day. But antioxidant enzymes can destroy thousands of free radicals over and over again. They're free-radical eating machines.

At higher levels, polyphenols activate anti-inflammatory genes that inhibit the activation of nuclear factor kappa B, the master gene that turns on inflammation. At still higher levels, polyphenols activate the antiaging gene SIRT1, which makes your cells more powerful and younger. Polyphenols also contain fermentable fiber, which feeds the good bacteria in your gut, so much that Dr. Sears calls them the "master sculptors of the gut."

According to Dr. Sears, you need about a gram of polyphenols a day to turn on your anti-inflammatory genes. A lot of people love to believe that they're getting the benefits of polyphenols from drinking wine, but to get enough of them to make a difference, you would need to drink eleven glasses a day of red wine or more than a hundred glasses of white wine. That would definitely cause more harm than good!

Dr. Sears recommends taking concentrated polyphenol supplements; good food sources of polyphenols include blueberries, grapes, and other blue, red, and orange foods, as well as dark chocolate and my personal favorite source, coffee.

Since I interviewed Dr. Sears and did the research for *Head Strong*, it's become clear to me that eating veggies alone won't provide enough polyphenols for optimal health, even if you really like veggies. I decided to make it a point to get at least four grams of polyphenols a day, so I started adding far more herbs and spices to my food (curry powder, ginger, cumin, cinnamon, oregano, sage, rosemary, thyme, and parsley are all great sources of polyphenols) and drinking decaf coffee in the afternoon. I even formulated a very-high-polyphenol supplement called Polyphenomenol.

When I recently took a test to analyze my gut bacteria using Viome, a company founded by Naveen Jain (you may remember him from chapter 4), I got both some good news and some bad news. The bad news was that nearly two decades of taking antibiotics as a young man had harmed the balance and diversity of my gut bacteria. The good news was that the high levels of polyphenols in my diet had worked. They are keeping the bad guys in check and keeping inflammation down, and I'm leaner and healthier than I ever was before. It is not humanly possible to get that level of polyphenols from food alone; you'd have to eat more pounds of vegetables every day than your stomach can handle! So do what Grandma said: eat your damn veggies. And consider supplemental polyphenols for even more gut support.

4. Grandma said that you're not going to leave the house until you take your tablespoon of cod-liver oil. Of course, she said that because she couldn't get purified EPA and DHA fish oil or its even stronger cousin, krill oil. Dr. Sears's work focuses on omega-3 fatty acids, one of two types of unsaturated fats that our bodies need but cannot produce. The other one is omega-6 fatty acids, which are available in our food supply in much greater quantities than omega-3s. Omega-6s are the building blocks of inflammatory hormones, and omega-3s are the building blocks of anti-inflammatory hormones, both of which are healthy and necessary at the right levels.

Ideally, your ratio of omega-6s to omega-3s should be between $1:1^{1}/_{2}$ and 3:1. That is, for every 3 grams of widely available omega-6 you eat, you need 1 to 2 grams of hard-to-get omega-3 oils. Dr. Sears says that this is the sweet spot for controlling inflammation, but most people following the standard American diet have an intake that is closer to *eighteen* to one. Ever wonder why you perform worse when you eat junk food? Look no further than your omega-6 intake.

Our levels of inflammation as a society have increased dramatically since Grandma's time. Dr. Sears says that almost every disease we're currently fighting—obesity, diabetes, heart disease, cancer, and Alzheimer's—are all known to be inflammatory diseases. Yet we are fueling that fire by adding more and more omega-6s to our diets.

Vegetable oils are a major source of omega-6s that most people eat way too much of because they are the cheapest source of fat calories in the world. This may sound extreme, but Dr. Shanahan says that we should be calling vegetable oils "liquid death" because they are so chemically unstable and promote the formation of free radicals that can directly damage our DNA, having effects similar to those of radiation. In her interview, Dr. Shanahan said that eating vegetable oils is like ingesting radiation. Neither one is a good choice for people who want to improve their health.

Yet there are far more vegetable oils in our diet now than ever before in history. Canola oil, which is the second largest source of vegetable oil in the United States, didn't even exist until 1985. The average American is now made up of more of these fats than ever before. Dr. Shanahan says that if you biopsy human fat tissue, it is different from what it was fifty years ago. Today, it is composed of more liquid fat, which is prone to degradation and inflammation.

If you're not scared off of vegetable oils yet, think about the fact that your brain is made of 50 percent fat. If your body does not have access to healthy fats, it will use whatever fats you've eaten to build your brain. Dr. Shanahan compares this to being at a construction site and the contractor saying, "I know you wanted your house to be made of brick, but the bricks never showed up. We did get these Styrofoam balls, and we've got to get this show on the road, so let's just use these and see what happens." Like a contractor, the body does its best with the materials it has on hand, but if your brain is made of inflammatory oils, chances are that you're not going to perform at your best. You'll get a muffin top in your brain!

Dr. Shanahan tells her patients that they don't even know who they are until they rebuild their brains with healthy fats. She says that it usually takes them anywhere from two to six months to feel as though their brains are back on. That was my experience, as well. When I cleaned up the fat in my diet and added a lot more of the right kinds of stable fats from butter, avocados, coconut and Brain Octane oil, and ghee from grass-fed cows, I tapped into huge amounts of energy and resilience I hadn't known were there.

Nina Teicholz is another one of my guests who has railed against the pervasive use of vegetable oils. Nina is an investigative journalist whose work has appeared in publications such as the *New York Times*, *The New Yorker*, and *The Economist*, and she is the author of the *New York Times* bestselling book *The Big Fat Surprise: Why Butter, Meat, and Cheese Belong in a Healthy Diet*. (Don't you love that title?)

Nina told me about the history of the American Heart Association, which was a sleepy little society of cardiologists back in the 1940s, when food manufacturers such as Heinz, Best Foods, and Standard Foods were starting to really grow in size and influence. In 1948, Procter & Gamble said it wanted to make the American Heart Association the beneficiary of a contest.

Overnight, almost $2 million flowed into the American Heart Association's coffers. It was suddenly opening chapters all over the country with research budgets, and it began to develop the kind of influence and authority for which it's known today. When it released its first set of nutritional guidelines in 1961, it suggested that Americans switch from saturated fats to unsaturated fats, including vegetable oil. Coincidentally (or not), Crisco (solidified vegetable oil) was one of Procter & Gamble's major products.

But our bodies and our brains need saturated fats. They're the only type of fat that raises high-density lipoprotein (HDL, or "good") cholesterol, they're the building blocks of our hormones, and they're the most stable type of fat. They do not have any extra double bonds that can react with oxygen, which is why they are solid at room temperature. This means that when they are heated, they do not create toxic oxidation by-products.

Meanwhile, vegetable oils are polyunsaturated, meaning that they have lots of double bonds that can react to oxygen. They are much more reactive at high temperatures, especially when they are exposed to high temperatures for prolonged periods of time. Can you say "restaurant fryer"?

The food industry attempted to solve this problem by developing trans fats, which are a by-product of hardening vegetable oil, to make them more stable and mimic saturated fat. Companies such as McDonald's used to fry their french fries in saturated animal fat (tallow), but when they cut costs by getting rid of saturated fats, they brought in hardened vegetable oils (trans fats). Then, starting in 2007, as we became aware of how toxic trans fats are, restaurants swapped them out for regular vegetable oil.

This is dangerous because not only are heated vegetable oils exceptionally inflammatory, they are also so unstable that they can cause fires. That's right. Nina told me about an interview she conducted with a vice president of a big oil company who told her about the horrible problems the major fast-food chains have been having ever since they switched over to frying with vegetable oils. All sorts of junk was building up on the walls and clogging their drains. And when they put the restaurant uniforms that were saturated in vegetable oil in the back of a truck to be cleaned, they would spontaneously combust.

Do you know what is a great cooking fat that is solid and stable at room temperature and does not oxidize? Saturated fat. And guess what Grandma used to cook with? Most likely lard or butter, both of which are healthy and delicious, don't smoke up the kitchen, and have been used in Western civilization since antiquity. Dr. Barry was right: Grandma was smarter than we ever gave her credit for.

Action Items

- Don't eat vegetable oils such as soy, corn, or canola, especially in restaurants. Use saturated fat (butter, lard, ghee, coconut oil, Brain Octane oil, or MCT oil) instead. Use olive oil on finished dishes, not for cooking.
- Adjust your diet if you get hungry within five hours of eating.
- Order a Viome test, the best way to see what your food is doing to your gut bacteria: www.viome.com.

- Consume more omega-3s and fish oils, but don't go nuts.
- Get adequate but not excessive protein from healthy animals or high-leucine vegetables, about 0.5 grams per pound of body weight, or up to 0.8 grams if you are looking to build muscle.
- Eat a lot more herbs, spices, coffee, tea, chocolate, and colored veggies to get more polyphenols. Consider a high-quality supplement to get even more. (I use Polyphenomenal because I created it!)

Recommended Listening
- Barry Sears, "Fertility & Food, Flavonoids & Inflammation," *Bulletproof Radio*, episode 300
- "Vegetable Oil, the Silent Killer" with Dr. Cate Shanahan, *Bulletproof Radio*, episode 376
- Mark Hyman, "Meat Is the New Ketchup," *Bulletproof Radio*, episode 288
- Nina Teicholz, "Saturated Fats & the Soft Science on Fat," *Bulletproof Radio*, episode 149

Recommended Reading
- Barry Sears, *Mastering the Zone: The Next Step in Achieving SuperHealth and Permanent Fat Loss*
- Catherine Shanahan, *Deep Nutrition: Why Your Genes Need Traditional Food*
- Mark Hyman, *Eat Fat, Get Thin: Why the Fat We Eat Is the Key to Sustained Weight Loss and Vibrant Health*
- Nina Teicholz, *The Big Fat Surprise: Why Butter, Meat and Cheese Belong in a Healthy Diet*

Law 27: Feed the Little Bastards in Your Gut

The bacteria in your gut control a lot more than you might imagine. They have the power to make you fat, tired, and slow, to give you extra energy to tap into new power, and even to make you de-pressed. They are in the driver's seat, and if you treat them poorly, your performance will suffer. When you treat them well, they will serve you. Learn how to make them do your bidding.

Dr. David Perlmutter is well known for his bestselling book *Grain Brain: The Surprising Truth About Wheat, Carbs, and Sugar—Your Brain's Silent Killers*, but he's also a physician at the top of a field who has changed the way we think about the relationship between our brains and the food we eat. He's one of the very few board-certified neurologists who is also a fellow of the American College of Nutrition. This dual expertise enables him to publish extensively in peer-reviewed scientific journals such as *Archives of Neurology, Neurosurgery*, and *The Journal of Applied Nutrition*. You'll find him lecturing frequently at symposia sponsored by such medical institutions as Columbia University, Scripps Research Institute, New York University, and Harvard University when he's not at the University of Miami Miller School of Medicine, where he's an associate professor. Few medical professionals are qualified as broadly in multiple disciplines, and on top of that he's a fantastic human being.

Dr. Pearlmutter describes your relationship with your gut micro-biome, the complex community of bacteria, viruses, fungi, and other microscopic critters that have been living in our gut for millions of years, as beautiful, self-supportive, and mutualistic. These bacteria may have been inside of us for a long time, but they have remained a mystery until quite recently. According to Dr. Pearlmutter, 90 percent of the literature peer-reviewed journals have ever published about the human microbiome has been within the past five years.

So why are we suddenly taking the microbiome so seriously? First, because the science is brand-new: researchers from the National Institutes of Health completed the mapping of the microbiome only about five years ago. And second, we're learning how badly we've threatened that symbiotic relationship, leading to many of today's health crises. Dr. Pearlmutter believes that the overuse of antibiotics, which deplete microbial populations in the gut, has caused tremendous damage to the human microbiome. This damage may be permanent, and research has linked our diminished microbes to the current obesity epidemic, particularly in children.

The idea that antibiotics are connected to weight gain is not new. In the 1950s, the livestock industry discovered this fact when they fed antibiotics to animals that subsequently got fat. Today, 75 percent of the antibiotics manufactured in the United States are fed to cattle for precisely this reason: it fattens them up for slaughter and enables farmers to save money on feed.

Antibiotics cause animals to gain fat even when they consume the same amount of calories as other animals. If cutting calories were the secret to losing weight or it was true that "a calorie is a calorie," it would be impossible for antibiotics to make cows—or people—fatter on the same number of calories. Quick sidetrack: artificial sugars also dramatically reduce the diversity of gut bacteria, which explains why people who drink diet soda have higher rates of obesity even though they don't consume any extra calories. In short: *it's not about the calories; it's about the microbiome.*

There is also a connection between our gut health and our cardiovascular health. In several studies on mice, the ones who exercised had a much greater diversity of gut bacteria than those that were sedentary.[1] The same connection exists in humans. In 2016, scientists analyzed the fecal microbiota (poop) of thirty-nine healthy participants who were similar in age, body mass index, and diet but had varying cardiovascular fitness levels. They found that the participants with higher levels of cardiovascular fitness had greater biodiversity. And they specifically had an abundance of the three types of bacteria that create butyrate, a short-chain fatty acid found in butter from grass-fed cows that is essential for a healthy brain, and consequently increased levels of butyrate itself.[2] (My Viome test showed that my gut bacteria make 1.5 times more butyrate than average, which means I eat lots of butter from grass-fed cows.) Another recent mind-bending study showed that the microbes in our gut produce nearly *all* of the fatty plaque in people with heart disease.[3] It is not formed from the fat they eat.

This is one reason it's so important to eat only grass-fed meat from a farmer who you know does not use antibiotics or feed the animals grains, particularly grains that have been treated with glyphosate (the active ingredient in Roundup), which is—guess what?—an antibiotic! Glyphosate changes the human microbiome, affects our ability to utilize vitamin D, and alters how we digest our food. Nearly 19 billion pounds of glyphosate have been released into the environment. Compare that to the fact that, according to Dr. Pearlmutter, taking one course of antibiotics will change your microbiome for the rest of your life.

In addition to making us fat, Dr. Pearlmutter says that our aggressive overusage of antibiotics is paving the way for antibiotic-resistant "superbugs," which the World Health Organization has categorized as one of the top three health risks to the planet over the next decade. With all of the other current threats to our planet (no, I'm not going to get political), this is pretty scary.

In my research for *The Bulletproof Diet* and *Head Strong*, I came to believe that we are really here to serve our gut bacteria. Your particular balance of microbes determines a great deal of your biology, including your metabolism, skin, digestion, and weight. In the past few years, researchers have discovered that your gut bacteria dabble in mind control, too. Your gut and brain are in constant contact thanks to a pathway called the gut-brain axis, and some bacteria actually make neurotransmitters, which directly influence your brain activity.

What can we do about all this? Well, although she may not have known it at the time, all of your grandma's advice (see Law 26) is beneficial to your gut microbiome. In addition to avoiding processed foods, factory animals, grain-fed meat, and all genetically modified foods (which are more likely to have been treated with glyphosate), take antibiotics only when you absolutely need them and focus on eating foods that nurture healthy gut bacteria. These include polyphenols and a special kind of fiber called *prebiotic fiber*, which is the food that your gut bacteria eat.

Dr. Pearlmutter says that prebiotic fiber is the key to health. It can be found in high levels in foods such as Jerusalem artichokes, jicama, dandelion greens, onions, garlic, leek, asparagus, and radicchio. Even cooked and cooled white rice contains some resistant starch to feed your bacteria. (Sushi time!) Fermented foods are also hugely important for feeding gut bacteria. Once again, this taps into the wisdom of our ancestors. Fermented foods have been a traditional part of the human diet for as long as we've been eating food off of the ground, and it turns out that they nourish the microbiome, because as food ferments, bacteria multiply. Kimchi, cultured yogurt, sauerkraut, and kombucha are all good examples of fermented foods that are rich in healthy bacteria. You don't have to be a foodie or a health nut to choose these foods. They are what high-performance people eat.

Dr. Mark Hyman says that you basically change your gut microbiome with every bite you eat and that at the end of the day you're only as healthy as your gut. When you eat, you are literally gardening. Your gut microbiome is your inner garden, and if you fertilize your garden with the right foods, you're going to grow the right "plants."

Fixing his patients' guts is the most important thing that Dr. Hyman does to change their lives and their health. Once their nutrition is in order and their gut is healed, he says, 90 percent of their symptoms go away. That's pretty stunning. Dr. Hyman's dietary principles are simple: eat foods that don't have a bar code or a nutrition label. That means eating real food such as avocados, almonds, grass-fed meat, and tons of vegetables.

In other words, eat according to the wisdom of our ancestors. Eat like your grandma did.

Action Items

- Eat some fiber or resistant starch and lots of vegetables at each meal.
- Focus on whole, unprocessed, organic foods, and skip meat if it is not organic and grass fed.
- Avoid antibiotics whenever possible, as well as meat and other products from animals that were fed antibiotics.
- Eat fermented foods that agree with you.
- Consider a Viome test from www.viome.com/bulletproof to see what's growing in your gut and what tweaks you can make in your diet.

Recommended Listening
- David Perlmutter, "Autism, Alzheimer's & the Gut Microbiome," *Bulletproof Radio*, episode 250
- "Connecting Your Gut and Your Brain" with David Perlmutter, *Bulletproof Radio*, episode 359

Recommended Reading
- David Perlmutter with Kristin Loberg, *Brain Maker: The Power of Gut Microbes to Heal and Protect Your Brain—for Life*

Law 28: If You Get Toxins from Only Nature, You Can Get Nutrients from Only Food

You evolved in a clean environment to feel great and live long enough to reproduce as long as you had enough high-quality food. Those days are gone. High performance now requires that you overcome the decline of clean air, food, and water by going beyond what you can get from eating even the most nutritious food. The highest performers use supplements to perform better now and live longer, too. Take your vitamins.

Looking at the data and seeing how many game changers mentioned the importance of taking supplements, it's clear that people who are at the top of their games don't just take their vitamins; they also credit doing so with being a vital part of what put them at the top of their field. So do I.

Take Bill Andrews. He's out to either cure aging or die trying. As the CEO of Sierra Sciences, Bill is one of the world's top experts on antiaging. Like many others, he was motivated by personal interest to get into this field. His motivation began more than fifty years ago when he was a little boy and his father said to him, "I don't understand why nobody's cured aging yet. Bill, since you're so interested in science, when you grow up you should become a doctor and find a cure for aging." He's been obsessed with it ever since.

After studying hundreds of thousands of compounds, Bill has focused his research on telomeres, the protective end caps on your DNA that shield your chromosomes from damage when they replicate. As you get older, your telomeres shorten and are less able to protect your DNA. Eventually, the ends of your genetic code become frayed, putting you at increased risk for disease and premature death. Ever since 1993, when Bill learned that telomeres shorten over time and that this may be the cause of aging, he has had one mission: to prevent that shortening and actually relengthen them. His company, Sierra Sciences, is committed to that mission.

The telomerase gene is in charge of maintaining the telomeres. Bill explains that any gene in the body can be turned on and off like a light switch, and that light switch is typically a protein located adjacent to the gene and the chromosome. He started out looking for the telomerase switch, but after seven years he still hadn't found it, and neither had any other lab in the world. He decided to put that approach on hold and move on to plan B, which was to screen for synthetic chemicals (drugs) that when added to the cells could turn the switch on or off. He assumed that those drugs would bind to the protein he wanted to identify. The drugs would essentially be fishing hooks to pull up the right protein, while at the same time acting as a potential treatment to lengthen telomeres and extend longevity.

Bill and his team have been very successful with that approach. Yet when he started doing it, scientists all over the world told him it was impossible and he would never be able to find a molecule that could turn on the telomerase gene. Today, he has found close to nine hundred different chemicals that turn on the telomerase gene. Talk about changing the game!

Dr. Elissa Epel, whom you'll read more about in chapter 15, co-authored *The Telomere Effect: A Revolutionary Approach to Living Younger, Healthier, Longer* with Nobel laureate Dr. Elizabeth Blackburn, who discovered the role of telomeres and telomerase. Dr. Epel came on *Bulletproof Radio* to discuss telomeres and stress, and we talked about whether there is a role for supplements in antiaging. Her short answer is "Probably," but she also feels that lifestyle factors and stress are at least as important.

In any case, both Bill and Dr. Epel believe that keeping telomeres longer and/or decreasing their rate of shortening will have an impact not just on aging but on every disease that has anything to do with health and especially that involves cell division. These include cancer, heart disease, Alzheimer's disease, osteoporosis, muscular dystrophy, immune disorders, and many others. Even people who have HIV or other degenerative diseases could potentially benefit from taking something that can extend their telomeres. A major cause of all the ailments that stem from AIDS is accelerated telomere shortening in the immune cells. This is why T-cells disappear in people who are infected with the AIDS virus.

These highly specialized supplements are expensive today, but that won't always be the case. As more of us embrace the idea of having better immune systems and aging backward, the cost of supplements like this will fall, the same way the cost of a cell phone went from $25,000 in 1985 down to almost free today. I have a hard time waiting for that day.

Since impatience is a virtue when it comes to not dying, I sought out experts in nutrient deficiencies to help learn how to make the meat hardware I have now work better and last longer. Dr. Kate Rhéaume-Bleue has spent the last decade using her medical and biological training to examine the role of vitamin K2 and speaks internationally about this little-known but powerful supplement.

Dr. Rhéaume-Bleue first became interested in vitamin K2 in 2007 after reading the dentist Weston Price's book *Nutrition and Physical Degeneration: A Comparison of Primitive and Modern Diets and Their Effects*, a groundbreaking book in 1939 that documented the decline in health of native communities such as Native Americans, pygmies, and aborigines when they started eating industrial foods. A few months later, she began researching vitamin K2 and noticed amazing parallels between its effects and what she'd read in Price's book.

When Weston Price traveled around the world from Switzerland to

Africa in the 1930s, he found communities of people who had beautiful, perfect, straight, white, healthy teeth that didn't get cavities, even
though, shockingly, they didn't brush or floss or even have dentists.
They were able to maintain this dental health with good diets. They
ate a wide variety of foods, and their diets provided high levels of vitamins and minerals, particularly fat-soluble vitamins. He saw very high
levels of vitamins A and D, as well as high levels of another fat-soluble
vitamin that he had never seen before. He didn't know what it was, so
he just called it Activator X because he observed that it activated the
DNA that would enable people to benefit from and utilize the other
vitamins and minerals in their diet.

Price studied Activator X and found it very useful in conjunction with vitamins A and D for healing dental cavities. He actually
stopped drilling and filling teeth and started giving his patients a nutritional protocol instead. Later he published before-and-after images
of mouths full of open cavities that had completely sealed over. He
found that it's actually possible for your teeth to heal. They're designed to do that if they have the right nutrients. Price found that certain foods were high in Activator X, particularly my favorite source:
butter from grass-fed cows.

For ages, Activator X remained a mystery and a subject of debate
in the medical and nutritional world. It wasn't until 2008 that scientists learned that it was none other than vitamin K2. Also around
that time, a lot of research was being published about the problems
with calcium supplements causing increased risk of heart attack and
stroke. Dr. Rhéaume-Bleue says that calcium supplementation is not
inherently safe or unsafe; we simply need to find out how the body
can safely use calcium, get it to the right places, and keep it out of
your arteries. That's precisely what vitamin K2 helps it to do.

We need calcium in our bodies for our bones and our teeth, and
that's exactly where it tends to be lacking. When this happens, the
mineral leaches out of the areas where it should be and leaves behind
little holes in either bones or teeth. This is how we get osteoporosis
and cavities. The flip side is that in the same people who suffer from
osteoporosis and cavities, there is often a buildup of calcium in places
where it shouldn't be, such as the arteries, kidneys, heel spurs, and

breast tissue. It is a paradoxical situation of our needing calcium but it being dangerous if it gets into the wrong places.

It turns out that this is vitamin K2's role: to keep calcium in its place at all times. It's incredible that you can boost your bone health and your dental health and even maintain a healthy heart by taking a vitamin. I take my vitamin K2, because the rewards outweigh the risks.

I have been sold on the amazing powers of vitamin K2 for years, and I've also been using supplements to detox my body with great results. Part of this journey involved interviewing one of the luminaries in the field, Dr. William J. Walsh, who discovered the connection between nutritional deficiencies and mental illness. For the past thirty years, he has developed biochemical treatments for patients diagnosed with behavioral disorders, attention deficit disorder, autism, clinical depression, anxiety, bipolar disorders, schizophrenia, and Alzheimer's disease.

It all began more than thirty-five years ago, when Dr. Walsh was a prison volunteer in the Chicago area and started looking at the biochemistry of some violent offenders. He found that many violent criminals and ex-convicts had very high levels of trace metals in their blood. Further study showed that metals such as copper have a direct impact on neurotransmitter levels. Dr. Walsh was able to treat many of those people using nutritional therapies, and since then he has used similar protocols to treat the wide variety of issues listed above.

This is the far end of the spectrum of supplement therapy, but it's not binary. Even if you're not suffering from a mental health issue, it's quite possible that the right supplements can push your performance forward enough to make a real difference. I'm fortunate that my volunteer work running an antiaging nonprofit group for more than a decade introduced me to this knowledge early on, because it has profoundly changed my brain and my ability to show up as a husband, father, and entrepreneur. Over the past ten years, there has been a quantum shift in how popular it is for elite performers to use supplements to round out their nutritional intake. We're not talking just pro athletes—people at elite levels in almost every field are using them.

Not long ago, I had the good fortune of meeting Dan Pena, a self-made man who has raised $50 billion in capital. When he accepted my invitation to speak at the Bulletproof Conference, I noticed how vibrant and youthful he was, with more energy than most people half his age, which is considerably greater than mine. I found out why during dinner at his castle in Scotland when I pulled out my bag of supplements. Most people laugh when they see how many pills I take with each meal, but Dan just looked at me and said, "Mine's bigger than yours," as he pulled out his own bag. Then he showed me the spreadsheet he uses to track them. I was surprised, but I really shouldn't have been; the highest performers in all fields invest in supplements because the return is so high. If you're not taking supplements, you're leaving some of your capacity on the table.

If you're worried that your body won't use some of the supplements and you'll end up peeing them out, you can relax. My pee is probably more expensive than yours.

Action Items
- Cover your bases by taking these supplements: vitamin D3, vitamin K2, vitamin A, magnesium, krill oil/omega-3, copper, zinc, iodine, tyrosine, and methyl vitamin B12 with methyl folate.
- Supplement with polyphenols extracted from plants.
- Consider seeing a functional medicine doctor to get your nutrient levels tested.
- Look for supplement formulas designed to deliver the results you're seeking, and try them to see if they work for you.

Recommended Listening
- Bill Andrews, "The Man Who Would Stop Time," *Bulletproof Radio*, episode 10
- Kate Rhéaume-Bleue, "The Power of Vitamin K2," *Bulletproof Radio*, episode 106
- William J. Walsh, "Gain Control of Your Biochemistry," *Bulletproof Radio*, episode 132
- Elissa Epel, "Age Backwards by Hacking Your Telomeres with Stress," *Bulletproof Radio*, episode 436

THE FUTURE OF HACKING YOURSELF IS NOW

For years, I felt like an outlier as I used myself as a human guinea pig in my efforts to understand the biological secrets of human performance. But it turns out I'm not alone. The idea of self-experimentation was one of the top twenty priorities identified by more than 450 highly successful people. You could argue that it's because *Bulletproof Radio* has an inherent bias toward featuring other biohackers, which is true. It's also true that people from all walks of life who are at the top of their games get there because they are interested in finding new ways to drive their performance forward. These efforts require two steps: quantifying what is currently going on in your body and then taking action to make changes.

Despite all the evidence to the contrary, some people still remain skeptical of biohacking because they don't believe that what goes on in their bodies can impact your mental performance. To these people I say: Try solving a difficult problem the morning after a particularly festive late night. Now do you see the connection? Your performance—the way you show up in the world emotionally and cognitively—is a direct reflection of how well your body is doing. That's why measuring your biology matters. But quantifying by itself is like collecting little bags of mismatched buttons—great as a hobby (if you're into that kind of thing) but not very productive. Data are meaningful only when they are useful. Biohacking requires knowledge *and* action: first, you have to quantify what is going on in your body; second, you have to determine what changes need to be made; and third, you have to implement those changes.

As it happens, our bodies come with some onboard sensors that are pretty handy biofeedback mechanisms. Those sensors are called "feelings," and they offer real-time data when technology isn't available. You can try everything I've ever written about nutrition, but if you still feel like crap, what you're doing is not working, no lab tests required. At the end of the day, the "I feel like crap" and "I feel like a great golden god or goddess" tests are the most reliable ones you can use to assess your progress. They're worth more than every data point in the universe because you won't perform the way you want to when you feel like crap, but you can change the world when you set yourself up to feel great. Of course, if you can get some more detailed biological data, you might be able to pinpoint the reason why you feel like crap and come up with a solution that will help you reach states far beyond what you've ever imagined.

My history as a biohacker started with my love of technology and computer science. I got my undergrad degree in an artificial intelligence field called decision support systems. At the time, AI was a controversial field; no academic wanted to bet tenure on it, and my class graduated with the warning that if we called it AI, we'd be unemployable. Whatever. Since that time, we built the cloud, and the world now has so much computing capacity that we can waste it tracking the most trivial details, organizing them, and comparing them to other seemingly trivial details. That was my passion, the most important thing I could imagine doing. It was the way I was going to change the game, and it worked. I made a lot of money doing what I loved (and lost it!), and I dreamed about computers at night. Until one morning I woke up to discover that building technology itself wasn't my passion anymore. I wanted to *use* technology to figure out some important stuff. That's when I turned to biohacking.

One reason I lost my passion for building technology was because at the time, computers sucked at finding meaningful patterns in batches of unrelated data. But in the last few years, a new generation of coders has done something way more important than building the cloud: they've figured out how to make computers operate much like our brains using technology called neural networks, or machine learning. We can finally tell a computer to go figure out what matters and let us know when it's done. Well, pretty close, anyway.

We are just starting to apply machine-learning algorithms to biological data from hundreds of thousands of people to find new correlations that reveal what kinds of interventions work. For example, Dr. Paul Zak (whom you'll read more about later) has used these techniques to reliably determine what will raise someone's oxytocin levels (and by how much) even without doing a blood test. Researchers can use these data to investigate the *why* and find the specific mechanisms at work—but that kind of research often takes years. In the meantime, the rest of us can benefit from the *what*. If machine learning reveals that a specific intervention—whether it's nutrition, supplements, sleep, or meditation—offers significant benefits for 90 percent of people, we can choose to do it without having any idea why it works.

It used to take generations for this kind of knowledge to trickle down. Monks sat in monasteries and meditated using onboard sensors called feelings, taking notes for the next generation about what worked and what didn't. Today, my neurofeedback start-up is gathering brain waves from super-high-performing people—24,000 samples per second—and feeding them into a machine that can find patterns almost immediately. Imagine if those supermeditating monks had had access to that technology!

Many visionaries in the field of health have followed the data and ignored the dogma, sometimes with astounding results. More and more of us have decided to take the radical step of doing what works even if we aren't sure why, and we're seeing massive benefits. We use data to verify what's working and correct course when needed. This is a sea change for humanity, and I'm really excited about it.

Law 29: Track It to Hack It

You have the ability to target any state of high performance you choose. Decide what you want to change, measure where you are, and get moving. Check again later. Rinse and repeat. You can surpass previous generations because you have access to more data about yourself and others than was available throughout history.

The playing field is more level than it has ever been, and technology will help you correct course when necessary.

Dr. William Davis is a cardiologist who has gone against the grain (wait for it) to change the way people think about nutrition and health. A crusader for a grain-free lifestyle (do you get it now?), Dr. Davis is the author of the well-known Wheat Belly books as well as *Undoctored*. Dr. Davis was one of the first physicians to sound the alarm about the dangers of gluten. It's rare for such a well-regarded member of the medical community to risk his career by speaking out against the standard American diet. But Dr. Davis is a game changer.

In our interview, Dr. Davis shared that he is seeing an extraordinary shift in the way people are managing their health. Instead of relying on doctors to tell them how to feel better, they're figuring it out on their own thanks to increased access to medical research and data, as well as the multitude of affordable tracking devices (everything from heart rate monitors to fitness trackers to devices that monitor sleep and basal temperature) on the market. Dr. Davis sees this as a wonderful thing because, in his view, the mainstream health care system is failing.

In the United States, health care consumes 17.5 percent of the gross domestic product. By comparison, residential and commercial construction combined makes up only 7.5 percent. From the pharmaceutical industry to insurance companies to hospitals to medical device manufacturers, it is a massive—and massively profitable—business. The health care industry is booming, and Americans are sicker than ever. According to Dr. Davis, that's because the industry is focused more on the bottom line than on patient care. It's not that the people who work in these industries are evil. It's that the companies involved have become very good at making decisions in service of a goal. They often have the wrong goals, so their decisions create emergent behavior that looks evil. In my opinion, it actually is pretty evil. But I understand that it wasn't intended to be that way.

The good news is that today, an extraordinary library of information, experts, studies, and data is only a few keystrokes away. The idea that doctors are the only ones who can access and understand medical information is no longer true. Dr. Davis believes that over the next few years, more and more people will use technology to take ownership of their health and become "undoctored."

Dr. Davis said that in his experience, patients who educate themselves about their health and take matters into their own hands usually experience better results than people who rely solely on doctors for information and recommendations. That's because when you track your own data, you can make observations that no one else can, such as the impact of a specific food or supplement on your blood pressure or inflammation level. And you can learn to hone your onboard sensors, the ones that tell you when something doesn't feel right, and add those data to your solution.

One of the simplest diagnostics Dr. Davis suggests to people is to take their temperature first thing in the morning. Your temperature is a reflection of your thyroid function, and if it's too low, it's a good indication that your thyroid is sluggish (that you are hypothyroid). Dr. Davis said that his next-door neighbor once told him about some hypothyroid symptoms he was experiencing. He had a morning temperature of 94.5, which indicates hypothyroidism. (My morning temperature was an unhealthy 96 in 2005, when I first tried this technique.) Dr. Davis told him, "You probably have an iodine deficiency. Start taking iodine." Iodine is needed for your body to create thyroid hormones. Low iodine level is a main cause of hypothyroidism, a major symptom of which is temperature fluctuations. Within two weeks, his neighbor's temperature was up to 96.5 in the morning and on its way to a healthy 97.3.

In my case, iodine didn't work, so I tried a body temperature reset method designed by a control systems engineer: drinking hot water all day, wearing fleece in front of a heater, taking targeted doses of T3 thyroid hormone, and generally feeling like a boiled lobster for a long, sweaty week. It worked, and my body temperature rose and stayed up. (Do not try this, especially taking large doses of thyroid hormone, without medical knowledge or a doctor's help. You could die.)

It doesn't matter whether you use the latest technology or an old-fashioned thermometer. Taking your health into your own hands is empowering. I've been experimenting with trackers for years and have a deep well of knowledge in this area. Years ago, I designed the data system for the first stick-on internet-connected cardiac monitor, and later I was the chief technology officer of a wristband tracker company that Intel acquired. I have a drawer full of various health trackers, and I could never make myself wear one for more than a week or two because the data weren't very useful and the devices were clunky and uncomfortable.

Thankfully, those days are gone. I now sleep wearing an Oura ring, which tracks my sleep states, heart rate, heart rate variability (stress level), body temperature, breathing rates, activity levels, and more. It looks like a normal ring, stays charged for a week, and is totally waterproof. You can't even tell I'm a cyborg when I wear it. It gives me all the information I need to know what's going on in my body and choose my activities based on my biological state.

Being able to adjust your inputs as needed is central to successful biohacking. Though it's often useful to develop daily routines or to "automate" certain decisions such as what to wear or what to eat for breakfast (as discussed in chapter 1, this can help prevent willpower fatigue), routines do come with a risk: if you do them on autopilot, you may be missing important signals from your onboard sensors. Your body is a dynamic, complicated organism with an internal state that varies from day to day, based on countless variables. It will let you know when something isn't working. When you track your biology using technologies that help assess what's going on in your body at any given time, you can hone your inputs so they will complement your body's current state instead of making the choices that have worked for you in the past.

For example, if my ring tells me that I didn't cycle into the deepest stages of sleep last night and therefore didn't get enough restorative sleep, I'll skip a workout today to let my body recover. If my heart rate variability (the range from my maximum to minimum heart rate) is low, indicating that my body is in a stressed state of fight or flight, I'll take a break and do some meditation or yoga to prepare for the day's events. When I know that my body is primed to perform because it is well rested with high heart rate variability, I'll choose to take on a big challenge with the confidence that I can really bring it. Best of all, every time I get data from the Oura, I can correlate it with how I'm feeling. The data are teaching me which signals in my nervous system (aka feelings) are worth listening to.

Stress is not inherently good or bad, but your body can handle only so much of it at a time before it starts to take a toll. There are various kinds of stress: psychological, emotional, physical, and environmental. Not all of these types of stress have the same impact, but they do all affect your body. For example, psychological stress leaves you depleted. So hitting the gym really hard or challenging your body with a full-day fast may not be the best way to recover from a difficult breakup. You'd actually be better off doing what your body is probably telling you to do: get into bed and pull the covers over your head.

Sometimes stress isn't something you're consciously aware of, so it's important to find out how much unconscious stress your body is under before choosing to add additional stress. You may feel great, but if your data say that today is not a good day to work out, you need to listen to that. If your data show that you have chronically low heart rate variability, it means that your body is holding on to a lot of unconscious stress. It's important to find out why. What are you doing (or not doing) on a regular basis that is making you weak? You might have a chronic low-grade infection, sensitivity to a food that you eat regularly, or something in your environment may be affecting you. Try changing specific parts of your routine to see what kind of impact it has.

Of course, you can use information from your health trackers the opposite way, too—to determine how your body is currently responding to the inputs you choose. Is intermittent fasting putting your body into a state of fight or flight because you're doing it too often? You don't have to worry or wonder. Just check your heart rate variability during your intermittent fast. Are you wondering if drinking coffee late in the day is interfering with your sleep? Check your sleep report the next day and find out. (But seriously, you don't need an app for that!)

The number of actions you can take based on biological feedback is seemingly endless. Petteri Lahtela, the CEO and cofounder of Oura, explained that you can even use the ring to help determine your chronotype, or the manifestation of your personal circadian rhythms. You can figure this out based on your body's temperature fluctuations at night.[1]

As Dr. Davis explained, temperature changes can also be a sign of medical conditions. If your temperature is abnormally low, it's time to start considering what may be causing a thyroid problem, such as eating too many whole grains or being exposed to mold toxins in your environment. For women, being aware of temperature fluctuations can also help manage fertility cycles. When a woman is ovulating, her temperature rises by about half a degree. Tracking basal temperature can help a woman become aware of when she is most fertile, which is powerful knowledge whether or not she's planning a family.

Another company that uses machine learning to crack the code of what's going on inside your body is Viome. As I mentioned in chapter 4, I am an adviser to this company, which offers a kit to monitor the health in your gut. It does this not by assessing your heart rate, body temperature, or daily steps but by testing your poop. That's right. It uses $2 billion worth of technology to rapidly identify bioweapons, to identify every bacteria, fungus, and virus in your gut at a level of detail previously unheard of. The really exciting part is that Viome compares what's in your gut with what's in everyone else's gut using machine learning, so you can see how likely it is that your gut microbes are helping you or hurting you and what will work to fix this balance. Naveen Jain, the founder and CEO of Viome, says that his ultimate goal is to use technology to make sickness optional. He believes—as do many doctors and scientists—that health begins in the gut and an imbalanced microbiome is a precursor of disease.

Naveen looks at the human body as an ecosystem that is only 10 percent human and 90 percent microbial. Ninety percent of the cells in your gut make up the microbiome, and 25 percent of the metabolites in your body are created in your gut. So if you can figure out what's happening in your gut, you can better predict how your body is going to react to specific inputs. For example, you can tell that you've been on a ketogenic diet for too long without a break if you are lacking the bacteria that make beneficial short-chain fatty acids.

Viome also allows users to see the bacteria, phages, and viruses that are living in their blood and shows them which enzymes and cofactors (compounds that enzymes need to function) are lower than normal. You can easily correct these imbalances with the right supplements. The exciting part is that we can use this information to become aware of such imbalances before we experience symptoms. Naveen believes that this will eventually enable us to find predictive biomarkers of diseases and cure them before they manifest into physical problems.

That is a future I definitely want to stick around to see. The body has long been a mystery, and the idea that we can now use these tools to find out what is going on inside of us is incredibly exciting. Your physiological state can make all the difference to your performance. So why wouldn't you want the information you need to change the state of your body at will?

At Bulletproof, data are built into the company culture. Members of the team measure and share our chronotypes, our instincts for how much information we need to make a decision, and even a quantified measure of how we like to be shown gratitude. It may sound out-there, but this stuff is deeply wired into our biology, and being aware of our individuality helps us know how to communicate and work well together. If data can show me that one person really appreciates a hug to say thanks but another really likes praise, I'll use the data, and everyone wins.

As a human being, I would argue that you have a moral imperative to hack yourself—but is it moral to hack your employees? I believe the answer is yes. You are setting them up to win. When leaders help people in their companies develop greater self-knowledge and self-awareness, it makes for happier employees who are both more compassionate with themselves and others and more passionate about the jobs they do. So go ahead, hack yourself. Help those around you hack themselves, too! Life will never be the same.

Action Items
- Track your sleep using a sleep tracker such as the Oura ring. Do less intense training or fasting on days when you slept like crap

the night before, and go hard on the days when you're at full power.

- If you don't have a sleep tracker, use your onboard sensors instead. On a sheet of paper rate your sleep on a scale of 1 to 10 when you first wake up. Base the score on how good you feel, how stiff you are, how anxious you are, and how easy it was to wake up.
- Stop using toys to track the number of steps you take per day or fictional "calories burned" metrics. They distract you from the useful data you want: heart rate, heart rate variability, temperature, and sleep quality. Knowing those will change your life.
- If it's in your budget, a full panel of health metrics from your functional medicine doctor is a great investment. Ask for all hormones, full thyroid, inflammation markers, and nutrient analysis, plus whatever else your doctor thinks is helpful.
- Have your poop tested by Viome (www.viome.com) to see what is going on in your gut.

Recommended Listening
- William Davis, "How the Health Care System Keeps You Sick & What You Can Do to Change It!," *Bulletproof Radio*, episode 402
- "Hack Your Chronotype to Improve Sleep & Recovery by Wearing a Ring," *Bulletproof Radio*, episode 437
- Naveen Jain, "Listen to Your Gut & Decide Your Own Destiny," *Bulletproof Radio*, episode 452

Recommended Reading
- William Davis, *Undoctored: Why Health Care Has Failed You and How You Can Become Smarter than Your Doctor*

Law 30: What Doesn't Kill You Makes You Stronger

Every system in your body benefits from intense, brief bouts of stress followed by recovery. It's what makes us stronger. Only fearful people choose chronic, unending stress from work, relationships, or the environment around them. Apply the cycling principal to all the stress in your life. Ruthlessly remove useless stressors from everything you do, and from your body itself.

Dr. Ron Hunninghake, the chief medical officer at the famous Riordan Clinic in Wichita, Kansas, has developed a seemingly counterintuitive protocol that is changing the way we fight some cancers: by using vitamin C and oxidation. Normally, we tend to think of oxidation as a bad thing, but as Dr. Hunninghake explains, brief, intense oxidation (cellular stress) can be beneficial to your health as long as you follow it with reduction (cell recovery).

Oxidation is the process by which our bodies process oxygen and use it to create energy. As a by-product, this creates free radicals, unstable and highly reactive molecules with an unpaired electron. These free radicals can damage our cells, mitochondria, and even DNA. Many researchers believe it is a primary cause of aging.

Reduction is the opposite process, during which a molecule with an unpaired electron gains an electron, which stabilizes the molecule and prevents further damage. All the energy in your body comes from rapid cycling between these two states. The only cells in your body that don't consistently lose and gain electrons are dead cells. The better your cells are at vacillating between these two states, the better you will be at everything you do. We won't go into too much detail here—hacking that process is the topic of an entire book, *Head Strong*.

Back to vitamin C. When you consume it, it functions as an antioxidant (a substance that inhibits oxidation), but Dr. Hunninghake explains that giving it intravenously has a different effect. (Humans are actually one of the only animals that have lost the genetic ability to make their own vitamin C, but I believe our ability to produce it synthetically and use it effectively is part of the beauty of being human.) Administering intravenous vitamin C creates an oxidative effect in the body, which of course scares off many people from doing it, including most mainstream doctors. Dr. Hunninghake compares it to intermittent fasting or high-intensity training on a cellular level. The oxidation kills off cells that are dysfunctional or weak, including cancerous and precancerous cells.

Dr. Hunninghake's cancer protocol involves administering intravenous vitamin C to kill off the diseased cells. He then supplements with strong antioxidants such as glutathione to make the cells that did survive stronger. This is classical hormesis, the process of giving something stressful or toxic to the body in order to stimulate a healing response. What doesn't kill your cells makes them stronger. And in cancer treatment, killing weak cells with stress so that strong ones can replace them is a great strategy.

A core biohacking principle is that you should stop doing the things that make you weak and start doing more of the things that will make you stronger—in that order. As you read earlier, your body can handle only so much stress at a time. It can't take advantage of hormesis or any form of productive stress if something is already making it weak. That's why knowing when to push yourself hard is as important as knowing when *not* to push yourself hard, and knowing how to relax and recover is as important as maintaining good form when you're lifting weights. People who rise to the top master both sides of the equation; they apply it at work, at home, in the gym, in bed, when they eat, and even in their cells when they need it.

The idea of using intravenous vitamin C to fight some types of cancer sounds like a brilliant therapy, and I look forward to seeing more research on it in the future. If I were facing cancer, I would use it. Then again, I used intravenous vitamin C extensively in the past when I was recovering from exposure to environmental toxic mold, which doctors had diagnosed as fibromyalgia, chronic fatigue, and Lyme disease. I added an independent intravenous vitamin clinic to Bulletproof Labs in Santa Monica, California, because this therapy is powerful enough to bring about recovery even when people aren't sick. We can learn a lot about how the body recovers from observing how these therapies work for patients with Alzheimer's disease, Parkinson's disease, diabetes, and cancer. By using the data from innovative treatments used to help those who are suffering the most, we can help guard against some of the same kind of suffering in our own future.

Action Items

- Switch to high-intensity interval training (either sprints or heavy lifting) followed by high-quality recovery and sleep to see more returns on less exercise.
- When your data show that you are stressed, avoid putting additional stress on your body.
- When you have exceeded your stress threshold, recover like a boss. Consider IV nutrients. Get a massage. Try cryotherapy. Go to a sauna. Watch a movie!

Recommended Listening

- Ron Hunninghake, "Vitamin C Is Taking the Fight to the Big 'C,'" *Bulletproof Radio*, episode 379
- Erin Oprea, "Tabatas: Like Getting HIIT by a 4×4," *Bulletproof Radio*, episode 313

Law 31: Heal like Wolverine, Age like Benjamin Button

The most important thing to invest in is not Bitcoin. It's not the stock market. It's the investment in your biology that counts. Chronic injuries, chronic pain, and simple aging will slow you down and take away energy from important things. Do what it takes to heal what you have before you replace it or cut it out. Before you go under the knife, exhaust every other possible option. Keep all your systems young.

Most of us learn at some point in our lives to ignore chronic pain. Coaches tell us to "walk it off," which is great advice if you're whining and terrible advice if you are actually injured. By the time we hit our twenties, a lot of us have chronic injuries—parts of the body that still work but hurt more than they should. Over time, these inefficiencies cause dysfunctions in other parts of the body, create subtle stress, and waste energy you can put to much better uses.

I have my fair share of chronic pain, thanks to thirteen years of playing soccer as an obese, inflamed teenager, ski injuries, and a knee with a screw in it after three surgeries. Given my plan to live to at least 180 years old, this is simply unacceptable! I've used medical lasers, electrical stimulation, injections, pulsed electromagnets, and other stuff straight out of science fiction to help heal some of those injuries, and I've had a lot of success. But nothing compares to stem cells, which have become far more affordable in the last couple of years and are already far cheaper than the cost of most surgeries. I plan to get stem cell injections every six months for the rest of my (very long) life.

To learn more about this cutting-edge therapy, I sought out three experts: Dr. Matthew Cook, who runs BioReset Medical in Los Gatos, California, and treats many Major League Baseball pitchers when their shoulders get injured; Dr. Harry Adelson at Docere Clinics in Park City, Utah, an early stem cell adopter who specializes in spinal pain; and Dr. Amy B. Killen at Docere Medical, also in Park City, who uses stem cells for cosmetic procedures. All three of these doctors treated me, and of course I interviewed them to learn more about how they had developed their game-changing techniques.

I started with Dr. Harry Adelson. Years ago, when stem cell therapy was unheard of in the United States, he traveled to Venezuela to learn about it from Dr. Carlos Cecilio Bratt. Dr. Bratt is one of the best-known stem cell doctors in South America, and his practice inspired Dr. Adelson to search for the "golden ratio" of affordable and effective treatments, which I experienced myself.

For years, most people thought that using stem cells to treat chronic pain, enhance recovery from injury, or even improve the skin was science fiction, a treatment reserved for the ultrarich, or worse, something that was controversial, because thirty years ago, stem cells came from embryos (what opponents called fetal stem cells). Today, stem cell therapies using cells from your own body are widely available, and I believe their popularity will only increase as time goes on.

The human body's ability to heal on its own is impressive, and with a little help from stem cell therapy, it goes from impressive to almost unbelievable. Stem cell therapy has been used to restore sight to blind people, restore hearing in deaf rodents, repair connective tissue, heal spinal injuries, and even restore cognitive function in patients who have suffered strokes. Suzanne Somers, one of America's most popular and beloved personalities and a *New York Times* bestselling author, told me in an interview that she is the first woman in the United States to regrow a breast after a partial mastectomy using her own stem cells.

But stem cell therapies aren't used only for healing illnesses and injuries. Reversing aging is all about recovering from stress and strain so that your body becomes young again, and stem cell therapy can slow the effects of aging by keeping your skin collagen and elastin rich. It makes your joints stronger and more pliable, and it can even increase (ahem . . .) the length and girth of certain areas.

Stem cell therapy involves extracting stem cells from one part of your body, usually fat from your lower back or bone marrow, mixing them with growth factors, and injecting them into another part of your body. Dr. Adelson removed stem cells from my bone marrow and fat and remarked that I had the "yellowest" marrow he'd ever seen (that's a good thing) before he injected them into every injury site. It was an intense procedure—I had dozens of injections. Within just a couple of days, though, my pain levels decreased noticeably. You don't realize how much background pain there is until it suddenly goes away! I was so impressed with the results that I decided to visit Dr. Adelson again, this time with my wife, Dr. Lana. After her procedure, she said that the pain from several of her childhood injuries had simply gone away.

We also stopped in to see Dr. Amy B. Killen, a physician who focuses on stem cell–related antiaging procedures, specifically related to sexual health. Yes, that's right. Dr. Killen injects stem cells into places that would probably make you cringe. She uses the growth factors in the platelets to regenerate different parts of the body, in her case the skin, hair, and sexual organs.

Why would I want anything injected into that most sensitive area? Dr. Killen explains that the cells in blood vessels and in the penis that enable men to have erections age over time. Some even die. This is one thing that can cause erectile dysfunction. Introducing new cells and growth factors into the corpora cavernosa, the little tubes on the sides of the penis that create erections, results in increased blood flow and nerve response. Most of Dr. Killen's patients are experiencing some degree of erectile dysfunction. I was not, frankly, but I wanted to do whatever I could to keep the equipment lasting as long as possible. And since I had fresh stem cells, they had to go somewhere . . .

The side effect of this treatment on men is an increase in size, especially if you follow it up with a vacuum pump that encourages blood flow. You are supposed to use it daily for a month, but honestly that's a lot of time spent pumping. I tried it twice and decided that I'm happy with what I've got, thank you very much! I used all the time I saved not pumping to write a chapter of this book for you instead.

However, since we're on the topic of upgrades in that region, it's worth mentioning GAINSWave, a shock-wave therapy that doctors use on the penis. A fifteen-minute noninvasive procedure has a profound effect on the male organ. When I tried it at another clinic in Seattle, I experienced spontaneous erections like a twenty-year-old. It's usually used for erectile dysfunction, but it works on most men to improve responsiveness, and a version for women is in the works. Sometimes being a professional biohacker is tough!

My very brave wife, Dr. Lana, also went to Dr. Killen and got what she calls "the turbo O shot." In women, Dr. Killen injects stem cells and growth factors into two locations—the clitoris (ouch) and the anterior upper vaginal wall, right above the G-spot. Her patients experience an improvement in their vaginal tissues, better lubrication, and even improved orgasm strength. Fortunately, topical numbing cream makes it far less painful than it sounds.

I know that Dr. Lana doesn't mind my sharing the fact that she experienced profound changes within a week. She had renewed vigor and says she felt as though she were twenty-five again (although she was already perfectly beautiful and vigorous to me). From my perspective, the experience was pretty amazing, too. Dr. Lana says she recommends vaginal stem cell therapy to all of her friends and to many of her fertility coaching clients after they go through childbirth to help them feel rejuvenated.

The last stop on my stem cell tour was Dr. Matthew Cook, a co-founder of BioReset Medical, who treats professional sports and celebrity patients in the San Francisco Bay area with a huge number of rejuvenation technologies, including stem cells. Dr. Cook recorded a fantastic interview for *Bulletproof Radio* during which he explained all the types of stem cell therapies available and some of the groundbreaking work he's doing.

Dr. Cook found that the muscles in my neck were putting pressure on the nerves in my arms, a problem that many baseball players develop. Because Dr. Cook treats members of the Washington Nationals and many other athletes, he knew exactly what to do. He used a procedure he had pioneered as an anesthesiologist to inject stem cells and fluid around the nerve to free it up. And it worked! Other doctors I'd seen had suggested removing one of my ribs as a possible treatment—which would have resulted in lifelong structural imbalances and chronic pain. Dr. Cook's one-hour treatment solved my problem for good.

This procedure has provided so much value to so many people that Dr. Cook left a successful career in anesthesiology to focus on regenerative medicine, where he has pioneered a type of stem cell treatment that uses ultrasmall stem cells, such as stem cells extracted from your own blood. Another innovation Dr. Cook has developed is a stem cell treatment for trauma. Using an anesthetic nerve block, he carefully injects stem cells next to the vagus nerve to reset the body's stress response. This procedure is like a hard reset of a computer. It turns off the fight-or-flight nervous system for eight hours; when it comes back on, you are in a "rest and relax" mode.

If you've ever experienced a highly stressful event, even as a child, chances are that parts of your nervous system are locked in fight-or-flight mode. This heightened stress reactivity is commonly found in patients with PTSD. When I had the reset procedure done, my resilience and cognitive function went through the roof. Dr. Cook also placed cells along my sinuses so they could enter the base of the brain, and within a half hour my vision noticeably improved, and I already had good vision. It was a shockingly effective procedure.

I truly believe (and hope) that in the not-so-distant future we'll be using stem cell therapy to eliminate the majority of degenerative diseases and stay forever young. The costs are falling rapidly. This could be a game changer not just for you and me but also for our children and all of humanity. Whether or not stem cell therapy is accessible to you, I highly recommend doing everything you can to repair old injuries. Your body will fix them well enough to make sure you can reproduce, but you want to fix them so well that you are free to do your work in the world for as long as you choose. Today we have the power to stay younger for longer and even to reverse some of the degenerative effects of aging. The world's highest performers are investing in innovative treatments to help them perform at their best for as long as humanly possible and to avoid the pain and suffering that could slow them down.

Action Items

- What are your three most significant accidents or injuries you recall right now?
- Do you experience *any* lingering pain or stiffness or lack of mobility in any of those areas? If so, it's time to get hacking until they're back to full strength.
- If you have chronic pain in a part of the body that's never been injured, it may be the result of an unresolved emotional trauma. Revisit the laws in this book about healing from trauma for guidance.

Recommended Listening
- Matt Cook, "Everything There Is to Know About Stem Cells," *Bulletproof Radio*, episode 512
- "The Healing Powers of Stem Cells" with Dr. Harry Adelson, *Bulletproof Radio*, episode 332
- Harry Adelson, "The Real Deal on Stem Cell Therapy for Pain Conditions," *Bulletproof Radio*, episode 412
- Amy Killen, "Treating & Curing Erectile Dysfunction with Stem Cell Therapy," *Bulletproof Radio*, episode 407

HAPPIER

BEING RICH WON'T MAKE YOU HAPPY, BUT BEING HAPPY MIGHT MAKE YOU RICH

One of the most revealing facts in the data I collected from top performers is that not one person, neither incredibly successful and wealthy entrepreneurs nor university professors, mentioned money as being one of their top three priorities. Money is simply not what drives or rewards this group of high-impact people. Though many of them have managed to accumulate vast wealth, it came as a side effect of pursuing their great passions and transcending their primitive minds. Indeed, when you master your base instincts and find lasting happiness, you free up huge amounts of energy that you can use to become more successful and wealthy.

This is a lesson that has taken me many years to learn. When I was a kid, I had a poster hanging in my bedroom that said, "Business is a game and you keep score with money." I cringe when I think back on that now, knowing that business is not a game; it's a skill and an art, and you measure your performance by the impact you make. Your team relies on your business for their livelihood, for their sustenance, and to provide for their families, and your customers trust you to do what you say you will and to provide more value than your service costs. If you think it's a game, it's one you're sure to lose.

I spent years chasing money, and the more I chased it, the less happy I was. Making money didn't make me happy, because money doesn't do that. After some reflection, I realized that my basic needs were being met and I was living well enough, so I focused on helping other people because that actually did make me happy. You can't put a price on the feeling you get when someone looks you in the eye and sincerely thanks you for making his or her life better. The financial rewards followed. And people who are far wealthier than I don't prioritize money, either. They know that money comes from happiness, not the other way around. Sure, you can make money—lots of it—by taking from others or doing things that you hate. But as long as you have enough to eat, it's just not worth it.

Law 32: You *Can* Put a Price Tag on Happiness

Once your basic needs have been met, focus your energy on doing great things that matter deeply to you. Making more money beyond a basic financial safety threshold does not substantially increase happiness or joy. So roll up your sleeves and do whatever it takes to know you've got your bases covered, and then swing for the fences.

If there's anyone who knows what does and doesn't make you happy, it's Genpo Roshi, a Zen priest and teacher in the Soto and Rinzai schools of Zen Buddhism. Since his spiritual awakening more than forty-five years ago, he's dedicated his life to helping others to realize their true nature and deepening his own journey. Genpo says that there is a sustainable state of happiness that is not predicated on conditions. In this state, happiness is your basic foundation.

Conditional happiness, on the other hand, is dependent on an outside factor. This is the "I'll be happy when . . ." mentality. *I'll be happy when I meet the right person. I'll be happy when I get a raise or a promotion.* I chased that form of happiness for years. When I made $6 million at the age of twenty-six, I'm embarrassed to admit that I actually told a friend who had also found sudden wealth, "I'll be happy when I have ten million." When I lost it all two years later, my stress levels increased, obviously, but my happiness (or lack thereof) didn't change.

When we're in that state of seeking, sometimes referred to as a scarcity mind-set, we can never be truly happy because we're focused on what we don't have. Happiness is always a carrot stick away. To be sustainably happy, you must be satisfied with what you have right now. Genpo says that when he realized he had enough money, he stopped seeking. He wasn't wealthy, but he had enough.

Once he stopped seeking and started simply allowing, he became happier and capable of achieving more than ever before. Genpo says that finding sustainable happiness is possible only when a few standards are met, including both mental and physical freedom. This means having enough money so that you feel somewhat secure instead of being constantly stressed about finances. It's hard to be happy when your body is in panic mode focusing on survival.

However, it's not impossible. After I finished business school, I spent some time in Cambodia, where the average income was about one dollar per day and the population had been traumatized by war. It was common to see people missing limbs due to land mine explosions. Even though those people often didn't know where their next meal would come from, I was humbled by how much happiness I saw in their eyes. Quite often, they had more happiness than I did. It might have come from their community, their families, or possibly their belief system, but it certainly didn't come from money. None of my previous experiences had prepared me to go to that war-torn area and see such happiness and resilience.

In the West, however, research has found that there is a baseline income that produces happiness. A 2010 study out of Princeton University determined it to be $75,000. The study revealed that this annual salary is the benchmark at which people can more easily feel sustainably happy and satisfied with the direction their life is going in.[1] (The number may be slightly higher or lower, depending on where you live, and inflation may have raised that number a bit, but it's a good starting point for thinking about your financial safety set point.) People who did not reach this threshold weren't necessarily sadder, but they were more stressed and worn down by worrying about basic needs than were their higher-earning counterparts. (You can find that theme throughout this book: nagging, continuous stress from *any* source whittles away at your game-changing energy.) But the most interesting thing about this study was that no matter how much more than $75,000 people earned, their happiness levels plateaued after their basic needs were met. Some studies put the minimum number higher, but all of them show that adding more income above a certain level doesn't meaningfully increase your happiness.

Not all of my podcast guests are financially supersuccessful, but all have reached a level of prominence in their fields, and the vast majority of them get a lot more satisfaction from their work than from the financial rewards it brings them. Several of them spoke about another threshold that most people never reach but many dream about: becoming a millionaire. There are about 11 million millionaires in the United States now (not counting Bitcoin holders). That's enough money to ensure that your basic needs are met *for life* if you manage it well.

Many of the millionaires I've spoken to have mentioned the personal freedom that reaching this threshold provides and warned against the entrepreneurial desire to risk losing it. I first heard about this from John Bowen, who helps incredibly wealthy families manage their money. He says that if you are ever fortunate enough to amass even a modest nest egg (also known as "failure capital," also known as "F-you money"), never put it at risk. If you are reading this book, you might be the type of person who is inclined to put everything on the line to pursue your passions. This is how I am, too, as are most of the entrepreneurs I know. It's that instinct that caused me to lose the amazing windfall I earned as a young man. When you're passionate about what you're doing and comfortable with risk, it's all too easy to put it all on the line. But the wealthiest and most successful people I know say to fight that instinct and guard your nest egg with your life. If only someone had taught me that sooner!

I spoke with Shazi Visram, the founder and CEO of Happy Family, an organic baby food company that she founded and later sold for a reported $250 million. It was enough money for her to retire and maintain a luxurious lifestyle. Yet she says that when she earned that money, she didn't earn the right to be happy forever. What she earned was the ability to stop worrying about money forever (unless she lost it). The daughter of immigrants, Shazi grew up in a motel room in Alabama for the first seven years of her life, so gaining the ability to never have to worry about money again was a pretty big deal. She says that immigrants and the children of immigrants never forget being hungry. It's imprinted in their DNA.

The fear of not having enough once she actually had enough was what drove Shazi to protect her nest egg at all costs. But apart from that fear sitting on one shoulder, she is an ambitious hard worker who believes in the magic of creating her own opportunities. Her desire to take some chances and try to double, triple, or quadruple her nest egg has frequently threatened its core. To avoid that, she has chosen to focus on joy, not success. Once you've tasted success, it's hard not to want more and more. And you likely will have more and more, but that's not the endgame. Shazi advises to take the time to up your game. Make it about amassing joy, not just successes in the form of accolades or money.

Shazi also advises leveraging your nonfinancial assets after a big win. For her that meant investing her time, energy, creativity, and ability to work through difficult challenges for businesses she believes in rather than risking too great a portion of her net worth to purchase equity. (I am greatly honored that my company is one she believes in.) Shazi recommends preserving your financial assets with discipline and support. Invest wisely, and stick to the rules. Find a trustworthy financial adviser who understands the spirit of your money and will help you define the liquidity you have for taking risks on investments and new ventures. It may be zero, and that's okay. The odds are that you probably aren't the best person to determine how to allocate your assets—even modest ones—because you're too close to them.

In addition, she recommends that you be careful of becoming a deal junkie, because sometimes the thrill of the deal or the charm of the entrepreneur or the excitement of the mission clouds your judgment. The same thing is true of day-trading stock options or buying into that hot new ICO you read about online. If you are looking for thrill-seeking adventure and activity, go elsewhere (like maybe try kite surfing) until you really have true F-you money, which both Shazi and I truly hope you do one day.

But remember that real success is the joy you derive from your life. Money can help with that, but it is not the one and only or even the main pathway to joy. Think of it as a slightly nicer car with a smoother ride and a good sound system. It's enjoyable to ride in, but any other decent working car will get you to your destination, too.

Coincidentally, one of my favorite stories about the power (or lack thereof) of money is also about cars, and it comes from my good friend, the legendary marketing guru Jay Abraham, who has significantly increased the bottom line for more than ten thousand clients worldwide. Jay has studied and solved almost every type of business question, challenge, and opportunity. I call him when I'm stuck. He has an uncanny ability to see hidden assets, overlooked opportunities, and undervalued possibilities.

Jay started out at age eighteen holding three jobs at a time and always felt insecure and undeserving; he felt the need to have external trappings to prove his worth to others. He made the equivalent of $35 million at the age of twenty-six, which he actually doesn't recommend unless you are exceptionally mature, well grounded, and exceedingly focused on making a difference long term. For Jay, it led to his having three midlife crises. Each time he asked, "Is that all there is?" Money wasn't making him happy. In other words, he was still seeking.

When Jay initially started making a lot of money, the first thing he did was go out and lease a top-of-the-line Mercedes-Benz, which he'd always wanted. He then drove over to a colleague's house from a previous low-paying job, parked his magnificent new Mercedes out front and all five feet, seven inches of him sauntered up to show off his new material trapping of success. His friend opened the front door, looked at him, looked at the big, expensive Mercedes out front, looked at Jay again, and said, "Funny, you don't look any taller!"

Jay says that he should have learned from that, but coming from a low-income background he initially craved external acknowledgment from the world. So every time he got stressed, he would go out and buy a ludicrously senseless luxury car. The funny thing was that he'd get maybe a week or two of joy out of owning it and then rarely drive it before ultimately realizing it couldn't give him the internal certainty, confidence, purpose, passion, or therapeutic comfort he was after. Then he would quickly sell it for a significant loss. Finally, he realized that the greatest enjoyment most people get from owning exotic cars and other flashy toys is the vicarious thrill they give others for the fleeting moments when you zip by them.

Jay tried everything to become happier. He went to his therapist for the usual fifty-five minutes but always felt as though his time was up just when they were getting to the good stuff. So he paid his therapist to work with him for several hours at a time for a full week. That cost plenty of money, but he gained profound insights that shifted his entire perspective on his life and business.

The therapist told him that most entrepreneurs are focused on attaining an end product: the fastest-growing company, the biggest house, the most toys, the best-looking spouse, whatever. However, if you are unlucky enough to achieve any or all those things for mere achievement's sake, it's anticlimactic: the skies won't open, the angels won't sing, pure happiness and joy won't automatically befall you. In actuality, your problems, challenges, and stress only multiply. The real thrill of business and life is the process, the quality of interactions and relationships, and the value you contribute to others. The lesson was simple yet profound: the success that you think is going to rock your boat (or yacht, as the case may be) will actually just poke holes in it if the journey isn't meaningful and enjoyable.

It's okay to want to be rich. Just make sure your happiness isn't tied to your money.

Action Items

- If your basic needs are met, stop seeking. Money won't make you happy. What annual income do you actually *need* to have your needs met? _____
- What would you do if you made twice that amount tomorrow?

  _____

- That's a good hint about what makes you happy. Start doing more of that now!
- If you've been lucky enough to secure a nest egg, protect it with your life. Get help managing it carefully, and focus on leveraging your nonfinancial assets to achieve interest payments in joy, not dollars.

- Focus on the journey, not the destination. If you don't enjoy yourself along the way, you won't be happy when you get there, either.

Recommended Listening
- Genpo Roshi, "Learn How to Meditate from a Zen Buddhist Priest," *Bulletproof Radio*, episode 425
- Jay Abraham, "Biohacking Secrets for Success from the Greatest Executive Coach & Marketing Strategist in the World," *Bulletproof Radio*, episode 396
- Jay Abraham's miniseries of interviews with me at The Abraham Group, www.abraham.com

Recommended Reading
- Dennis Genpo Merzel, *Big Mind Big Heart: Finding Your Way*
- Jay Abraham, *Getting Everything You Can Out of All You've Got: 21 Ways You Can Out-Think, Out-Perform, and Out-Earn the Competition*

Law 33: Wealth Is a Symptom of Happiness

Happy people are engaged, productive, and successful. You must focus on what makes you happy today because being happy unlocks a new level of potential in everything you do. Happiness makes it far easier to change your circumstances, your neighborhood, or maybe the whole world.

Happy people are more successful than people who are less happy. That may seem like an exaggeration, but it's not. Specifically, happy people on average have 31 percent higher productivity than their less happy peers, their sales are 37 percent higher, and their creativity is three times as high.[2] Researchers attribute these differences to the power of positive thinking. Happy people think more positively, and that "can-do" perspective leads to increased success.

But happiness isn't just linked to personal success. Happy people also earn more money for both themselves and their employees. A study by Gallup Healthways showed that employees with low life satisfaction stay home from work an average of 1.25 more days per month than their happy peers do. This translates into a loss of fifteen days a year.[3] In addition, researchers at Gallup found that retail stores that scored higher on employee life satisfaction generated $21 more in earnings per square foot of space than other stores, adding $32 million in additional profits for the whole chain all together.

Perhaps no one knows more about the connection between happiness and productivity than Vishen Lakhiani, whose company, Mindvalley, has been certified as one of the world's best workplaces by the Great Place to Work Institute. Vishen says that happiness is fuel that gets you to your vision faster. Most people miss out on that fuel because they believe they'll be happy *after* they achieve their vision. They are stressed out and unhappy because they have not decoupled their happiness from their vision. They're waiting to get to a destination. As Genpo would say, they are seeking. But when you realize that you can find happiness along the journey, everything changes.

In his book, *The Code of the Extraordinary Mind: 10 Unconventional Laws to Redefine Your Life and Succeed on Your Own Terms*, Vishen talks about his concept of "Blisscipline," the discipline of bliss. He has formulated a daily methodology to hack your happiness levels and transform happiness into rocket fuel to get you to your vision faster. This involves changing the way you set goals for yourself. Vishen explains that there are two kinds of goals: means goals and end goals. For example, wanting to get a college degree, get a job, get married, and have a million dollars in your bank account are means goals. They don't really speak to your happiness because they're all really a means to something else. You want a college degree so that you can do something else (for example, get a job and make money). You want a million dollars so that you can be something else (a millionaire whom everyone respects). You want to get married so you can feel something else (such as connected and supported instead of lonely or afraid).

The "something else" is the end goal. These goals are typically feelings-oriented, such as, I want to travel the world, I want to wake up every day next to the love of my life, or I want to experience the joy (and frustration) of raising a child. When Vishen created his company, he did it with an end goal in mind: "I want to build a company for the sake of learning how to function as a team and develop my leadership skills and have the thrill of building something unique." That focus has brought true happiness to Vishen and the rest of his team.

Vishen says that end goals fall into three distinct buckets: things you want to experience, ways in which you want to grow as a human being, and ways in which you want to contribute to or leave your mark on the world. When you're setting practical goals for yourself, Vishen says, it's important to take the time to consider these end goals.

When you do so, you stop aiming for the million dollars, though it may come to you anyway. Because Vishen says that focusing on end goals leads to creative output that will help you become successful. But when you plan this way, you can avoid the trap that so many millionaires fall into of having money in the bank but hating their lives. Those people make the mistake of focusing on the means goals and sacrificing their end goals.

When Vishen refactored his goal list, he decided to completely give up one of his companies because it was making him miserable. He sold all his shares, took a loss, and escaped. As soon as he did, he instantly felt happier. Next, he decided to start his own festival, which became Awesomeness Fest and is now called A-Fest. When he had the idea, Vishen knew it made no business sense to start a festival, but he felt compelled to do it. It was aligned with his end goals. Today A-Fest is one of his greatest legacies. Every year, thousands of people apply to join him in a beautiful location and learn from amazing teachers. That was never a part of his plan, but when he created his list of end goals, he found a path to success and happiness.

Action Items

- Set new means goals by asking yourself these questions to determine your end goals:
  - What do I want to experience?

- How do I want to grow?
- How do I want to contribute to the world around me?

Recommended Listening

Vishen Lakhiani, "10 Laws & Four-Letter Words," *Bulletproof Radio*, episode 309

Recommended Reading

- Vishen Lakhiani, *The Code of the Extraordinary Mind: 10 Unconventional Laws to Redefine Your Life and Succeed on Your Own Terms*

Law 34: The Less You Have, the More You Gain

A certain amount of belongings is necessary and valuable, but society programs you to believe that objects will make you happy. The opposite is true: when you get rid of the things that don't bring true value and make room in your life for the things that do, you become happier and more content.

Joshua Fields Millburn is a minimalist who has helped more than 20 million people pare down their lives through his popular podcast, website, books, and documentary. But several years ago, he was living a very different life. He says that he was successful in a narrow sense. But he was out of shape and overweight, his relationships were in shambles, and he didn't feel creative or passionate about what he was doing even though he had a financially successful career.

Joshua felt that he wasn't growing or contributing to the world around him, two of Vishen's all-important end goals. He was focused instead on so-called success and achievement, and in our culture that means the accumulation of what he calls the "trophies of success": things. He was living in a big house with more toilets than people to use them and more TVs than people to watch them. He had multiple luxury cars, closets full of expensive clothes, and a full basement that was jam-packed with stuff he thought was supposed to make him happy. But instead of feeling successful, he was discontent, anxious, and overwhelmed. He was making good money, but he was spending even more money, and before he knew it he'd racked up six figures' worth of debt and felt trapped under its weight.

Then, within a month, Joshua's mother passed away and his marriage ended. Those two events forced him to look around and take an inventory of his life, and he stumbled onto the idea of minimalism. He asked himself, "How might my life be better with less?" His answer was that he could improve his health because he would have more time to focus on taking care of himself. He could invest time in his relationships and finally make room to work on a passion project. He realized that he'd been using things as barriers to protect him from being vulnerable and taking risks.

Joshua began by taking a long look at his belongings and paring down as much as he could. He says that after that he derived more value from the things he owned. These days he sometimes tests his choices by sporadically depriving himself of something to see whether or not it truly adds value to his life. For instance, he might live without a cell phone for a month or go without home internet. When he brings those small luxuries back into his life, he does so in a much more deliberate manner and is intentional about how he uses them. He sees how they can enhance his life while remaining conscious of the ways in which they are wasting precious time and energy.

Ultimately, this minimalist approach has allowed Joshua to make room for life's most important things, which of course aren't *things* at all. To make room in your own life, Joshua recommends starting with the simple goal of getting rid of one item a day for thirty days. You will probably end up getting rid of more than thirty items because once you start searching your cabinets and drawers you'll gain momentum.

If you want to ramp it up a little bit, add some accountability and friendly competition. To do this, partner with a friend or a family member at the beginning of the month. Make a bet. It can be a dollar or a meal or whatever you want. (Try not to make it a material thing.) On the first day of the month, you both have to get rid of one item.

On the second day, you both have to get rid of two items. And so on. It starts off easy, but it gets pretty difficult by the middle of the month. Whoever goes the longest wins the bet. If you both make it to the end of the month, you'll each have gotten rid of almost five hundred items, so you'll really both have won.

When deciding what to keep and what to get rid of, ask yourself if you really need each item. Is it essential? Does it augment your experience of life, or is it a pacifier you use to sooth yourself or fulfill an emotional need?

Like Vishen, Josh warns against seeing "things" as an end goal. If you're working only for money to buy stuff, you're not going to feel fulfilled in the long term. Quite often the stuff ends up being the point until you realize, like Joshua, that it's not actually making you happy.

But is being happy the right end goal? Joshua doesn't think so. He believes that the pursuit of happiness in our society is a problem because it leads us to chase the wrong things. We mistake ephemeral pleasure for long-term happiness or contentment. To him the point is actually living a more meaningful life, aligning your short-term actions (the work you do, the ways you contribute, and the people you spend time with) with your long-term values. If you're able to do that, happiness is just a really great by-product.

After I spoke with Joshua, I sought out James Altucher, a self-made millionaire, serial entrepreneur, and bestselling author. James has taken minimalism to the next level: about three years ago, he gave away nearly all of his earthly possessions and decided to live the life of a nomad with no place to call home.

About a year prior to our conversation, James was traveling and had leases on two different apartments he was renting that were expiring. One was in the city where he worked, and the other was in the town where his kids lived. While he was away, James asked a friend of his to go to both apartments and sell, keep, donate, or throw out every single one of the items. He didn't want to ever go to those apartments again and have to deal with the fatigue of trying to figure out, once again, how to manage all of his objects and possessions.

He hadn't really been living a maximalist lifestyle before that, yet he had accumulated thousands of items. When his friend sent him photos of a hundred garbage bags full of stuff, James was shocked. He decided not to go through the process of renting again and accumulating more stuff and instead became a nomad. To experience other lifestyles and vary his lifestyle, he rented spaces via Airbnb and stayed as long as he liked in each one.

That lifestyle not only liberated James from being tied down by an apartment lease, it also helped him cut down on having to make thousands of small decisions about how to maintain and update a home and all of its possessions. He wanted to spend a larger percentage of his day making choices about what he really wanted to do instead of what he had to do, and dramatically cutting down on his possessions allowed him to do so.

Most people discover the hidden "management burden" of owning things when they buy a house for the first time. The amount of energy you spend repairing things, decorating things, and cleaning things is hard to imagine until you start doing it. What if you were to spend that energy on improving yourself instead of improving your home?

James kept two bags, one containing three outfits and the other containing a computer, a tablet, and a phone. He uses other items, but he doesn't own them. Instead of the sharing economy, James calls it the access economy. He has a gym membership to access the items he needs for exercise and a library card to access the books he wants to read. He prioritizes having access to everything he needs to make a living and be productive. He can take an Uber for $10 instead of spending tens of thousands of dollars on his own car. He can stay in an apartment in New York City for $300 a night instead of spending $2 million to own one.

James says that this is not minimalism, it's *choiceism*. He has eliminated as many difficult choices from his life as possible. That has freed up energy for him to focus on the things he loves to do. It's not always possible to do that, but if you stop seeking, focus on your end goals, and let go of your anchors, you can drastically improve your odds of focusing on the things you love to do.

About a year after my interview with him, James did stop his nomadic life, but he still practices the art of having less.

Action Items
- Make a commitment to getting rid of at least one item every day for the next thirty days.
- When going through items, ask yourself, "Does this add value to my life?"
- Explore choiceism by eliminating items and responsibilities that constantly force you to make decisions.

Recommended Listening
- "Minimalism: Living a Richer Life with Less" featuring The Minimalist, *Bulletproof Radio*, episode 372
- "How Giving Away All His Possessions & Living like a Nomad Made Millionaire James Altucher Happier & More Successful," *Bulletproof Radio*, episode 405

Recommended Reading
- Joshua Fields Millburn and Ryan Nicodemus, *Minimalism: Live a Meaningful Life*
- James Altucher and Claudia Azula Altucher, *The Power of No: Because One Little Word Can Bring Health, Abundance, and Happiness*

YOUR COMMUNITY IS YOUR ENVIRONMENT

Have you ever noticed how brainstorming aloud with a friend leads to more creative outcomes than when you do it alone, or how spending time with the right people sheds a new light on whatever obstacle you're currently dealing with? Or maybe you've simply noticed how much happier you are when you know you can count on seeing the same friendly faces at your weekly poker game or yoga class or even happy hour.

If any of these examples resonates with you, you know firsthand the power of community. And so do game changers: being a part of a community was their second most popular piece of advice. An astounding number of the innovators I interviewed praised the power of community to improve performance, boost success, and cultivate happiness. They see high-quality relationships as a fundamental element of a high quality of life. The people who are making a difference in this world prioritize connection.

Of course, not all connections are created equal. The wrong ones can create a tremendous amount of stress and sideline your performance or weigh you down and keep you stuck in the status quo. But when you find the right friends, relationships, and communities, they can bring happiness, fuel growth, foster security, offer insight and support, and challenge you to change your game.

I wish someone had given me this advice early in my career. I wasted a lot of time trying to succeed through fierce independence rather than acknowledging the power of connectedness. The truth is that no one can change the game by himself. It not only takes a village, it takes the right village. Build yours with intention.

Law 35: Get High With a Little Help from Your Friends

Social interaction impacts your brain chemistry—for better or worse. Seek out a strong community that inspires you, and reap the benefits in all areas of your life. Community leads to happiness, and happiness leads to success.

Recent research has shown that the benefits of connection and community are more than just anecdotal or experiential; they are neurological. The right kind of human connection helps your brain become stronger. As someone who grew up more than a little socially awkward and prone to introversion, I wanted to learn more about the cognitive benefits of social connection. So I reached out to Dr. Paul Zak. He is a scientist, prolific author, and public speaker whose research on oxytocin and relationships has earned him the nickname "Dr. Love." His current work applies neuroscience to improving marketing and consumer experiences. As such, he calls himself a "neuro-economist," a title few people in the world hold.

I first met Dr. Zak at an "influencer dinner" hosted by Jon Levy. Jon's dinners have gotten a lot of media attention because he insists that all guests refrain from disclosing their name or profession until after they've prepared a meal together. Instead of shaking my hand, Dr. Zak hugged me. That was how he greeted everyone. It didn't even feel (very) weird.

Decades ago, Dr. Zak was studying economics and biology and investigating how trust impacts international economic decisions when the legendary anthropologist Helen Fisher asked him, "Have you ever heard of oxytocin?" That question changed the course of Dr. Zak's career. He realized he'd found a biological mechanism that influenced not only individual behavior and decision making but also the process of international policy making.

When you interact with another person whom you perceive to be trustworthy, your brain sends a hormonal signal that the relationship is safe and you should therefore proceed with it. The hormone is oxytocin. When you get a hit of oxytocin, you are motivated to continue interacting with the other person because it makes you feel good. It works against our built-in fear system, which warns you to be cautious and hide or run away from strangers.

Understanding oxytocin is important because a lot of good things can come from interacting with other humans. Everyone is a stranger to everyone else at first. But another person might become a friend, a professional collaborator, even a life mate. Whether or not you pursue a connection is largely determined by your body's chemical response to an individual.

Oxytocin also amplifies empathy, which is a critical component of any authentic human connection. Empathy allows you to imagine another person's pain. When you feel empathy for someone, you are motivated to treat him or her better because you can put yourself into his or her shoes emotionally. New research shows that only 10 percent of empathy is hardwired. The other 90 percent is a learnable skill.[1] Studies also reveal that oxytocin is heavily implicated in the mirror neuron system,[2] which makes perfect sense since mirror neurons fire when you act and when you observe someone else completing the same action, as if you were doing it yourself.

Dr. Zak has run hundreds of experiments measuring oxytocin levels in participants' tissues and blood and manipulating it using oxytocin injections or nasal spray, and has been able to observe that an increase in oxytocin makes people more generous and trusting and less suspicious. It also makes them better able to read social cues. Once it is stimulated, your brain's production of oxytocin stays active for about twenty minutes. During that time, the divide between you and others is narrowed. Your ego recedes into the background, and you see more commonality than division between you and your fellow humans.

Any type of human interaction boosts your oxytocin level, but some are more effective than others. Face-to-face communication stimulates the greatest oxytocin release. Videoconferencing is second best, then talking on the phone, then texting, and finally social posting. Empathy is actually decreasing in the younger generations because of their reliance on technology to connect with friends and peers.[3] I may be a tech guy, but I still value face-to-face interactions, and so should you.

Another great benefit of oxytocin is that it reduces your stress response and dramatically boosts your happiness. And social interaction is an incredibly simple way to get a quick hit of oxytocin. Dr. Zak suggests that the next time you're feeling stressed, isolated, or depressed, turn to someone you care about and say, "I'm having a bad day; I could use a little extra love right now." This is a powerful way of prioritizing your own happiness and the health of your relationships.

I have put this advice to use in a lot of really beneficial ways. Bulletproof followers were getting some benefits of oxytocin when they interacted on my online forums, but I created physical cafés so they would have places to meet in person, build community, and boost their oxytocin levels even higher. That was also one of the motivating forces behind the creation of Bulletproof Labs in Santa Monica, where people can connect with one another while upgrading both their minds and bodies. In addition, I've learned to prioritize face time with my staff as well as my friends and fellow entrepreneurs. I live on an organic farm on an island in a rural area, and there are lots of benefits to it, but one downside is that I have to get onto a plane to connect with my team and some of my favorite communities around the country. When I don't take time to do so, my performance goes down, and so does my happiness. Connection is not optional; it is essential.

Action Items
- Shake less, hug more. Physical contact stimulates oxytocin release.
- Schedule a massage to raise your oxytocin.
- Videoconference instead of calling when you can.
- Take the time to meet face-to-face when you can.

Recommended Listening
- "Hugs from Dr. Love" with Paul Zak, *Bulletproof Radio*, episode 334
- Lindsey Berkson, "How Our Toxic Environment Is Impacting Our Sexy Brains and Hormones," *Bulletproof Radio*, episode 418

Recommended Reading

- Paul J. Zak, *Trust Factor: The Science of Creating High-Performance Companies*

Law 36: You Are a Reflection of Your Community

Create a safety net of people who will be there for you when you need them long before you ever need them. Make sure they bring out the best in you and push you to think bigger and be better. The motivational speaker Jim Rohn said that you are the average of the five people you spend the most time with. Choose them carefully.

You read earlier about bestselling author and wellness expert JJ Virgin's son, Grant's, miraculous recovery from life-threatening injuries after he was the victim of a hit-and-run accident. Long before that happened, JJ had built a strong community of wellness experts whom she frequently brought together through conferences and events. Many of them credited JJ with helping them reach their goals and become the success stories they are today.

Then the accident happened. JJ's first big book, *The Virgin Diet*, was about to launch. She had everything invested in that book. Not only had she spent the entire advance she'd received from the publisher on marketing and publicity efforts, but she had even invested her own savings. As the primary breadwinner for her two sons, JJ had to make that book a success. She cared deeply about its message, she was counting on it to provide for her family, and now her son's life literally depended on it.

Of course, when JJ was building her connections, she wasn't planning on needing them to help launch her book. But when Grant was in the hospital, they showed up in force to help with everything from the book launch to Grant's care. Someone whom JJ had barely known before the accident was Dr. Anne Meyer, a rehabilitation doctor who works in the brain trauma unit at Cedars-Sinai Medical Center. She showed up one Friday night armed with essential oils that helped reawaken Grant's senses. One of JJ's girlfriends put her in touch with Dr. Donald Stein, who'd been studying progesterone therapy in the treatment of traumatic brain injuries for decades. Another friend put her in touch with Dr. Barry Sears, who in 2006 had consulted on the first-ever case of using high-dose fish oil to treat traumatic brain injuries (and was a guest on *Bulletproof Radio*). JJ began using progesterone cream and fish oil on Grant, who came out of his coma soon after.

JJ's community sent word to their own networks, and JJ started to receive kind gestures from complete strangers. One family she had never met before drove three hours to the hospital just to pray at Grant's bedside. Before long, there were prayer circles for Grant all over the world. When she sat by his bedside, JJ could feel all of that love and healing energy being directed at him from people around the globe.

Who's to say how much each of those interventions ultimately helped Grant recover? JJ is confident that each of them played a role. They also did the meaningful work of helping her feel cared for during the most difficult time in her life. That was valuable, and it wouldn't have happened if she hadn't already invested so much of her energy in creating a deep and supportive community. In fact, before Grant's accident, JJ had twisted my arm to make me start going to networking events with her, because she knew the value of building a community of people who could inspire me to up my game. It worked, and as I connected with more game changers, their desire to help others—even me—was infectious and inspiring.

It turns out that happiness is literally contagious. In a longitudinal study of nearly five thousand people, researchers saw that happy people cluster together, and the relationship between people's happiness extends up to three degrees of separation (for example, to the friends of one's friends' friends).[4] This isn't just a coincidence or a result of happy people naturally gravitating toward each other. Researchers concluded that people who are surrounded by many happy people are actually more likely to become happy in the future. And you already know that happy people are more successful.

This leads to a positive feedback loop of relationships and happiness. Happy people have more and better-quality relationships, which extends their own happiness to others and helps make them even happier. When researchers compared the upper 10 percent of consistently very happy people with average and very unhappy people, they found that the happiest people were more social and had stronger romantic and other social relationships than those in the less happy groups.[5] Being part of a community also creates a sense of safety, which is calming for your primitive brain.

I took JJ's advice and began spending more time with other game changers, including many of the ones in this book, and along the way I have learned so much from them that has made an enormous difference in my life. One of those people is Tony Robbins, who helped teach me which things can be learned from others and which things you need to learn yourself. He says that we can all learn the science of achievement, or how to take your vision and make it real, from others. We should all be standing on the shoulders of the people around us instead of reinventing the wheel. But you won't learn what he calls the "art of fulfillment," or what is going to fulfill you, from anyone else. You have to figure it out for yourself. This is crucial, because, as Tony says, success without fulfillment is the ultimate failure.

Tony says he gets phone calls all the time from multibillionaire entrepreneurs, politicians, and people who just won an Academy Award but are depressed. They feel they can't tell anyone how they really feel because they've reached all of their goals but still don't feel fulfilled. They don't have a sense of meaning in their lives. Tony says the antidote to this is to focus on things outside you. This requires not only thinking bigger but also thinking beyond your own ego. There is a reason that so many of the game changers in this book have dedicated their lives to making the world better for the rest of us. Success comes more naturally after you stop thinking about what you want and start thinking about what other people need. Most people believe they can improve only in small incremental steps, but Tony advises you to think ten times bigger about the impact you can make. This shifts your focus from making a little bit more money to making a difference in a way you truly care about and that is bigger than yourself. That is what leads to true fulfillment and happiness.

Another person who has helped me start thinking bigger is Peter Diamandis, the founder and executive chairman of the X Prize Foundation, named one of the world's fifty greatest leaders by *Fortune* magazine, who is literally creating robots to mine asteroids. I am grateful to Peter for calling me out years ago and telling me that I wasn't thinking big enough about the impact I could have. That advice and my friendship with Peter have profoundly impacted many areas of my life.

Peter's advice is to think about the group to which you most want to be a hero. Whom do you want to inspire, and what do those people need? Answering this question will help you determine your purpose. Once you have a better sense of your purpose, you can ask yourself: What is your "moon shot"—your big, bold idea—within that purpose? Peter told me to come up with a bold idea that I could really get excited about and to let go of what I thought I knew about why it was impossible.

That's how I came up with my moon shot: to disrupt industrial food production because I believe the most important thing food does is change how you feel, but food manufacturers are stuck in a loop of making cheap, addictive food that makes you feel bad. Bulletproof Coffee was the start, but Peter made me think even bigger. Before learning from him I thought that remaining a small, privately held e-commerce company was the best route because I could sell directly to people without a middleman, but thinking bigger allowed me to see that my real goal was to help millions of people feel good, and remaining small wouldn't allow me to do that. In the last few years, people have consumed more than a hundred million cups of Bulletproof Coffee. That wouldn't have happened without a community of people who helped me see where I was thinking small.

This doesn't mean that you should spend time only with people who think and act just like you do. I thoroughly enjoyed a hilarious and surprisingly profound conversation with JP Sears, a life coach and comedian who is best known for his satirical parodies of veganism, new-age beliefs, gluten-free foods, and, yes, even the Bulletproof

Diet. JP says that he doesn't like hanging out with like-minded people because they don't help him grow. He prefers seeking out like-*hearted* people who are accepting of him but think differently. And he said it while wearing his wife's leopard-skin tights.

It's comfortable to be with people who think like you. Everyone agrees with you, so you feel safe, but you're not being challenged. When you are faced with something you disagree with, you have an opportunity to grow. Instead of creating resistance and more division, JP recommends seeking to understand it from an opposing or just different point of view. The goal isn't to change your mind or convince someone else to change theirs. Rather, it's to land in a space in between, which JP says is the definition of understanding and tolerance. Of course, empathy is a huge part of this, which is why we tend to get along better with people we disagree with in person than we do in online interactions. Face-to-face interactions lead to increased oxytocin levels, which lead to more empathy, which leads to stronger connections.

This is not only important advice to practice externally, it also applies to our own internal discord. Many of us don't give ourselves permission to be conflicted. Instead, we have conflict about our conflict. But if we can be okay with having opinions or emotions that aren't always in sync, we can find a sense of peace and connection within ourselves. JP says that just as nutrition comes from compost, accepting conflict can lead to peace, both internally and externally. You'll save a lot of energy when you stop fighting your inner conflict and embrace the full range of your thoughts and feelings without judgment.

Our tendency to seek the familiar and fight everything that challenges us is a product of our basic instincts to stay safe. But nobody has ever changed the game by playing it safe. As JP puts it, it's when we're in the mystery—when we're walking through the proverbial dark forest and stepping off the cliff, and we don't know exactly what we're going to land in, when we're going to land, and even if we're going to land at all—that we find exhilaration and inspiration. In JP's opinion, a necessary ingredient for a great life is the willingness to scare yourself to death in order to actually live and not just survive. This is what allows you to get out of the coffin of your comfort zone where you live on autopilot, repeating the same patterns. Break out of that coffin and actually embrace the mystery and the unknown. Connect with people who challenge you to grow in unexpected and sometimes uncomfortable ways.

Seriously, how much better would your life be if you were constantly surrounded by people who were as profound and inspiring (and funny) as JP? The people you choose to spend time with matter. Pay attention to whether or not your community consists of people who bring out the best in you or drag you down to their level. Never be afraid to change things up and create new connections. The people around you play a huge role in setting your limits or encouraging you to exceed them.

Action Items

- Set goals that reflect your desire to impact the world in a way that's ten times greater than you are now.
- Ask yourself whom you want to be a hero to and what those people need. This will help you determine your moon shot—your big, bold goal.
- Actively seek out people who challenge you to think differently and bigger, and spend more time with them.

Recommended Listening

- Tony Robbins and Peter Diamandis, "Special Podcast, Live from the Genius Network," *Bulletproof Radio*, episode 306
- Peter Diamandis, Part 1, "The Space Episode," *Bulletproof Radio*, episode 448
- Peter Diamandis, Part 2, "What the Hell Is a Moon Shot?," *Bulletproof Radio*, episode 449
- JP Sears, "Using Humor & Sarcasm to Improve Your Life, Revitalize Mitochondria & Defeat Self-Sabotage," *Bulletproof Radio*, episode 393

Recommended Reading

- Tony Robbins, *Unshakeable: Your Financial Freedom Playbook*
- Peter H. Diamandis and Steven Kotler, *Abundance: The Future Is Better Than You Think*

- JP Sears, *How to Be Ultra Spiritual: 12 ¹/₂ Steps to Spiritual Superiority*

Law 37: No Relationship Is an Island

Your intimate relationships have the power to drive you to new levels of success or failure. Fix or end a bad relationship to free up energy so you can do what matters most to you. Invest in any type of great relationship that works for you in order to unlock more power than being alone. Ignore tradition if it doesn't serve you, but seek the support of your community. The relationship that serves you will be stronger and last longer with a community backing it.

Though it may not always seem that way (ahem) if you're married or in a long-term committed relationship, studies consistently show that people who are in a long-term committed relationship, across age and gender, are generally happier than people who are not.[6] Of course there are lots of happy single people, too, but science shows that people in relationships are, on average, happier. From an evolutionary stand-point, intimate relationships support two of your three F's. Knowing that you have a stable partner provides feelings of safety and a sense of community, which lessens background fear. And as for that other F-word, if your body believes you have a hope of reproducing the species, it lowers background stress (even if you have no plans to do so).

Less fear, more sex—who wouldn't be happier? Lots of people. But when you're in a relationship that doesn't work, the opposite is true: your happiness—and your performance—plummet.

That's not to say that marriage is the only type of relationship that offers happiness. Many of the young people I work with are embracing polyamory and other "nontraditional" types of relationships that may be extreme but seem to make them happy and enable them to perform at their best. When I spoke with Christopher Ryan, a coauthor of the

New York Times bestseller *Sex at Dawn: How We Mate, Why We Stray, and What It Means for Modern Relationships,* he told me that the way we view sexual relationships today is largely a product of culture. After studying primatology, human anatomy, contemporary psychosexuality research, and anthropological literature, he believes the vision of our ancient ancestors' sexuality is clear: They were more egalitarian, fluid, and interdependent. They mitigated risk by sharing their resources instead of hoarding private property (and spouses) the way we do now. Chris reminds us that we didn't *descend* from apes; we *are* apes. We are living in an artificially created environment that is in conflict with our natural appetites and doesn't necessarily make us happy.

Knowing how deeply our intimate relationships affect our performance, I sought out one of the world's top relationship experts, Esther Perel. Esther is a psychotherapist and *New York Times* bestselling author who is one of the most insightful voices around on modern relationships. Like Chris, she believes that relationships are more complex and multilayered than we as a society like to admit. Our ideas about what constitutes a relationship are always changing. For instance, we have shifted the definition of monogamy from mating with one person for life to being with one person at a time. We often have multiple partners over the course of our lives due to breakups, death, and divorce.

Today the rules for relationships are shifting under our feet. We as individuals are navigating a host of challenges and opportunities that didn't exist a century ago, when decisions were made for us by legal and religious institutions. None of us knows where this is going to go. Just a generation ago, interracial, intercultural, interreligious, and gay couples were unheard of. Today they are the norm.

Interestingly, Esther says that any type of relationship—even a nontraditional one—will work better with the support of community. Every time a cultural norm begins to shift, people say it's impossible, it will never work. Esther reminds us that the first intermarriage in the United States was between a Catholic and a Protestant. People said it would never work. Then it was marriage between Jews and gentiles. People said it would never work. Then it was marriage between black and white, which was criminal until not too long ago.

People said it would never work. But those marriages were initially difficult because the couples were isolated. Not having the support of their communities, they had fewer resources and were less happy. As norms have shifted and mixed couples have gained the support of the people around them, such relationships have become more successful. It turns out that having a relationship doesn't fully quell the subtle biological fear that a relationship is supposed to address unless the relationship also has community support.

So maybe it's not so crazy to think that having more than one partner at a time will eventually become the norm again, as Chris believes it once was. Esther says that many people today want long-term relationships that combine all the values of a traditional marriage—companionship, economic support, family life, and social respectability—with a romantic partner who is their best friend, passionate lover, and confidant. They also want what Esther calls a self-actualization marriage, which includes the value of authenticity and truth to the self. According to Esther, this leads a surprising number of people to try open relationships. People want a committed, stable, secure relationship, but they don't want it at the expense of their personal freedom, self-expression, or authentic self.

In a passionate argument during the interview, Esther explained that although it's not done to avoid infidelity, ultimately polyamory might make a relationship last longer because both partners can experience a sense of self-actualization inside the relationship and therefore become a stronger couple. That's the goal: to last, to be stronger, and not to compromise the self in the context of a connection. If this is done with honesty and transparency, people may also be able to avoid the secrecy, lying, and deception that accompany infidelity.

Of course, this is not for everyone. Esther stresses the importance of knowing and being honest about what works for you. This, too, requires coming out of isolation. If you do not have the support of your community, any relationship will be more difficult. Esther says that the majority of people who practice polyamory keep it a secret out of fear of judgment, which leaves them lacking in the kind of community support that is critical for relationship success.

No matter the type of relationship, Esther stresses the importance of community. Look for examples of couples that inspire you. She says that when she asks her patients to name couples that inspire them, the majority of them come up blank. Yet when she asks them to name businesspeople or creatives or musicians or artists who inspire them, the list is endless. Treat your relationship with as much intention as you would any other part of your life and performance. Find examples of couples who inspire you, and work to gain their support. The more integrated into your community your relationship is, the more it will thrive and help fuel your performance.

People who do great things can take a lesson here. Work as hard on your relationships as you do at the gym or in your career, and make sure that whatever relationships you have are tied to a community. It's not self-indulgent to spend your time and energy working on your relationships; it's necessary in order to be happy, and happiness is critical to your success.

Action Items

- Ask yourself how happy you are in your current relationship. If it's making you miserable, it is hindering your performance. Either invest in fixing it or redirect your energy elsewhere.
- List three couples who inspire you. Don't know any? Start paying attention until you find some.

  - _____
  - _____
  - _____

- Are you in a community that supports the type of relationship you have or are looking for? If not, start with finding your community as a strategy for improving—or starting—a world-class relationship.

Recommended Listening

- Christopher Ryan, "Sex, Sex Culture & Sex at Dawn," *Bulletproof Radio*, episode 52
- Neil Strauss, "Relationship Hacks for Dealing with Conflicts, Monogamy, Sex & Communication with the Opposite Sex," *Bulletproof Radio*, episode 406

- "Sex, Marriage, and Business: Relationship Therapy" with Esther Perel, *Bulletproof Radio*, episode 456
- John Gray, "Beyond Mars and Venus: Tips That Truly Bring Men and Women Together," *Bulletproof Radio*, episode 414
- John Gray, "Addiction, Sexuality & ADD," *Bulletproof Radio*, episode 222
- Genpo Roshi, "Learn How to Meditate from a Zen Buddhist Priest," *Bulletproof Radio*, episode 425
- "Make Bad Decisions? Blame Dopamine" with Bill Harris, *Bulletproof Radio*, episode 362

Recommended Reading
- Christopher Ryan and Cacilda Jetha, *Sex at Dawn: How We Mate, Why We Stray, and What It Means for Modern Relationships*
- Esther Perel, *The State of Affairs: Rethinking Infidelity*

RESET YOUR PROGRAMMING

As I looked at the data from hundreds of successful people, it was incredible to see how many of them had shared their experiences with meditation. It's true that every so often I've sought out a guest with specific expertise in meditation, but most of the leaders who mentioned it as one of their most important pieces of advice were not meditation experts at all but high achievers in unrelated fields—the type of people you might not expect to be interested in something as "woo-woo" as meditation.

If you're under the age of thirty, you may not understand what's so incredible about successful people disclosing the fact that they meditate, but twenty years ago meditation was viewed a lot like smart drugs are today: very few people would admit to benefiting from it, but many top performers actually did. Years ago I listed meditation on my LinkedIn profile along with my use of smart drugs, and I'm sure the people who noticed it thought I was crazy. But it was Silicon Valley; engineers are already crazy, California is known for weirdos and out-there thinkers, and I was good enough at what I did to get away with being a little eccentric.

Occasionally someone would approach me after a meeting and say quietly, "So, you meditate? Me, too." People kept it a secret because they didn't want it to be held against them. Fast-forward to Silicon Valley today, and in the top ranks of almost any company, it's more likely to be held against you if you *don't* meditate.

It's a huge step in the right direction that we are able to publicly acknowledge the value of meditation, but we have a long way to go in terms of learning how to meditate efficiently and effectively. The idea that a meditation practice was one of the top twenty pieces of advice from high performers shows just how effective it can be. No matter what type of meditation you choose, a sustained practice helps you become more aware of your automatic thoughts and impulses, and with that increased awareness comes increased control. When you're able to live in the present moment and choose your responses to life instead of having them chosen for you by your primal operating system, you set yourself up for success. In other words, meditation creates awareness, and awareness creates choice.

Law 38: Own the Voice in Your Head

The critical voice in your head holds you back. It causes you pain, distracts you, and limits your potential. Meditation can help you understand when the voice in your head is distracting you with lies and when it's helping you. There is no excuse for living your life without owning the voice in your head. Meditate. Your happiness and performance are waiting for a huge upgrade.

In chapter 6, I shared Bill Harris's story about the tough period he went through in 2008 when the economy crashed and he went through a stressful divorce. During that time, he let his meditation practice slip, and before he knew it, he had racked up six speeding tickets and lost his driver's license.

What's the connection between a suspended meditation practice and a suspended driver's license? Meditation helps lessen your body's chemical response to stress. It does this, Bill said, by enhancing the workings of the parasympathetic nervous system, which is the source of rest and relaxation, while slowing the sympathetic nervous system, which triggers the fight-or-flight response. Meditation has also been shown to strengthen the prefrontal cortex, the part of the brain involved in decision making. So when you meditate regularly and somebody cuts you off in traffic, instead of feeling as though you are under threat and need to flee (or drive away fast, in Bill's case), your stress response stays in check and your prefrontal cortex can step in and help you make a good decision.

So how can you begin a meditation practice? Bill recommends that when you begin meditating, it's important to let go of expectations and just let things happen. Many people deal with life by resisting or hiding from the things they don't like. So when those repressed feelings come up in a meditation practice, they feel uncomfortable. But it's not the feelings themselves that are causing the discomfort; it's their resistance to those feelings. When you give yourself the space to feel and accept whatever comes up, it stops feeling uncomfortable, and you can then deal with those feelings appropriately.

When you begin meditating, try to step back from your brain for a moment and observe your thoughts with curiosity. Most people don't realize that there is a space between a trigger and a feeling. When you are triggered, you think that a stimulus is making you feel a certain way, but there's a system inside your head that interprets data from the outside from a fear-based perspective and translates it into a feeling. Your mitochondria, after all, want you to notice and obsess over potential dangers. But that just keeps you stuck in a vicious cycle of fear and reaction. The fear is what gets our attention and prompts us to take action. Someone cuts you off in traffic, your stress response is activated, you feel angry, and you scream obscenities out the window. When you can interrupt that system, you are able to see that you are not in danger even when your brain says you are. Then you can consciously choose to react with anger or fear or to simply drop it and not react at all.

With repetition and time, new neural pathways will develop that favor being happy, calm, peaceful, focused, and creative as opposed to reactive, angry, and resistant. Bill admits that he used to be really angry, rough around the edges, difficult to get along with, unhappy, and depressed. A consistent meditation practice changed him at his core and led him into a completely different life.

Vishen Lakhiani also credits meditation with turning his life around. Years ago, after working extremely hard to become an engineer at Microsoft, he realized that he hated programming and quit.

He then spent years trying to find something that he found meaning-ful and fulfilling. After starting a few companies that failed and being fired twice, he was out of money and sleeping on a couch he'd rented from a Berkeley college student.

That was in 2001, after the dot-com bubble burst, and the only job Vishen could find was dialing for dollars for a technology company that sold its product to law firms. He had to go through the yellow pages and call all the lawyers in the book to pitch them on the compa-ny's technology. There was no base salary, so if he didn't close a sale, he wouldn't earn any money.

In desperation, Vishen went to Google and searched for tips to help him succeed. The results led him to a meditation class. The teacher was a pharmaceutical sales representative who said that learning and applying meditation techniques had helped her boost her sales, so Vishen decided to try it. He used the techniques he'd learned in his meditation class at work. Before choosing a name from the yellow pages, he went into a deep state of meditation. Then he opened the yellow pages, and rather than calling lawyers to pitch at random, he ran his finger down the list of names, closed his eyes, and waited for an impulse. Then, when he opened his eyes, he called the name his finger was on.

Yes, this sounds weird. Vishen himself can't quite explain it. But within a week he doubled his sales. It was as if he were magically call-ing the lawyers who were more likely to buy. Indeed, the voice in his head was sending him a signal, telling him whom to call and how to tailor his pitch to each person. He continued to deepen his meditation practice. Before calling an attorney, he set an intention that the sale would go well only if it was in the best interest of everyone concerned. Then he visualized connecting his heart to the attorney's heart and imagined a friendly conversation during which he was receptive to the other person's needs and empathetic to them.

Once again, he doubled his sales. Within four months, he was pro-moted four times and eventually became the director of sales and opened a New York office for the company at the age of twenty-six. He became passionate about meditation. Knowing how much it had helped him, he wanted to share the knowledge with others, and that's how his company, Mindvalley, was born.

If you aren't convinced by Vishen's story, that's okay. I know lots of skeptical venture capitalists who admit that they go by "gut feel" when they decide to invest. (I also pitched an investment to one billionaire who did a Chinese astrology analysis on a start-up team I was working with before he'd invest!) Being skeptical and meditating are not mutually exclusive—just ask Dan Harris, an Emmy Award–winning journalist and self-described skeptic who admits he was surprised by how much he benefited from meditation. Like Vishen, he is on a mission to share it with others. He believes that meditation will be at the forefront of a public health revolution centered on physical *and* mental wellness, one that will address issues such as bullying, education, parenting, marriage, politics, and pretty much every other aspect of life and performance.

Long before Dan became a guest on *Bulletproof Radio* and an author, he was a correspondent on ABC's *Nightline*. He flew up to my home on Vancouver Island to interview me about how I'd used modafinil to get ahead in Silicon Valley. That interview put modafinil into the national spotlight as a smart drug. After the interview we meditated together in my backyard. I could tell he was a little skeptical about meditation, but he had done it before and was willing to go all in. My dog, Merlin, must have felt it, too, because he wandered over and sat on Dan's feet. Merlin always finds meditators and joins them; dogs can feel when someone's energy shifts during meditation.

As Dan developed a more serious meditation practice, he began to see that the reason he did things he didn't want to do was because he was unaware of his fear-based thoughts—and he'd let them take the driver's seat. For him, meditation was the building of an internal telescope that allowed him to see the activity of his mind so that it no longer controlled him. While there are a lot of other things that meditation can do, this is a simple goal for beginners or skeptics. It's not complicated. It's not mystical. It does not involve believing in anything, joining a group, wearing special outfits, or sitting in a funny position. It's actually very simple. But it still takes learning and practice.

Dan believes that his function on the planet now is to say this as clearly as possible, as loudly as possible, and in as many places as possible so that people start to see meditation as an option that is viable for them. What meditation or mindfulness allows anyone to do is to draw the line between useful and constructive anguish and useless rumination. If you are going to make an impact, there is going to be some mental churn and anguish at times. Some worries. Some plotting. Some planning. Some strategizing. Even some legitimate fear. But the seventeenth time you're catastrophizing some problem that has arisen, imagining every worst-case scenario in minute detail, meditation allows you to stop and ask yourself, "Is this useful?" That is one powerful result of meditation in action.

For example, when I spoke to Dan, his son was one and a half years old and going through a phase where he refused to brush his teeth. Dan's mind immediately began to tell him a story: He's never going to brush his teeth. He'll have meth mouth and will never be able to get a job, and his life will be ruined. Dan's mind had been telling him stories like that for years, but what meditation allowed him to do was simply become aware of them. Then he could choose to get off the train before becoming frustrated and reacting. That is precisely the space between the trigger and the reaction that Bill spoke about, and in my mind, it is one of the greatest benefits of meditation.

Dan wants everyone to understand that the mind is trainable. And the methodology for training it is available to anybody who's willing to do the work. You won't make the things that you don't like about yourself simply go away, but over time you can reduce the likelihood that you will be an asshole, that you will be impatient, or that you will be cruel to yourself or others. If that isn't a game changer, I don't know what is.

Action Items

- Find a meditation class online or in person. Sign up!
- Some tools I like:
  - 10% Happier meditation app from Dan Harris at www.10percenthappier.com.
  - Energy For Success meditation from Dr. Barry Morguelan at

www.energyforsuccess.com (it's playing in the background as I type this).

- For the first month, commit to doing at least five minutes of meditation every day. More is better. Just build the habit, and you'll naturally find the right type and amount for you.

Recommended Listening

- Bill Harris, "Hacking Meditation with Holosync," *Bulletproof Radio*, episode 186
- Vishen Lakhiani, "10 Laws and Four-Letter Words," *Bulletproof Radio*, episode 309
- "Mind, Buddha, Spirit" with Dan Harris, *Bulletproof Radio*, episode 343
- Barry Morguelan, "The Ancient Energy Discipline That Stimulates Healing and Vitality," *Bulletproof Radio*, episode 413

Recommended Reading

- Dan Harris, *10% Happier: How I Tamed the Voice in My Head, Reduced Stress Without Losing My Edge, and Found Self-Help That Actually Works—A True Story*
- Vishen Lakhiani, *The Code of the Extraordinary Mind: 10 Unconventional Laws to Redefine Your Life and Succeed on Your Own Terms*

Law 39: Hijack Your Body's Attention

Your breath controls your brain and your heart because a lack of oxygen will get your body's attention faster than anything. Train your body to stay calm during stressful situations by using your breath to your benefit. Train your body to use oxygen better. There is untapped energy available when your body stops stressing and gets more oxygen. Unconscious breathing lessens your impact in the world. And you are here to make an impact.

Wim Hof, who holds twenty Guinness world records for withstand-ing extreme temperatures, has climbed Mount Everest and Mount Kilimanjaro in only shorts and shoes. Wim is best known as "The Iceman," and you may have seen him on TV swimming among gla-ciers without a wet suit. He has developed a breathing technique that provides short bursts of oxygen to his cells, which trains them to use oxygen more efficiently. The breathing technique is a meditation technique, and it works because it teaches the body not to be stressed when it normally would be.

The first time I met Wim, he had dropped in on a Bulletproof Bio-hacking Conference, and I invited him onstage. Within a minute, he had me practicing his breathing technique while doing push-ups in front of three thousand people. It made me feel a little drunk, but he egged me on. As I staggered to my feet, I asked myself, "Who is this guy?" It turned out that Wim really does live fearlessly. You can hear it in his passion for what he does in our podcast interview.

Wim says that we have lost the ability to connect with our bodies at the most basic level, to use oxygen to change the chemistry deep in our tissues. The effects of this disconnection are worsened by the typical Western diet and lifestyle, which, he says, lay the ground-work for disease. If you drink polluted water or eat processed food, the body uses up a lot of resources and energy trying to detox itself, which creates cellular stress. One way to combat that stress is to use the breath to help restore balance. Wim's deep breathing technique not only protects him against the cold, it also gives him control of his body chemistry, enabling him to cleanse his tissues from the inside and create more cellular energy. And he's got the data to prove it.

His method is made up of three elements: deep breathing, gradual exposure to cold, and mind-set. It is based on forty years of fieldwork and has had impressive results. His first test group of eighteen people had no prior experience in the cold. After four days of training, they were able to endure for five hours in their shorts outside in wintertime in below-zero temperatures.

The reason this technique is so effective is that it optimizes the vascular system, which enables your body to distribute oxygen to the cells and throughout the bloodstream more effectively. This brings your resting heart rate down and reduces stress on your body. Your respiration rate (breath) directly affects your heart rate, and gradual exposure to cold slows the activation of the sympathetic nervous system (your fight-or-flight response). In other words, deep breathing in the cold calms the heart rate and alleviates stress in the body. Wim says that when we do this, we bring the body from a mode of stress and anxiety to relief mode, which leads to a surplus of energy that the body can use to heat and heal itself.

Wim suggests starting slowly. Once a week, finish your warm shower with a burst of cold water for thirty seconds, and gradually increase from there. To do his breathing technique, sit down, get comfortable, and close your eyes. Make sure you're in a position where you can freely expand your lungs. Wim suggests doing this practice right after waking up, when your stomach is still empty. Warm up by inhaling deeply and drawing the breath in until you feel a slight pressure. Hold the breath for a moment before exhaling completely, pushing the air out as much as you can. Hold the exhalation for as long as you can. Repeat fifteen times.

Next, inhale through your nose and exhale through your mouth in short, powerful bursts, as if you're blowing up a balloon. Pull in your belly when exhaling, and let it expand when you inhale. Do this about thirty times at a steady pace, until you feel that your body is saturated with oxygen. You may feel light-headed or tingly or experience a surge of energy that's literally electric. Get a sense of which parts of your body are overflowing with energy and which ones are lacking it—and where there are blockages between those two extremes. As you continue breathing, send the breath to those blockages.

If the cold is not for you, there are plenty of other ways to benefit from breathing exercises. I sought out Emily Fletcher, the founder of Ziva Meditation, to learn her meditation techniques for busy and active people. Emily began her meditation training in Rishikesh, India, and was inspired to become a meditation teacher after experiencing the profound physical and mental benefits it provided her during her ten-year career as a performer on Broadway.

I asked Emily which breathing technique she felt provided her students with the most profound benefits, and she instructed me in what she calls a "balancing breath" to balance the left and right sides of the brain. Emily says that a simplified way of looking at the brain is that the left side is in charge of the past, the future, and critical and analytic thought, all activities that have taken over our modern lives to an unhealthy degree, which is one reason we find it so difficult to stay focused on the present moment and even harder to surrender to a state of flow. Our poor little right brain, which controls creativity and problem solving, present-moment awareness, and intuition, is atrophying. The balancing breath is something you can do in your waking state to begin to correct the imbalance between the right and left sides of the brain.

Emily says that one of the benefits of meditation is that it thickens the corpus callosum, the thin white strip that connects the right and left hemispheres of the brain. This is valuable because the thicker your corpus callosum is, the better able you are to bridge the gap between the two hemispheres no matter what is going on around you. So even if your boss is yelling at you, you're stuck in traffic, or you're arguing with your spouse, you become better able to access creative solutions and remain focused on the present moment instead of reacting out of fear or anger. Incidentally, on average women naturally have a thicker corpus callosum than men do.

To practice the balancing breath, use the thumb and ring finger of your right hand. Gently press your right nostril closed with your thumb and exhale completely through your left nostril. Then inhale completely through the left nostril and close your left nostril with your ring finger. Release your thumb and exhale completely through the right nostril. Then inhale completely through the right nostril. Continue this pattern on each side, ideally ending the same way you started, with an exhale through the left nostril.

Emily says to do this fast if you're feeling tired and need a hit of energy to focus; do it slowly if you're feeling amped up or nervous and need to relax. It's also a good way to ease yourself into meditating. It's almost like pulling back on a bow and arrow so that when you go into your meditation your body can really surrender and let go.

Emily explains that the reason so many meditation teachers and yoga teachers use breath work as a doorway into the practice is that our breath and thoughts are two functions that we can control to some extent but that are both autonomic. We breathe involuntarily all the time, yet we can get in there and slow down our breath, speed it up, or change the nostril that we're breathing through. And we can do the same thing with our thoughts.

The mind thinks involuntarily, just as we breathe and the heart beats involuntarily. We will never get the mind to stop thinking—and that's not the goal of meditating, anyway. But we can get in there and monkey with it to a certain degree. And the more we meditate, the more we can move beyond the left brain's critical voice and become able to tap into that still, small voice inside us. When you start meditating, you are taking your right brain to the gym. It doesn't clear your mind. It's not about clearing your mind during the meditation itself. But it does turn the volume down on that critical voice, and then you can hear that little tiny whisper of an intuition. The more you cultivate and listen to that soft, guiding voice, the louder it gets.

Action Items
- Finish your morning shower with thirty seconds or more of cold water. Work up to it if you need to. Let the water hit your face and chest for maximum benefits.
- Practice a "balancing breath" for a few minutes a day, ideally before meditating.

Recommended Listening
- "Climb Everest in a T-Shirt and Shorts. Survive Submersion in Freezing Water for Hours. Wim Hof Tells You How He Did It!," *Bulletproof Radio*, episode 403
- Emily Fletcher, "Greater Sex, Better Sleep with Ziva Meditation," *Bulletproof Radio*, episode 224

Recommended Reading
- Wim Hof and Koen De Jong, *The Way of the Iceman: How the Wim Hof Method Creates Radiant, Longterm Health*

- Scott Carney, *What Doesn't Kill Us: How Freezing Water, Extreme Altitude, and Environmental Conditioning Will Renew Our Lost Evolutionary Strength*

Law 40: Hurry! Meditate Faster

Meditation costs you only the time and energy it takes to do it. The return is higher performance and happiness. Get a better return on your meditation investment by reducing the time it takes and increasing your benefits. Meditate. But once you know the basics, meditate better.

As you know, I've been meditating for twenty years. In that time, I've meditated with monks in Tibet, I've meditated with electrodes strapped to my head, and I've meditated in pretty much every possible way in between. What I've learned along the journey is that there are tons of people spending a lot of time meditating and getting far fewer benefits than they could, just as there are a ton of people exercising but not getting all the benefits of the effort they're exerting. Your time and energy are your most precious assets. Why would you spend more time to get energy than necessary? Game changers learn how to be badass meditators. Of course, if longer bouts of meditation give you personal or spiritual fulfillment, have at it! But if you're looking to get the best return on your time investment, take advantage of tools that will help you meditate faster.

Back when I was starting out as an engineer, a colleague invited me to come with him to learn breathing techniques from an Indian guru. I said no. The idea of a bunch of people sitting in a room breathing together seemed cultish and weird. It wasn't until a couple of years later, when the same program was described to me as a performance-enhancing technique, that I became interested in checking it out.

I attended an Art of Living weekend seminar for executives in a beautiful mansion in Saratoga, California, and was blown away. For the next five years, I did the program's breathing exercises every morning. I woke up at the crack of dawn every Saturday and drove forty-five minutes to do those breathing exercises with a small group of technology executives who had collectively made somewhere around a billion dollars. I learned the power of breathing and the incredible things it can do, and it was transformative. I performed better, I was more productive, and I was nicer to the people around me. My relationships, along with everything else in my life, improved.

The executives in that room took the time to get together because they found it equally worthwhile. It wasn't just the breathing that made the practice so effective, it was the sense of community we gained from doing it together. One of them told me, "I keep doing this because it's like taking a mental shower every week." Those game changers stacked the deck in their favor in every possible way. And I encourage you to do the same thing.

So many people begin a meditation practice only to give up a few weeks later because they don't see results. That's because they aren't practicing effectively or their egos get in the way. Others keep at it but spend years barely moving the needle when they could see results much faster. Meditation seems so simple that some people are resistant to hiring a teacher or coach, but it's actually much more complicated than it seems. Without the use of a teacher or technology to help you gauge if you're doing it right, it's very difficult to know when you are tapping into the correct brain states that will actually make a difference. Plus, since meditation is so popular these days, it's easy to do a quick internet search and find a lot of low-quality information that can lead you in the wrong direction.

To continue evolving my practice, I've relied on the people I interviewed for this chapter—Bill Harris, Emily Fletcher, Dan Harris, Vishen Lakhiani, and Wim Hof—all of whom teach meditation using high-quality tools and techniques. I've also sought out experts in the latest technology to take my meditation practice to the next level and get greater benefits in less time, culminating in opening my own neurofeedback facility in Seattle to advance my meditation and that of many game changers.

One fundamental technology of meditation is called heart rate variability (HRV) training. As we discussed in chapter 10, HRV is used to assess stress response. It has nothing to do with your heart's number of beats per minute. HRV measures the spacing between each heartbeat and compares it to the spacing of other individual heartbeats. When you are in a state of fight or flight, your HRV becomes very flat, with equal spacing between heartbeats. But when you are in a restful state of flow, the variability of your heart rate may go up or down, but the HRV increases dramatically. The spacing between two heartbeats will be much different from the spacing between two other heartbeats that come a moment later. Your HRV impacts everything from your brain waves to your cardiovascular health and even the people around you.

The HeartMath Institute, which has been researching HRV for years, makes technology that you can use to see what it feels like to have high HRV and consciously learn to put yourself into that state. It measures your heart rate, and as you breathe you get a signal (green for high HRV, red for low HRV) that tells you how well you're doing. I became proficient years ago and found it so effective that I began using it with executives I trained in human performance.

One of my coaching clients was a billion-dollar hedge fund manager who was in a chronic state of fight or flight but didn't know it. I recommended HRV training along with the right food, sleep, meditation, and other hacks. He was resistant to HRV at first, but after practicing for six weeks he felt a huge difference in being able to change his stress levels at will. He decided to try measuring his HRV at work. He got to his trading console early, clipped on the sensor, and the opening bell rang. He went into the red "stress zone" and stayed there all day. It took him another six weeks to be able to operate in a state of calmness while on the trading floor. His ability to get into a relaxed, focused state of flow at work allowed him to make better decisions, become a more successful trader, and have more energy at the end of the day. If you're wasting the energy in your nervous system all day without knowing it, is it any wonder you're tired?

Another option is to introduce elements into your meditation practice that actually alter your brain state. One way to do this is through sound, which has a vibrational frequency that affects your mental state. The audio soundtracks from Bill Harris's company, Holosync, provide specific sounds to play during meditation. There are also specific mantras you can use to help activate the state you're trying to achieve. Light also impacts the experience of meditation. Light-sound goggles blink lights outside your closed eyes to help you achieve a different brain state faster while meditating.

As with HRV training, once you are familiar with the feeling you achieve when meditating with some technological help, you know what brain states to aim for when you're meditating solo. More than a few times, I've been that weird guy on the airplane wearing blacked-out goggles with blinking lights leaking out the edges. I can't see other people, but I'm pretty sure I'm getting strange looks as I take control of my brain at 30,000 feet. To date, no one has kicked me off a flight for it, but I know that a few flight attendants have picked up their own light-sound goggles after we chatted about it. Do what it takes to gain mastery of your mind, and don't worry about what people think.

Even the color of light can have an impact on your brain state. I use TrueDark glasses with patented optical filters designed to induce deep sleep. It turns out that when I wear them, my brain quickly moves into a calm and relaxed alpha brain wave state, even if I'm not planning to sleep. Sure, I could meditate to get there, but if I can get there and answer emails in midair at the same time, that's awesome.

My final and most important meditation hack is meditating with electrodes stuck to my head that track my brain waves. Scientists have been monitoring brain waves for fifty years but almost always looking at dysfunctional brains. We now know what the brain waves of advanced meditation practitioners look like and how to train them.

I got my first EEG machine at home in 1997 and have upgraded that technology—and my brain—ever since. Having experimented with every type of meditation I could, I found that there is nothing that compares to having a computer give you feedback a thousand times a second. That's why I created 40 Years of Zen, a neuroscience facility in Seattle that trains successful people to perform at even higher levels. We have created custom hardware and software for taking the brain to another level, compressing years of meditation into five days of intense work in a place that looks suspiciously like Xavier's School for Gifted Youngsters. The goal is to be able to manifest the same brain states as people who have spent decades meditating. This is the ultimate cheat at meditation, and lots of studies show that neurofeedback can raise your IQ.[1] Seriously. The moon shot for 40 Years of Zen is to make meditation so accessible that we can raise the average IQ on the planet by fifteen points.

Over the past several years, I've been measuring the brain waves of high-performance people, and now we are analyzing them with machine learning so that for the first time in history we can understand the brain patterns common to people who are changing the world—and then make them teachable. The next step is to make this technology available in schools, offices, and homes in a safe and effective manner, which I am working on as I write. Hopefully by the time you read this book, you will be able to use the ultimate meditation cheat anywhere in the world, begin editing the voices in your head, and take a fast and efficient journey toward better performance and increased self-awareness.

Action Items

- Sign up for a meditation class, already. It's not that hard.
- Measure or train your heart rate variability. I use HeartMath for training and the Oura ring for monitoring my HRV while I'm asleep.
- Try other meditation hacks, for example light-sound goggles, Bill Harris's Centerpointe soundtracks, and/or TrueDark twilight glasses (disclosure: I helped to start TrueDark and am an investor). Do whatever it takes. There is value in unassisted meditation, but the tech will help you get it faster.
- Consider going to www.40yearsofzen.com to get your EEG work done.

Recommended Listening

- "Lyme Disease, Heart Rate Variability & Skincare," *Bulletproof Radio*, episode 297
- Eric Langshur, "Be a Boss with Your Brain, Heart & Gut," *Bulletproof Radio*, episode 457

(14)

GET DIRTY IN THE SUN

I would not have predicted that out of any possible piece of advice in the world, something as simple as going outside and getting dirty would be one of the top twenty responses from the people I've interviewed. Then again, I decided to leave the Silicon Valley tech world behind but to stay connected and move into the forest of Vancouver Island almost a decade ago in order to spend more time outdoors. My experience showed that the greatest gift I could give my kids was growing up in nature. It boosted my mood and cognitive performance immeasurably, and it turns out that I'm not alone. Spending time in nature nourishes your brain and your gut, helps your cells create more energy, and is at least as effective at treating depression as pharmaceuticals. No matter where you live, it is possible and essential to find the time and place to do something so basic that many people make the mistake of overlooking it: going outside. It helps you perform better when you're inside, too.

Law 41: Make Your Environment Less like a Farm and More like a Zoo

Most people live in a domesticated environment that is economically useful and efficient but devoid of the type of energy that can power you to new levels. Spend more time outdoors. See trees. Smell plants. Taste real food. Sweat in the sun. Shiver when it's cold. Give your nervous system a taste of the environment it evolved in so you can reap the returns as your biology changes to increase your performance.

Daniel Vitalis is in love with the idea of human wildness—as in free, sovereign, and undomesticated human life. His passion resides at the intersection of human zoology and personal development. In other words, he is keenly focused on understanding how we can use the wisdom of our ancestors and the benefits of their natural environments to reinvigorate our wild nature while simultaneously thriving in today's world. For two decades, he's been developing and applying practices modeled on the lives of early humans to help people get in touch with their wild sides. Some of the things he does are a little nuts, but he is inspiring a lot of people to maximize their performance in ways that are in line with mine.

Daniel uses the term "rewilding" to refer to the idea of restoring something to its natural, uncultivated state. It is the antonym of *domesticating*, which is derived from the same word as *domicile*— another word for house. In other words, *domesticated* means "of the house," and for thousands of years humans not only have been domesticating plants and animals but also domesticating ourselves. Along the way, we've created a domestic version of many naturally wild entities. The romaine lettuce we eat is a domesticated version of the wild lettuce *Lactuca serriola*. The dogs we have as pets are domesticated versions of wolves. And Daniel claims that humans today are not actually *Homo sapiens* but rather a domesticated subspecies he calls *Homo sapiens domestico fragilis*. Maybe a little over the top, but he's got your attention.

How has domestication changed us? Daniel says we are less robust and more graceful physically than our wild ancestors. We're leaner and thinner and smaller. We mate and breed in captivity. We eat a diet of domesticated food. We are therefore a domestic subspecies. That's radical thinking.

This means that there is a "wild" form of humans—indigenous people who still live in isolated pockets around the world. Daniel says that these wild humans are healthier, stronger, and fitter than the rest of us. But there aren't many of them left. Daniel believes that we are on the brink of a monumental change for human history, which is the extinction of wild humans. When this happens, he says, we'll lose the strength of our gene pool. This is why we must reawaken the wildness that's still alive in our DNA with daily practices that will kindle the fire in our wild roots.

This *rewilding* process entails taking a look at your lifestyle and asking yourself how you can reinstate some of the things that are natural to our species. Daniel says to imagine pulling a chimpanzee out of the jungle and bringing him home to live in North America. Is your interest in keeping that animal healthy so it can live a long and productive life? If so, you would set up a habitat for the chimp that resembled its natural setting as much as possible instead of sticking it in an apartment, handing it a remote, and feeding it processed foods. But the latter is exactly what we are doing to ourselves, so much so that Daniel believes we are halting our own evolution and harming our DNA for future generations. He suggests that there is a direct link between this degeneration of our genetic code and the increase in modern illnesses such as cancer, heart disease, diabetes, tooth decay, and bone decay. We're coming unglued.

Right now, Daniel says, we are living in a human factory farm. The purpose of a farm is not to promote the animals' health, happiness, well-being, and longevity. It's about achieving maximum productivity at any expense with the goal of ending that animal's life shortly. We're born in captivity. We're snipped and cut right after birth. We're traumatized. We're indoctrinated. We're brainwashed. Then we produce products, services, and taxation money nonstop until we die prematurely. That's a factory farm for humans. It's a dark interpretation of our lives, for sure, and it ignores the benefits of civilization. But this perspective does offer us some useful insights when it comes to maximizing human performance.

Daniel believes we can instead create a human zoo—a place that promotes an animal's maximum health, the expression of its wild behavior, and the preservation of its genetics so that the animal can live a long life. To live in a zoo, you must re-create a habitat and diet that's as similar to the wild version as possible, even though it can be only an approximation. That exactly meets the definition of biohacking: changing the environment around you so you have full control of your own biology. Daniel isn't suggesting that you need to go off the grid completely and start living in the woods. Instead, ask yourself:

If you were going to bring a wild human being into your house, how would you prepare? What would you have available for him or her to eat? What kinds of activities would you plan? Then consider how you could take advantage of the same changes to set up your life so that it's more of a zoo and less of a farm.

Of course, Daniel has faced a lot of criticism. He suggests that this is because the idea of wildness is taboo in a "civilized" society. In order to maintain our civilization, we have programmed ourselves to believe that there is something scary, unorganized, and inherently "other" about wildness and that if we get in touch with that part of us, it will erode all of the progress we've made and we'll become barbaric again.

Not only is wildness normal, it is healthy. We've seen how every step we've taken away from nature has led to a breakdown in our health, whether it's a result of sitting too much, not getting enough nutrients from plants and healthy animals, or the backbreaking labor of farming at the beginning of the Neolithic revolution. We were healthier in our wild environment. Before humans lived indoors, they had constant access to fresh air and didn't have to deal with things such as dust, which is dead skin that we now breathe in all day long in addition to the chlorofluorocarbons that air-conditioning and refrigeration have been releasing into the air since the 1930s and all of the toxins in our factory-produced carpeting and furniture.

We're never going to be able to go back to being completely wild, but Daniel and others recommend a few simple actions that can help awaken the wildness in your genes—all of which mirror the advice throughout this book: reduce your toxic load, improve the quality of your diet, increase your exposure to fresh air, sunlight, soil, and clean water. Basically, begin the rewilding process by immersing yourself in a natural environment when you can get outside and changing your environment inside to be more natural.

Action Items

- Get some indoor plants. (Be sure to get organic plants without pesticide on them and control for mold growth in the soil. I use Homebiotic spray, which contains natural soil bacteria that combat indoor fungus.)

- Go for a hike in nature every time you travel.
- List three ways you can make your environment more like a zoo than a farm:

  - _____
  - _____
  - _____

Recommended Listening

- Daniel Vitalis, "ReWild Yourself!," *Bulletproof Radio*, episode 141
- Zach Bush, "Eat Dirt: The Secret to a Healthy Microbiome," *Bulletproof Radio*, episode 458

Law 42: Allow Your Body to Make Its Own Sunscreen

Sunlight is a nutrient. Just as eating too much food can give you diabetes, getting too much sunlight can give you cancer. But replacing sunlight with junk light is like replacing real food with junk food. You will perform better and live longer when real, unfiltered sunlight bathes your naked skin and enters your eyes for at least twenty minutes a day. It will improve your sleep, act as an antidepressant, and give you more energy. Sunlight is not optional.

You read earlier about Dr. Gerald Pollack's incredible work discovering a fourth phase of water that is not a liquid, gas, or solid but a gel called exclusion zone, or EZ, water. This is the type of water that is in our cells and that your mitochondria (the millions of power plants in your cells) need to create energy. Recently, scientists have discovered mysterious cell structures called microtubules that are required for you to build new mitochondria and move them around in neurons,[1] and it turns out that EZ water is essential to movement within micro-tubules.

There are a few ways to create more EZ water. You get EZ water naturally when you drink raw vegetable juices, fresh spring water, or glacial melt water, and it forms spontaneously when regular water is vibrated or blended. Recent research by Dr. Pollack shows that even more EZ water forms when you blend butterfat into water. Better yet, EZ water forms in your cells when you expose your skin (and your eyes, the gateways to the brain) to unfiltered sunlight for a few minutes every day without sunglasses, clothing, or sunscreen.

Specifically, it's 1,200-namometer light that creates EZ water, although sunlight also has other spectra with beneficial effects. For instance, the red light found in sunlight is absorbed by the hemoglobin in your blood and by mitochondria, which adds electrons to your cells. They are the same type of electron your body normally makes from combining food and air.

There is so much confusion and fear about sun exposure that many people take great pains to cover every inch of their skin before going outside. We slather on sunscreen, wear sunglasses, and cover up with clothing. But our bodies thrive in natural sunlight. Of course, it is not healthy to get so much sun exposure that you get sunburned, but a small amount of sun exposure every day stimulates collagen production in your skin and is good for your brain, your mood, and the water in your cells.

To get some information on sun exposure and sunscreen, I sought out Dr. Stephanie Seneff, a senior research scientist at the MIT Computer Science and Artificial Intelligence Laboratory, whose research concentrates mainly on the relationship between nutrition and health. She has written ten papers on modern-day diseases and the impact of nutritional deficiencies and environmental toxins on human health. She's my favorite type of game changer—an expert in one field who moved to another field and disrupted it because she saw things a different way.

Dr. Seneff says that melanoma rates have increased in step with the increased use of sunscreen. Though causality has not been proven, there is a strong correlation between sunscreen use and melanoma, which doesn't make sense since sunscreen is supposed to protect you from the harmful sun's rays. But Dr. Seneff explains that the connection actually goes back to glyphosate, the herbicide in Roundup, which, she says, disrupts the skin's natural ability to protect itself from the sun.

Gut microbes normally produce tryptophan and tyrosine, amino acids that serve as precursors of melanin, the dark compound in tan or dark-skinned types. They are meant to soak up UV light and protect you from any damage it might cause. But when your food is exposed to glyphosate, it affects your gut microbes and they cannot produce enough of these amino acids. Your natural mechanisms for sun protection stop functioning. This contributes to dangerous sunburns and/or melanoma—not because of exposure to the sun itself but because of exposure to chemicals that kill off the bacteria you need to protect yourself from the sun. You also need plenty of polyphenols (compounds from brightly colored plants) in your diet for your skin to manufacture melanin because melanin is made out of cross-linked polyphenols.

With the right diet and a healthy gut, you can safely expose yourself to the sun in moderation, enabling your cells to make more EZ water. When regular water is exposed to infrared (and maybe UV) light, it is transformed into EZ water. If you expose yourself to infrared light via an infrared sauna or simply by going outside on a sunny day without sunglasses or sunscreen, your body will soak up that light energy and build EZ water. Light enters your body through your eyes and makes its way directly into your brain, where you'll first feel its impact. Light matters greatly to your brain because of its ability to help make EZ water and because you build melanin deep inside your brain, where it can create extra oxygen and electrons to fuel cognitive function. Other research shows that exposure to UV light can prevent or lessen nearsightedness.[2]

Dr. Pollack told me about an experiment in his lab in which he flowed water through a narrow tube. When he exposed the water to UV light, it flowed through the tube five times faster. If your blood and lymphatic fluid can flow through your narrow capillaries more quickly, you will experience less chronic inflammation. The tiny microtubules in your mitochondria also benefit from this "turbocharge" effect when you are exposed to sunlight.

As you read in chapter 7, adequate exposure to sunlight is also necessary to support your circadian rhythm so you can get good-quality sleep. When you're exposed to daylight, your body produces serotonin, the "feel-good" neurotransmitter. Your body breaks down serotonin into melatonin, the hormone that helps you sleep. If you're not exposed to enough natural sunlight during the day, you won't have enough melatonin to sleep well at night. And you already know that not sleeping well is the key to sucking at basically everything.

One of the first people to really sound the alarm about junk light (artificial light that can hinder performance) was T. S. Wiley, an author who was fifteen years ahead of her time in identifying the importance of sunlight and darkness for human health. Since that time, the Nobel Prize has been awarded for work in circadian biology, and a few thought leaders in the wellness space have joined me in taking up the cause of using light and darkness to improve our biology. Perhaps the best known is Dr. Joseph Mercola, an osteopathic physician who has run the most trafficked health site on the internet for twenty years. He's consistently been ahead of the curve with many of his recommendations. As you'd expect from a disruptive game changer, he has his share of critics, even though he's been vindicated many times. In addition to interviewing him on the show, I've gotten to know him as someone who really practices what he preaches. To support his own biology, Dr. Mercola spends about ninety minutes every day walking on the beach, most of the time barefoot and without a shirt on to get electrons, photons, negative ions from the ocean, microbes from the seabirds, and, most important, UVB exposure. This has allowed him to maintain high vitamin D levels without taking supplements for the past several years. Ninety minutes a day is not possible for most people, but you can still benefit from spending a few minutes walking in nature as often as possible.

Our bodies are designed to make all the vitamin D we need when we are exposed to adequate UVB light via the sun's rays. Yet Dr. Mercola estimates that today 85 percent of people are deficient in vitamin D, which is linked to a huge multitude of problems: cancer, diabetes, osteoporosis, rheumatoid arthritis, inflammatory bowel disease, multiple sclerosis, cardiovascular disease, high cholesterol levels, neurological system disorders, kidney failure, reproductive system disorders, muscle weakness, obesity, disorders of the skin, and even tooth decay.

There is another reason that vitamin D is so important: vitamin D deficiency can lead to sleep disorders. In fact, studies show that the epidemic of sleep disorders is caused in part by widespread vitamin D deficiency.[3] If you can't move to Florida and spend more than an hour at the beach every day as Dr. Mercola does, I suggest eating foods that are rich in vitamin D, such as salmon, egg yolks, and tuna, and supplementing in addition to getting some UVB exposure from sunlight or a tanning lamp if you live in a northern climate as I do. Before supplementing, have a blood test done to make sure you're getting the right amount of vitamin D. Just as too little vitamin D is bad, so is too much. Vitamin D temporarily pauses melatonin production, so take it in the morning instead of at night, when you want to go to sleep. And please, please do not take vitamin D3 unless you also take vitamin K2. New research shows that taking vitamin D3 without having enough K2 in your diet may calcify tissues over decades, and some preformed vitamin A (not just beta-carotene) can help balance these ratios.

Exposure to sunlight is essential to your mental health and overall happiness. You're likely already familiar with one of the most pervasive types of depression, which hits during the darker months. Clinically, this is called seasonal affective disorder (SAD), and its symptoms can range from lack of motivation and trouble focusing to full-blown depressive symptoms. People who suffer from SAD usually find that it starts in the autumn, as the days grow shorter, and gets better in spring, when the days get longer. Location also clearly plays a role— those living farther from the equator have a higher incidence of SAD than those closer to the equator. Only around 1 percent of Florida residents experience SAD, whereas it affects 9 percent of Alaska residents.[4] I believe there are many people who don't have full-blown SAD but whose performance and overall wellness are negatively impacted in the winter, especially in the northern latitudes. This is a huge problem if you're looking to be more successful at what you do but have less energy for several months of the year!

For decades, the most effective and popular treatment for seasonal depression has been light therapy. Research has shown it to be as effective as pharmaceutical antidepressants, and some studies have even indicated that it can work faster.[5] The most effective version of light therapy is simply to go outside and expose your eyes and skin to natural sunlight for twenty minutes a day. To max out your vitamin D, expose as much of your skin as the temperature and local laws allow.

To set your brain's sleep and wake timer, don't wear sunglasses, and don't look directly at the sun. The right spectrum of light will bounce off of your surroundings. Even if you don't suffer from seasonal depression, doing this will improve your mood, help you sleep, and help you build more beneficial EZ water in your cells. And it's free.

If exposure to natural light is not an option, try to find an indoor full-spectrum light that emits at least 2,500 lux (lux is a unit of light) without using LED lights. Set your lights at eye level and angle them away from your direct field of vision. As with the sun, don't look directly at it. You want to expose your eyes without frying your retinas. Start at just five or ten minutes of exposure a day, depending on your light's power, and work your way up to no more than sixty minutes. Make sure to follow the manufacturer's directions. Protect your eyes from excessive UV light.

I have been using light therapy since 2007 to upgrade my performance, and it works. One of the people who helped me figure it out was Steven Fowkes, a biochemist who was one of the first people to pull together the research on smart drugs and share it. His influential newsletter, Smart Drug News, which is no longer being published, was the very beginning of the revolution in nootropics we are living through today. Without Steve's work, I wouldn't have had the Silicon Valley career I've enjoyed. Steve was onto something twenty years before everyone else.

Steve helped me fine-tune my light therapy, which has boosted my cognitive function and helped me enjoy noticeably better sleep. He says that if you're in harmony with your day and your biorhythms are in phase with the light-dark cycle, you want to expose yourself to red light in the morning to mirror the sunrise. Then the light needs to shift toward blue in the middle of the day and for most of the day before phasing back down into red again as you prepare for sleep. This replicates the sun's natural cycle, although blue LEDs are a poor way to get daytime blue light because of their intensity.

If you're out of sync with the natural phases of day, meaning that you stay up late or wake up early (before sunrise), you can use light therapy to nudge yourself back into alignment with the day. For example, if you have to wake up earlier than is ideal for your biology, you really want red light exposure first thing when you wake up. Set up some red lights above your bed, kick off the covers, turn on the red lights, and bake your body in red and infrared photons. This will turn on your mitochondria, improve your circulation, and give you a noticeable boost in energy. At night, the blue light that is a part of the spectrum of LED bulbs suppresses melatonin production, so set dimmer switches in your house for evenings and avoid the lights of electronic screens.

Exposure to the sun helps your body create vitamin D and EZ water and sets your circadian rhythm to boost your performance. Getting outside is critical, which leads us to the next law . . .

Action Items

- Choose organic foods that have not been exposed to glyphosate.
- Get adequate exposure to the sun—twenty minutes a day without sunscreen and without glasses of any type (glasses block the sun's UV rays). Listen to a podcast, go for a walk, make a call, or meditate during that time so you get a bigger return on the investment of your time.
- Consider supplementing with vitamins D, K2, and A. Be sure to get tested first so that you know the appropriate dosage to take. Wild salmon and egg yolks are good nutritional sources of vitamin D, but they don't come close to the dose in supplements.
- Spend a week in a sunny place in the middle of the winter if you live somewhere with dark winters.
- Consider light therapy if you feel even slightly less energy during the winter months.

Recommended Listening

- Stephanie Seneff, "Glyphosate Toxicity, Lower Cholesterol Naturally & Get Off Statins," *Bulletproof Radio*, episode 238
- Joseph Mercola, "The Real Dangers of Electric Devices and EMFs," *Bulletproof Radio*, episode 424
- Steven Fowkes, "Hacking Your pH, LED Lighting, and Smart Drugs," Part 1, *Bulletproof Radio*, episode 94

Recommended Reading

- T. S. Wiley with Bent Formby, *Lights Out: Sleep, Sugar, and Survival*
- Joseph Mercola, *Effortless Healing: 9 Simple Ways to Sidestep Illness, Shed Excess Weight, and Help Your Body Fix Itself*

Law 43: Bathe in the Forest Instead of the Tub

Our society's obsession with cleanliness has led to a dramatic re-duction in our gut biodiversity, which has a negative impact on our overall health and happiness. It is not necessary or beneficial to be 100 percent sanitary all the time. For optimum health and hap-piness, get dirty, bathe in nature, and keep yourself no more than moderately clean.

Dr. Maya Shetreat-Klein is a neurologist and herbalist and the author of *The Dirt Cure: Healthy Food, Healthy Gut, Happy Child*, which describes an integrative and spiritual approach to treating health issues in both kids and adults. I find her work particularly interesting because not only is Dr. Shetreat-Klein a neurologist, she's also an herbalist and urban farmer, and she has done a lot of impor-tant work with indigenous communities.

Dr. Shetreat-Klein wants to change the way you think about dirt and bacteria. She says that exposing yourself to bacteria is transformative for the whole body, from the development of the gut to the development of the immune system to healthy brain function. Our culture is obsessed with being hygienic. We have come to believe that the cleaner you are, the better, and that being dirty is a bad thing. As a result, we've sanitized our lives and our bodies to a fault using antibiotics, factory-farmed food, and antibacterial cleansers.

This has all conspired to make us less healthy and less happy instead of more. Dr. Shetreat-Klein says that the first step in reclaiming our well-being is to shift the way we think about dirt. Most bacteria are neither good nor bad. There are definitely a few nasty ones, but the strength of your body's immune system—which includes your gut microbes—determines how much of a threat is present. So what determines the health of your gut? Microbial biodiversity is the Holy Grail. When you have a diverse community of bacteria living inside you, they keep the gut balanced and prevent any one type of bacterium from growing out of control. You'll never be completely free of bad organisms. They're in us all the time, including parasites and viruses. But they can live synergistically and keep one another in check as long as you have a wide variety of other organisms, as well.

The best way to promote gut microbe diversity is through exposure to good, old-fashioned dirt—in particular, soil, which contains organisms that can literally make you happier. Scientists discovered this, like many other good things, by accident. Back in 2004, Dr. Mary O'Brien, an oncologist at the Royal Marsden Hospital in London, injected lung cancer patients with a soil bacterium called *Mycobacterium vaccae* to see if it could prolong their lives. It did not. However, it did significantly improve the patients' quality of life. They were happier, expressed more vitality, and had better cognitive functioning after being injected with the bacterium.

A few years later, neuroscientists at the University of Bristol injected the same bacterium into mice and found that it activated groups of neurons in the mouse brains responsible for producing serotonin. That boosted serotonin levels in the brain to similar levels as antidepressant medications. So instead of taking medications with well-known and well-documented side effects, it's possible to get similar results from tending to your organic garden. Sign me up for that.

Scientists are currently studying whether they can replicate these results in humans and use soil bacteria to treat depression and even PTSD. Until they find funding and jump through the necessary hoops to complete a double-blind study, I'm going to risk wasting my time playing in the mud.

There is a reason we enjoy playing in the mud as kids: we instinctively gravitate toward it because it makes us feel good. We naturally want to get dirty. Even as babies, we crawl on the ground and constantly put out hands and feet into our mouths. As we do this, we're actually seeding our microbes again and again during this critical period of development.

Dr. Shetreat-Klein says that this is only one way that humans naturally engage in plant medicine. We all know that taking a walk in nature makes us feel good. So does receiving flowers, which, she suggests, is another form of plant medicine. Our culture tells us to give flowers to people when we're happy, when we love them, when we want to congratulate them, or when they're sad or have experienced a loss. We do it because it transforms the way we feel physically and emotionally. Having living plants from the outdoors in our homes shifts our mood. Perhaps the cloud of soil bacteria that accompanies the flowers is one reason for this.

Another cultural behavior based in plant medicine is the Japanese practice of *shinrin-yoku*, or forest bathing. In this tradition, people immerse themselves in the beauty of the forest. The concept was developed in the 1980s as many Japanese moved from the countryside to more urban areas and felt compelled to get back to the land and bathe in it to soak up some of what they were missing in the city. The therapy has become a mainstay of Japanese medicine.

Forest bathing doesn't just improve your gut biome; walking in nature is a nonstrenuous physical activity, which in and of itself can improve mood, decrease stress hormone production, and increase longevity.[6] But it's not just the movement that reduces stress in forest bathers. Studies have shown that the average salivary cortisol concentrations of forest bathers are 12 to 13 percent lower than those of urban hikers, meaning that nature itself reduces stress hormones.

Forest bathing can also decrease sympathetic nerve activity, blood pressure, and heart rate.[7]

Forest bathing also boosts immunity. This may be due in part to increased biodiversity from spending time in nature. In addition, many evergreen trees give off aromatic compounds called *phytoncides* that increase natural killer (NK) cells, your immune system's lead defense against viruses and disease. NK cells are suppressed by chronic exposure to stress hormones, which can lead to a weakened immune system and even cancer. But NK cell activity is always higher after forest bathing and rises as your body is exposed to more phytoncides. Cognitively, forest bathing improves mood and increases mental performance and creative problem solving.[8] It's possible that some essential oils from evergreen trees contain these compounds, too.

Another *Bulletproof Radio* guest, Dr. Zach Bush, began his career in oncology research. When he discovered molecules from microbes in soil that looked like the chemotherapy chemicals he was studying, a lightbulb went off in his head. He realized that soil microbes communicate directly with our mitochondria and our cellular DNA and changed his career to study this phenomenon. In his interview, Dr. Bush recommended that we all spend time in a larger variety of natural environments, just breathing deeply. Our sinuses pick up microbes from natural environments, and microbial diversity in our bodies makes us far more resilient. He makes a practice of visiting deserts, rain forests, and any other unusual natural environments he can find as a way of diversifying his gut bacteria. He has also created a supplement made from ancient soil bacteria containing the compounds he discovered, called Restore. I now make it a point to breathe deeply in unusual environments full of undisturbed soil microbes. It's called hiking, and it beats using a treadmill on so many levels.

Even if you live in an urban environment, there are ways to benefit from being in nature. Spend time in public parks, try composting, get a dog to run around outside with, or spend more time with other people to boost your gut biodiversity. Being clean and washing your hands is fine, but cut back on antimicrobials and hand sanitizers and use regular soap instead.

Basically, be moderately clean and encourage your kids to get dirty. Let them roll down hills and play outside as much as they can. Play outside with them, and then wash off at the end of the day with a bar of soap. It's actually pretty simple, like all the best game changers are.

Action Items

- Let your kids play in the dirt. Better yet, join them.
- Take a walk in nature once a week. Increase your return by adding community (bring friends!).
- Eliminate antibacterial cleansers and bleach.
- Bring potted plants (including dirt!) into your home to benefit from soil bacteria.

Recommended Listening

- "Talking Dirty About Spiritual Plants and Microbial Biodiversity," *Bulletproof Radio*, episode 426
- Evan Brand, "Forest Bathing, Repairing Your Vision & Adaptogens," *Bulletproof Radio*, episode 268
- Zach Bush, "Eat Dirt: The Secret to a Healthy Microbiome," *Bulletproof Radio*, episode 458

Recommended Reading

- Maya Shetreat-Klein, *The Dirt Cure: Healthy Food, Healthy Gut, Happy Child*

USE GRATITUDE TO REWIRE YOUR BRAIN

One thing that nearly every law in this book has in common is that they take you out of a stressed state of fight or flight by making your primitive defense systems feel safe. This is how the world's most successful people find the power to change the world. And the absolute best way to ensure that your body knows it's safe is to cultivate gratitude. The people who are at the top of their fields, do noteworthy things, have power, and use it to serve others know that gratitude is not just something that is pleasant to feel; it is vital to having the energy to do what they do and to enjoy life while doing it.

It's easy to be grateful when life is going well, but having gratitude for everything, even your worst traumas, setbacks, and obstacles, is not simple. Yet, as these luminaries have attested, it is essential. Instead of falling into the trap of self-pity or creating a narrative that the odds are stacked against them, they did the hard work of seeing the beauty in their darkest moments. Many of the people I interviewed said they wouldn't be as happy or as successful as they are today if they hadn't found a way to be thankful for their struggles. The same goes for me.

I'm grateful that I lived in a house full of toxic mold that completely jacked up my biology. I'm grateful that I lost all my money and had to keep working. If I hadn't lived through the pain and difficulty of those moments, I wouldn't have learned the valuable lessons that inspired me to create Bulletproof and share what I've learned about how to create more energy than I thought I was supposed to have. It took work to make myself feel that way, because my natural response was to feel pretty pissed off about the whole situation. But that work pays off every day because I don't carry the burden of anger anymore.

If you were to skip every other chapter in this book and read just this one, you'd still be ahead of the game. Gratitude is that important. And it's a skill you can learn to develop. With regular practice, gratitude leaves a lasting imprint on your nervous system, making you more sensitive to positive thinking. This means that the more you practice gratitude, the more you will default to positivity instead of negativity. Basically, *life takes less work when you practice gratitude*. The more you naturally tend toward positive thinking, the better you are able to transcend your base instincts and spend your precious energy moving the needle for yourself and perhaps the rest of humanity, too.

Law 44: Gratitude Is Stronger than Fear

Overcoming fear that does not serve you is necessary to access your greatness. Courage works, but it takes a lot of energy to maintain. Save courage for when your life is actually on the line. The rest of the time, use gratitude to turn off fear at the cellular level. Freedom from fear leads to happiness, and happiness is what makes you perform your best at whatever you choose to do.

One of the most impressive guests I have learned from is Dr. Stephen Porges, who is a distinguished university scientist at Indiana University, where he directs the Sexual Trauma Research Consortium at the Kinsey Institute. In 1994, Dr. Porges changed the face of medicine when he proposed the Polyvagal Theory, which links the autonomic nervous system to social behavior and provides a physiological explanation for behavioral problems and psychiatric disorders. His work has profoundly changed the way scientists approach the topic of mental health and offers insights into the functionality of stress that can benefit us all.

Known as the "wandering nerve" (*vagus* is Latin for "wandering"), the vagus nerve starts at your brain stem and wanders throughout the body, connecting your brain to your stomach and digestive tract, as well as your lungs, heart, spleen, intestines, liver, and kidneys. The vagus nerve's main job is to monitor what's going on in your body and report information back to your brain. It is a key component of your parasympathetic nervous system, which is responsible for calming you down after your fight-or-flight response revs you up. The strength of your vagus nerve activity is known as your vagal tone. If you have a high vagal tone, you are able to relax more quickly after experiencing a moment of stress. Low vagal tone is the opposite and can keep you in a chronic state of fight or flight.

Clearly, being able to override your default programming and calm down more quickly after experiencing a moment of stress is important. Luckily, according to Dr. Porges, it is possible for anyone to improve his or her vagal tone. One way to enhance vagal tone is through social interaction. We as mammals did not evolve in isolation; we evolved in communities. As such, we benefited from and continue to need the help of others. Caregiving is not a selfless, one-directional act. It is bidirectional, or at least it should be. We naturally feel good when we help other people, as long as they are pleasant recipients of that help. Children and dogs are perfect examples of this. They are needy and respond lovingly to our care, and that makes us feel good and want to continue caring for them.

Another human experience that impacts vagal tone is feeling gratitude. Dr. Porges explains that when you're in a state of gratitude, your nervous system is bathed in cues of safety. This makes sense from an evolutionary standpoint—you're not going to feel grateful when a tiger is chasing you. But you need more than just the absence of a tiger to feel grateful. He reminds us that the removal of a threat is not the same thing as safety. Your body needs to receive cues that you are truly safe in order to feel gratitude. He suggests that there is a decision process of sorts that determines how your body responds to perceived danger. You are not conscious of this process—it happens in the background, and different branches of the vagus nerve activate in response to different situations.

When you experience a frightening stimulus, your body responds first to social communication: verbal language, body language, vocal tone, and other nonverbal cues.[1] If the stimulus is too strong for these responses to provide adequate comfort, your brain activates your stress hormones—your fight-or-flight response. If you have poor vagal tone and are not able to return to baseline, you may freeze completely and become unable to act. Dr. Porges suggests that this is common in survivors of trauma or abuse.

When you know your fear is irrational, you can use safety cues to stop panic and keep your body from going into full-blown fight or flight. One of these safety cues is to use a soothing voice. Dr. Porges explains that this phenomenon is hardwired in us. Think of young children, who are measurably calmed by soothing, singsong tones. Parents often use these tones instinctively with their children, but altering your tone of speech works for adults, too. Guided meditations, either in person or recorded, adopt a slow, rhythmic tone of speaking. Using the voice as a relaxation cue coaxes your brain into a relaxed state faster than a normal conversational tone would. (There's a reason I don't talk fast on *Bulletproof Radio*!) The implication is that if you're stressed, Rage Against the Machine may not be the right soundtrack for you, even if it is energizing; calm music may pay higher dividends for your nervous system.

Another way to activate a safety cue for your brain is to imagine your happy place. I know this sounds cliché, but it works. To do this effectively, you'll need to determine a "safe place" or "happy place" while you're calm. Close your eyes and think about an environment in which you're completely at ease, content, and peaceful. Imagine as much sensory information and detail as you can—sights, smells, and sounds. Practice this visualization often. That way, when you start feeling fearful or angry, you can conjure up your "safe place" without much effort. It's there for you when you need it. Mine may or may not look like a Bat Cave.

Another top expert who taught me a lot about gratitude is Dr. Elissa Epel, who, as you read earlier, is a professor at UCSF who studies how stress can impact our biological aging via the telomere/telomerase system and how meditation modalities may buffer stress effects and boost physical and spiritual well-being.

Dr. Epel told me about a study she did with the mitochondria researcher Dr. Martin Picard at Columbia University. They examined participants' blood to determine the activity of their mitochondrial enzymes. These chemicals play an important role in producing energy for your cells. Dr. Epel and Dr. Picard found that as a group, caregivers—such as mothers who had a child with a chronic condition—had reduced enzyme activity. Yet within that group there were some notable exceptions.

To learn the origin of these differences, the researchers took an inventory of the participants' daily lives and asked them questions such as: From the moment you wake up, how much are you looking forward to the day? How much are you worrying about the day? How happy are you? How stressed or anxious are you? They were looking not just for the participants' affect and emotion but for their appraisals of what was going to happen to them, good or bad. In other words, were they locked in a cycle of always anticipating a threat, or did they also experience hope and gratitude? They checked participants' mitochondrial enzymes in the morning, after a moment of stress, and then again in the evening. They found that the people with the most mitochondrial enzymes had a higher positive affect when they woke up and when they went to bed, especially around bedtime. It was their recovery mood and whether or not they held onto the residue of everything that happened to them throughout the day that determined how well their mitochondria were functioning.

To help people improve their mood and not wake up anticipating stress, Dr. Epel suggests that they think of something they are grateful for in the evening before bed. That simple gratitude exercise could potentially boost the participants' mitochondrial enzymes and made them happier.

Although it's understandable that mothers of sick children might be prone to fearing the worst, Dr. Epel explains that many of us anticipate moments of stress without even realizing it. The question is: Are you carrying that perceived danger or threat with you throughout the day and ruminating over it? Are you putting yourself into a state of fight or flight by anticipating stress before it happens? Or are you bathing yourself in cues of safety by feeling grateful? An easy way to tell if you are spending your days anticipating threats is by paying attention to how you feel in the evening. At night, your mood is really important because it reflects how well you've recovered from your stress. How positive is your mood when you get home from work in the evening and before bed?

Several years ago I instituted a gratitude practice at Bulletproof. Our weekly executive team meetings begin with each team member sharing what he or she is grateful for. Sometimes it's a big win at work. But most often it's time with family, a volunteer project, or maybe a Seahawks win. Starting a meeting with gratitude makes for a more powerful interaction and builds connection among the team members. I see it as an act of service I can offer to the people who so passionately support the company's mission: to help people tap into the unlimited power of being human.

I value gratitude so much that I don't save it for Team Bulletproof. Every night before bed since my kids were old enough to talk, I've been asking them to relate an "act of kindness," something they did that day to help another person. Their vagal tone increases when they recall something nice they've done. We follow with a nightly gratitude practice. Lana and I ask them for three things they're grateful for. Sometimes it's a little thing, such as being grateful for having had grass-fed rib eye for dinner. (I love having foodie kids!) But sometimes it's profound. Once when my son was five, he got a strange look on his face and said, "Daddy, I'm grateful for the Big Bang because without it there wouldn't be anything." Then he rolled over and happily went to sleep with his nervous system calm and his mitochondria running at full power. It works for adults, too. Try it.

Action Items

- Stop putting yourself into a stressed state by anticipating problems before they occur (worrying). If you sense this happening, work on going to your "happy place."
- Do something kind for someone else every day to improve your vagal tone.

- Every night before bed, think of three things you are grateful for to boost your mitochondrial enzymes. In fact, try it now and feel what it does to your nervous system. You get bonus points for locating where in your body you feel intense gratitude.

  - _____

  - _____

  - _____

- Speak in a calming, more soothing voice when you want to turn off the fight-or-flight response in yourself or others.
- Listen to high-energy music when you need the energy—but if you're already stressed, focus on music with calm voices.

Recommended Listening
- Stephen Porges, "The Polyvagal Theory & the Vagal Nerve," *Bulletproof Radio*, episode 264
- Elissa Epel, "Age Backwards by Hacking Your Telomeres with Stress," *Bulletproof Radio*, episode 436

Recommended Reading
- Stephen W. Porges, *The Pocket Guide to the Polyvagal Theory: The Transformative Power of Feeling Safe*
- Elizabeth Blackburn and Elissa Epel, *The Telomere Effect: A Revolutionary Approach to Living Younger, Healthier, Longer*

Law 45: Forgive, but Don't Be Sorry

Gratitude by itself improves your performance. But the most advanced performers know that gratitude is also the doorway to forgiveness. When you forgive, you reprogram your nervous system to no longer automatically react to memories of past trauma, suffering, and perceived slights. To forgive, identify the false stories you tell yourself, then find a way to be grateful for even the worst things you've experienced. You don't have to say you're sorry to forgive. Forgiveness is the single most powerful upgrade to human performance. Forgive with the same intensity you bring to your mission in life, and you will access new levels of energy and happiness.

On my path to becoming Bulletproof, I spent some time in a sweat lodge after completing a week of Alberto Villoldo's advanced shamanic meditation training. An old and powerful Native American sun dancer led the experience, which I was honored to share with a group of a dozen people. One of those people was a woman who was extremely unhappy, even though just being there was an incredible gift. She kept saying things such as "I've hit rock bottom; it can't get any worse," and when she had the opportunity to ask the earth for anything, she said, "I just wish I had enough energy to make it through the day." I was floored to witness her belief in her story and blurted out, "Why not at least ask for enough energy to dance through the day?" I'll chalk that indiscretion up to the incredible heat, but it provided an important lesson in believing your own story.

The wise elder who was overseeing the sweat lodge looked at her and said, "You are suffering from something called self-pity. We know what to do about that," before he poured more water on the hot stones. Indeed, that woman had plenty of things she could have been grateful for. She was still standing. She was able to afford that relatively expensive experience, and she'd had an opportunity to learn from an amazing game changer like Alberto Villoldo before being invited by an elder to participate in a sacred ceremony.

This is a matter of reframing. Every one of us has both things we can feel self-pity about and things we can feel grateful for. Which ones are you going to focus on? Even if your life is really hard right now—or if your life has always been hard—you can find something tiny to be grateful for. When I've felt as though things were bad, I've always gone back to being grateful for having two good legs. Things can always be worse. You're still standing. You have this book and the wonderful chance to learn from hundreds of high performers. You can handle this. You are not *enough*—you are *way more* than enough.

In part, gratitude is so powerful because it takes you out of your own story of self-pity. Imagine that someone cuts you off in traffic. Most of the time when this happens, we immediately tell ourselves a story without even thinking about it: That guy thinks he's better than me. What a jerk. But what if you change the story? Imagine that person is rushing to the hospital to see his or her dying mother for the last time. In that case, wouldn't you be grateful that you were able to let them go ahead of you?

It's the feeling of gratitude for even a perceived slight that opens the door to forgiveness. Of course, neither story has any validity. You'll never really know why that person cut you off. But you can choose a story that allows you to feel grateful and forgive, or you can choose to hold on to resentment. The person who cut you off won't know the difference. His or her life won't change no matter what you tell yourself about why he or she did it. At its core, forgiveness lets you stop carrying other people's grudges. You have more important things to carry.

Many of us make the mistake of doing this halfway. Someone cuts us off, and we decide to forgive the other person without creating a narrative that allows us to feel gratitude. In other words: *He cut me off because he thinks he's better than me, but I forgive him.* This is a step in the right direction, but it results in merely a cognitive level of forgiveness that won't affect your brain waves or nervous system and allow you to experience the full benefits of gratitude. Thinking about forgiveness is not the same as feeling it. In other words, it's easy to pretend that you don't care about how a jerk treats you, but if it's secretly sucking your energy on the inside, you will still end up paying the price.

Finding gratitude even for the corrosive jerks in your life, on the other hand, will actually boost your happiness. Having a thick skin isn't very useful, because it forces you to keep taking hits, it blocks positive emotions, and it is energetically expensive to build and maintain your thick skin. When you can learn to feel gratitude and compassion for a jerk, however, his or her behavior will pass right through you without costing you any energy. That is called forgiveness. The best part, of course, is that showing and actually *feeling* gratitude for a jerk makes that person even madder than when you ignore him or her. And that costs the jerk even more energy than it takes to act like a jerk in the first place. There is no possible way for your secretly hating anyone to improve your life or theirs.

Hz]   30   40   50   60   70   80   90   100
                                                                    M

40 Years of Zen Neurofeedback Augmented Reset Protocol showing forgiveness and gratitude impact on brain waves during executive cognitive enhancement training

In one of his interviews, I asked Tim Ferriss of *The 4-Hour Workweek* fame what three pieces of advice he'd have for someone who wanted to perform better as a human being. He replied with a quote from B. J. Miller, a palliative care physician who is a triple amputee: "Don't believe everything you think." Tim says that when people question their deep-rooted philosophies and basic assumptions, they very often find them to be completely off base. He experienced this in his own life. In response to BJ's advice, he started telling himself: *Don't retreat into the story.* If you wake up in a funk or you're in a depressive period and you retreat into a disabling story about yourself or the world, you are never going to be able to change the game.

While I learned from many spiritual teachers and personal development experts to phrase affirmations in a positive way—focused on doing something rather than *not* doing something—Tim says that *don't retreat into the story* has worked well for him. It's like a stop sign that he uses to interrupt the pattern of self-deception. This allows him to look at what's in front of him nonreactively and without the emotional baggage of trauma or past mistakes. The positively phrased version of that would be "See things as they actually are, and live in that world." You can do both!

For instance, if someone on the phone appears to be very curt and rude to you, don't assume that he or she has some personal vendetta against you and that he or she is trying to ruin your day. Maybe he's just hungry. Maybe she needs to go to the bathroom and her boss won't let her take a break until the next hour clicks through. Choosing a positive story enables gratitude and therefore forgiveness for a small slight, but if you retreat into a story that fosters self-pity, you're not going to like your life.

Perhaps no one has mastered the art of reframing self-pity into gratitude better than Tony Robbins, the world-famous motivational speaker, personal finance guru, and multiple-time *New York Times* bestselling author. In a special episode of *Bulletproof Radio*, Tony, Peter Diamandis, and marketing guru Joe Polish discussed Tony's story and how he believes that nothing is impossible. Impossible, he says, is not a fact; it's an opinion. Technically, everything is impossible until somebody does it. Even in the field of science, many things that have been shown to be impossible were later proven to be possible. Therefore, Tony says that anytime a business is not growing or a person is not succeeding, it's not because it's impossible. It's because that person has a story about why his or her strategy isn't working. As Tony says, "If you can just divorce the story of your limitation and marry the truth of your unlimited capacity, then the whole game changes." Having met Tony and shared his stage, I can assure you that there is no one who lives that motto more!

The truth of the matter is that the stories that are holding you back are *all* the result of past traumas when your nervous system believed you were seriously threatened. Trauma is held in the body. The stories exist as your body's primitive way of making sure you don't fall victim to the same situation again. Feeling gratitude and offering true forgiveness is the way to untangle these stories and see things as they really are.

- Think about the worst thing that has ever happened to you and come up with one good thing that came from it:

  _____

- What is one limiting story you absolutely believe to be true about yourself or the world?

  _____

- Can you imagine one thing that would make the story not true, at least one time? If the answer is yes, stop believing the story. If the answer is no, keep digging or ask a close friend for his or her take. Self-limiting stories are never, ever real.
- Make a list of people or things you hold a grudge toward:

- Those grudges are costing you energy, causing you pain, and not affecting the other party at all. Find gratitude and seek forgiveness for everyone on this list, and watch your limits fall away.

Recommended Listening

- Alberto Villoldo, "Brain Hacking & One Spirit Medicine," *Bulletproof Radio*, episode 220
- Gabrielle Bernstein, "Detox Your Thoughts to Supercharge Your Life," *Bulletproof Radio*, episode 455
- "Address Invisible Patterns, Find Joy in Solving Problems & Other Lessons with the Founder of TOMS Shoes," *Bulletproof Radio*, episode 442

- "Mashup of the Titans" with Tim Ferriss, Parts 1 and 2, *Bulletproof Radio*, episodes 370 and 371
- Tim Ferriss, "The Tim Ferriss Experiment," *Bulletproof Radio*, episode 215
- Tony Robbins and Peter Diamandis, "Special Podcast, Live from the Genius Network," *Bulletproof Radio*, episode 306

Recommended Reading

- Tony Robbins, *Awaken the Giant Within: How to Take Immediate Control of Your Mental, Emotional, Physical and Financial Destiny!*
- Peter H. Diamandis and Steven Kotler, *Abundance: The Future Is Better than You Think*

Law 46: Use the Tools of Gratitude

Don't leave gratitude to chance. Take advantage of simple, effective tools to build gratitude into your day the same way you build in exercise or healthy food. Gratitude is a muscle. Exercise it.

UJ Ramdas is an entrepreneur and behavioral change specialist with a background in cognitive science. He's also a certified hypnotist who is passionate about bringing together practical psychology and business to create a better world and has changed the game for his many consulting clients. But I wanted to speak to UJ because of his focus on gratitude and setting up habits to foster more of it throughout his life. UJ suggests that you must experience gratitude both cognitively and physiologically in order for it to be effective, meaning you have to think it and feel it. When those two elements connect, you can reshape your thinking in a powerful way.

For years, UJ had a nightly ritual that enabled him to experience the power of gratitude. Every night, he used a journal to review all of the good things that happened that day. But when he looked at the science, he saw that the effects of gratitude were more powerful when people asked themselves what they were grateful for first thing in the morning, so he shifted to a morning routine that consisted of asking himself and writing down the answers to three questions: What am I grateful for? What can I do to make today great? What kind of person do I want to be today?

UJ says that answering these questions first thing in the morning allowed him to take advantage of the primacy effect, the idea that doing something as soon as you wake up has a disproportionate effect on your entire day. The second and third questions prime the brain to anticipate positive actions and results, which boosts feelings of gratitude. For example, UJ says that when people think they are going to watch their favorite movie, their endorphin levels automatically increase. Anticipation is therefore an incredible source of well-being and happiness, as long as you are anticipating something positive.

Instead of giving up his nightly ritual, before bed UJ began reviewing three good things that had happened to him that day. He says that when we write down something we're grateful for, we sleep better, experience a better quality of sleep, share a greater sense of closeness with our family and friends, and have an increased desire to do kind things for others.

Then UJ asks himself, "What's one thing I could have done to make the day better?" This keeps him in the mind-set of constantly improving. UJ is so passionate about these gratitude habits that he created a custom notebook called the Five Minute Journal to make it easy for people to adopt them into their own lives.

UJ says that these simple habits can make you more resilient, increase your prefrontal cortex activation, and help you stay calm and focused in moments of stress instead of panicking, because they improve vagal tone. Just as important, these gratitude habits lead to other positive changes. In one groundbreaking study on gratitude back in 2003, the scientist Robert Emmons had participants write down five things they were grateful for just once a week. Ten weeks later, the participants who had practiced gratitude were exercising one and a half hours a week more than a control group (without being told to) and reported feeling a sense of reciprocity toward their family, friends, and colleagues that inspired more kind acts. In other words, they wanted to do nice things for the people in their lives because they were grateful for them.

The energy Tony Robbins extends to help others is legendary, so it only makes sense that he has a personal gratitude practice. Tony says he spends just three minutes thinking about three things he's grateful for and visualizing each one of them in great sensory detail. For example, instead of thinking "I'm grateful for that roller coaster over there," Tony mentally puts himself into the front seat and feels himself going over the edge, becoming completely present in the visualization of the thing he is grateful for. He also makes sure that at least one of his three things is something really simple, such as the wind on his face or his child's smile, to train himself to be grateful for the little things in his life.

After doing this for three minutes, Tony does a three-minute blessing, during which he imagines life, God, or energy coming into his body, healing every muscle and nerve, and strengthening his passion, love, generosity, creativity, and humor. Then he visualizes any problem he's facing as being solved. Once he feels that fully, he imagines a circle of energy around himself, his intimate family, and his friends. Then he continues the circle all the way out to his clients and imagines them being healed, getting what they want, and having the lives they deserve.

Last, he thinks of three specific outcomes that matter to him, and instead of thinking about achieving them, he sees, feels, and experiences them as done and imagines the impact that completing them would have. He sees people's lives being touched and experiences their joy, and he feels grateful. This entire practice should take about ten minutes, but Tony says that he often lets it go for fifteen or twenty minutes because he's having such a good time.

To experience the same effects, use UJ's technique, Tony's technique, or the one I use with my kids. Add in any combination of these tools:

KEEP A GRATITUDE JOURNAL

This is probably the most popular gratitude practice, in part thanks to UJ's Five Minute Journal app. Writing down the things you're grateful for is tangible, and it's easier to remember to be grateful daily when it involves a physical object. The process is simple: write down three things you're grateful for in the morning and three more before bed. If that's too much, write in just the morning or the evening.

PRACTICE MINDFULNESS

Slow your life down. If you find that you're rushing to get to work, notice it and relax. Being a few minutes late won't kill you. Next time you go up the stairs, pay attention to every step. Look at the trees and flowers and the grass growing through cracks in the pavement when you take a walk. Literally stop to smell the roses. There's tremendous beauty all around us, and most of us blow right by it on the way to the next goal or obligation. Life is too short not to appreciate the little things. Take your time. This bathes your nervous system in safety cues, which shuts off your default programming and allows for the power of gratitude.

RETHINK A NEGATIVE SITUATION

Here's an old parable. A farmer's horse ran away. His neighbors said, "What a shame!" He said, "Maybe." The next day, the horse came back, and it brought more wild horses with it. The neighbors said, "How wonderful!" The farmer said, "Maybe." The next day, a horse stepped on the farmer's son's arm, breaking it. The neighbors said, "How horrible!" The farmer said, "Maybe." The next day, the government came to the village, drafting people for the war. They passed over the farmer's son because of his broken arm. "How wonderful!" the neighbors said. The farmer said, "Maybe."

It's a silly parable, but it makes a good point: situations are neutral;

how you perceive them is what makes them good or bad. Find the silver lining in everything. Often the silver lining is that each hardship makes you learn something new or become a stronger, more resilient human being. Don't force yourself to feel a certain way if you're not ready. This isn't about being happy and positive all the time. Some situations suck, and it's important to feel your negative emotions. Just get into the habit of finding positives, as well.

APPRECIATE ACTIVELY

Look for opportunities to be grateful throughout your day. This is especially useful when you're having a bad day or find yourself focusing on negative emotions. This isn't about being fake or lying to yourself. It's about actively looking for things in your life that you authentically appreciate. This might start out as just being grateful for your (buttered!) cup of coffee every morning, the fact that you're healthy, or the fact that you have two working legs.

FILL A GRATITUDE JAR

This is a play on journaling but a bit more creative. Choose a large jar or a fishbowl, and as a family (or by yourself), write down what you're grateful for each day and pop it into the bowl. As the bowl fills, it will serve as a physical representation of all the things you have to be grateful for.

PRACTICE GRATITUDE WITH LOVED ONES

Share your gratitude as a family at the dinner table. This is a great little ritual to introduce, especially if you have children. If you want, add some ground rules. First, each thing you mention should be new; second, it should have something to do with the events of that day; and third, it should be different from another person's gratitude that night. This cultivates creativity and engagement. Reflecting back on the day in a positive way can have some really powerful benefits. And since gratitude in general can help with sleep, the evening is a good time to do this. As a group of friends or roommates or as a family, choose a time to share your gratitude with one another. Not only will you gain the benefits of more positive thinking pathways, you'll also foster closeness with the people you love.

TAKE A GRATITUDE WALK

Go for a walk (bonus points if you get some sunshine at the same time), and pay close attention to everything you see and experience. Notice all the beauty, the feeling of each step in the soles of your feet. This will calm your mind and foster gratitude. Focus on the feeling that gratitude creates in your body, and enjoy it.

WRITE A THANK-YOU NOTE

Write a letter of love and gratitude to someone who has touched your life in a big or small way. It can be a parent, a friend, a teacher who shaped your life, or anyone you want to thank. Tell them what they've done for you. This has the added bonus of deepening your connections with those you care about.

PRACTICE COMBINING GRATITUDE AND FORGIVENESS

You can carry around a lot of stress—even unconsciously—from anger and hurt. To practice a combination of gratitude and forgiveness, write down something that has hurt you, or maybe just acknowledge some of your anger or pain. Feel the negative emotion, think of a way the situation that caused it benefited you or shaped you into who you are today, and let go of the negativity. Forgiveness has a profound effect on boosting your alpha brain waves—those associated with a calm, focused mental state. I guarantee that spending more time in that state will be a game changer for you.

Action Items
- What are the three most appealing tools of gratitude from this section?

  - _____
  - _____
  - _____

- Now try them!

Recommended Listening
- UJ Ramdas, "Success and Gratitude," *Bulletproof Radio*, episode 80
- Tony Robbins and Peter Diamandis, "Special Podcast, Live from the Genius Network," *Bulletproof Radio*, episode 306

AFTERWORD

Over the past several years, as I've interviewed hundreds of people who have created meaning and impact, more than a few have tried to turn the tables by asking me for my own three most important pieces of advice. I've resisted providing an answer until now, because those interviews—just like this book—are not about me. They are about distilling new knowledge from amazing experts and thought leaders and sharing it with the many people who care enough to put it to use in their lives. I am one of those people!

I am also loath to tell you that because one successful person does something one way, you should do it that way, too. We're all different, and what works for one person, even me, might not work for you. But when you analyze the data to find out *what matters*, rather than how someone does something, you can choose your own priorities more wisely. Compared to setting priorities, finding the tools to get there is just a detail.

But now, after compiling the data and revisiting all of those interviews, I am excited to share my three most important things with you. They are not tips or tricks—they are compass points that I hope you will use to move in the right direction with whatever methods work best *for you*.

My first answer is something that has profoundly changed my life. I teach it to my kids, to my team at Bulletproof, and to world-class executives at 40 Years of Zen. That thing is the power of gratitude. Simply telling my wife and my kids about three things that I'm grateful for every day has completely shifted my attitude and given me more energy to put toward all of my endeavors. I am certain that I wouldn't be the father, husband, or CEO I am today if I hadn't made a gratitude practice nonnegotiable.

As you read earlier, to experience the true power of gratitude, it's essential to find a way to be grateful for everything, even your greatest obstacles and failures. To teach my kids to celebrate failure so they won't live in fear of it, I include one failure that I'm grateful for each night when we list our three things. This has helped me forgive, let go, and keep pushing boundaries in my efforts to change the game.

My second most important piece of advice is to understand your wiring and the fact that you have a mitochondrial network that wants you to do three things in order: run away and hide from or kill scary things, eat everything you can, and reproduce. Once you acknowledge the fact that you have a built-in intelligence that moves faster than you can think, encouraging you to prioritize these three things over everything else, the amount of shame and guilt you experience will be reduced tremendously. If you fall down on any of these three things, it's okay. You're built to do that. Now get up and try those things again but with yourself in charge instead of the primitive consciousness living inside you. Once you reach this level of acceptance, you can put that energy toward things that energize you instead of the things that make you weak. For many game changers, including me, this includes a mission I am passionate about.

Finally, I want you to understand that your body doesn't listen to you very well, except when it comes to gratitude and love. Fortunately, it does listen to the environment around you. This may sound scary, but it actually gives you a tremendous amount of control. After all, you decide what you eat, how you sleep, when you move, the air you breathe, and the type of light you expose yourself to. All of this matters tremendously. It's part of the matrix that supports you and contributes to how smart, fast, and happy you are going to be. If you manipulate these variables in your favor, you can gain more willpower and resilience than you ever realized was possible.

Of course, all three of these pieces of advice interact with one another. When your environment supports your biology and you bathe your body in safety cues using a gratitude practice, you gain the necessary energy to transcend the wiring that wants to keep you focused on your survival. On the other hand, focusing on gratitude can help your body cope with a stressful environment. Like every law in this book, the benefits you gain in one area will compound as they impact other aspects of your life. Once you see which changes create the greatest benefits, you can prioritize your actions accordingly.

And because breaking rules is something that game changers do, I'm adding a fourth answer. It is tied to my company's mission statement and my own, to help people tap into the unlimited power of being human. The fourth most important thing is simply to understand that you have unlimited power and you can do impossible things when you find the right way to tap into that power. I've learned the hard way that every time I think I've hit a limit, I'm wrong. I'm just not thinking big enough. So think bigger.

Now it's your turn. You now know what hundreds of highly impactful people say makes them stronger, more creative, and resilient. This is life-changing information, but it won't change anything if you don't take action. So what are you going to do first? What impact do you most want it to have? And how are you going to use the energy you gain to change *your* game?

ACKNOWLEDGMENTS

The acknowledgment section of a book could perhaps best be called the gratitude section. Because you're at the end of the book, you already know how important gratitude is to your own happiness and performance. That doesn't mean it's easy to write, because there are so many people I am grateful for. I'm grateful for the people who listened to the hundred million episodes of *Bulletproof Radio* they have downloaded, especially the people who've taken the time to stop me when they see me on the street to tell me how it's made a difference in their lives. That's one of the things that keeps me doing two interviews a week, every week. It's also that kind of interaction that inspires me to do the work to write a book like this.

Thanks to the team who directly supported the writing of this book, including Jodi Lipper, my trusted writing partner; Matthew Swope, who did the statistical analysis of the data behind the book; Julie Will, editorial director at Harper Wave; and Celeste Fine, the most awesome agent there is. And thanks to Bulletproof Radio Executive Producer Selina Shearer, who keeps lining up world-changing guests.

Thanks also to my assistants Anie Tazian, Kaylee Harris, and Bev Hampson, who performed impossible scheduling miracles to carve out time on my calendar to write this book and took on so many other tasks I'd otherwise have to do myself instead of writing.

And speaking of time, thanks to my lovely wife Dr. Lana and my kids, Anna and Alan, for letting me sleep in after some long nights of writing, and understanding that a book is a mission that must be achieved once it is started. This book wouldn't exist without your love and flexibility, and I hope the time spent writing it instead of playing with you creates a big enough impact on the world to make your lives better, too.

It's a full-time job to be the CEO of a company working to disrupt Big Food, and I could only have written this book with the rock-solid support of the entire team at Bulletproof, who kept the focus on our customers at the times when my focus went to writing. Thank you for that and the tireless energy you put into changing people's lives every day.

Extra thanks to JJ Virgin, Joe Polish, Jay Abraham, Jack Canfield, Dan Sullivan, Mike Koenigs, Dr. Barry Morguelan, Michael Wentz, Peter Diamandis, Naveen Jain, Craig Handley, Dr. Amen, Dr. Perlmutter, Dr. Hyman, and Ken Rutkowski for your advice and friendship along the way.

A special shout-out to Dr. Drew Pierson from 40 Years of Zen who set up custom neurofeedback protocols for me to help my brain write this book, and to Dr. Matt Cook and Dr. Harry Adelson for all the stem cells!

I become enriched with every interview and conversation I have on *Bulletproof Radio*, and with five hundred episodes completed, listing each name here won't be helpful. Extra shout-outs to the guests featured in this book, including JJ Virgin, Jack Canfield, Stew Friedman, Tony Stubblebine, Brendon Burchard, Robert Greene, Vishen Lakhiani, Robert Cooper, Gabby Bernstein, Dan Hurley, Tim Ferriss, Steve Fowkes, Dennis McKenna, Rick Doblin, Amber Lyon, Patrick McKeown, Brandon Routh, Ravé Mehta, Bruce Lipton, Jia Jiang, Naveen Jain, Subir Chowdhury, Dr. Izabella Wentz, Mark Bell, Genpo Roshi, Pedram Shojai, Hal Elrod, Dr. John Gray, Christopher Ryan, Emily Morse, Dr. Jolene Brighten, Paul Zak, Eli Block, Mistress Natalie, Geoffrey Miller, Bill Harris, Dr. Pooja Lakshmin, Dr. Michael Breus, Dr. Jonathan Wisor, John Romaniello, Phillip Westbrook, Dan Levendowski, Dr. Dwight Jennings, Arianna Huffington, Kelly Starrett, BJ Baker, Dr. Doug McGuff, Charles Poliquin, Mark Sisson, Dr. Bill Sears, Mark Divine, Catherine Divine, Mattias Ribbing, Jim Kwik, Stanislov Grof, David Perlmutter, Alberto Villoldo, Daniel Amen, Gerald Pollack, Cynthia Pasquella-Garcia, Mark David, Barry Sears, Dr. Cate Shanahan, Mark Hyman, Nina Teicholz, Bill Andrews,

Dr. Kate Rheaume-Bleue, William J. Walsh, PhD, Dr. William Davis, Dr. Ron Hunninghake, Dr. Matthew Cook, Dr. Henry Adelson, Dr. Amy Killen, Jay Abraham, Joshua Fields Millburn, James Altucher, Tony Robbins, Peter Diamandis, JP Sears, Christopher Ryan, Esther Perel, Dr. Barry Morguelan, Dan Harris, Wim Hof, Daniel Vitalis, Zach Bush, Dr. Stephanie Seneff, Dr. Joseph Mercola, Evan Brand, Dr. Maya Shetreat-Klein, Stephen Porges, Dr. Elissa Epel, Dr. Elizabeth Blackburn, Steven Kotler, and UJ Ramdas.

Thanks also to caffeine, nicotine, aniracetam, modafinil, Unfair Advantage, Smart Mode, KetoPrime, red light, and all the other nootropics that powered my consciousness as this book evolved. And last of all, thanks to my mitochondria (those little bastards!) for doing my bidding (at least most of the time)!

NOTES

CHAPTER 1: FOCUSING ON YOUR WEAKNESSES MAKES YOU WEAKER

1. Shai Danziger, Jonathan Levav, and Liora Avnaim-Pesso, "Extraneous Factors in Judicial Decisions," *Proceedings of the National Academy of Sciences of the United States of America* 18, no. 17 (April 26, 2011): 6889–92; http://www.pnas.org/content/108/17/6889.full.pdf.

CHAPTER 2: GET INTO THE HABIT OF GETTING SMARTER

1. Peter Schulman, "Applying Learned Optimism to Increase Sales Productivity," *Journal of Personal Selling & Sales Management* 19, no. 1 (1999): 31–37; http://www.tandfonline.com/doi/abs/10.1080/08853134.1999.10754157.

2. Susanne M. Jaeggi, Martin Buschkuehl, John Jonides, and Walter J. Perrig, "Improving Fluid Intelligence with Training on Working Memory," *Proceedings of the National Academy of Sciences of the United States of America* 105, no. 19 (May 13, 2008): 6829–33; http://www.pnas.org/content/105/19/6829.abstract.

CHAPTER 3: GET OUTSIDE YOUR HEAD SO YOU CAN SEE INSIDE IT

1. https://www.goodreads.com/quotes/542554-taking-lsd-was-a-profound-experience-one-of-the-most; http://healthland.time.com/2011/10/06/jobs-had-lsd-we-have-the-iphone/

2. Enzo Tagliazucchi, Leor Roseman, Mendel Kaelen, et al., "Increased Global Functional Connectivity Correlates with LSD-Induced Ego Dissolution," *Current Biology* 26, no. 8 (April 25, 2018): 1043–50; https://www.cell.com/current-biology/fulltext/S0960-9822(16)30062-8.

3. Daniel Wacker, Sheng Wang, John D. McCoy, et al., "Crystal Structure of an LSD-Bound Human Serotonin Receptor," *Cell* 168, no. 3 (January 26, 2017): 377–89; https://www.cell.com/cell/fulltext/S0092-8674(16)31749-4.

4. D.W. Lachenmeier and J. Rehm, Comparative risk assessment of alcohol, tobacco, cannabis and other illicit drugs using the margin of exposure approach, *Scientific Reports*. 2015; 5:8126. doi:10.1038/srep08126.

5. David Baumeister, Georgina Barnes, Giovanni Giaroli, and Derek Tracy, "Classical Hallucinogens as Antidepressants? A Review of Pharmaco-dynamics and Putative Clinical Roles," *Therapeutic Advances in Psycho-pharmacology* 4, no. 4 (August 2014): 156–69; https://www.ncbi.nlm.nih .gov/pmc/articles/PMC4104707/. Briony J. Catlow, Shijie Song, Daniel A. Paredes, et al., "Effects of Psilocybin on Hippocampal Neurogenesis and Extinction of Trace Fear Conditioning," *Experimental Brain Research* 228, no. 4 (August 2013): 481–91; https://link.springer.com/article/10.1007 /s00221-013-3579-0.

6. David A. Martin, Danuta Marona-Lewicka, David E. Nichols, and Charles D. Nichols, "Chronic LSD Alters Gene Expression Profiles in the mPFC Relevant to Schizophrenia," *Neuropharmacology* 83 (August 2014): 1–8; https://www.sciencedirect.com/science/article/pii/S00283908 14001087?via%3Dihub.

7. Peter Gasser, Katharina Kirchner, and Torsten Passle, "LSD-Assisted Psy-chotherapy for Anxiety Associated with a Life-Threatening Disease: A Qualitative Study of Acute and Sustained Subjective Effects," *Journal of Psychopharmacology* 29, no. 1 (January 1, 2015): 57–68; http://www.maps .org/research-archive/lsd/Gasser2014-JOP-LSD-assisted-psychotherapy -followup.pdf. Peter Gasser, Dominique Holstein, Yvonne Michel, et al., "Safety and Efficacy of Lysergic Acid Diethylamide-Assisted Psychother-apy for Anxiety Associated with Life-Threatening Diseases," *The Journal of Nervous and Mental Disease* 202, no. 7 (July 2014): 513–520; http://www .ncbi.nlm.nih.gov/pmc/articles/PMC4086777/.

8. Teri S. Krebs and Pål-Ørjan Johansen, "Lysergic Acid Diethylamide (LSD) for Alcoholism: Meta-analysis of Randomized Controlled Trials," *Journal of Psychopharmacology* 26, no. 7 (July 1, 2012): 994–1002; http://jop.sagepub .com/content/26/7/994.

9. R. Andrew Sewell, John H. Halpern, and Harrison G. Pope Jr., "Response of Cluster Headache to Psilocybin and LSD," *Neurology* 77 (June 2006): 1920–22; http://www.maps.org/research-archive/w3pb/2006/2006_Sewell _22779_1.pdf.

10. Tania Reyes-Izquierdo, Ruby Argumedo, Cynthia Shu, et al., "Stimulatory Effect of Whole Coffee Fruit Concentrate Powder on Plasma Levels of To-tal and Exosomal Brain-Derived Neurotrophic Factor in Healthy Subjects: An Acute Within-Subject Clinical Study," *Food and Nutrition Sciences* 4, no. 9 (September 2013): 984–90; https://www.scirp.org/journal/Paper Information.aspx?PaperID=36447.

11. M. P. Gimpl, I. Gormezano, and J. A. Harvey, "Effects of LSD on Learning as Measured by Classical Conditioning of the Rabbit Nictating Membrane Response," *The Journal of Pharmacology and Experimental Therapeutics* 208, no. 2 (February 1979): 330–34; http://jpet.aspetjournals.org/content /208/2/330.long.

12. Robert C. Spencer, David M. Devilbiss, and Craig W. Berridge, "The Cognition-Enhancing Effects of Psychostimulants Involve Direct Action

in the Prefrontal Cortex," *Biological Psychiatry* 77, no. 11 (June 15, 2015): 940–50; https://www.biologicalpsychiatryjournal.com/article/S0006-3223 (14)00712-4/fulltext.

13. Kenta Kimura, Makoto Ozeki, Lekh Raj Juneja, and Hideki Ohira, "L-Theanine Reduces Psychological and Physiological Stress Responses," *Biological Psychology* 74, no. 1 (January 2007): 39–45; https://www.sciencedirect .com/science/article/pii/S0301051106001451?via%3Dihub.

14. Scott H. Kollins, "A Qualitative Review of Issues Arising in the Use of Psychostimulant Medications in Patients with ADHD and Comorbid Substance Use Disorders," *Current Medical Research and Opinion* 24 (April 1, 2008): 1345–57; https://www.tandfonline.com/doi/abs/10.1185/03007 9908X280707.

15. Irena P. Ilieva, Cayce J. Hook, and Martha J. Farah, "Prescription Stimulants' Effects on Healthy Inhibitory Control, Working Memory, and Episodic Memory: A Meta-analysis," *Journal of Cognitive Neuroscience* 27, no. 6 (June 2015): 1069–89; https://www.mitpressjournals.org/doi/abs/10.1162 /jocn_a_00776?url_ver=Z39.88-2003&rfr_id=ori%3Arid%3Acrossref.org &rfr_dat=cr_pub%3Dpubmed.

16. Anna C. Nobre, Anling Rao, and Gail N. Owen, "L-Theanine, a Natural Constituent in Tea, and Its Effect on Mental State," *Asia Pacific Journal of Clinical Nutrition* 17 suppl. 1 (2008): 167–68; http://apjcn.nhri.org.tw /server/APJCN/17%20Suppl%201//167.pdf.

17. "Review of 'Smart Drug' Shows Modafinil Does Enhance Cognition," University of Oxford, August 20, 2015; http://www.ox.ac.uk/news/2015 -08-20-review-%E2%80%98smart-drug%E2%80%99-shows-modafinil -does-enhance-cognition.

18. Jared W. Young, "Dopamine D1 and D2 Receptor Family Contributions to Modafinil-Induced Wakefulness," *The Journal of Neuroscience* 29, no. 9 (March 4, 2009): 2663–65, http://www.jneurosci.org/content/29/9/2663.

19. Oliver Tucha and Klaus W. Lange, "Effects of Nicotine Chewing Gum on a Real-Life Motor Task: A Kinematic Analysis of Handwriting Movements in Smokers and Non-smokers," *Psychopharmacology* 173, nos. 1–2 (April 2004): 49–56; https://link.springer.com/article/10.1007%2Fs00213 -003-1690-9. R. J. West and M. J. Jarvis, "Effects of Nicotine on Finger Tapping Rate in Non-smokers," *Pharmacology Biochemistry and Behavior* 25, no. 4 (October 1986): 727–31; https://www.sciencedirect.com/science /article/pii/0091305786903771?via%3Dihub.

20. Sarah Phillips and Pauline Fox, "An Investigation into the Effects of Nicotine Gum on Short-Term Memory," *Psychopharmacology* 140, no. 4 (December 1998): 429–33; https://link.springer.com/article/10 .1007%2Fs002130050786. F. Joseph McClernon, David G. Gilbert, and Robert Radtke, "Effects of Transdermal Nicotine on Lateralized Identification and Memory Interference," *Human Psychopharmacology: Clinical and Experimental* 18, no. 5 (July 2003): 339–43; https://onlinelibrary.wiley .com/doi/abs/10.1002/hup.488. D. V. Poltavski and T. Petros, "Effects of

Transdermal Nicotine on Prose Memory and Attention in Smokers and Nonsmokers," *Physiology & Behavior* 83, no. 5 (January 17, 2005): 833–43; https://www.sciencedirect.com/science/article/abs/pii/S00319384040 04548.

21. Johathan Foulds, John Stapleton, John Swettenham, et al., "Cognitive Performance Effects of Subcutaneous Nicotine in Smokers and Never-Smokers," *Psychopharmacology* 127 (1996): 31–38; https://www.gwern.net /docs/nicotine/1996-foulds.pdf.

22. William K. K. Wu and Chi Hin Cho, "The Pharmacological Actions of Nic-otine on the Gastrointestinal Tract," *Journal of Pharmacological Sciences* 94 (2004): 348–58; https://www.jstage.jst.go.jp/article/jphs/94/4/94_4_348 /_pdf. Rebecca Davis, Wasia Rizwani, Sarmistha Banerjee, et al., "Nico-tine Promotes Tumor Growth and Metastasis in Mouse Models of Lung Cancer," *PLOS One* 4, no. 10 (October 2009); https://www.ncbi.nlm.nih .gov/pmc/articles/PMC2759510/pdf/pone.0007524.pdf; Helen Pui Shan Wong, Le Yu, Emily Kai Yee Lam, et al., "Nicotine Promotes Colon Tumor Growth and Angiogenesis through -Adrenergic Activation," *Toxological Sciences* 97, no. 2 (June 1, 2007): 279–87; http://toxsci.oxfordjournals.org /content/97/2/279.html.

23. Katherine S. Pollard, Sofie R. Salama, Nelle Lambert, et al., "An RNA Gene Expressed During Cortical Development Evolved Rapidly in Hu-mans," *Nature* 443, no. 7108 (September 14, 2006): 167–72; https://www .nature.com/articles/nature05113.

24. According to Teresa Valero, "Mitochondrial Biogenesis: Pharmacological Approaches," *Current Pharmaceutical Design* 20, no. 35 (2009): 5507–09; http://www.eurekaselect.com/124512/article, "Mitochondrial biogenesis is therefore defined as the process via which cells increase their individual mitochondrial mass. . . . This work reviews different strategies to enhance mitochondrial bioenergetics in order to ameliorate the neurodegenerative process, with an emphasis on clinical trials reports that indicate their poten-tial. Among them creatine, Coenzyme Q10 and mitochondrial targeted anti-oxidants/peptides are reported to have the most remarkable effects in clinical trials." According to Fabian Sanchis-Gomar, Jose Luis García-Giménez, Mari Carmen Gómez-Cabrera, and Federico V. Pallardó, "Mitochondrial Biogene-sis in Health and Disease. Molecular and Therapeutic Approaches," *Current Pharmaceutical Design* 20, no. 35 (2009): 5619–33; http://www.eurekaselect .com/120757/article: "Mitochondrial biogenesis (MB) is the essential mech-anism by which cells control the number of mitochondria." See also Gerald W. Dorn, Rick B. Vega, and Daniel P. Kelly, "Mitochondrial Biogenesis and Dynamics in the Developing and Diseased Heart," *Genes & Development* 29 (2015): 1981–91; http://genesdev.cshlp.org/content/29/19/1981.long.

25. Florian Koppelstaetter, Christian Michael Siedentopf, Thorsten Poeppel, et al., "Influence of Caffeine Excess on Activation Patterns in Verbal Work-ing Memory," scientific poster, RSNA Annual Meeting 2005, Chicago, Illi-nois, December 1, 2005; http://archive.rsna.org/2005/4418422.html.

26. Flávia de L. Osório, Rafael F. Sanches, Ligia R. Macedo, et al., "Anti-depressant Effects of a Single Dose of Ayahuasca in Patients with Recurrent Depression: A Preliminary Report," *Revista Brasileira de Psiquiatria* 37, no. 1 (January–March 2015): 13–20; http://www.scielo.br/scielo.php?script=sci _arttext&pid=S1516-44462015000100013&lng=en&nrm=iso.

27. Gerald Thomas, Philippe Lucas, N. Rielle Capler, et al., "Ayahuasca-Assisted Therapy for Addiction: Results from a Preliminary Observational Study in Canada," *Current Drug Abuse Reviews* 6, no. 1 (March 2013): 30–42; http://www.maps.org/research-archive/ayahuasca/Thomas_et_al_CDAR.pdf.

28. James C. Callaway, Mauno M. Airaksinen, Dennis J. McKenna, et al., "Platelet Serotoin Uptake Sites Increased in Drinkers of *Ayahuasca*," *Psychopharmacology* 116, no. 3 (November 1994): 385–87; https://link.springer .com/article/10.1007/BF02245347.

29. Ibid.

CHAPTER 4: DISRUPT FEAR

1. M. C. Brower and B. H. Price, "Neuropsychiatry of Frontal Lobe Dysfunction in Violent and Criminal Behaviour: A Critical Review," *Journal of Neurology, Neurosurgery, & Psychiatry* 71, no. 6 (2001): 720–26; http://jnnp.bmj.com/content/jnnp/71/6/720.full.pdf.

CHAPTER 5: EVEN BATMAN HAS A BAT CAVE

1. Aaron Lerner, Patricia Jeremias, and Torsten Matthias, "The World Incidence and Prevalence of Autoimmune Diseases Is Increasing," *International Journal of Celiac Disease* 3, no. 5 (2015): 151–55; http://pubs.sciepub .com/ijcd/3/4/8/.

CHAPTER 6: SEX IS AN ALTERED STATE

1. Ed Yong, "Shedding Light on Sex and Violence in the Brain," *Discover*, February 9, 2011; http://blogs.discovermagazine.com/notrocketscience /2011/02/09/shedding-light-on-sex-and-violence-in-the-brain/#.WgSzGY Zrw6g.

2. Eliana Dockterman, "World Cup: The Crazy Rules Some Teams Have About Pre-game Sex," *Time*, June 18, 2014; http://time.com/2894263/world -cup-sex-soccer/.

3. Madeline Vann, "1 in 4 Men over 30 Has Low Testosterone," ABC News, September 13, 2007; http://abcnews.go.com/Health/Healthday/story?id =4508669&page=1.

4. Tillmann H. C. Krüger, Uwe Hartmann, and Manfred Schedlowski, "Prolactinergic and Dopaminergic Mechanisms Underlying Sexual Arousal and Orgasm in Humans," *World Journal of Urology* 23, no. 2 (July 2005): 130–38; https://link.springer.com/article/10.1007%2Fs00345-004-0496-7.

5. Michael S. Exton, Tillman H. C. Krüger, Norbert Bursch, et al., "Endocrine Response to Masturbation-Induced Orgasm in Healthy Men Following a

3-Week Sexual Abstinence," *World Journal of Urology* 19, no. 5 (November 2001): 377–82; https://link.springer.com/article/10.1007/s003450100222.

6. James M. Dabbs Jr. and Suzanne Mohammed, "Male and Female Salivary Testosterone Concentrations Before and After Sexual Activity," *Physiology & Behavior* 52, no. 1 (July 1992): 195–97; https://www.sciencedirect.com/science/article/abs/pii/0031938492904539.

7. Umit Sayin, "Altered States of Consciousness Occurring During Expanded Sexual Response in the Human Female: Preliminary Definitions," *Neuro-Quantology* 9, no. 4 (December 2011); https://www.neuroquantology.com/index.php/journal/article/view/486.

8. Sari M. Van Anders, Lori Brotto, Janine Farrell, and Morag Yule, "Associations Among Physiological and Subjective Sexual Response, Sexual Desire, and Salivary Steroid Hormones in Healthy Premenopausal Women," *The Journal of Sexual Medicine* 6, no. 3 (March 2009): 739–51; https://www.jsm.jsexmed.org/article/S1743-6095(15)32435-8/fulltext.

9. Navneet Magon and Sanjay Kalra, "The Orgasmic History of Oxytocin: Love, Lust, and Labor," *Indian Journal of Endocrinology and Metabolism* 15 suppl. 3 (September 2011): S156–61; https://www.ncbi.nlm.nih.gov/pmc/articles/PMC3183515/.

10. Margaret M. McCarthy, "Estrogen Modulation of Oxytocin and Its Relation to Behavior," *Advances in Experimental Medicine and Biology* 395 (1995): 235–45; https://www.researchgate.net/publication/14488327_Estrogen_modulation_of_oxytocin_and_its_relation_to_behavior.

11. Cindy M. Meston and Penny F. Frolich, "Update on Female Sexual Function," *Current Opinion in Urology* 11, no. 6 (November 2001): 603–09; https://journals.lww.com/co-urology/pages/articleviewer.aspx?year=2001&issue=11000&article=00008&type=abstract.

12. Case Western Reserve University, "Empathy Represses Analytic Thought, and Vice Versa: Brain Physiology Limits Simultaneous Use of Both Networks," ScienceDaily, October 30, 2012, https://www.sciencedaily.com/releases/2012/10/121030161416.htm.

13. Daniel L. Hilton, Jr., "Pornography Addiction—A Supranormal Stimulus Considered in the Context of Neuroplasticity," *Socioaffective Neuroscience & Psychology* 3 (July 19, 2013); https://www.ncbi.nlm.nih.gov/pmc/articles/PMC3960020/.

14. Aline Wéry and J. Billieux, "Online Sexual Activities: An Exploratory Study of Problematic and Non-problematic Usage Patterns in a Sample of Men," *Computers in Human Behavior* 56 (March 2016): 257–66; http://www.sciencedirect.com/science/article/pii/S0747563215302612.

15. Simone Kühn and Jürgen Gallinat, "Brain Structure and Functional Connectivity Associated with Pornography Consumption: The Brain on Porn," *JAMA Psychiatry* 71, no. 7 (2014): 827–34; https://jamanetwork.com/journals/jamapsychiatry/fullarticle/1874574.

16. Valerie Voon, Thomas B. Mole, Paula Banca, et al., "Neural Correlates of Sexual Cue Reactivity in Individuals with and Without Compulsive Sexual Behaviours," *PLOS One*, July 11, 2014; http://journals.plos.org/plosone /article?id=10.1371/journal.pone.0102419.

17. Norman Doidge, "Brain Scans of Porn Addicts: What's Wrong with This Picture?," *The Guardian*, September 26, 2013; https://www.theguardian .com/commentisfree/2013/sep/26/brain-scans-porn-addicts-sexual-tastes.

CHAPTER 7: FIND YOUR NIGHTTIME SPIRIT ANIMAL

1. Scott LaFee, "Woman's Study Finds Longevity Means Getting Just Enough Sleep," UC San Diego, September 30, 2010; http://ucsdnews.ucsd.edu /archive/newsrel/health/09-30sleep.asp.

2. R. J. Reiter, "The Melatonin Rhythm: Both a Clock and a Calendar," *Experientia* 49, no. 8 (August 1993): 654–64; https://link.springer.com/article /10.1007/BF01923947.

3. Toru Takumi, Kouji Taguchi, Shigeru Miyake, et al., "A Light-Independent Oscillatory Gene *mPer3* in Mouse SCN and OVLT," *The EMBO Journal* 17, no. 16 (August 17, 1998): 4753–59; http://emboj.embopress.org/content /17/16/4753.long.

4. Ariel Van Brummelen, "How Blind People Detect Light," *Scientific American*, May 1, 2014; https://www.scientificamerican.com/article/how-blind -people-detect-light/.

5. Micha T. Maeder, Otto D. Schoch, and Hans Rickli, "A Clinical Approach to Obstructive Sleep Apnea as a Risk Factor for Cardiovascular Disease," *Vascular Health and Risk Management* 12 (2016): 85–103; https://www .dovepress.com/a-clinical-approach-to-obstructive-sleep-apnea-as-a-risk -factor-for-ca-peer-reviewed-article-VHRM.

6. Michael Tetley, "Instinctive Sleeping and Resting Postures: An Anthropological and Zoological Approach to Treatment of Low Back and Joint Pain," *The British Medical Journal* 321, no. 7276 (December 23, 2000): 1616–18; https://www.bmj.com/content/321/7276/1616.long.

7. Sydney Ross Singer, "Rest in Peace: How the Way You Sleep Can Be Killing You," Academia.edu, February 1, 2015; http://www.academia.edu/10739979 /Rest_in_Peace_How_the_way_you_sleep_can_be_killing_you.

CHAPTER 8: THROW A ROCK AT THE RABBIT, DON'T CHASE IT

1. Liana S. Rosenthal and E. Ray Dorsey, "The Benefits of Exercise in Parkinson Disease," *JAMA Neurology* 70, no. 2 (February 2013): 156–57; https:// jamanetwork.com/journals/jamaneurology/article-abstract/1389387.

2. Hayriye Çakir-Atabek, Süleyman Demir, Raziye D. Pinarbaşili, and Nihat Gündüz, "Effects of Different Resistance Training Intensity on Indices of Oxidative Stress," *Journal of Strength and Conditioning Research* 24, no. 9 (September 2010): 2491–98; https://insights.ovid.com/pubmed?pmid=20802287.

3. Ebrahim A. Shojaei, Adalat Farajov, and Afshar Jafari, "Effect of Moderate Aerobic Cycling on Some Systemic Inflammatory Markers in Healthy Active Collegiate Men," *International Journal of General Medicine* 4 (January 24, 2011): 79–84; https://www.dovepress.com/effect-of-moderate-aerobic-cycling-on-some-systemic-inflammatory-marke-peer-reviewed-article-IJGM.

4. Bharat B. Aggarwal, Shishir Shishodia, Santosh K. Sandur, et al., "Inflammation and Cancer: How Hot Is the Link?," *Biochemical Pharmacology* 72, no. 11 (November 30, 2006): 1605–21; https://www.sciencedirect.com/science/article/abs/pii/S0006295206003893. Dario Giugliano, Antonio Ceriello, and Katherine Esposito, "The Effects of Diet on Inflammation: Emphasis on the Metabolic Syndrome," *Journal of the American College of Cardiology* 48, no. 4 (August 15, 2006): 677–85; https://www.sciencedirect.com/science/article/pii/S0735109706013350?via%3Dihub.

5. Farnaz Seifi-skishahr, Arsalan Damirchi, Manoochehr Farjaminezhad, and Parvin Babaei, "Physical Training Status Determines Oxidative Stress and Redox Changes in Response to an Acute Aerobic Exercise," *Biochemistry Research International* 2016, 9 pages; https://www.hindawi.com/journals/bri/2016/3757623/.

6. Lanay M. Mudd, Willa Fornetti, and James M. Pivarnik, "Bone Mineral Density in Collegiate Female Athletes: Comparisons Among Sports," *Journal of Athletic Training* 42, no. 3 (July–September 2007): 403–08; https://www.ncbi.nlm.nih.gov/pmc/articles/PMC1978462/.

7. "Preserve Your Muscle Mass," Harvard Men's Health Watch, February 2016; https://www.health.harvard.edu/staying-healthy/preserve-your-muscle-mass.

CHAPTER 9: YOU GET OUT WHAT YOU PUT IN
1. Begoña Cerdá, Margarita Pérez, Jennifer D. Pérez-Santiago, et al., "Gut Microbiota Modification: Another Piece in the Puzzle of the Benefits of Physical Exercise in Health?," *Frontiers in Physiology* 7 (February 18, 2016): 51. https://www.frontiersin.org/articles/10.3389/fphys.2016.00051/full.

2. Mehrbod Estaki, Jason Pither, Peter Baumeister, et al., "Cardiorespiratory Fitness as a Predictor of Intestinal Microbial Diversity and Distinct Metagenomic Functions," *Microbiome* 4 (2016): 42; https://microbiomejournal.biomedcentral.com/articles/10.1186/s40168-016-0189-7.

3. Tian-Xing Liu, Hai-Tao Niu, and Shu-Yang Zhang, "Intestinal Microbiota Metabolism and Atherosclerosis," *Chinese Medical Journal* 128, no. 20 (2015): 2805–11; http://www.cmj.org/article.asp?issn=0366-6999;year=2015;volume=128;issue=20;spage=2805;epage=2811;aulast=Liu.

CHAPTER 10: THE FUTURE OF HACKING YOURSELF IS NOW
1. "Temperature Rhythms Keep Body Clocks in Sync," ScienceDaily, October 15, 2010; https://www.sciencedaily.com/releases/2010/10/101014144314.htm.

CHAPTER 11: BEING RICH WON'T MAKE YOU HAPPY, BUT BEING HAPPY MIGHT MAKE YOU RICH

1. Daniel Kahneman and Angus Deaton, "High income improves evaluation of life but not emotional well-being," *Proceedings of the National Academy of Sciences of the United States of America* 107, no. 38 (September 21, 2010): 16489–93; http://www.pnas.org/content/107/38/16489.

2. Shawn Achor, "Positive Intelligence," *Harvard Business Review*, January–February 2012; https://hbr.org/2012/01/positive-intelligence. Sonja Lyubomirsky, Laura King, and Ed Diener, "The Benefits of Frequent Positive Affect: Does Happiness Lead to Success?," *Psychological Bulletin* 131, no. 6 (November 2005): 803–55; https://www.apa.org/pubs/journals/releases/bul-1316803.pdf.

3. Michael Como, "Do Happier People Make More Money? An Empirical Study of the Effect of a Person's Happiness on Their Income," *The Park Place Economist* 19, no. 1 (2011); https://www.iwu.edu/economics/PPE19/1Como.pdf.

CHAPTER 12: YOUR COMMUNITY IS YOUR ENVIRONMENT

1. "Genes Play a Role in Empathy," *ScienceDaily*, March 12, 2018; https://www.sciencedaily.com/releases/2018/03/180312085124.htm.

2. Mackenzie Hepker, "Effect of Oxytocin Administration on Mirror Neuron Activation," *Sound Ideas*, University of Puget Sound, Summer 2013; https://soundideas.pugetsound.edu/cgi/viewcontent.cgi?article=1267&context=summer_research.

3. Kathy Caprino, "Is Empathy Dead? How Your Lack of Empathy Damages Your Reputation and Impact as a Leader," *Forbes*, June 8, 2016; https://www.forbes.com/sites/kathycaprino/2016/06/08/is-empathy-dead-how-your-lack-of-empathy-damages-your-reputation-and-impact-as-a-leader/#429c3d353167.

4. James H. Fowler and Nicholas A. Christakis, "Dynamic Spread of Happiness in a Large Social Network: Longitudinal Analysis over 20 Years in the Framingham Heart Study," *The British Medical Journal* 337 (December 4, 2008): a2338; https://www.bmj.com/content/337/bmj.a2338.

5. Ed Diener and Martin E. P. Seligman, "Very Happy People," *Psychological Science* 13, no. 1 (January 1, 2002): 81–84; http://journals.sagepub.com/doi/abs/10.1111/1467-9280.00415#articleCitationDownloadContainer.

6. "Are We Happy Yet?," Pew Research Center, February 13, 2006; http://www.pewsocialtrends.org/2006/02/13/are-we-happy-yet/.

CHAPTER 13: RESET YOUR PROGRAMMING

1. Michael A. Tansey, "Wechsler (WISC-R) Changes Following Treatment of Learning Disabilities via EEG Biofeedback Training in a Private Practice Setting," *Australian Journal of Psychology* 43, no. 3 (December 1991): 147–53; https://onlinelibrary.wiley.com/doi/abs/10.1080/00049539108260139, reported improvements averaging 19.75 points on the WISC-R Full Scale IQ score for twenty-four children with "neurological or perceptual

impairments or attention deficit disorder." Using a random assignment wait list control design, Michael Linden, Thomas Habib, and Vesna Radojevic, "A Controlled Study of the Effects of EEG Biofeedback on Cognition and Behavior of Children with Attention Deficit Disorder and Learning Disabilities," *Biofeedback and Self-regulation* 21, no. 1 (March 1996): 35–49; https://link.springer.com/article/10.1007/BF02214148, reported that the eighteen participants who received EEG biofeedback showed a statistically significant gain of 9 points on the K-Bit IQ Composite. Joel F. Lubar, Michie Odle Swartwood, Jeffery N. Swartwood, and Phyllis H. O'Donnell, "Evaluation of the Effectiveness of EEG Neurofeedback Training for ADHD in a Clinical Setting as Measured by Changes in T.O.V.A. Scores, Behavioral Ratings, and WISC-R Performance," *Biofeedback and Self-regulation* 20, no. 1 (March 1995): 83–99; https://link.springer.com/article/10.1007/BF01712768, reported gains averaging 9.7 points for twenty-three children. Siegfried Othmer, Susan F. Othmer, and David A. Kaiser, "EEG Biofeedback: Training for AD/HD and Related Disruptive Behavior Disorders," in *Understanding, Diagnosing, and Treating AD/HD in Children and Adolescents*, ed. James A. Incorvaia, Bonnie S. Mark-Goldstein, and Donald Tessmer (Northvale, NJ: Aronson, 1999), 235–96, reported an average gain of 23.5 points with a sample of fifteen children. L. Thompson and M. Thompson, "Neurofeedback Combined with Training in Metacognitive Strategies: Effectiveness in Students with ADD," *Applied Psychophysiology and Biofeedback* 23, no. 4 (December 1998): 243–63; https://link.springer.com/article/10.1023%2FA%3A1022213731956, reported ninety-eight children gaining an average of 12 points. Thomas Fuchs, Niels Birbaumer, Werner Lutzenberger, et al., "Neurofeedback Treatment for Attention-Deficit/Hyperactivity Disorder in Children: A Comparison with Methylphenidate," *Applied Psychophysiology and Biofeedback* 28, no. 1 (March 2003): 1–12; https://link.springer.com/article/10.1023/A:1022353731579, reported an improvement of only 4 points in a study of twenty-two children. See also Joel F. Lubar, "Neurofeedback for the Management of Attention-Deficit/Hyperactivity Disorders," in *Biofeedback: A Practitioner's Guide*, 2nd ed., ed. Mark S. Schwartz (New York: Guilford, 1995), 493–522. Vincent J. Monastra, Donna M. Monastra, and Susan George, "The Effects of Stimulant Therapy, EEG Biofeedback, and Parenting Style on the Primary Symptoms of Attention-Deficit/Hyperactivity Disorder," *Applied Psychophysiology and Biofeedback* 27, no. 4 (December 2002): 231–49; https://link.springer.com/article/10.1023/A:1021018700609. John K. Nash, "Treatment of Attention Deficit Hyperactivity Disorder with Neurotherapy," *Clinical Electroencephalography* 31, no. 1 (January 2000): 30–37; http://journals.sagepub.com/doi/pdf/10.1177/155005940003100109. Siegfried Othmer, Susan F. Othmer, and Clifford S. Marks, "EEG Biofeedback Training for Attention Deficit Disorder, Specific Learning Disabilities, and Associated Conduct Problems," January 1992; https://www.researchgate.net/publication/252060569_EEG_Biofeedback_Training_for_Attention_Deficit_Disorder_Specific_Learning_Disabilities_and_Associated_Conduct_Problems.

CHAPTER 14: GET DIRTY IN THE SUN

1. Laken C. Woods, Gregory W. Berbusse, and Kari Naylor, "Microtubules Are Essential for Mitochondrial Dynamics—Fission, Fusion, and Motility—in *Dictyostelium discoideum*," *Frontiers in Cell and Developmental Biology* 4 (2016): 19; https://www.ncbi.nlm.nih.gov/pmc/articles/PMC4801864/.

2. Hidemasa Torii, Toshihide Kurihara, Yuko Seko, et al., "Violet Light Exposure Can Be a Preventive Strategy Against Myopia Progression," *EBioMedicine* 15 (2017): 210–19; https://www.ebiomedicine.com/article/S23 52-3964(16)30586-2/fulltext.

3. S. C. Gominak and W. E. Stumpf, "The World Epidemic of Sleep Disorders Is Linked to Vitamin D Deficiency," *Medical Hypotheses* 79, no. 2 (August 2012): 132–35; https://www.medical-hypotheses.com/article/S03 06-9877(12)00150-8/fulltext.

4. Sherri Melrose, "Seasonal Affective Disorder: An Overview of Assessment and Treatment Approaches," *Depression Research and Treatment*, 2015, 6 pages; https://www.hindawi.com/journals/drt/2015/178564/.

5. Raymond W. Lam, Anthony J. Levitt, Robert D. Levitan, et al., "The CanSAD Study: A Randomized Controlled Trial of the Effectiveness of Light Therapy and Fluoxetine in Patients With Winter Seasonal Affective Disorder," *The American Journal of Psychiatry* 163, no. 5 (May 2006): 805–12; https://ajp.psychiatryonline.org/doi/abs/10.1176/ajp.2006.163.5.805.

6. Sokichi Sakuragi and Yoshiki Sugiyama, "Effects of Daily Walking on Subjective Symptoms, Mood and Autonomic Nervous Function," *Journal of Physiological Anthropology* 25, no. 4 (2006): 281–89; https://www.jstage.jst .go.jp/article/jpa2/25/4/25_4_281/_article.

7. Ibid.

8. Marc G. Berman, Ethan Kross, Katherine M. Krpan, et al., "Interacting with Nature Improves Cognition and Affect for Individuals with Depression," *Journal of Affective Disorders* 140, no. 3 (November 2012): 300–05; http://www.natureandforesttherapy.org/uploads/8/1/4/4/8144400/nature _improves_mood_and_cognition_in_depressive_patients.pdf.

CHAPTER 15: USE GRATITUDE TO REWIRE YOUR BRAIN

1. Stephen W. Porges, "The Polyvagal Theory: New Insights into Adaptive Reactions of the Autonomic Nervous System," *Cleveland Clinic Journal of Medicine* 76 suppl. 2 (2009): S86–90; https://www.ncbi.nlm.nih.gov/pmc /articles/PMC3108032/.

INDEX

ABOUT THE AUTHOR

DAVE ASPREY is a Silicon Valley tech entrepreneur, professional bio-hacker, the *New York Times* bestselling author of *Head Strong* and *The Bulletproof Diet*, the creator of Bulletproof Coffee, and the host of *Bulletproof Radio*, the Webby Award–winning, number one–ranked podcast. He lives in Victoria, British Columbia, and Seattle, Washington.

Joined Up

Joined Up

An introduction to
youth work **and** *ministry*

DANNY BRIERLEY

LIFESTYLE

First published in 2003 by Spring Harvest Publishing Division
and Authentic Lifestyle

09 08 07 06 05 04 03   7 6 5 4 3 2 1

Authentic Lifestyle is an imprint of Authentic Media
PO Box 300, Carlisle, Cumbria CA3 0QS, UK
and
Box 1047, Waynesboro, GA 30830–2047, USA
www.paternoster-publishing.com

British Library Cataloguing in Publication Data
A catalogue record for this book is available from the British Library

ISBN 1–85078–483–3

Cover design by Sam Redwood
Typeset by Waverley Typesetters, Galashiels
Printed in Great Britain by Cox & Wyman, Reading, Berkshire

Contents

Part Three: Practice of youth work *and* ministry

Preface

This is the first title in a new *Youthwork* series published by Authentic Media, in association with Youthwork – the Partnership. Books in the Going Deeper series are:

- Designed for those who are serious about youth work and ministry
- Sometimes controversial, always challenging, never dogmatic
- Written by Christians from many traditions and experiences, united by a common commitment to Jesus Christ
- Doorways to influential Christian and non-Christian thinkers, concepts, models and literature
- Reliant upon youth work, theology and youth ministry, as well as other disciplines
- Willing to engage with, and be challenged by, different world-views.

My desire is that this book will stimulate debate among those committed to serving the young. I hope it will provide a useful apologetic for those working in church settings, as well as a challenge to pursue deeper under-standings of practice. Likewise, I hope those working in

statutory settings will find the book a helpful introduction to faith-based youth work. Above all, I hope all readers will find fresh insights about the person and work of Jesus Christ. I neither expect nor want readers to agree with everything I have written. For this reason I have invited critical responses to some of the chapters and I am grateful to Nick Margesson, Malcolm Rittman, Dr Nigel Wright, Claire Leas and Dr Sally Nash.

Some of the content for this book first appeared in a series of articles written for *Youthwork Magazine*. As well as providing a helpful writing schedule, this also enabled me to respond to feedback from readers. I am grateful to all those who took the time to write or e-mail. They challenged and at times changed my thinking. Steve Adams and John Buckeridge deserve a special mention for their patience and constant encouragement.

I am also grateful to the following for commenting on earlier drafts of the text: Steve Chalke, Dr John Colwell, Jonathon Dutton, Lyn Green, Simon Johnston, Alan Mann, Robin Parry, Colin Sinclair and Jeremy Thomson. Thanks are also due to Mark Finnie, Sheila Jacobs and Nancy Lush at Authentic and Steve May-Miller at Spring Harvest.

DANNY BRIERLEY
March 2003

Foreword

Work with young people has, during the past three years, moved to the centre of both the government's and the churches' agenda. After more than a decade in the wilderness and drastic financial cuts the Youth Service is again being taken seriously by the government.

'Youth Service gets Funding and Budget Line Boost' was a headline in the December 2002 edition of *Young People Now* magazine which the National Youth Agency publishes for everyone working with young people. At the same time a whole variety of church reports have focused on the need to re-evaluate the churches' work with young people; from the positive comment of the Salvation Army in their report 'Burden of Youth' that 'The Salvation Army will prioritise it's mission and invest its resources and expertise in the UK's youth', to the almost panicky response of the Church of England in the much publicised report 'Hope for the Church' that stated: 'The Church of England must learn to attract younger adults in greater numbers.'

Danny Brierley's book is therefore being published at a very critical time for both the future of the Youth Service and the mission of the churches in the twenty-first century. It doesn't pull any punches about the current struggle between youth work *and* youth ministry which has led to

real divisions particularly among evangelical Christians
and real suspicions about motives from those in the
secular youth work world. I am personally grateful for
Danny's exploration as I face the same struggle between
being Chair of the National Youth Agency and a member
of the College of Evangelists.

Danny believes the core values of youth work –
Voluntary Participation, Informal Education, Empowerment and Equality of Opportunity – 'provide a strong
philosophical framework in which youth ministry can
operate'. He explores in chapters 5–8 how these core
values can be shown to be consistent with the teaching
of Scripture and particularly how 'the life and work of
Christ Jesus makes them biblically justified.' This exploration, he believes, can 'result in new theological understanding'. I recently shared with the ecumenical borough
deans of London his insight into the way 'Jesus used
healing as a way of countering social inclusion' and how
this gives a whole new meaning to Jesus' manifesto for
mission and call to give priority to proclaiming 'good
news to the poor' in Luke 4:18. This led to a very lively
discussion over tea!

If the book provides ways in which 'youth work *and*
youth ministry are providing the church with new theological insight' it also explores the important challenge of
values in all youth work. At my first board meeting of
the National Youth Agency we had a fascinating debate
about the inclusion of the word 'justice' in our mission
statement. As one who has written a book called *Justice
on the Agenda* I was particularly interested in the strong
feelings this raised on both sides. Danny quotes with
approval Maxine Green's words that 'Young people have
a right to their spiritual, political, and ideological heritage'.
Of importance at this present time is the chapter on
Equality of Opportunity, particularly the section on Race

for justice. Both his statement that 'It is wrong to talk of different races; there is only one human race' and his illustration from the West Midlands where 'Christians stood alongside Muslims in the campaign for justice' show how important values should be in youth work. In the National Youth Agency one of our big concerns is the challenge of faith-based youth work and community cohesion and it is here the values Danny explores in this section are very important. His conclusion that 'Equality of opportunity requires that all religions be given equal access to resources and status' would be supported by the National Youth Agency provided those who receive funding are prepared to work in partnership with others. Tom Wylie, Chief Executive of the National Youth Agency, has recently asked a question about the 'danger that some sectors of the voluntary sector are now directing prodigious energy not to work in partnership but to secure competitive advantage and to wrest power from the state, especially from local authorities' (*YPN*, December 2002].

While it is important for the state to recognise that the Church now 'is the largest employer of full-time paid youth workers in England and Wales' it is equally important that this is not used as an excuse for the State and local authorities to under-fund the Youth Service or for the Church to misuse this power.

Danny Brierley recognises that much Church-sponsored youth ministry 'has traditionally benefited socially and economically "included" young people in suburbia' and he calls in his chapter on Incarnation for Christians to see that 'the value of the incarnation calls us to prefer identification with the socially and economically "excluded"'. His statement that 'The incarnation ... reminds us that people matter' made connections in my mind with George Burton's classic on youth work with excluded young people in Canning Town called *People*

Matter More Than Things. It is important today when many excluded young people are written off by the tabloid press as yobs, for us to recognise all 'Young people are individuals who deserve to be valued, respected and have their views and experiences taken seriously' (*Working with Young People*).

As someone passionately concerned with mission I particularly valued the section in the chapter on Informal Education on Conversation. 'Youth work *and* ministry relies significantly upon conversation. Quite often the significant work takes place immediately outside a youth centre.' This was something I found to be very true when I was a youth worker at Shrewsbury House in Liverpool and shared in my book *From a Mersey Wall*. Christian youth workers need to learn in the words of Michael Green in his book *Evangelism and the Early Church* how to 'gossip the gospel'. Danny Brierley in this section also challenges those 'Evangelicals [who] have traditionally understood conversion as something done to others' with his statement 'This egotistic understanding is challenged by informal education; empowered by the Holy Spirit, people convert themselves.' This is close to what John Drane calls 'midwife evangelism' in his book *The McDonaldization of the Church*. It is an approach to mission he believes 'requires youth workers and ministers to be vulnerable', something which David Bosch explores in his book *The Vulnerability of Mission* – 'Only if we turn our backs on false power and false security can there be authentic Christian Mission'.

I hope this book will be widely read by those Christians training as youth workers. It would certainly be a text book I believe would be of real value on those courses for Christian youth workers and ministers validated by the National Youth Agency. I also believe it will be very valuable not only for clergy and church councils

employing youth workers but also for all Christians because of the very valuable insights it gives on mission today.

Finally I hope it will be read by those involved in the secular youth service as it will help to dispel many of the widely held myths about the reasons for Christian involvement in youth work.

BISHOP ROGER SAINSBURY
Chair of the National Youth Agency
and former Bishop of Barking

References

Young People Now, December 2002

National Youth Agency: *The Burden of Youth* (Henley Centre/ Salvation Army, 2001)

Jackson, Bob, *Hope for the Church* (Church House Publishing, 2002)

Sainsbury, Roger, *Justice on the Agenda* (Marshalis, 1985)

Burton, George, *People Matter More Than Things* (Hodder & Stoughton, 1965)

Meha, Josie and Marilyn McGowan, *Working with Young People* (TSA, 2002)

Sainsbury, Roger, *From a Mersey Wall* (Scripture Union, 1970)

Green, Michael, *Evangelism and the Early Church* (Hodder & Stoughton, 1980)

Drane, John, *The McDonaldization of the Church* (Darton, Longman & Todd, 2000)

Bosch, David, *The Vulnerability of Mission* (Selly Oak, 1998)

Part One:

Foundations of youth work *and* ministry

Chapter 1

Introducing youth work
and ministry

Pistols at dawn

In the days of chivalry, when two individuals (usually headstrong men) could not agree, they would sometimes fight to the death in a duel. Seeing such acute and irreconcilable differences, each would rather die than accept the validity of the other's position. 'Pistols at dawn' was a bizarre and destructive ritual. This book is about a modern-day duel that many peace-loving Christians find themselves caught up in. It is the struggle between youth work and youth ministry. They see acute and irreconcilable differences of ideology and practice between the Church and State and, in the name of God, take up the challenge. In most cases 'pistols at dawn' leads, not to acts of violence, but to entrenched – and no less destructive – stand-offs between the estranged and non-communicative parties.

Sometimes evangelical Christians like me are quick to adopt dualist theology: good is pitched against evil; light against dark. Just as in Hollywood, we like to know there are 'goodies' and 'baddies' – and who is who. But to what extent is dualism necessary? Christian theology certainly affirms the existence of some forms of dualism.

For example, God and creation are not one and the same.
The Bible may declare God to be the Lord and the One
who sustains creation, but to hug a tree is not to hug God,
as pantheists and process theologians suggest. The Bible
supports a dualism between God and creation. Creator
God may be active in and through the work of his creation
but he and creation do not merge to become one and
the same. Some dualism is therefore biblically justified.
Yet the Bible also denies the validity of some forms of
dualism that seem to have found favour today. For
example, it refutes the possibility that good and evil
are locked together in a cosmic duel. It is not a match
between two opposing equals in which good is declared
the victor – but only just. It would be wrong to suggest
God's defeat of evil is simply due to his slightly quicker
reflexes or more accurate shot. Christ is the Supreme
Lord. It is an unequal match in which there was only
ever going to be one outcome. Some Christians get carried
away with dualism, seeing acute and irreconcilable
differences that don't necessarily exist in the eyes of God.
It is perhaps no surprise that a male dominated Church
should adopt masculine approaches to conflict; there
are few records of women using duels to settle their
differences.

To think about . . .

What other examples of dualism are suggested
in the Bible? What other popular dualisms are
not supported by the Bible?

The struggle between youth work and youth ministry
seems to be another unnecessary dualism. 'Pistols at

dawn' is called between *youth work*, representing the world and all that is secular, and *youth ministry*, representing the kingdom of God and all that is sacred. Youth work, or youth and community work as its practitioners prefer, is often associated with the caring professions and the work of local authority Youth Services. In contrast, youth ministry has emerged in the last twenty years as the evangelical Church's response to the spiritual needs of young people. There is no room for neutrality in this duel; we are asked to choose which side we are on: youth work or youth ministry; secular or sacred; the world or the kingdom of God. What could be simpler?

Consequently, youth work and youth ministry have developed their own distinct terminologies and professional infrastructures, involving, among other things, publishers, career paths, training courses and conferences. Practitioners display their allegiance by the type of books they read and the conferences they attend. Those that subscribe only to *Young People Now* or *Youthwork Magazine* reveal their adherence. Too often both 'sides' regard each other with suspicion and ignorance. Youth work often labels youth ministry as a religious brainwasher or amateur meddler, whereas youth ministry frequently judges youth work to be a social 'do gooder'. But who are these contenders and are their differences really that irreconcilable? My contention is that youth work and youth ministry both contain elements that are helpful but that separately neither can be considered sufficient. They each have strengths and weaknesses. However, when they are reconciled to each other, the combined youth work *and* ministry provides a genuinely holistic approach to working with young people. But, before reconciliation can be achieved, it is first necessary to review the alleged differences.

What is youth work?

Youth work has come to represent a particular approach to engaging with young people. Not everything involving young people is youth work, just as not everyone who works with a young person is a youth worker. A police officer may arrest a young person, but that does not make them a youth worker. The same is also true for other professionals, such as teachers and social workers. They may work with young people but they are not regarded as youth workers. Similarly, playing pool with a young person, even if at a Friday evening youth club, is not youth work *per se*. Yet, playing pool may provide a context in which youth work can take place. Purpose is all-important. Youth work is concerned with young people's personal, social and educational development. It offers young people both planned and spontaneous opportunities to learn through experience, about self, others and society. The purpose of youth work is defined in the *National Occupational Standards for Youth Work in the UK* as being

> To work with young people to facilitate their personal, social and educational development, and enable them to gain a voice, influence and place in society in a period of their transition from dependence to independence.

> National Youth Agency, 1999

Kerry Young believes youth work is primarily about moral philosophy, enabling young people to determine the central questions of life: what sort of person they are, how they want to relate to themselves and others, and what kind of society they choose to live in. It is concerned not so much with providing activities and imparting

knowledge, as enabling young people to take control of their own development. Youth work is not something done *to* young people but rather a process they engage in, in order to assume greater control of their own lives. A game of pool may then provide a context for a youth worker and young person to engage in dialogue from which both parties derive benefit. Whereas teachers, with their lesson plans and delegated authority, deliver *formal education*, youth workers, with their conversation and experiential learning, offer *informal education*. Young people are required to attend school but are free to choose whether or not to participate in youth work. Youth workers have to earn the right to be involved with young people and respect their decision to accept or reject what is offered.

Youth work has been shaped by four core values defined by the 1991 Second Ministerial Conference for the Youth Service. Activity that is not informed by these values is not considered to be youth work. These values are:

- *Voluntary participation* – young people and youth workers enter into a voluntary relationship in which young people are active partners in the learning process and decision making structures. Youth work cannot involve compulsory attendance
- *Informal education* – youth workers enable young people to gain skills, knowledge and attitudes needed to make the most of their rights and responsibilities as members of society. Youth work is responsive to the interests and needs of young people and involves both planned and spontaneous interventions
- *Empowerment* – youth workers support young people to understand, and act on, the personal, social and

political issues which affect their lives, the lives of others and the communities of which they are a part. Youth work promotes the value of young people

- *Equality of opportunity* – youth workers help young people to identify and challenge oppressions such as racism and sexism and all those that spring from differences of culture, ethnicity, language, gender, disability, age, religion and class. Youth work celebrates diversity and challenges discrimination.

> **To think about . . .**
>
> To what extent does the second Great Commandment (Mt. 22:39) provide a purpose for youth work?

Because youth work strives towards a holistic approach, recognition is given to the place of spirituality within the development of young people. Spiritual development is even enshrined within the *National Occupational Standards for Youth Work in the UK*. Yet youth workers are often unclear what this means in practice. Spirituality can cover anything from experimentation with eastern mysticism, an awareness of Islamic culture, or an appreciation of the environment. Sometimes it is reduced to being 'whatever moves me'. There is a place for spiritual development within youth work but who knows what that means?

What is this youth ministry?

In contrast, youth ministry has tended to be defined in almost exclusively spiritual terms. Its primary purpose is

often understood to be converting young people to Christianity. Nick Aiken asserts the basic aim of working with young people is to challenge them with the message of Christ and to nurture them in the way of Christian discipleship. This suggests that youth ministry and evangelism are one and the same, prompting Mark Ashton and Phil Moon to declare

> Christ does not teach us to support the potential development of young people so that they may realise their full potential. We are instead to call them to repentance and faith, because only in that way can they begin to realise their full potential.

Working towards improving young people's experience of life is of secondary importance to preparing them for the life to come. Pete Ward asserts that 'much of what passes for youth work in a secular setting is of a different genus to the new kinds of work being funded by the Church'. He believes 'ministry' is an appropriate distinction because youth ministry practitioners (youth ministers or pastors) have more affinity with clergy than with youth workers. In its broadest sense 'ministry' refers to service rendered to God and therefore 'ministers' are those set apart by the Church for such activity.

To think about . . .

To what extent does the Great Commandment (Mt. 22:37, 38), as well as the Great Commission (Mt. 28:19, 20) define the purpose of youth ministry?

Youth ministers have collectively become adept in using lively games, videos, discussion starters and other dynamic communication tools in their practice. They use these to illustrate their message. Youth ministers usually start from the premise that Jesus is the way, the truth and the life and that what is contained within Scripture is sufficient and necessary for all young people. This means that, despite their creative methods, youth ministry tends to rely upon more formal approaches. However, the issue is not the validity of the Christian gospel, but the attitude taken by practitioners to engagement with the young. Many youth ministers assume they know what's best for the young people they serve and that their role is to supplement the formal, but non-proselytising religious education they receive from school. It is this that the proponents of youth work find objectionable. Surely this is brainwashing?

So youth work and youth ministry, with their seemingly acute and irreconcilable differences, take up 'pistols at dawn'. But such a duel seems an unnecessary waste. Could an amicable resolution not be found?

Youth work *and* ministry

It seems to me unhelpful to pitch youth work and youth ministry as an 'either/or'. Both have strengths and weaknesses, suggesting the potential for 'both/and'. In this book I state the claim for youth work *and* ministry. The core values of youth work provide a strong philosophical framework in which youth ministry can operate. If youth work is the broad discipline involving all informal educators engaged with young people, then youth ministry is a 'specialism' within it. This becomes the domain of youth work *and* ministry.

The four youth work values of voluntary participation, informal education, empowerment and equality of opportunity are not merely 'politically correct' statements. It is my belief that they are ministry values best demonstrated in the person and work of Christ. In Part Two I shall critique each of these and provide a theological, as well as professional, justification. Having done this, I will argue that the unique contribution of youth work *and* ministry it to add a fifth value: incarnation. For it to be authentic, ministry must be ethical. The end does not always justify the means. It seems inconceivable that the will of God should be reliant upon less than honest means. Those who have confidence in the gospel have no need to manipulate or coerce young people into accepting the message of Christ. Providing an opportunity for genuine exploration of faith and belief is far more likely to result in lasting fruit. This is because it is based on personal conviction. Regrettably, there are too many examples of unethical youth ministry that aims to box young people in to making a decision for Christ. Youth ministry needs youth work if it is to be ethical and young person-centred.

Yet youth ministry has much to contribute towards the spiritual development of young people. It recognises the human capacity for belief and faith and provides a context for spiritual exploration. Youth work that does not support young people's spiritual transformation is not emancipating because the human condition cannot be changed by self-determination alone. Christian youth workers, believing that fullness of life is found only in Christ, provide an opportunity for young people to explore questions of faith and belief for themselves. They do not coerce; instead they provide safe places for young people's spiritual quest.

It is not just youth ministers who are interested in 'conversion'. In a way, so too are secular youth workers.

Youth work that does not lead to change, or conversion, in young people's attitudes to self, others and society is ineffective practice. After all, why should public money be used to fund a service that does not bring about any change? Youth work enables young people to identify and bring about their own change and so, whether they like it or not, effective youth workers are in the business of conversion. Youth ministry is sometimes more open and specific about its 'change' agenda but, as long as it is undertaken ethically and with due regards to the needs of young people, then it should not be dismissed. Youth work needs youth ministry if it is to be genuinely holistic in its approach to the development of young people.

I believe it is time to call a halt to the unnecessary and destructive duel between youth work and youth ministry. It should not be a case of secular youth work or sacred youth ministry. With a bit of humility, openness and respect on both sides it is possible to create genuine youth work *and* ministry. The political and spiritual climate certainly appears conducive to this.

Social policy is beginning, once again, to recognise the valuable contribution made by the Church in the community. In case you haven't heard, the largest employer of full-time youth workers in England and Wales is not central or local government. It is the Church. *Hello!* In 1998 Peter Brierley estimated the Church employed 7,900 full-time paid youth workers. That same year, research commissioned by the National Youth Agency calculated that Local Authorities employed just 2,860 full-time paid youth workers. Even if you include the 21,480 part-time paid youth workers this still only gives a full-time equivalent of 7,220 youth workers employed by local authorities. Critics argue that these statistics do not compare like with like. They rightly point to the significant number of unqualified workers employed by churches

on low wages. Yet, the fact remains, the Church is massively committed to working with young people and has become the largest employer of youth workers in England and Wales. Recognising the need for specialist training, the Church has developed courses such as the Oasis Youth Work and Ministry Degree.[1] These combine youth work, applied theology and youth ministry to train professionals to operate like spiritual amphibians in both secular and sacred settings.

The 'New Right' shift towards free enterprise and the privatisation of some state functions has opened doors for faith-based organisations to deliver services previously the domain of local authorities. At the same time, the Church has been vocal in its defence of the Youth Service, campaigning for increased public spending and the retention of services that benefit the young. The coming together of youth work and youth ministry is perhaps best symbolised in the appointment of a Bishop as Chair of the National Youth Agency, unthinkable a few years ago. There has never been a better time to practise youth work *and* ministry. But where is the line between secular and sacred? What is Christian about youth work *and* ministry?

---

[1] www.oasistrust.org/youthworkdegree

Chapter 2

What's so Christian about youth work *and* ministry?

Youth work *and* ministry brings together youth work and youth ministry, the secular and the sacred. But what role does faith play in such an approach? In essence, what's so Christian about youth work *and* ministry? This is a fundamental question because there can be no basis for youth work *and* ministry that is less-than-Christian. In this chapter I shall argue that a commitment to theology, mission and vocation help to establish its Christian basis. Let me declare at the outset, I am totally convinced that youth work *and* ministry must be underpinned by a systematic theology and biblical framework. Yet, theology is not an exact science; it can mean different things to different people. Equally, I see youth work *and* ministry as being a response to God's mission. Yet there is a need to answer the charge of brainwashing. Finally, I see youth work *and* ministry as being more of a vocation than an occupation. That said, I am not always confident with the language of 'calling' because it is not often clear where God's direction ends and my self-interest begins.

Youth work *and* ministry as Christian theology

There must be a link between youth work *and* ministry and Christian theology and the Bible, but what should

this be? And what comes first: practice or belief? Using John Hull's matrix, there are five possible ways in which the Bible and Christian theology could inform youth work *and* ministry practice. These are:

1 Christian theology is both necessary and sufficient for a complete understanding of youth work *and* ministry. There is no need to refer to other disciplines, such as psychology or sociology.

2 Christian theology is necessary but not able to provide a complete understanding of youth work *and* ministry. Additional insights can be supplemented by other disciplines.

3 Christian theology provides a sufficient but not a necessary understanding of youth work *and* ministry. Other disciplines and belief systems are equally capable of providing understanding.

4 Christian theology provides a possible and legitimate understanding of youth work *and* ministry but is neither sufficient nor necessary. Its contribution to understanding is debatable.

5 Christian theology does not provide a possible or legitimate way of understanding youth work *and* ministry. It adds nothing to understanding.

To think about . . .

How does the Bible and Christian theology interact with your practice? What does this say about:

a) Your view of the Bible?
b) Your view of the 'world'?
c) Your practice?

Theology is a much misunderstood discipline; broadly speaking, it is the study of God. Regular and systematic reading of the Bible is surely one of the primary spiritual disciplines and a foundation for theological inquiry. Yet, strange as it may sound, theology involves more than just Bible reading. For example, my reading of the Scriptures is greatly aided by use of Bible dictionaries, commentaries and other reference books. These help me to understand the subtle language differences, the significance of cultural references and the importance of reoccurring themes. The Bible is an assortment of ancient texts, addressing real issues faced by real people. Understanding the original context and culture of a scriptural passage aids its present-day translation and application. Inevitably we filter our understanding of the world, and therefore of the Scriptures, through, what Lesslie Newbigin described as the lenses of our culture. Just as sunglasses filter our perception of reality, so too our culture and upbringing can affect our interpretation of Scripture. For example, two visits to Hungary and Cuba have helped me to see that being born and brought up under a capitalist system has affected my outlook on faith and the world. It would be grossly arrogant to suggest that my interpretation is more valid than that of equally sincere Cuban Christians who, like me, base their understanding on the Bible. Martin Luther's (1483–1546) insistence on *sola scriptura*, or the primacy of the Bible, does not negate the importance of theology. Theology brings together the Bible texts, the historical context of the biblical writers, and our own traditions and values. Taken together, these provide us with fresh insight into biblical truth.

John Colwell of Spurgeon's College frequently reminds me that good theology is practical theology. Practical, or applied, theology is not so much the application

of Christian doctrine in pastoral settings as a critical dialogue between theology and praxis. It is concerned with how the Christian faith works out in practice and raises questions about what it sees, before addressing them back to theology. Being action-orientated, youth work *and* ministry requires a practical theology. Theology and youth work *and* ministry enjoy a symbiotic relationship. They inform and, in turn, are informed by each other. Theology enriches youth work *and* ministry practice. Likewise, experiences gained in youth work *and* ministry result in new theological understanding. Many believe the Bible to be God's complete and inspired revelation, but only a fool would claim to understand all its depths or have the monopoly on its interpretation. Some truths remain hidden within the biblical text for generations, waiting to be exposed.

For example, the 1960s charismatic movement provided the Church with a fuller understanding of the person and work of the Holy Spirit. God did not bring this about by issuing a new edition of the Bible containing previously unreleased material about the Holy Spirit. Rather, new significance came to be given to parts of the ancient text overlooked by previous generations. 1960s youth culture, with its experimentation, challenge to the *status quo* and new forms of music, brought about new theological understandings. Many of today's young Christians are incredulous that previous generations of believers failed to grasp the significance of biblical passages that highlight the work of the Holy Spirit in bringing about renewal and spiritual gifts. They say, 'But didn't people read the book of Acts?' and, of course, they are right. Young people and youth subcultures brought new theological insights that have enriched us all.

This should not be dismissed as liberal social theology. The Bible represents an emerging theology brought about over thousands of years. Though it is internally consistent, with the latter stages not undermining the former, there is nevertheless an unfolding story that becomes clearer with time. Abraham may have been saved by faith just as surely as Paul, but his understanding must have been less developed than that of Paul's. Being a Jew, the apostle Peter was used to abstaining from certain types of 'unclean' food. Whilst in Joppa, Peter dreamt that God was telling him to kill and eat unclean animals (Acts 10). This was sacrilegious. Yet it represented another part of the unfolding story of God's mission. The gospel was now to be inclusive of all people, Gentiles as well as Jews. Change necessitated new theological understanding. Hence, though the biblical text is now complete, and not to be added to, our understanding of God's revelation continues to develop. We must continually strive to be open to God's work in our lives and resist the temptation to revert back to the narrow dogmatism of the Pharisees.

The four values of voluntary participation, informal education, empowerment and equality of opportunity shape the development of youth work *and* ministry. It is my contention that these values, in turn, help us to see God's character and methodology in new ways. Today's young Christians find it difficult to believe that only a generation or two ago the Church gave tacit or even explicit support to institutional racism, backing the wicked system of apartheid. Of course, they have the benefit of living in an age that claims to promote empowerment and equality of opportunity. Because of this, their cultural lenses reveal more about God's justice and inclusion than those worn by previous generations. Youth work *and* ministry is providing the Church with new theological insight.

Youth work *and* ministry as Christian mission

Christianity is a missionary movement. All over the world the gospel is growing and bearing fruit (Col. 1:6) because Christians are open about their faith in Christ. For Christians, belief represents more than a philosophy of life. It is submission to the Creator and Lord. Christianity is exclusive, claiming to offer a universal and unique solution to the spiritual needs of humanity. Jesus is *the* way, *the* truth and *the* life (Jn. 14:6). Each person's experience of faith in Christ provides further assurance that it can work for others as well. It is inevitable, and to be welcomed, that Christians will stimulate other people's spiritual inquiry. There can be no youth work *and* ministry that does not have at its heart a love for both God and his creation. But this can also lead to misunderstanding.

Youth work *and* ministry is often regarded with suspicion by those outside of the Church. There is a popular perception that faith-based youth work is exclusively concerned with self-promotion, converting young people away from free-thinking, autonomous individuals into inculcated followers. In short, it is judgemental towards others. Regrettably, there is sometimes a hint of truth in this. It may not always be fair, but youth work *and* ministry must answer the accusation of religious indoctrination. That said, other world-views, such as the all-pervasive humanism, are often left unchallenged as if they are non-judgemental. Ironically, some humanist practitioners are judgemental in their non-judgement of others with the temerity to adopt different views to their own. It is time for everyone, Christian and non-Christian, to acknowledge that they hold personal and corporate views that influence their outlook.

Maxine Green has provided a much-needed apologetic for youth work *and* ministry. She argues that faith-based youth work is valid in a pluralistic society for the following reasons:

1 It is appropriate for older generations to offer young people their religious traditions, ideals and values. It promotes inter-generational dialogue

2 Young people have a right to their spiritual, political and ideological heritage; to deny them this right is to deny them opportunities for growth and development. Failure to do this increases their susceptibility to cults and extremist groups

3 The youth work profession has always viewed spiritual development as an important part of young people's holistic development. In reality, this is often either ignored or misunderstood by many Youth Services. Specific reference is made to spiritual development in the *National Occupational Standards for Youth Work in the UK*

4 Religions and, in particular, Christianity have played a seminal role in the development of youth work and the Youth Service in Britain. It is continuing a tradition.

In Part Three I will argue that evangelism and mission are not the same thing. Evangelism is concerned more exclusively with proclamation and calls on hearers to make a personal response to Christ. This is appropriate for those who are ready to make such a decision. However, reaping is dependent upon sowing (Jn. 4:35, 36). Asking those who are not yet ready to make a response to Christ can force them unnecessarily to reject him. I believe evangelism should enable those who want

to turn to Christ to do so. Too often evangelism is viewed as spiritual selling, with the end used to justifying the means. Surely grace is not dependent on indoctrination or manipulation?

Mission, on the other hand, is broader, and involves Christians joining in with God's activity in the world. It allows for dialogue and inquiry and is demonstrated through words, works and wonders. Christ was sent to effect reconciliation between God and humanity and this is shown when Christians demonstrate the power of reconciliation between broken communities. However, mission is not just a social activity. It maintains that people need saving from themselves and each other and that Christ alone is able to mediate forgiveness and reconciliation. Youth work *and* ministry provide a safe context in which young people can explore spiritual issues. Those who, like Paul, say 'I know whom I have believed' (2 Tim. 1:12) have confidence in the gospel. They don't need to resort to indoctrination or manipulation. If that is the theological basis then to what extent does faith provide a motivation? Is youth work *and* ministry an occupation or a vocation?

Youth work *and* ministry as Christian vocation

If medicine and law are established professions then youth work *and* ministry, like social work, is an emerging profession. The term 'profession' comes from the professing, or taking, of religious vows and implies a collective identification with a recognised tradition or occupation. Professions are by nature exclusive. For example, not everyone with an interest in medicine is recognised as being part of the medical profession. Professions are generally characterised by:

- A specialist skill enabling members to offer a specialist service
- A broad theoretical base
- A minimum entry requirement for prospective members, based on recognised experience and qualifications
- A direct and personal relationship between members and clients
- A collective identity between members who share responsibility for maintaining the competence and trust of the profession
- A representative governing body.

Youth work *and* ministry, as a separate and special issue within the broader discipline of youth work, shows all the signs of becoming a profession. The emergence of JNC-recognised training programmes, such as those offered by Oasis,[1] Moorlands College[2] and the Centre for Youth Ministry,[3] and the presence of Amaze,[4] the Association of Christian Youth and Children's Workers, are evidence of this. Though becoming 'professional' provides identity and recognition, there are also inherent weaknesses.

Professions maintain their status by controlling who they recognise as one of 'their own'. The language of profession can, at times, be misleading. 'Professional' and 'professionalism' are not necessarily the same: the former is associated with status and belonging, whereas

---

[1] www.oasistrust.org/youthworkdegree

[2] www.moorlands.ac.uk

[3] www.centreforyouthministry.ac.uk

[4] www.amaze.org.uk

the latter is concerned with quality and ethics. Non-professionals are not necessarily what Doug Nicholls, General Secretary of the Community and Youth Workers Union, calls 'glorious amateurs'. There are plenty of long-serving Christian youth workers who, by the above definition, do not qualify as professionals and yet who display greater professionalism in their practice than some of those that are declared members of the youth work profession. Youth work *and* ministry must not promote the status of its full-time professionals at the expense of its multitudinous extra-time workers (volunteers). To do so would be to undermine the four core values.

To think about . . .

What will enable you to sustain a long-term involvement, or career, in youth work *and* ministry?

Those engaged in youth work *and* ministry view their activity as being more than a personal response to the needs of young people. For them, it is a calling or vocation that originates beyond themselves. Vocation refers to God's call to women and men to serve him. The Puritans grouped callings into 'general' and 'particular'. They understood the former to be the general invitation given to all people to follow Christ. The latter referred to God's leading in specific tasks and roles and, as such, was context specific. Ministry is simply service (*diakonia*) and takes place when the gifts of God's grace (*charismata*) are employed in the service of others. Sam Richards under-stands youth work *and* ministry as

Participation in God's mission among young people. It should be undertaken by those called and sustained by God, who are willing to serve young people in obedience to God's saving purposes. This serving should be self-emptying rather than paternalistic or self-promoting.

Calling is not reserved for church office alone. Professional ministry was far less significant in New Testament times than it is now. God has arranged society in such a way that there are farmers, home makers, bakers and chariot makers. Their God-given skills can be used in his service. The artists who worked on the tabernacle (Ex. 31:1–6; 35:30 – 36:2) were engaged in ministry. All work that is dedicated towards fulfilling God's mission can therefore be considered 'ministry'.

Therefore youth work *and* ministry can take place in *and* beyond Christian settings. As well as those employed by churches, it may also include those working in 'secular' settings. A Christian employed as a Youth and Community Worker by a Local Authority Youth Service may see their activity as participating in God's mission among young people. It is their ministry. They extend the boundaries of the kingdom into areas inaccessible to those working from a local church setting. Though they may not actively promote Christian beliefs, their practice is inspired by their personal commitment to the God of love, justice and reconciliation, and their Christ-like attitude prompts inquiry from young people. Such an approach may not represent the totality of all that God intends but it is certainly an important part. Therefore, youth work *and* ministry operates in and beyond Christian settings. It refers more to the worker's motivation than to the organisational context.

To think about . . .

To what extent do you consider yourself called to work with young people? What difference does this make to your practice?

Summary

Youth work *and* ministry does not have a monopoly on quality work with young people. It does not claim to be the only effective methodology. However, it does offer a distinct and focused opportunity for young people to explore spiritual issues in a safe environment. Remove the spiritual dimension and youth work *and* ministry ceases to offer anything different to youth and community work. It is as distinctly Christian as it is professional. Its

effectiveness is, in part, due to a thorough grasp of the principles of youth work. Yet, youth work *and* ministry relies upon theology as well as sociology and psychology. The next chapter reviews the history of youth work *and* ministry up until 1939 and demonstrates just how significant the Church's role has been in the development of the modern Youth Service.

Chapter 3

History of youth work *and* ministry up to 1939

Why history?

In almost every village, town and city today there is evidence of youth work *and* ministry. Young residents at the YMCA, Girls' and Boys' Brigade Companies on parade, small groups meeting in people's homes and even the existence of local authority youth centres, all confirm this. These disparate activities are united by their history as much as by their involvement with young people. Despite protestations today from both sides of the false divide, those who in the eighteenth and nineteenth centuries pioneered engagement with the young saw no conflict between youth work (secular) and youth ministry (sacred). Recognising injustice and ignorance, they developed programmes that supported young people. Many of them were Christians whose faith in Christ served as a motivator. It is from these roots that the modern Youth Service has grown. A brief survey of history reveals that youth work *and* ministry is not a fad that is here today but gone tomorrow. It is a radical return to roots.

For practitioners who thrive on interaction with young people, taking time to research the history of youth work and ministry may seem both unnecessary and irrelevant. Add to this any negative and unresolved experiences of

school history lessons and such an attempt seems doomed from the start. Yet, I believe history can live for it has as much to do with the present and future as it does with the past.

First, we do not operate in a time vacuum. Today's actions and attitudes owe their origins to past events. To understand the present we have to appreciate the past. Thus history helps to shape identity and an awareness of who we are. There are a number of significant Christian organisations today, such as Crusaders[1] and the Salvation Army, which are rich in history. The key to their future success rests to some extent on an understanding of their heritage.

Second, history affords us the luxury of hindsight. It is as if we sit on the shoulders of those who have gone before us and, as a consequence, can see clearer and further than could our forebears. Reflecting on past successes and failures enables us to develop good practice in the future. We can not only learn from our own mistakes; we can also learn from the mistakes made by previous generations. Without such an appreciation of history there can be little room for progress.

Third, there are times when history guides us to confess the sins of the past. This ensures previous actions, now understood to be, for example, sexist or racist, can be confessed. This opens up the possibility of a new relationship in the future with 'those sinned against' in the past. This has been particularly effective in bringing about healing and reconciliation in South Africa. Some sections of the Church have had to come to terms with, and confess, their participation in Apartheid. Tragically, in the 1950s and 1960s those who answered the British government's

---

[1] www.crusaders.org.uk

invitation to leave the Caribbean and migrate to Britain, found many congregations to be unfriendly and evenly openly hostile to them. Left with little choice, they formed what are now termed Black Majority Churches. Some of the deep pain that is still felt today will only be healed when those who represent the guilty organisations come to terms with, and repent of, their past.

Finally, identifying past achievements gives credibility to today's practice. Some youth and community workers give the impression that youth work has always been a secular concern. Many do not appreciate just how big a contribution the Christian Church has made to their own work. The origins of the modern Youth Service can, in large part, be traced back to the pioneering work of Christians. The Youth Service wouldn't be what it is today without the Church. So, history is important, as the poet Steve Turner puts it

> History repeats itself
> Has to
> No-one listens.

That said, history is more art than science. The interpretation of facts is as important as the facts themselves. Any history is inevitably incomplete and this one is no different. Not all events are included or given equal weight. Therefore what follows can only be a subjective understanding of the development of youth work *and* ministry as I see it. Others may arrive at radically different conclusions from the same, or different, events.

It is also worth remembering that historians are never neutral. Their beliefs and experiences shape their analysis. Having the benefit of hindsight makes them infuriatingly 'know all'. Because they read the records of past events through the lenses of contemporary culture,

they sometimes find themselves drawn into conflict with their subjects. They use current values and attitudes to judge past events. What, at the time, was deemed positive by the prevailing culture then becomes labelled negative by today's standards. This can lead to the re-writing of history. Such revisionist history has, for example, led to a view of Winston Churchill that would have been inconceivable immediately after the Second World War. So, recognising the importance of history, and the challenges it presents, we review the origins of youth work *and* ministry.

First steps

The honour of being the first recorded youth worker is often reserved for Hannah More, a friend of William Wilberforce. She organised a programme of elementary education, religious instruction and vocational training in the 1790s. Though driven by a desire to see people come to faith in Christ, her commitment to both social action and mission brought her into sharp conflict with the Church. This has remained a tension for most youth work *and* ministry practitioners ever since.

In the late eighteenth century Sunday Schools were formed to teach reading, writing and Bible knowledge to young people beyond the reach of the Church. By the nineteenth century they had become a significant move-ment, one that was to inspire many developments in youth work and ministry. Evangelicals promoted literacy, not out of humanitarianism but, as a way of promoting the Christian faith. Why else did they tend to favour reading over writing? That said, many made the link between education and emancipation, as John Venn observed

Man cannot by education be made a real Christian; but by education he may be freed from the prejudices and delivered from the dominion of dispositions highly favourable to temptation and sin.

In 1844 George Williams, inspired by the Sunday School movement, founded the Young Men's Christian Society, later known as the Young Men's Christian Association (YMCA). This had an unambiguous missiological aim: to provide a structure of Christian fellowship in London for respectable clerks and other such 'white-collar' male workers and, in so doing, to win them to Christ. Its Christian aims were clear

> The Young Men's Christian Association seeks to unite those young men who, regarding Jesus Christ as the God and Saviour, according to the Holy Scriptures, desire to be his disciples in the faith and in the life, and to associate their efforts for the extension of his kingdom amongst young men.

Influenced by American revivalism, George Williams was concerned to protect young men moving into towns and cities from becoming disorientated and vulnerable to temptation. He organised frequent meetings for prayer and Bible study. Likewise, the Sunday School movement also inspired William Smith in 1883 to found the Boys' Brigade. Faced with a rowdy Sunday School class at North Woodside Mission Hall in Glasgow, he created a fusion of military-style drill and Bible study.

Following missions led by the international sensations, Dwight L. Moody and Ira D. Sankey, a number of Sunday Schools extended their provision for older young people. These groups became known as 'Christian bands' and were modelled on the work of American congregational pastor, Frances E. Clark. The International Christian

Endeavour Society which he founded required members
to commit to:

1 The pledge – an active commitment to the service of
   Jesus Christ as Lord and actively participate in the
   Society's prayer meetings.
2 The monthly experience or consecration meeting.
3 Systematic, definite and regular committee work –
   training by doing.
4 Private devotion, daily prayer and Bible reading.
5 Denominational loyalty including attendance at
   midweek prayer and Sunday evening services.
6 Interdenominational fellowship.

With the support of the Sunday School Union, Clark came
to Britain in 1888 and soon Christian Endeavour had
thousands of young members attracted by the Christian
band's emphasis on active service and committee work.
Christian Endeavour shifted the emphasis from 'telling'
to 'discovering, training and sharing'.

To think about . . .

What are the historical roots of your
organisation? To what extent are they evident
today?

Philanthropy and politics

In the absence of a State system of welfare, it was
left to individuals to fund humanitarian programmes.

Philanthropy, the act of using wealth to give to those in need, became the primary means of social welfare. Today it appears contradictory that many of those who owned the mines and factories should consider it their moral duty to care for the poor they so badly treated in their employment. Certainly it can be argued that philanthropy was used as a means of social control. Faced with bloody revolution across the channel, the English elite were keen to alleviate the misery of the poor just enough to stop them from revolting, but not too much so as to deny them access to power. Providing social welfare helped to reinforce the power of the factory and mine owners and created a dependency culture.

However, philanthropy was not just about giving money; it required the giving of self. The giver had to mix freely with the recipient in order to pass on their values, beliefs and lifestyle. Engaging directly and personally with young people promoted the importance of relationships in youth work and ministry. Such interactions were seen as being the means to moral, as well as spiritual, education. Lord Shaftesbury recognised the safety of middle class lives and property depended on there being a peaceful, happy and moral population. In 1878 the Archbishop of York declared

> If we in the Church of England do not deal with the masses, the masses will deal with us.

At a time when Britain's economic and military dominance was being stretched to the limit by the British Empire, there was a need to ensure 'the lower orders' were sufficiently submissive. As Bernard Davies puts it

> It was seen as essential that young people grew up patriotic, fit enough physically to defend their country and committed

to fulfilling it's 'white man's burden' – that is, transmitting its self-evidently superior values to the heathen and uncivilised peoples of the world.

Early developments in youth work *and* ministry were often quite militaristic in style. The Boys' Brigade practised drill in their uniforms and sought to be a disciplined and moral force for good. Hence the purpose of the Boys' Brigade was declared to be

The advancement of Christ's Kingdom amongst boys and the promotion of habits of obedience, reverence, discipline, self-respect and all that tends towards true Christian manliness.

In Wales the situation was quite different. Non-conformists were far more significant than Anglicans or Catholics, urbanisation was less prevalent and the 'middle classes' less powerful. Consequently, youth work *and* ministry was less philanthropic and few of the English voluntary organisations made it to the Welsh valleys. Positively, this meant youth work *and* ministry developed a strong local community emphasis. It was local people taking local action with local young people. By the beginning of the twentieth century, English voluntary organisations, such at the YMCA, were beginning to develop some work in Wales. However, as Jones and Rose point out, these were nearly always Anglican bodies with an apparent disinterest in non-conformism and the Welsh language.

Philanthropy receded with the end of the First World War. Whole youth groups had been slaughtered during the 'Great War'. No longer could the middle classes patronise the working classes with acts of charity to the families of those who had lost so much in service of their

country. They had proved their self-discipline, patriotism and industry. Just as the treatment of women could not return to the pre-war condition, so too, young people could no longer be ignored. Britain had expected and young people had answered.

Serving the middle classes

What originated with a focus on the socially excluded gradually began to drift towards the children of wealthy parents. This mirrors today's pattern: youth work often targets the disadvantaged whilst youth ministry concentrates on the advantaged. The Children's Special Service Mission (CSSM) began in 1867 after Josiah Spiers took his Sunday School class to a special children's meeting led by the American evangelist, Payson Hammond. Inspired by this, Spiers created a new kind of service especially designed for children and, with others, formed the CSSM. This further developed the work of the Sunday School movement and established precedent for age-appropriate service content. However, despite beginning with a broad appeal, the CSSM soon gravitated towards a focus on upper-middle class children. Spiers justified this by pointing to the range of religious societies that concentrated on the working class, such as Dr Barnado's. However, it appears others had similar ideas. Crusaders plus Varsity and Public School (VPS) camps concentrated their efforts on the children of wealthy parents. Meetings were often held in the drawing rooms of the 'upper class' and were strictly by invitation only. Pete Ward, in *Growing up Evangelical: Youthwork and the making of a subculture*, quotes one observer saying that 'everything unsuited to a drawing room is avoided and the graceful courtesies of the Christian life are

encouraged'. The CSSM later changed its name to Scripture Union.

Universities played a significant role in developing work among the young. Through the CSSM, privileged students of the Cambridge Inter-Collegiate Christian Union (CICCU) participated in camps and beach missions. CICCU provided a model for other universities and, to provide support to the growing number of Christian Unions, the Inter Varsity Fellowship (IVF) was formed. This was later called Universities and Colleges Christian Fellowship (UCCF). Privileged students, influenced by CSSM, CICCU and IVF, became the leaders of twentieth-century evangelicalism. Their involvement in camps and beach missions also led to a focus on youth work, albeit directed at middle class young people. Many of these models, intended to serve advantaged young people, have proved ineffective with the disadvantaged.

The gender agenda

It is clear that inequalities existed in the male and female provision. William Smith was the founder of the Boys' Brigade. His vision was of 'Christian manliness'. He declared

> By associating Christianity with all that was most noble and manly in a boy's sight, we would be going a long way to disabuse his mind of the idea that there is anything effeminate or weak about Christianity.

If boys were directed towards Christian manliness, girls were directed towards Christian subservience. In 1890, Maud Stanley made clear that clubs for the working girl were important because they could 'make her conscious

of her own responsibilities both towards God and man' and in doing so 'give her an influence over her sweet-heart, her husband and her sons'. The Girls' Friendly Society (GFS), founded in 1875, was the first Anglican organisation run entirely by lay women. At its peak in 1913 it had over 200,000 members and 40,000 'associates'. Associates were nearly always upper or middle class women who sought to save young women in domestic service from falling. The GFS could be criticised for failing to break down the class barriers that separated servants from masters and for not sufficiently backing the political emancipation of women. However, associates often became involved in advocacy work on behalf of young, exploited members. The GFS was not nicknamed 'The Great Fuss Society' for nothing.

Unlike the GFS, the Young Women's Christian Association (YWCA) did not deny membership rights to those who became pregnant outside of a marriage relationship. It made specific provision for those considered to be in 'moral difficulty'. Yet, for its time, such tolerance inevitably had its critics. In 1921 the breakaway Christian Alliance of Women and Girls was formed. The YWCA was also more political than the GFS, with many of its leading members being suffragists.

The beginnings of State involvement

By the beginning of the twentieth century tensions were beginning to appear between conservative and liberal wings of the Church. The evangelicals emerged as the champions of youth work *and* ministry. David Bebbington attributes the success of evangelicalism to this commitment to engagement with the young. 'Concentrate on young people,' said Bishop Taylor Smith, 'they bring you

in the biggest dividends.' This period also reflected a change in attitude of the State towards young people and youth work.

Though it is hard to imagine now, the British State did not begin to get involved with youth work until the inter-war years of the 1920s and 1930s. These were years of significant expansion for the voluntary organisations. The Scouts grew from a membership of 152,000 in 1913 to 438,000 in 1938. During the same period the Boys' Brigade grew from 65,000 to 161,000. But what had held back the State?

First, youth work was viewed by some at the time as being primarily about meeting young people's recreational needs. It could not compete with the economic and political necessity of providing the national work force with formal education and vocational skills training. The Great Depression provided a powerful reminder of this need. Second, State involvement was actively resisted by the voluntary youth organisations, keen to protect their own identity and *raison d'être*. They wanted the State to provide them with funding, but not competition. Third, British society was not as individualised as it is today. Notions of citizenship and community responsibility were part of the dominant culture. With individuals and groups willing to assume responsibility for meeting the needs of young people in their communities, there seemed little need for centralised youth provision. Finally, during the inter-war years State intervention came to be associated with the totalitarianism of fascist and communist regimes. There was apprehension of awakening the 'enemy within'.

The First World War had a dramatic effect on social policy. During the war, rising youth crime led the Home Office to recommend that local juvenile organisation committees should co-ordinate and stimulate youth

provision. The 1918 and 1921 Education Acts empowered local authorities to set up such committees where they weren't already in existence and to provide public funding of youth facilities. At a national level, the Juvenile Organisation Committee enabled voluntary organisations to contribute to public policy. Voluntary organisations and State were beginning to interact, with the former providing initiative and human resources and the latter much needed funding. However, by 1936 only thirty-six local committees were still functioning, and just six had full-time secretaries. Sadly, youth work still did not have the economic or political support enjoyed by formal educationalists.

The culling of so many men during the First World War, together with increasing paid employment oppor-tunities for women, led in the 1920s to a shortage of volunteers within the voluntary youth organisations. Local committees, traditionally protective of their inde-pendence, began to organise themselves into new national bodies. The National Association of Boys' Clubs and the National Federation of Young Farmers' Clubs were both formed as a result and, in 1936, eleven organisa-tions sponsored the Standing Conference of National Voluntary Youth Organisations. The Central Youth Council of the Church of England was launched in 1938.

During the 1930s a return to war looked inevitable. Policy-makers once again became concerned with the state of the nation's health and, in particularly with the combat-readiness of young males. Consequently, the 1937 Physical Training and Recreation Act empowered local authorities to fund facilities designed to raise the level of national fitness. As well as funding voluntary organi-sations, some authorities took this as an opportunity to establish their own youth centres. Local authorities were now not only funding youth work they were also capable

of organising it. Thus began the State's involvement in the Youth Service.

Just before the outbreak of war in 1939, the King George's Jubilee Trust published a report on the needs of young school-leavers. It acknowledged the responsibilities of the State towards meeting the needs of young people. Yet, it also reaffirmed the position of voluntary youth organisations, stating that

> This does not imply that the great amount of invaluable work done by the voluntary bodies should be taken over by public authorities today, or tomorrow. This is not our British way . . . while the voluntary system should be strengthened to carry on its already valuable work, the problem can be solved satisfactorily only by largely increasing the supply of public funds and services. If we are wise, we shall not abolish or strangle the voluntary system but, as in the past, public authorities will utilise and aid what exists and supplement it with their own services.

To think about . . .

How should voluntary organisations and the State relate to each other today?

Summary

In the absence of the Welfare State, philanthropy was the primary means of social investment. Christians proved to be some of the better employers, providing their young

employees with education, housing and basic health care. At the time this was seen to be a radical and caring response to social needs. Many such philanthropists were motivated by the Christian faith, seeing their actions as being a natural extension of their beliefs. That few other faith groups engaged in social welfare simply reflected the limited presence of non-Judaeo-Christian groups in Britain at the time.

Judging their actions by today's standards must cause us to question some of the motivations and methods. Were they concerned more with the needs of young people or their own privileged position and the promotion of their beliefs? However, judging with hindsight is easy. Christians reflected the culture of the day. They were no worse than their non-Christian peers. The fact remains, Christians helped pioneer the modern day Youth Service. They engaged with young people at a time when others didn't. Faith was not coincidental to their practice. It informed their approach and, as such, promoted a belief in youth work *and* ministry. The involvement of the State in youth work provision was gradual and originally intended to serve as a resource to the voluntary youth organisations, still dominated by the Church. In time, the State was to reduce the responsibility of local communities to support the needs of local young people. On the horizon was the emerging Welfare State.

Chapter 4

History of youth work *and* ministry from 1939 to 1999

As we have seen, in the absence of the Welfare State, philanthropy was the primary means of social investment and many philanthropists saw their actions as a natural extension of their Christian faith. Gradually, as the State took on more responsibility for the development of young people, the Church became less involved. Consequently, what had begun as youth work *and* ministry became separated into secular youth work and sacred youth ministry. What happened from 1939 to the present day to lead to this unnecessary and destructive duel? And what are the developments that are prompting a return to youth work *and* ministry?

The 1940s – war and peace

The return to war in 1939 signalled major social change. Urban young people and children were evacuated to the countryside to be cared for by other communities. Many fathers enlisted in the armed forces and were separated from their families whilst many mothers sustained the 'war effort' by working long hours in jobs previously reserved for men. 'Blackout' was a major disruption and community resources were commandeered. The 'home

front' required a stable and well-disciplined population. To make matters worse, youth crime was increasing at an alarming rate. Between 1939 and 1941 the number of young people aged under seventeen years found guilty by the courts in England and Wales rose by over a third. The government sought to strengthen the youth organisations in order to prevent a recurrence of the social problems experienced during the First World War, as well as once again improve the discipline and combat fitness of young people.

In November 1939 the government issued Circular 1486, *The Service of Youth*, which led to the launch of the modern Youth Service. This recognised the educational contribution made by voluntary youth organisations, giving this 'service of youth an equal status with the other educational services conducted by the local authority'. The principle of youth work *and* ministry was further enshrined in the Circular as it claimed

> The individual traditions and special experience of youth possessed by the voluntary organisations will be joined with the prestige and resources of the local education authority.
>
> Board of Education, 1939: para.8

Circular 1484 acknowledged that patchy youth provision required the Board of Education, predecessor of the modern-day Department for Education and Skills, to undertake direct responsibility for youth welfare. A National Youth Committee was formed to advise the Secretary of State for Education, and funds were made available to bolster provision. Local Education Authorities were required to form Local Youth Committees to 'strengthen the hands of local authorities and voluntary

organisations'. Money was made available to voluntary organisations, including Christian-based groups, to deliver youth work on behalf of the State. The State's role was to fund, not necessarily deliver, youth services. Even so, some voluntary organisations viewed the growing role of the State with some suspicion. Despite this, the principle of youth work *and* ministry was enshrined in the foundation of the modern Youth Service. Within a year, 1,700 new youth clubs had been opened, with new youth leaders trained by the Central Council of Recreative Physical Training.

In June 1940 Circular 1516, entitled *The Challenge of Youth*, provided a philosophy of youth work. It defined the primary purpose of youth work as being to provide young people with social and physical training. Character building was a reoccurring theme of this war-time initiative. After all, the armed forces needed a supply of physically and psychologically fit young men. The 1944 Education Act placed further responsibility on local authorities to provide 'adequate facilities' for the educational and recreational needs of young people without specifically mentioning the existence of the Youth Service.

The 'service of youth' initially enjoyed government support. By 1948 an estimated 1,800 full-time youth leaders were employed: the majority with voluntary organisations. Professional training was provided by four one-year university courses, with additional training provided by the YMCA and the National Association of Boys' Clubs.

The 1950s – rock 'n'dole

However, post-war gains were soon lost. Funding for voluntary organisations was significantly cut to pay for

the expanding Welfare State. By 1953 the number of full-time youth leaders had fallen by almost two-thirds. Few youth centres were constructed and what remained often had to make do with shabby premises. Young people presented society with new opportunities and threats. The post-war baby boom was projected to increase the number of fourteen to twenty year olds by 800,000 (20 per cent). And the challenges were significant.

Jobs needed to be found for 'de-mobbed' men returning to 'civvy street' and, despite much effort, women were not persuaded in large numbers to give up their new jobs. Why should they? To avert socially destructive mass un-employment, young people's entry into the labour market was delayed by extending compulsory education up till the age of 15. This pattern has continued today with the current New Labour government in Britain aiming to see 50 per cent of all young people completing Higher Education. This policy, together with the abolition of National Service in 1957, meant that young people had more time on their hands. The nation was gripped by a moral panic concerning the anti-social attitude of youth. The trial in 1952 of two teenagers, Derek Bentley and Christopher Craig, for the murder of a policeman was seen as symptomatic of a general rise in youth crime. In addition, prejudice against those immigrants from com-monwealth countries led to race riots involving, among others, 'Teddy Boys'.

The release in 1956 of Bill Haley's film, *Rock Around the Clock*, proved to be quite symbolic and, according to the magazine *NME*, led to cinema seats being ripped up from San Francisco to Scunthorpe. For Davies this marked the start of a distinctive and assertive youth culture. Young people used clothes, make-up, hairstyles and choice of music as never before to symbolise a break with their parent's generation. Furthermore, the increasing

availability of contraception enabled a more liberal attitude to sex.

The media played an important role in disseminating and promoting new expressions of youth subculture. Of particular importance were commercial and pirate radio stations, as well as the development of television. What for some was a threat to society was for others a commercial opportunity. Young people may have provided the creativity, but the means of production were definitely owned by adults eager to find new markets for work lost through the cessation of war. Advertising agencies, aided by the increasingly dominant sociology movement, coined the phrase 'teenager' to describe the target market. It could be argued that Macmillan's claim, 'You've never had it so good' should perhaps have read, 'You've never been exploited so bad'! It was in this context that the government commissioned a committee, chaired by Lady Albermarle, to review the needs of the Youth Service.

Meanwhile, the evangelical wing of the Church was actively looking for revival to sweep away the corrosive effects of popular culture. One man contributed to this more than any other. His name was Billy Graham. He had begun his ministry in Chicago in 1945 with Torrey Johnson, the first President of Youth For Christ. He became convinced that 'if they could sweep young people into a tide of revival, they could place Evangelical Christianity at the heart of a movement to revitalise American culture'. Billy Graham first came to Britain in 1954 on board the liner *United States*, bringing with him an American approach to faith, culture and diplomacy.

American post-war manufacturing adopted mass production techniques, known as 'Fordism', with the aim of assembling uniform products as efficiently as possible. Henry Ford was said to have told customers they could choose any colour so long as it was black. Billy Graham's

approach to mass evangelism was almost 'Fordian' in its use of efficient processes. Large-scale events were organised which featured music, singing and an evangelistic sermon by Billy Graham. He would always end by leading the audience through a formulaic and responsive prayer built around the 'four spiritual laws'. The event would close with Billy inviting those that had prayed the 'believer's prayer' to stand at the front of the arena to receive literature and prayer from a 'counsellor'. Overnight the details of respondents would be passed on to local churches to follow up, inviting them to attend a 'nurture group' for new Christians. This system was applicable from Cardiff to Calcutta.

Billy Graham 'crusades' generally attracted a younger audience and it was he who introduced Youth For Christ to Britain. Though popular, Graham's approach was in many ways not consistent with youth work *and* ministry. It was heavily event-orientated; relationship-building was only required to get people to attend. The meetings were lively but quite formal in style. There was certainly no room for dialogue between Graham and his audience. He spoke the truth and his audience either accepted or rejected it. Billy Graham's method has influenced a generation of Christian youth workers. Youth For Christ rallies became a feature of evangelical youth work on both sides of the Atlantic. So much for the Church: but what of the statutory sector?

The 1960s – duel in the crown

In 1960 the fortunes of the Youth Service changed with the publication of the Albermarle Report. Entitled *The Youth Service in England and Wales*, it maintained the purpose of youth work was to 'provide young people

with challenging opportunities for them to display and to respect forms of pre-eminence in fields other than academic' (HMSO, 1960: para. 137). In other words, it was educative, but not in a formal sense.

The Report led to a significant expansion in the Youth Service. For Davies the years that followed were the golden age of the Youth Service. Significant investment was made in new purpose-built youth centres. Their design reflected the open youth club model, with specialist provision for physical and social recreation. Being costly to maintain and staff, these youth centres limited the geographical coverage of youth work. It was impossible to provide a youth centre for every community. Furthermore, being building-based restricted the flexibility of the Youth Service. In some cases young people's participation served the buildings, instead of the buildings serving the needs of the young. Most of today's youth centres can be attributed to Albermarle. The most outlandish example of this is the enormous Bowes Lyon Youth Centre in Stevenage, Hertfordshire, which is simply vast.

The Albermarle Report also led to the statutory Youth Service becoming 'professional'. By 1968 the total number employed by local authorities had increased from 700 to 1,500. With this came the recognition of training qualifications, career structures and better terms and conditions. Debate raged about the nature of the profession. Would youth workers remain with the Youth Service indefinitely or would they transfer into related disciplines such as teaching or social work? If so, at what age? These are questions the Church is still wrestling with today. Negatively, this new emphasis weakened the role of volunteers.

The Albermarle Report also broke the long-established integration of youth work *and* ministry. It failed to

recognise that there is no such thing as a value-free system. Humanism is as ideological as Christianity in its proselytising. Though respectful of the faith-based origins of youth work, it questioned the relevance of Christian or even spiritual values for young people. Yet its language also stereotyped the role of girls as being to 'acquire technical competence as home makers' and implied ethnic tension was the result of immigration and, presumably therefore, not the racist attitudes of the white population. The Albermarle Report was far from perfect and yet it put youth work firmly on the government agenda.

During the 1960s the Church in Britain struggled with youth subcultures, appearing at times quite fearful of them. Pete Ward argues that the 'youth fellowship' was promoted as a safe alternative to popular youth sub-culture and the open youth club. Once in, young members could be shielded from some of the extremes of mainstream culture, much to the relief of Christian parents. A high priority was placed on retaining those already associated with the Church. Youth fellowships provided young people with spiritual formation and a social programme in equal measure. Personal and social development and informal education were less significant. Evangelical youth ministry in Britain tended to cater for those from privileged backgrounds, drawing primarily from grammar and public schools, to the exclusion of others. As Ward observes, like-attracts-like and a reliance upon peer evangelism inevitably meant the less privileged and academically able young people educated at 'secondary modern' schools were overlooked. There were, of course, notable exceptions, which must including the Mayflower Family Centre in London's East End and the work of Frontier Youth Trust. However, it was not only the Church that was questioning the role of youth clubs.

The 1970s – Flower praise

Nine years after Albermarle, a government review entitled *Youth and Community Work in the 1970s* recognised that youth clubs were not the only approach. It stated the Youth Service should 'meet the needs of young people by making contact with them wherever they are to be found and recognise them as part of the community'. The Fairbairn-Milson Report, as it was known, merged youth work and community work together. From then on, the statutory sector talked of youth and community work.

Ideologically, the Fairbairn-Milson Report advocated political, as well as physical and social, education, defining politics as being about life and how people live together. It championed young people's rights to question cherished ideas, attitudes and standards and, if necessary, to reject them. It advocated a more person-centred critical dialogue between youth workers and young people, rather than what was perceived to have been the indoctrination or training imposed upon young people by youth workers. It defined the primary purpose of youth work as being social education, stating

> We are not so much concerned today as in the past with basic education, or with economic needs, or with the communication of an agreed belief or value system; but we are concerned to help young people to create their place in a changing society and it is their critical involvement in their community which is the goal.
>
> HMSO, 1969: para. 152

Faced with secularisation and influenced by the hippie movement, evangelical youth work began to develop a subculture of its own. The Jesus Movement represented an interface between youth culture and faith. Music, hip

language, festivals, art and magazines all gave creative expression to young Christians keen to show the relevance of their faith. Record labels, publishing houses, conferences and merchandising helped to make this commercially viable. The Jesus Movement opened a dialogue with popular youth culture. In 1971 the Festival of Light drew thousands of young, hippie Christians to London's Trafalgar Square to celebrate their belonging to the 'Jesus revolution'. Middle class young people found in the Jesus Movement both a moderation and legitimisation of their counter-cultural lifestyle and values.

The Jesus Movement emphasised charismatic spirituality and community living. Whilst youth subcultures were experimenting with drugs, Christian young people were discovering the power of the Holy Spirit. The Jesus Movement contributed to today's widespread use of choruses and music groups in worship, the launch of Youth With A Mission (YWAM) and many of the house or 'new churches'. Faith and culture were beginning to develop a symbiotic relationship.

The 1980s – The Thatcher Years

In 1982 the Thompson Report, *Experience and Participation*, was published. This defined the fundamental purpose of the Youth Service as being

> To provide programmes of personal development comprising, in shorthand terms, social and political education ... The twin aims of this purpose are thus affirmation and involvement – affirming an individual in their proper identity and involving an individual in relationships with other individuals and institutions.
>
> HMSO, 1982: para. 7.3

Unlike Albermarle, the Thompson Report recognised some of the major structural divisions that existed within Britain, namely class, racism, sexism and attitudes towards people with disabilities.

The 1980s were dominated by 'Thatcherism'. Inflation and anti-competitive practice (and some would say Margaret Thatcher herself) became enemies of the State. Consumerism was the new religion, with choice being the creed. Osgerby notes the 'New Right' Conservative government championed the 'enterprise culture' of youthful 'wheeler-dealers' in the often London-based financial sector but failed to recognise that these young people represented only a tiny minority. The majority were struggling with the return of mass unemployment. Ironically, Thatcher's *laissez-faire* policy to reduce State involvement in the lives of citizens resulted in increased State intervention through quality audits, the National Curriculum and, later under John Major, the infamous 'Back to Basics' campaign and the 'Citizens Charter'. Local authority spending was cut and the Youth Service was one of the casualties. If the 1960s were the golden years of the Youth Service, then the 1980s were the dark ages.

During the 1980s the Church was also under considerable pressure. Between 1979 and 1989 it lost 155,000 teenagers, the equivalent of 300 a week. With the inclusion of children the loss was more like 320,000. The young had voted with their feet. Was it boring meetings, irrelevant teaching, lack of role models or a growing sense of disenfranchisement? Whatever the reason, local churches were struggling. To fill the gap, a number of local and national Christian youth organisations emerged, adopting the role of specialists. Steve Chalke, founding director of Oasis Trust, began to develop a number of youth initiatives that fused culturally relevant mission, social action and youth participation into a dynamic expression

of faith. He was a champion of youth work *and* ministry. Through the Video Express he pioneered the use of large-screen video projection that is so common today. By participating in Radio Cracker and the Christmas Cracker restaurants young people raised awareness and millions of pounds for third world programmes. The 1980s were creative, if tough, years.

The 1990s – turning the tide

Against the backdrop of urban riots, two Ministerial Conferences were held in 1989 and 1991 with the aim of defining the purpose and curriculum of the Youth Service. The first defined the Youth Service as comprising all voluntary, statutory and independent providers engaged in youth work. As the biggest member of the voluntary sector, the Church was able to stake its claim alongside that of local authorities. The Youth Service was seen similarly to the Merchant Navy; its existence was well known but comprised a diverse range of public and private service providers. The second conference adopted a more political definition of youth work, stating

> The purpose of youth work is to redress all forms of in-equality and to ensure equality of opportunity for all young people to fulfil their potential as empowered individuals and members of groups and communities and to support young people during the transition to adulthood.

It also stated that youth work offers young people opportunities that are:

- *Educative* – enabling young people to gain the skills, knowledge and attitudes needed to identify,

advocate and pursue their rights and responsibilities as individuals and as members of groups and communities locally, nationally and internationally

- *Promote equality of opportunity* – through the challenging of oppressions such as racism and sexism and all those that spring from differences of culture, race, language, sexual identity, gender, disability, age, religion and class, and through the celebration of diversity and strengths which arise from those differences

- *Participative* – through a voluntary relationship with young people in which young people are partners in the learning process and decision making structure which affect their own and other young people's lives and their environment

- *Empowering* – supporting young people to understand and act on the personal, social and political issues which affect their lives, the lives of others and the communities of which they are a part.

As will be seen in Part Two, these core values are directly relevant to youth work *and* ministry and offer fresh theological insights into the nature and ministry of God. They appear to reflect an approach that mirrored that adopted by Jesus during his earthly ministry. During the 1980s those that recognised this risked being labelled 'liberals' by the evangelical wing of the Church.

By the 1990s the Church had woken up to its loss of young people. It responded with a dramatic increase in the employment of full-time youth workers. Churches, mainly in the more affluent suburbs, wanted their own youth specialist. In 1998 the total number of full-time youth workers employed by local authorities in England totalled 3,190, with a further 23,890 employed

on a part-time basis. This amounted to a full-time equivalent rate of 7,190. Peter Brierley's research suggested the Church was employing approximately 7,900 full-time paid youth workers. The Church was now the largest employer of youth workers in the country. Yet the quality was not always comparable. To address this, Oasis,[1] followed by the Centre for Youth Ministry, and Moorlands College, developed specialist training courses that combine professionally-recognised youth work, applied theology and youth ministry.

Many specialist youth workers, perhaps motivated by their own frustrations, experimented with alternative forms of Christian worship. The grandchildren of the Jesus Movement began to mix liturgy, icons and symbolism with music technology. The Nine O'Clock Service (NOS), linked to the respectable St Thomas' in Sheffield, provided both an example and a warning to those who sought a new wineskin. Failing to meet the needs of older young people, the Church gradually lowered its definition of youth. Increasing emphasis was placed on work with the 11–14s and there is evidence now to suggest this has, at least, stemmed the exodus.

Things can only get better?

In 1997, Tony Blair's New Labour government swept to power in Britain. Eighteen years of successive Conservative rule was brought to a dramatic end. In came the 'Cool Britannia' project to re-brand Britain, Youth Offending Teams, Community Service Volunteers, life-long learning, the New Deal for Communities programme

---

[1] www.oasistrust/youthworkdegree

and the Social Exclusion Unit. The Conservative Party had been ousted, but Margaret Thatcher's 'New Right' agenda lived on in New Labour. Privatisation of State services, 'managerialism', target setting and new roles for both the business and voluntary sectors continued to feature alongside a social democratic emphasis on social policy. In the new economic and political climate the Youth Service benefited from increased public funding but, in return, had to accept increased external control. Local authorities were increasingly viewed as service purchasers, not necessarily service providers. Some local Youth Services are still coming to terms with the idea that they must bid alongside 'not-for-profit' voluntary organisations and 'for-profit' companies to deliver the services they once viewed as their domain.

Since 1997, the Church has continued to champion the cause of young people and the Youth Service. But the increasing role ascribed to the voluntary sector is creating new opportunities for the Church in Britain to work with young people 'at risk'. If companies and charities can deliver public services, then why shouldn't the Church also? Government legislation is increasingly recognising the role of the voluntary sector, even specifying the inclusion of the Church and other faith groups. For example, Oasis Youth Inclusion[1] is now working with socially and educationally excluded young people across a growing number of local authorities. It was one of the first organisations to be awarded National Mentoring Network Approved Provider standard, is part-funded by the Department for Education and Skills and is subject to annual inspection by Ofsted.

---

[1] www.oasistrust.org/youthinclusion

As always, there is a disparity between the national Whitehall and local 'town hall' politics but the gap is gradually closing with each new requirement to involve the voluntary sector. In February 2001 Oasis launched the Faithworks Movement[1] to advocate the role of faith groups in the provision of community services and faith-based welfare. It called on the government to value the significant work undertaken by churches and other faith communities in delivering 'community benefit' and to remove explicit and implicit obstacles to the provision of funding. Likewise, it called on the Church to be proud of its contribution whilst, at the same time, learn to re-engage with other community agencies and statutory bodies. One consequence of this is that all local authorities in England and Wales have been issued with guidelines relating to partnership with faith groups.

Summary

When war broke out in 1939, the principle of youth work *and* ministry – if not the term – was widely accepted by both Church and State. Christian organisations worked alongside the embryonic statutory sector without having to renounce their faith. In the post-war years this partnership was gradually eroded, with youth work becoming separated from youth ministry. The statutory sector labelled youth ministry as unprofessional and proselytising and the Church responded with the claim that youth work was devoid of spiritual significance. There are now signs that the duel is being brought to a peaceful end. The 'New Right' agenda at the end of the twentieth

---

[1] www.faithworks.info

Part Two:

Values of youth work *and* ministry

Chapter 5

Voluntary Participation

Not all activity involving young people is youth work *and* ministry. The police may be involved with young people – by arresting them – but its officers are not engaged in youth work *per se*. One of the core values of youth work is voluntary participation. This requires the relationship between youth worker and young person to be based on a voluntary contract, agreed by both parties. Because few choose to be arrested the judicial system gives the police statutory powers to enforce young people's participation. Likewise, in Britain those aged under 16 years have no choice but to participate in full-time education. Whether they like it or not, the law requires them to attend school. This obligation contributes in part to the label of formal education. In contrast, youth work *and* ministry is based on voluntary participation. Youth workers and ministers invite young people to participate in youth programmes; they never use coercion or enforcement. For this reason, youth work *and* ministry is described as informal education. (This is developed further in Chapter 6.) Voluntary participation requires that young people must have genuine freedom to opt in or opt out. Without it there can be no youth work *and* ministry.

Whilst the term 'voluntary participation' originates from the Albermarle Report, I believe the principle is

consistent with God's character and actions. For this reason, we begin with a theological introduction to the nature of God and apply this to an understanding of pre-destination and election.

God is love

The Bible is the unfolding story of God as revealed over thousands of years through the writings of many con-tributors. Though God does not change (Mal. 3:6), the understanding of his people does. What is hinted at in the Old Testament becomes clearer in the New Testament. This is known as 'progressive revelation'. For example, Abraham may have been justified by faith in Christ Jesus (Rom. 4:18; Heb. 11:8) just as surely as was Paul, but few would deny he had less understanding. After all, he pre-dated the law, exile, death and resurrection of Christ, as well as the outpouring of the Holy Spirit at Pentecost. Abraham's *Introduction to Systematic Theology* would have been wafer thin. Understandably the later biblical writers brought greater clarity. And so it was that the apostle John, with all the benefit of those who had gone before him, simply wrote 'God is love' (1 Jn. 4:8). He understood that the essence of God is love in its purest form. It is not just that God loves people but that God *is* love. He is the source of love and everything he does stems from it. Paul used the same principle to describe God the Father as being the source of all fatherhood (Eph. 3:15). For John Stott, it is not just that God is a better father than any human dad; he is the source of all fatherhood, from which all earthly fathers take their lead. So it is that he is also the source of all love. Christianity's emphasis on love makes it quite different from other philosophies.

According to Friedrich Neitzsche (1844–1900), the basic principle of humanity is the 'will to power'. He claimed that all human behaviour displays power and aggression. The weak form herds to collectively assert their will over the strong. Likewise, the strong use their position to repress the weak. In short, 'when the going gets tough', Neitzsche believed, 'the tough get rough'. However, according to Sigmund Freud (1856–1939), the basic principle of humanity is lust and sexual attraction. He believed that all human behaviour is the consequence of repressed sexual desires, many of which stem from the sexually charged relationship between child and parent. Both Neitzsche and Freud helped to explain complex aspects of human behaviour. In so doing, they both adopted a determinist view that renders human behaviour subject to forces beyond its control. In contrast to aggression and lust, the message of Jesus was love. Instead of using and abusing others, he talked about giving and forgiving. But how should we understand this love?

In considering God's love, care must be taken not to rely too much upon our human understanding of love. Process theologian Alfred Whitehead (1861–1947) argued that, 'It is as true to say that God creates the world as that the world creates God.' This must be challenged because God is not a human construct (Num. 23:19; 1 Sam. 15:29; Is. 40:18; 55:8, 9). Therefore, the language of romantic fiction, erotic pleasure or emotional intelligence cannot provide a sufficient definition of God's love. And yet, because we are made in God's image, something of his character and nature is revealed in our human experience. These forensic clues are useful in so far as they help us to build up a picture. On this basis we can continue.

God's love is offered unconditionally. It matters neither whether it is deserved nor recognised (1 Jn. 4:10), God *is*

love and so loves all people all of the time. This is good news because, despite our best efforts, we are unable to satisfy God's standards. Who can honestly claim to have never mistreated anyone or anything at any time? He does not treat us as we deserve. Instead, God's love compels him to seek reconciliation with his creation. This was why John claimed

> For God so *loved* the world that he gave his one and only Son, that whoever believes in him shall not perish but have eternal life.
>
> John 3:16 (my emphasis)

Because God is love, he does not override people's freedom to make choices. Being internally consistent, he does not use unethical methods to achieve his goals. Jesus told the parable of the prodigal son, in part, to demonstrate this principle. Whilst most attention is focused on the two sons, it is worth reflecting on the role played by the father. Henri Nouwen, Catholic priest, observes

> As Father, he wants his children to be free, free to love. That freedom includes the possibility of their leaving home, going to a 'distant country' and losing everything. The Father's heart knows all the pain that will come from that choice, but his love makes him powerless to prevent it. As Father, he desires that those who stay at home enjoy his presence and experience his affection. But, here again, he wants only to offer a love that can be freely received . . . But he cannot make them love him without losing his true fatherhood.

Some see a God of love in the New Testament but a God of wrath in the Old Testament. In so doing they struggle to reconcile an internally consistent

understanding of God (Deut. 6:4) with, what at times appears to be, two different portrayals. Whilst God may display temporary signs of anger, he permanently displays love (Ps. 30:5; Is. 54:8). God's love is evident in the Old Testament just as surely as in the New Testament. For example, it was the God of love that introduced the law so as to limit the effect of sin and prompt people's search for salvation (Rom. 7:7). Religious authorities understood this. On one occasion Jesus asked a religious expert to summarise the law. This man knew the Scriptures inside and out. He concluded that the essence of the law was love: love the Lord your God with all your heart, mind, soul and strength, and love your neighbour as yourself (Lk. 10:25–28). It is as if 'God is love' appears as a watermark on all the pages of the Old and New Testaments. Any understanding of God must start and end with this assertion for he can do nothing that is inconsistent with this. So does God invite us to participate voluntarily in his kingdom or does he enforce it?

Volunteers or conscripts?

My Bible College years were full of passionate debate. As communal students we thrived on argument – in the name of truth. Eschatology, or study of the end times, was a frequent topic. When was Christ likely to return, at what altitude would his people meet him and just how bad would it be for those left behind? Tony Campolo's quip that 'Christians are on the welcoming committee, not the planning committee', fell on deaf ears. However, the most passionate debate was usually reserved for the 'P' word – predestination. Did God choose us or did we choose him? Does God's army of believers comprise conscripts or volunteers? Calvinist conscripts lined up

against Arminian volunteers to fight it out just as surely as the Royalists did against the Roundheads in the English civil war. Though it generated more hot air than the ancient heating system, it was nevertheless an important debate.

Those who adopt a reformed theology broadly follow the work of John Calvin (1509–64). He was curious as to why, when the same gospel is proclaimed, some respond but others do not. He concluded that this was because God chooses some, but not others. Timothy George summarises Calvin's view of predestination in three words: absolute, particular and double. He maintains it is *absolute* because election is based solely on God's will and nothing to do with any human response. It is *particular* because election is only offered to certain individuals, not everyone. This led him to conclude that Christ did not die for everyone, but only for the chosen. It is *double* in that God predestines all people to eternity, some to heaven and others to hell. Calvin's theology was more pastoral than systematic and placed a high emphasis on the saving work of Christ, as extended to the elect.

Some 'strict and particular' Calvinists reject the notion of voluntary participation, believing that God chooses not to accept some people before they are even born. Only God knows whom he has predestined to eternity in heaven. Far from sounding harsh, they say it is only by God's grace that any, never mind all, are saved; that he should save some is better than none. After all, how can those who are pronounced 'dead in their transgressions and sins' (Eph. 2:1) be considered free to accept or reject the gospel? Because only God knows people's election, it is not for others to judge. Clearly such language is emotive but does at least remind us of God's sovereignty; as Lord of Lords he is answerable to no one. Therefore, at least

the value of voluntary participation is not annulled by this 'strict and particular' theology.

However, not all Calvinists think alike. The majority of reformed theologians believe that God's sovereignty does not undermine the notion of voluntary participation. They maintain that people are free to exercise their own self-determination whilst, at the same time, God works sovereignly behind the scene to bring about his will. In reality people freely make the choices that God has predestined for them. In effect, we are both conscripts and volunteers. Calvinists believe it is not just that people *think* they are free agents; they genuinely *are* free to make choices. This combination of divine election and human responsibility is known theologically as 'compatablism'. Most Calvinists are therefore happy to embrace the principle of voluntary participation.

> *To think about . . .*
>
> How do you respond to Calvinist theology?
> What, if anything, does it have to say about
> your youth work practice?

The question is, to what extent was Calvin's work consistent with John's declaration that 'God is love'? Though reformed theology undoubtedly reminds us of the horrific consequences of 'sin' and the richness of God's grace, I believe it tells only half the story. Whilst I agree with its conclusions, I cannot accept the reasoning. It would appear to me tautological to speak of people having freedom to enact only what God has predestined for them. This sounds manipulative to me and therefore incompatible with the all-loving God.

In contrast to Calvin stands the work of Jacobus Arminius (1560–1609). He maintained that God seeks to save all those who choose to accept the free offer of salvation. Election is then predetermined only by people's response, and not by a pre-set master plan. Because all-loving God wants people to make free choices he voluntarily chooses not to foreordain, or predetermine, their responses. He does, however, have complete fore-knowledge of how each person will respond. Arminius conceded that salvation appears, at times, precarious because people are equally capable of rejecting or accepting God. Those from an Arminian position also place a high emphasis on the voluntary nature of participation in God's kingdom. This, for me, appears more consistent with the understanding that 'God is love'.

God's love is not dependent on our response to him. God is love to all people, not just to those who respond to him. Why would God knowingly condemn some to eternal separation from him if he has the means to save everyone? The mystery is that he first loved us (1 Jn. 4:10), and loves us whether or not we choose to love him in return. Such love is unique and, therefore, appealing to those with knowledge of it. That so many people respond to God's love does not mean their freedom to choose is violated in some way. They are simply responding to an offer that seems too good to ignore. That said, Arminian theology still leaves some questions unanswered. For example, if all-loving God knows in advance some are heading towards eternal disaster why does he not save them from their folly? Even this appears inconsistent with God's love. However, before moving on, we should remember that the principle of voluntary participation can be supported by both Calvinistic and Arminian theology.

To think about . . .

How do you respond to the Arminian theology? What, if anything, does it have to say about your youth work practice?

The openness of God

In recent years, Clark Pinnock has taken the Arminian approach still further by advocating an 'open' view of God. Some conservative evangelicals have judged this to be a step beyond historic orthodoxy, whilst many charismatic evangelicals have seen this as a return to passionate spirituality. The debate has quite rightly been robust! Certainly Pinnock's model of 'inclusivism' appears close at times to pluralism; something I find quite challenging. Just as Calvin's work often elicits knee-jerk reactions from those who give it only casual attention, so too does the work of Pinnock. Both are worthy of consideration – if not acceptance.

'Open' theology asserts that God's relationship with the world is dynamic, not static. He neither controls people's response to him (foreordains) nor wants to have prior knowledge of their decision (foreknowledge). Instead, prompted by pure love, he risks rejection in order to secure a genuine heart-response from his people.

God's relationship with us can be likened to the kind of relationships we enjoy with each other. I can still remember the feeling of excitement and slight apprehension when I asked Sally to marry me. I could not have been more sure I wanted to marry her and, in my rational moments, was confident of her response. But

still, as I popped the question, there was a nagging thought that she might say no. I had no contingency plan for this. So it was with much joy and relief that she said yes. Freedom to accept must be based on an equal freedom to reject. It is not love that manipulates someone into choosing them, neither is it love that only risks asking the question when the answer is already known. Exchanging our marriage vows during the wedding service was a great delight but made easier by our prior knowledge of each other's planned response. You could argue that it would have been easier still if we had had an 'arranged marriage'; our role would then simply have been to affirm what had already been predetermined for us. Yet, with my Western conditioning, I cannot comprehend entering into a lifelong relationship with someone I have not freely chosen. Using the same argument, I cannot see that the God of love is in the business of arranging people's relationship with him without their genuine consent.

The 'open' view of God maintains that God knows all that there is logically to know. He is uniquely omniscient (all-knowing). But, philosophically, that does not mean he knows what is logically unknowable. Just as it would be wrong to suggest God has limited power because he cannot make a round square, so too it is wrong to suggest God's knowledge is limited simply because he doesn't know the future. The future has not yet happened and is therefore unknowable. Therefore 'open' theists are adamant that God is omniscient. It is not that God is incapable of knowing the future; he simply prefers a more dynamic relationship with creation. When God tested Abraham it was because he genuinely wanted to know the answer. *'Now I know'* declared God (Gen. 22:12). On occasion, God appeared exasperated with wayward Israel's action, admitting 'it never entered my mind that they should do such a detestable thing' (Jer. 32:35).

Open theology maintains that, though the future cannot be known as a matter of fact (because it hasn't yet happened), it can nevertheless be predicted with some certainty. Prophecy then becomes a prediction of what is most likely to happen, given the facts that are known at the time. And who better to make that prediction than God, who knows everything there is to know about us (Ps. 139:1). God's prophecy is therefore accurate because God is wise, not because the predicted event has already happened. Furthermore, most prophecies describe what God promises to do, enabling him to say with absolute certainty what he will do in the future. However, if circumstances change then he is not averse to altering his plans.

Positively, I believe the 'open' view of God breaths new life into prayer. Intercession then becomes a dynamic interaction between God and humanity, capable of bringing about significant change. Sometimes prayer causes God to alter direction and even to change his mind altogether (Gen. 6:6, 18:23–32; Ex. 32:14; 1 Sam. 15:35; Jon. 3:10). Not all Arminian's, let alone Calvinists, feel comfortable with this. Likewise, the 'open' view provides fresh insight into the joy God experiences when just one person repents (Lk. 15:7). Many of Jesus' parables communicate this sense of relief and excitement (Mt. 13:44–46; 18:10–14; Lk. 15:1–7, 8–10, 11–32). As Pinnock points out, the thrill of recovery is quite different from the satisfaction of predictable achievement (1994:41). Then, if God can experience joy then surely he can also feel pain and sadness?

As already acknowledged, the 'open' view of God is not without its critics. Some refuse to acknowledge that it is Christian, never mind Arminian. Tony Gray and Christopher Sinkinson provide a critical assessment. They are uncomfortable with any suggestion that God's power

and ability is limited, albeit by his own imposition, or that God's grace might extend to those beyond the Church. They draw attention to verses that speak of God's unchanging, immutable character. This follows the conservative evangelical tradition of claiming that God is incapable of change of any kind. The difficulty with this position is that it denies the possibility of love. 'Open' theists, on the other hand, are the first to acknowledge that God's *character* does not change; it need not because it is perfect. But his *actions* with people do.

What seems clear is that both conservative and 'open' evangelicals find biblical evidence for their approaches but neither can claim a monopoly on answers. Whilst acknowledging the openness of God leaves some big questions unanswered, I personally believe it offers fresh insight into the dynamic relationship God seeks with his creation. Both Arminian and Calvinistic theology support the principle of voluntary participation, even if the term is not normally associated with the latter. Open theology equally supports the notion of voluntary participation but, if authentic, is able to offer a more coherent and internally-consistent rationale. So how should this inform the practice of youth work *and* ministry? If involvement in the kingdom of heaven is based on voluntary participation how much more so should involvement in youth work *and* ministry?

To think about . . .

How do you respond to 'open' theology?
What, if anything, does it have to say about
your youth work practice?

Youth work *and* ministry

As far back as 1960, the Albermarle Report identified young people as the fourth partner in the Youth Service, alongside government, local authorities and voluntary organisations. Later reports, including the Thompson Report in 1982, have built on this with a commitment to experiential learning. Young people are not consumers of a service, they are participants within it. It affirmed

> The primary purpose of participation in the youth service is to give the young individual a sense of belonging, a sense of identity, and the skills, confidence and assurance needed to participate not only in their club or organisation but also in society at large.

Kerry Young points out that voluntary participation is not just concerned with young people's willingness to attend. It goes deeper than that. First, the intention – as well as the process – must be made explicit to young people. Second, young people should be encouraged to ask questions in order to gain a real sense of what is involved. Third, young people must give their conscious and informed consent to engage, not just in the immediate activity, but also in the underlying process. This is important for youth work *and* ministry. Voluntary participation is not activated by inviting young people to a free concert whilst failing to mention that the gig is sponsored by the church and will include a presentation about the Christian faith. Such an approach does not provide young people with all the necessary information they need to make an informed decision. This may be how cults operate but, as has been seen, this is not the way God chooses to deal with his creation. The end does not always justify the

means. We are mistaken if we think God needs that kind
of help.

> *To think about ...*
>
> To what extent are young people able to make
> informed decisions about your youth
> programme as a result of the information you
> provide?

Prisoner Cell Group H

The value of voluntary participation raises important
issues for those involved in church-based youth work *and*
ministry. To what extent are young people free to participate in church activities on a voluntary basis? Parents
and carers have a God-given duty to pass on to children
their spiritual heritage (Deut. 6:7; Prov. 22:6; Col. 3:21).
As parents, it is the responsibility of my wife and me to
bring up our children 'in the faith'. We cannot ask anyone
to do this for us. Difficulties arise when parents abdicate
their responsibilities or confuse the supportive, but
distinct, role of youth workers and ministers. Youth work
and ministry offers young people a safe and inspiring
context in which to explore matters of belief and personal
development. It is a supplement to, but never a replacement for, the role of parents and carers. Some Christian
parents insist their children attend at least one church
activity a week in the belief that, in time, they will thank
them for it. Their young people are forced to submit to
this for as long as they remain economically dependent

on their parents. Though intended to be positive, such enforced participation can damage the relationship between parents, young people and youth workers. Denied an opportunity to opt out, young people may record their dissatisfaction with their parents by blaming the nearest youth worker, who then becomes guilty by association. Such an arrangement rarely makes for conducive youth work *and* ministry. Young people who ordinarily might have engaged with the youth programme then become completely switched off by their lack of liberty. They display a combination of apathy, antipathy and antisocial behaviour to record their resistance. And who can blame them? This may be a necessary defence mechanism to protect their self worth and identity as an individual. Prisoners in Young Offenders Centres wear their regulation-issue jeans at almost half-mast for the same reason. Faced with almost total control by others, this becomes the only way to assert their individuality.

Youth workers sometimes fail to recognise the dilemma many 'churched' young people face and mistakenly accept the role of surrogate parent. Having not dealt adequately with their own insecurities and past hurts, they take young people's negative attitudes as a personal attack. Consequently, they respond negatively to young people's antisocial behaviour. Matters are made worse if they enforce young people's compliance by threatening to inform parents, who may be their personal friends. Tragically, this renders church an unsafe place for young people because whatever they do creeps back to their parents. Therefore, it is vitally important that youth workers and ministers protect their unique relationship with young people. They are not parents and do not act as agents for them. Youth workers and ministers maintain independence from parents in the belief that, in time,

parents will thank them for it. However, this is not easy in a church community where everyone is known. The brutal reality that most youth work *and* ministry is funded by church members, many of whom are parents, only serves to complicate matters.

Sometimes the value of voluntary participation requires youth workers and ministers to find ways of enabling young people to record their conscientious objection to attending church. Recognising their dilemma, I have sometimes asked young people 'How can I help you not be here?' I would rather work with a small number of those who positively want to participate than with larger numbers of those whose attendance is enforced.

To think about . . .

To what extent does parental control determine young people's participation in your programme? How do you maintain the unique youth work *and* ministry relationship with young people in a church setting?

Participants not consumers

Voluntary participation is not only concerned with freedom of involvement. The quality of involvement is equally important. Youth work *and* ministry enables young people to become participants in, not just consumers of, a service. As Mike Breen observes, the role of youth workers should never simply be to 'put something on' for young people. However, many fall into the provider-client trap.

Youth workers adopt the role of providers and then feel burdened by the pressure to deliver a programme that attracts clients (young people). Labelled as clients, young people feel uninvolved and disinterested in what is clearly not their programme. Too many youth workers respond by working even harder to improve their programme, with ever more ambitious trips, lock-ins and other forms of entertainment. Not only do youth workers have to sustain a continually improving programme, they must also be 'one up' on competing providers to deter clients from switching allegiance. The provider-client trap is set.

By contrast, voluntary participation liberates both youth workers and young people alike. Young people gain far more satisfaction and developmental opportunities when they are empowered to become full participants. They are more likely to engage in programmes that they consider belong to them, and not just to youth workers. Voluntary participation ensures their needs and aspirations are reflected in the programme, thus demonstrating the significance of their involvement. Through participation, young people gradually adopt the programme's struggle as their own. They begin to assume responsibility for its future success and failure. Young people need to see just how important their time, creativity and other resources are. Some providers, with the best of motives, seek to provide their clients with everything served on a plate. They see this as an act of service. However, this was not an approach taken by Jesus. Again, as Breen observes, when commissioning disciples, Jesus reminded them to involve those they sought to reach (Lk. 9:4; 10:8). Promoting participation helps to communicate value and respect.

All this is good news for youth workers. Who wouldn't want young people actively engaged in the programme? However, this rarely happens by chance. It requires a

conscious decision to involve young people throughout
the programme and to entrust them with responsibility.
Promoting voluntary participation is never easy. It can
take some time for a programme caught in the provider-
client trap to free itself from bad habits and for youth
workers and young people to recognise the new commitment to participation.

> *To think about...*
>
> What role do young people play in your youth
> programme? To what extent are they clients or
> participants? How do you enable young
> people's participation?

Summary

Voluntary participation is not just a value that originates
from a secular framework. It is a value of youth work
and ministry because it accurately reflects the invitation
that God extends to his creation. It would be inconsistent
for the all-loving God to coerce people into submitting to
his will. Likewise, youth workers and ministers that
model God's love do not use manipulative methods to
engage young people. The value of voluntary participation is not an optional extra. There can be no youth
work *and* ministry without it. The stark choice is cult or
church. What do you choose? So much for voluntary
participation, but what about the value of informal
education?

Voluntary Participation –
a response from Nick Margesson

In many ways the principal of 'voluntary participation' goes without saying. It's obvious, isn't it? Since there is no natural or legal obligation for young people to be involved in 'youth work *and* ministry', their participation must, necessarily, be on a voluntary basis.

Those involved in youth work *and* ministry will have to work hard to make sure that young people *want* to participate. When principals in ministry are clear-cut and obvious, as in this case, there are dangers in trying to find a theology which supports the principle. It may just be common sense . . .

In this chapter much of the argument is based on the 'Openness of God' teaching of Clark Pinnock. Pinnock presents a god who limits his power and knowledge to such an extent that he chooses not to know the future. He is restricted to making guesses because what has yet to happen can be predicted but not known for sure ('the future cannot be known as a matter of fact') and is so uncertain of himself that he seems to be hanging around waiting for humans to give him instructions.

This dangerous theology displays so tiny a view of God, so over-inflated a view of mankind, so small a grasp of the horror of sin and so weak an understanding of God's love that it cannot help but sell young people short.

The irony, in a chapter on 'voluntary participation', is that most young people will clear off when they realise that they are being offered an emaciated Christianity that offers no real answers, no real hope, no real relationship with the living God and no real rescue from hell.

This god is a million miles away from the infinitely powerful, all-knowing Creator God of the Bible. The references, which are often used to support Pinnock's argument, and which appear in the chapter, are far from convincing: in Genesis 18, God doesn't change his mind, and (if you read on) he destroys Sodom and Gomorrah just as he said he would. In Exodus 32, the very basis of Moses' prayer is God's *unchangeable* promise. As for 1 Samuel 15:35, you have to try really hard to ignore the context, because v. 29 states explicitly that God doesn't change his mind!

What's more shocking is the amount of biblical material you have to ditch to come up with Pinnock's weak and impotent god. What do you do with Creation, the Flood, the Exodus, the conquest of Canaan, the miracles of Jesus and the promised return of Jesus as Judge of all? What do you do with all of the passages that speak of God's Sovereignty in election (e.g. Mal. 12–3 [cf. Rom. 9:13], Rom. 8:29–30, Eph. 1:4)? Brierley finds he 'cannot reconcile this' with the statement that God is love. Yet in Scripture, God's love and election belong together (Deut. 7:7–8, Ps. 78:68, Jn. 15:12–16, Col. 3:12, 1 Thess. 1:4).

The Bible speaks of a terrifyingly powerful God who sustains and rules the universe and yet who wonderfully and inexplicably loves us. This is a God who is fully in control so that he can always keep his promises. This is the God that I can trust. This is a God that I can turn to when life is tough and messy, as it often is. This is the God whose side I want to be on. Surely youth work *and* ministry which introduces me to this God – the God of

the Bible – is youth work *and* ministry that young people will want to be participate in and on a voluntarily basis.

NICK MARGESSON
Youth Minister at St Helen's Bishopsgate, London

Chapter 6

Informal Education

It seems there is more acceptance of 'informal education' as a value than there is understanding of its meaning. Too often informal education is described negatively as being what it isn't, rather than what it is *per se*. It is usually contrasted with a simplistic view of formal education, being the antithesis of classrooms full of desks controlled by teachers. But this is no longer adequate. First, the maturation of youth work *and* ministry demands a more solid foundation and, second, the distinctions between formal and informal are becoming blurred as some youth workers begin to operate in semi-formal contexts.

Formal education relates to both the setting and method. It takes place in formal institutions such as schools and colleges, with their rules, systems and controls, and relies upon formal teaching methods. Here learning occurs at set times and in set places. When the bell goes, the potential for learning stops. In contrast informal education can take place anywhere. For the informal educator, street corners, a basketball court or church youth group are all potential places of learning. In its most basic form, informal education suggests an intention to foster learning in others using an informality of approach. Working with individuals and groups in the community, it uses both spontaneous and planned

opportunities to draw out learning. To understand this more we'll start by focusing on education before then moving on to look at informal methods and, in particular, the example set for us by Christ.

Education and learning

Education refers to the processes by which a person of any age grows in knowledge, awareness and life skills and, as such, is a means to growth and development. Some view education as a narrow, mechanistic product used to fill empty vessels (if not minds) with society's accumulated knowledge and wisdom. For others it is an enriching process that enables individuals to reach their full, God-given potential. 'Product educators' generally require individuals to follow predetermined patterns of learning. For example, the primary aim of maths teachers is for their pupils to reach prescribed standards of numeracy, not a love for the arts. 'Process educators', on the other hand, tend to create space in which individual's can determine their own interests and learning. In reality both product and process approaches are required. Formal education places greater emphasis on the former and youth work *and* ministry the latter.

Learning is the response people make to education and is normally characterised by changes in behaviour, attitude or skill. Recognising this, Jesus commanded his followers not simply to teach people what he had taught them, but rather to educate in such a way that enabled others to respond to what they heard (Mt. 28:19, 20). However, teaching and learning are not the same thing. It is possible for educators to teach in such a way that no learning takes places. My numerous French teachers are evidence of this, *mon petit pois*. Conversely, learning can

take place without any teaching. Learning is a lifelong process that builds upon the cumulative interactions between individuals and their environment. Every conversation and experience becomes a learning opportunity. For example, through bitter experience we learn to trust some people, but not others. Similarly, by conducting a series of experiments we learn that some routes to work are quicker than others.

> *To think about . . .*
>
> What have you learnt today? How did you appropriate the learning?

John Dewey, the pioneering American educationalist, maintained that thinking is the first step towards learning. He talked of 'forked-road situations' that present dilemmas and demand intellectual responses. Through informal education, youth workers and ministers seek to create, and draw attention to, such 'forked-road situations' in order to help young people pursue growth. Following this principle, Willow Creek Community Church[1] use drama or perform songs to create what they profoundly call a 'moment': one that presents people with a powerful representation of spiritual truth that invites an intellectual or emotional response. More spontaneously, a conversation with a group of young people in a park could equally provide an opportunity to explore issues of faith or belief.

---

[1] www.willowcreek.org

Education and fun

Contrary to popular belief, youth work *and* ministry is not primarily concerned with entertainment. It is not enough simply to provide a fun programme that keeps young people off the streets or in church. It requires more than free access to table tennis, computer games and the occasional trip. Youth work *and* ministry is interested in young people's growth and development. Just as Jesus grew in wisdom and stature and in favour with God and people (Lk. 2:52), so youth workers and ministers look to foster the same intellectual, moral, physical, spiritual and social development in the young people they serve. Education contributes to this development. This is not to say that every activity must have a direct educational outcome. Sometimes it is necessary to create a social context in which youth work *and* ministry can take place. Though running a basketball team is not in itself youth work *and* ministry, enabling team members to work together, resolve conflicts and recognise the relevance of Christ in their lives most definitely is. Informal education is as much an attitude as a method.

Informal educators often seek to create fun environments in which to foster learning. If they didn't, the value of voluntary participation would dissuade many young people from opting in to the learning process. Crowd-breakers, games, role plays, residential experiences, sport and the creative arts can all be used to good effect. However, informal education does not have a monopoly on fun. There are plenty of schoolteachers that use formal methods to consistently create fun and inspiring learning environments, making even quantum physics both interesting and comprehensible. Regrettably, not all youth workers are able to use informal methods to such effect. Two crowd-breakers and a fist

full of video clips do not necessarily constitute informal education.

Education and indoctrination

There is often a fine line between education and indoctrination. Informal educators do not preach, they engage in conversation. Aware of their own values and beliefs, they show genuine interest in the values and beliefs of others. In so doing, they create a two-way dialogue. Some believe that informal educators should never impose their own agenda on other people's learning and, therefore, become nervous at the mention of conversion. Others reject informal education because they are aware of Christ's call to mission (Mt. 28:19, 20) and his desire that all might be saved (1 Tim. 2:4). Yet this is not necessary.

Education is concerned not so much with the activity of teaching as with the evidence of learning, and the responses it elicits. If conversion is primarily about change then all informal education is in the business of conversion. Any youth work that does not result in change must be deemed ineffective. Informal educators must surely hope that, as a result of their interventions, young people engaged in criminality will change their ways. So Christians are not alone in looking for conversion. The issue is what role youth workers play in the conversion process.

Evangelicals have traditionally understood conversion as something done to others. For example, Victorian missionaries set out to convert the 'lost tribes of Africa'. Even today some evangelists measure themselves by the number of people they convert. This egotistic understanding is challenged by informal education; empowered by the Holy Spirit, people convert themselves. People ultimately respond to the Holy Spirit (Jn.

14:26; 1 Thess. 4:9), not to us. Back in 1983, Luis Palau did not convert me to faith in Christ. Having listened to his talk and spent weeks questioning others, I chose to convert. Youth work *and* ministry provides an opportunity for young people to explore, among other things, issues of faith and belief in a safe environment, free from indoctrination, manipulation or religious abuse. Some will choose to convert, others will not. This requires youth workers and ministers to be vulnerable (Lk. 10:3), lay aside their power (Phil. 2:5–8) and to have confidence in both the gospel (Rom. 1:16; 2 Tim. 1:12) and the ability of young people to make informed decisions. It involves a willingness to embrace conversation, not preaching; questions, not answers. With this attitude it becomes quite appropriate for youth workers and ministers to share their own beliefs and values. Indeed, it would unethical not to. By withholding our values, we deny young people the necessary information they require to make informed value judgements about us.

Informal education therefore provides a means to facilitate Christian discipleship. However, youth work *and* ministry recognises that the spiritual liberation of young people cannot be effected by education alone. The total depravity of humanity, brought about by the rule of sin (Eph. 2:1–9; 1 Jn. 1:8) is inclusive of all people, including the young. Though informal education cannot liberate those hindered by sin, it can – and does – provide a means by which young people can discover Christ, the liberator, for themselves.

Jesus the informal educator

Jesus is the supreme educator. Because all four Gospels refer to him as a teacher (e.g. Mt. 19:16; Mk. 4:38; Lk. 9:38;

Jn. 1:38), we tend to imagine he was a more divine version of our own schoolmasters – with gown, if not mortarboard. Today, teachers are generally labelled as those who stand in front of people and talk at them. Nothing could be further from Christ's approach. Jesus was not brought up in a social or political vacuum. He was born into a Jewish family, spoke Aramaic, was educated in both the home and synagogue and was familiar with the religious customs and practices of the time. To understand Jesus it is necessary to have some appreciation of his context.

Without access to printed material, first-century rabbis relied upon the oral tradition, passing on teaching to their disciples or *talmîd*. Masters had to teach succinctly so that their disciples could memorise the teaching word for word. Only this would protect the integrity of the oral tradition. To aid memorisation, the rabbis would use repetition, story telling and catch phrases. However, being a disciple was not just about reciting sacred teaching. It involved each *talmîd* entering into a life-sharing companionship with his rabbi so as to become more like him (Lk. 6:40). The disciples would accompany their masters to the synagogue, law courts and anywhere else to see how they conducted themselves (Mk. 3:13, 14; 10:32). Everyday situations were seen as opportunities for the *talmîd's* learning. This was the pattern that Jesus was brought up with and which can be seen to emerge through his own ministry.

The Sermon in the Mount is probably the best known, and yet least understood or obeyed, part of Christ's teaching. It stands out in the gospels as a rare occasion when Jesus delivered a set piece of formal teaching. Some scholars maintain that the sermon is not one historical event, but rather a compilation of Christ's teaching or sayings collected over a period of time. This view has to be accepted if it is to be argued that formal teaching was

a regular feature of his ministry. Certainly Matthew uses this literary technique to group together seven parables about the kingdom (Mt. 13). Whether you accept the Sermon on the Mount is a compilation or not, the fact remains Matthew chose to give relatively little space to Christ's formal teaching events. Like Mark, Luke and John, he gave far more significance to the everyday events that Christ turned into learning opportunities.

Unlike the rabbis, who only taught in one fixed location, Jesus viewed any setting as having potential for learning. For example, he taught in the temple (Mt. 21:23; Jn. 7:14), in towns and villages (Mt. 9:35; Mk. 6:6), in synagogues (Mt. 9:35; Lk. 4:15, 16), in homes (Mk. 2:1–11), whilst travelling (Mk. 10:32–34) and even from an anchored boat (Mk. 4:1; Lk. 5:3). Jesus was comfortable educating outside as much as inside. Furthermore, Jesus attuned his teaching to the needs and questions of his audience. He did not appear to come with a pre-loaded curriculum to follow. His teaching was formed around the question of those he came into contact with. Jesus did not simply bring revelation about God; he *was* the revelation of God. Again, he did not simply speak the words of God; he *was* the Word of God (Jn. 1:1, 2). He was both the medium and the message. Unlike formal educators, youth workers and ministers cannot always rely upon a script or session plan. Instead, they draw upon a repertoire of experience, creativity and internal resources to tailor learning to people's needs. Informal education is no easy option.

Conversation

Surprising perhaps for a teacher, Jesus was not a one-way communicator. He was comfortable with, and even

seemed to thrive on, dialogue. He listened, asked questions and was generally willing to engage in conversation. The Gospels record 125 incidents when Jesus communicated with others. Of these, others initiated 54 per cent. As Lewis and Lewis acknowledge

> The Son of God, who had all the answers to the worlds needs, who was *the* answer, so respected the personalities and individualities of his listeners that he allowed them to determine his communication agenda more than half the time.

People's questions not only revealed something about themselves and their needs but also provided an opportunity for informal education. The Gospel writers all chose to portray a dynamic and responsive approach to Christ's work. It was only in response to his disciple's request to teach them how to pray that he introduced the Lord's Prayer (Lk. 11:1–13). It was during a crowded dinner that Jesus helped his followers understand the importance of welcoming the poor, marginalised and powerless (Lk. 14:7–14). When James and John asked to reserve a privileged position with Christ in heaven, he helped prepare them for his death. Today we are able to understand salvation and grace because of the conversations Jesus entered into with Nicodemus (Jn. 3:1–21) and the woman at the well (Jn. 4:4–26). Unlike the Pharisees, Jesus did not exclude anyone; he was open to all. With Jesus, every situation became a potential learning opportunity. Through conversation, Jesus enabled people to become active participants in the education process. Perhaps no other religious leader has ever been so reliant upon informal education as was Jesus.

Maxine Green and Chadhu Christian, in their book *Accompanying*, argue that Christ's appearance on the

Emmaus Road (Lk. 24:13–35) provides a classic example of his use of informal education. They argue that: Christ kept to the traveller's direction and pace; respected their space and autonomy; engaged in their conversation; asked and responded to questions; and maintained the focus on the travellers, not on himself. Youth work *and* ministry relies significantly upon conversation. Quite often the significant work takes place immediately outside a youth centre, not in it, or at the close of a session, not during it. For it is then that conversation has opportunity to flourish. Residential experiences are so effective because they create such opportunities for conversation. Both young people and youth workers become more relaxed and willing to engage in more challenging dialogue.

To think about . . .

Take a few minutes to reflect on a significant conversation you have had with a young person. How were you both changed by it? How much opportunity do you have for conversation in your practice?

Story-telling

Jesus must surely be the greatest story-teller of all time. His audiences were consistently enthralled by what they heard. He painted pictures in people's minds and pointed them towards the good news of the kingdom. The term parable, meaning literally to 'throw alongside', implies

the stories pointed to something else. Each parable had both surface and deep meanings. Jesus drew upon everyday situations that were familiar to his listeners. For example, he told parables about sowing and harvesting, weddings, baking, bread, lamps and journeys. Similarly, he used characters that people could easily identify with. These included farmers, home makers, sons, fathers, widows and merchants. At a surface level, the parable of the wise and foolish builders (Mt. 7:24–29) communicated the folly of building a house on a foundation of sand, but at a deeper level it challenged people to put his teaching into practice. Those who heard him concluded that he taught with far more effect than did the Pharisees. As youth workers and ministers, we surely aspire to this.

Story-telling remains an important tool in youth work *and* ministry. Practitioners use stories to create 'forked-road situations' that make people think. Jesus deliberately used parables so as to prompt questions and to enable people to think for themselves. At times, this was deeply frus-trating for his followers who preferred to be told what to believe (Lk. 8:9, 10). Evangelical Christians, with their emphasis on truth and proclamation, have sometimes been uncomfortable with questions and 'loose ends'. However, it is a sign of maturation that reflection, medi-tation and story telling are beginning to find favour once again.

Symbolism and pictures

Isaiah dramatised his message by walking naked and barefoot (Is. 20), Jeremiah smashed pots (Jer. 19) and Ahijah tore his coat into twelve pieces (1 Kgs. 11:29–31). These are just some of the examples of prophetic sym-

bolism and pictures found in the Bible and used to reveal truth. Faced with apathy and intolerance, symbolism was often used to good effect. Jesus continued this tradition, using symbolic language and pictures in his communication. John's gospel is particularly rich in pictorial language with its inclusion of the seven 'I am' sayings (Jn. 6:35; 8:12; 10:7; 10:11; 11:25; 14:6; 15:1). For example, Jesus said, 'I am the bread of life' (Jn. 6:35). By this he meant, not literally that he was a never-ending loaf of sliced bread, but that he was the sole means of eternal sustenance. Like with parables, his use of such imagery was designed to make people stop and think. And it worked!

Perhaps the greatest example of Christ's use of symbolism occurred during his last meal with the disciples. From this informal setting emerged a pattern of communion or Eucharist that has been repeated (and sometimes distorted) by successive generations of followers. Jesus gave new symbolic meaning to what was left over from the meal. Who could not have been captivated by this visual representation of his forthcoming sacrificial death as he broke the bread into pieces and poured out what was left of the wine. Remarkably, by keeping their eyes closed, many evangelical Christians miss the full impact of this sacrament. In this piece of high drama, Christ communicates to us through all our human senses. As well as seeing, we also hear, smell, touch and eventually taste the symbols of his body that are broken and his blood that is poured out for us. It is incredibly symbolic. Today, both the 'alternative worship' scene and the charismatic movement have done much to promote the use of symbolism and pictures. In a multimedia age the evangelical Church is becoming more visually rich and discovering what other Christian traditions have always known.

To think about . . .

When was the last time you used prophetic symbolism in your practice? How effective was it?

Signs and wonders

Without saying a word, Jesus was able to demonstrate the good news of the kingdom by utilising signs and wonders. Roger Forster, founder of Ichthus,[2] often speaks of the 'words, works and wonders'. As Jesus healed the blind or disabled, people could see that the kingdom was at hand and that it was essentially good news. John's gospel in particular links the use of signs and wonders to Christ's teaching. Whereas all informal educators can use conversation, story-telling and symbolism, only those engaged in youth work *and* ministry can draw upon signs and wonders. As Christians, we recognise that our ministry is empowered by the work of the Spirit and, just as the early Church witnessed the miraculous, so too we should expect to see God at work in mysterious and profound ways. We do this, not to enhance our own power or position, but rather to draw attention to the goodness of God. There is nothing more powerful than hearing a young person testify as to how God has worked miraculously in her or his life.

---

[2] www.ichthus.org.uk

> *To think about . . .*
>
> What space is there for the miraculous in your practice?

Personal example

Finally, Jesus demonstrated the validity of his message through his lifestyle and witness. He 'walked the talk'; what he did was consistent with what he taught. It was not just that he spoke about good news, he *was* the good news. He was the message. This distinguished him from the Pharisees and, consequently, people recognised him as one who taught with authority (Mk. 1:21, 22). It is not enough for youth workers and ministers to represent Christ when 'on duty'. What they say, do and are in private is just as relevant.

Summary

Far from being a modern fad, informal education can be seen in the ministry of Christ. His use of conversation, story-telling, symbolic language, signs and wonders and personal example were all used to facilitate people's learning and response. There can be no greater recommendation for those engaged in youth work *and* ministry.

Informal Education –
a response from Malcolm Rittman

Education is a process of stimulation, where learners are exposed to a variety of methods leading to personal change, understanding of concepts and improved skills.

The author focuses on informal approaches to learning and proposes that Jesus was an informal educator using a variety of methods, including stories, conversation, symbolism, pictures, signs and wonders.

I am not convinced you can draw such a clear distinction between formal and informal education as the author suggests. I prefer to view approaches to education as a continuum in which all learning environments and experiences will include opportunities for both formal and informal learning to take place. For either formal or informal education to happen experiences need to be well planned and the educator requires a range of skills for effective learning outcomes to be achieved.

Informal educators need to know their learners, how they learn and what encourages their learning, and then determine plans to create the experiences and the environment, which stimulates and encourages learning. Informal education is not an excuse for not engaging in effective planning.

The author does not emphasise the effectiveness of using informal approaches in the development of

personal and social education with young people or that to be effective informal education needs to be culturally relevant. This was probably one of Jesus' main techniques as he related and engaged people through familiar experiences and used examples from the society in which they lived or worked.

In order to make learning effective, the environment needs to be developed in a way which enables learners to be relaxed and receptive to challenge. This is where the creativity of youth workers requires much skill. Effective youth and ministry workers are able to establish a culture and climate with a group to be receptive to learning. Jesus was able to do this in a range of situations and with different groups.

The skills of an effective educator could have been more clearly defined by the author. An effective informal educator in youth work *and* ministry, needs to

- Understand the process of education
- Recognise how learning takes place – formally and informally
- Be able to create a climate of learning for both individuals and groups
- Be clear about the outcomes for learners
- Ensure experiences are culturally relevant
- Be prepared to challenge attitudes and values.

As the author suggests we have much to learn from Jesus as we engage young people in youth work and ministry.

MALCOLM RITTMAN
Principal Youth Officer, Hampshire County Council

Chapter 7

Empowerment

New-born babies are great. After you've finished cuddling them you can put them on the floor, go out of the room and return a few moments later safe in the knowledge they will be just where you left them. That's because, without developed movement, or motor skills, they can't roll over or even control their hands. Powerless and totally dependent on others for their survival, they lie there and gurgle uncontrollably. But things don't stay that way for long. Soon they learn to co-ordinate their arms and legs, and then they're off. I can still remember the feeling of sheer panic the first time I came back into the room to discover my little baby had vanished. I eventually found her in the next room behind the curtains looking pretty pleased with herself. She had exercised the power of mobility.

Life, it seems, is one long struggle for power. This chapter looks at what people need to exercise power. It considers the value of empowerment in youth work *and* ministry and challenges some of the assumptions that often accompany this term. It begins, however, with a theological review of power as a concept.

Understanding power

In the beginning God created the heavens and the earth. So begins the opening chapter of the Bible. The following pages have helped millions of people to discover what it means to be truly human. Built into creation is the natural process of growth and development. Healthy plants, animals and humans all embark on a journey from immaturity to maturity. Though we sometimes take this for granted, such development does not happen automatically. To develop from a helpless babe into a responsible and mature adult requires, among other things, a combination of the right genetics, protection, sustenance and love. Within creation there is a hierarchy, with humans given the special responsibility of exercising dominion, or power, over the cosmos (Gen. 1:28). Part of being human is the exercising of power and therefore to limit people's capacity for power is to render them less human. Before this goes to our heads, it must be remembered that, theologically, all power comes from, and belongs to, God (Jn. 19:11). It was by his power that the world was first created and is now sustained (Is. 40:10–18, 21–26). God delegates his power to those made in his image but can reclaim it from those who misuse it. Infirmity, calamity and death serve as a reminder of our loose grip on power. We can develop new medical treatments but cannot 'cure' death. But what do we mean by power, and how should young people be helped to exercise such power, and on whom?

Being derived from the Latin *potestas* and *potentia*, 'power' is often understood to be the ability or potential to achieve a particular end. Power is an inevitable, and even necessary, part of living. We can't do without it. Someone is considered to be powerful if they can impose their own values, actions or rules on others. Inevitably,

for some to be considered powerful there must be those who are considered less powerful. The popular view of human development is that people should move from dependence to independence. Whilst that sounds noble, theologically, this is only a half-way solution. The ultimate goal is to see people develop from dependence to independence and then grow into *inter*-dependence. Christians point to the communal aspect of living and challenge the individualistic view that is so often promoted today. To say otherwise would be to join Margaret Thatcher in claiming there is no such thing as society, just a nation of individuals.

The question is, how is power to be used? After all, history is full of examples of those who have abused power to manipulate or eradicate others. We begin by looking to the Bible.

To think about . . .

Think of examples of when power has been used to abuse you and why you have abused power. How did it make you feel?

God of power and love

The Gospels portray Jesus as being supremely powerful. Yet power is not the same thing as authority. The New Testament contrasts power, or *dynamis* (Col. 1:16), with authority, or *exousia* (Mt. 21:23–27). Revolutionaries demonstrate how power can be exercised without any official authority. Likewise, those in authority may

sometimes be rendered powerless by their inability to command respect. The Pharisees were disturbed that, despite not appearing to have any official authority, Jesus obviously exercised significant power (Mt. 21:23–27). The religious and political authorities attributed great power to Jesus as a result of the huge crowds that followed him (Lk. 4:15; 5:14, 15; 9:10, 11; 12:1; 19:1–3, 47, 48). They could hardly afford to ignore such a popular figure. Those who heard Jesus marvelled at the power of his message, and contrasted this with the lacklustre teaching of the Pharisees (Mt. 7:29; Mk. 1:22; Lk. 4:32). His message was backed up by powerful demonstrations of the kingdom of God that resulted in the blind receiving their sight, the disabled being helped to walk again and even the dead being brought back to life (Mk. 2:9–12; Lk. 4:31–37). To do all of this, Jesus was anointed with the power of the Holy Spirit (Lk. 4:14). Taken together, it was no wonder he was considered powerful.

Yet, Christ's understanding of power was totally different to that of others. Ever since Israel's captivity Jews had waited eagerly for the promised Messiah. Expectations were running at an all-time high, as indicated by Simeon's example (Lk. 2:25–32). With Israel under military occupation and subject to Roman rule, the popular expectation was that God would raise up from the genealogy of David a political and military deliverer who would defeat the Roman army and liberate Israel. There was no shortage of young would-be messiahs willing, and yet unable, to take on the Romans. Every Jewish mother dreamt that her eldest boy would turn out to be the Messiah. Such a misconception was deeply ingrained. Jesus had to rebuke Peter severely when even he objected to the Messiah having to suffer (Mt. 16:15–23). What people expected and what they got were two completely different things.

God's chosen Messiah turned out to be not a powerful military commander but rather a suffering servant (Mk. 10:45) who was willing to empty himself of all but love in service of God and his people. To avoid confusion with the popular image of what a messiah should be and do, Jesus referred to himself as the Son of Man. By creating a new term, he could define it as he wished. Unlike us, Christ's power was not dependent on other people's response to him. He was not powerful because others said he was; he was powerful because he was (and still is) the source of power (Col. 1:16, 17). His power stemmed from his 'being in very nature God' (Phil. 2:6). He humbled himself and became obedient to death (Phil. 2:8). For mere humans, the greatest statistic in life remains death: 1 in 1 people die. But for Christ, death was not inevitable; it was a selfless act of obedience. Though Christ's death was horrific, it was by no means unique. For example, Luke tells us that Jesus was crucified along with at least two others (Lk. 23:32, 33). Theologically, the cross is significant, not because of its barbarity, but because it was the place that God the Son submitted to death. The religious and political authorities wrongly viewed his death as a sign of defeat. Three days later his resurrection demonstrated the limitless nature of his power.

Having destroyed the power of sin and death (2 Tim. 1:10), he now holds the keys to death (Rev. 1:18). He uses this power to give others the promise of resurrection and eternal life (1 Cor. 15:20–24). Knowing that he was returning to the Father, Christ told his followers they would do even greater things than he had done (Jn. 14:12). But he healed the sick and even raised people from the dead? Now, call me lacking in faith but somehow I can't quite believe I can improve on raising people from the dead! However, I can believe that my pathetically small contribution, when added to your slightly bigger contribution

and that of all those who have gone before us, will – in quantitative terms – result in more people being healed than ever the incarnate Christ could have achieved. Jesus gave his followers power and authority to act on his behalf (Lk. 9:1) and promised them the power of the Holy Spirit (Acts 1:8).

All this demonstrates that Christ was supremely powerful and yet willing to lay down his power for the sake of others. In doing so, he ensured that those dis-empowered by injustice were empowered as fellow members of society. Once again, Jesus provides a power-ful example of what all youth workers and ministers should be striving for; the empowerment of others.

Power games

There is no doubt that empowerment has become trendy. Ironically, it is often the very powerful who talk most about it. Jeffs and Smith challenge the notion that one person can empower another. For them, such a view creates a dependency culture in which one individual or group, thought to be more powerful than the other, benevolently hands over power. In most cases, just enough power is given away to ensure the 'empowered' remain indebted to those doing the 'empowering', but not so much that the balance of power actually changes. This is not true empowerment.

Instead of talking about empowering others, it is better to create positive environments in which people can empower themselves. Jesus perfectly demonstrated this. All but the most religious types came away from encounters with him feeling just a bit more beautiful, more capable and valued than they had felt beforehand. Without condoning her lifestyle, Jesus engaged with the

woman at the well (Jn. 4:4–26) in such a way that left her skipping elatedly back to town. Whereas I might have left her feeling guilty, I suspect Jesus left her feeling able to live a godly life. The challenge for youth workers and ministers is to create the same effect, deflecting attention from themselves onto the young people they serve.

Regrettably, it is necessary to create empowering environments because, it seems, it is part of fallen human nature to misuse power at the expense of others. Some individuals and groups are disempowered by barriers to their growth and self-determination that are erected by those who deny them a voice, responsibility or respect within society. As we have seen, this is a dehumanising experience and must be challenged.

The temptation can sometimes be for those engaged in youth work and ministry to step in as saviour figures, taking on young people's struggles. Though undertaken with the best possible motives, this approach reinforces the powerless position of the young people and the all-powerful position of the youth worker. As Green and Chadhu wisely point out, human growth is achieved through struggle. Remove the challenges and we deny young people opportunities for their learning and development. For example, over-anxious parents will hinder their child's development if they never let their offspring attempt to walk for fear of them falling. The role of youth workers and ministers is not to be the saviour of young people but rather to create an environment in which young people can discover the Saviour for themselves. Only then will they be empowered to be fully human, as God intended.

Encouraging people is one thing, giving them false expectation or mere flattery is quite another. Empowerment does not set people up to fail. Though the outward justification may be a desire not to offend, more often

this is prompted by our own lack of personal security or sufficient concern for others. To avoid potentially demanding conversations, we do not confront the issue. This helps nobody. Instead, youth work *and* ministry involves using a combination of reflection, conversation and questions to enable young people to learn from their own experiences. Empowerment should, therefore, not be seen as something soft. It is often a very demanding value to pursue with young people.

> *To think about . . .*
>
> How do you exercise power in youth work *and* ministry? What makes you feel more powerful? When do you feel least powerful?

Ethics of empowerment

On occasion youth workers are presented with ethical dilemmas that test their commitment to empowerment. I believe empowerment means allowing people freedom to adopt positions and roles that potentially conflict with our own. I cannot claim to have created an empowering environment if I block someone's attempt to travel in a different direction. This sometimes presents youth workers and ministers with ethical dilemmas. What should they do if a group of young people ask questions about another religion? Do they challenge the validity of their inquiry, quietly do nothing or actively help them to find out more? Thinking they are serving the faith, many evangelical Christians find the latter unacceptable. As by

now you might expect, I want to challenge this, both as a fellow evangelical believer and as someone engaged in youth work *and* ministry.

If I am unconvinced about the validity or standing of the Christian faith then I will react nervously when young people look at the competition. I may be tempted to deflect their attention or even prevent them from looking elsewhere. After all, didn't Jesus state, 'I am the way and the truth and the life. No-one comes to the Father except through me' (Jn. 14:6)? However, if, like Paul, I can say with complete assurance, 'I *know* whom I have believed' (2 Tim. 1:12) then I will have confidence in Christianity's ability to withstand the toughest of challenges. Jesus promised, 'For everyone who asks, receives; he who seeks, finds; and to him who knocks, the door will be opened' (Mt. 7:7, 8). Therefore, the challenge is not to stop young people looking in the wrong places, but rather to promote genuine spiritual inquiry in the first place. If they do that I believe the gospel will prove irresistible to them. But the decision is theirs, not mine, to make. So, back to the question of the young people interested in another religion. Out of respect for the other religion, I would not attempt to speak on its behalf. I would not feel equipped or authorised. Instead, I would look for ways of introducing the young people to someone from that faith group. As a result of showing respect for both the young people and the other religion, I would anticipate maintaining a positive relationship with them.

Occasionally youth workers and ministers are presented with more extreme dilemmas. For example, imagine that a group of young people asks you to help them organise a far-right extremist programme that you consider inherently racist. Does the value of empowerment require you to always do what young people ask, or are there occasions when, for their sake or that of

others, you should impose your own agenda? Here the value of empowerment must be weighed against the values of informal education and equality of opportunity. Rather than simply refusing to co-operate, such a situation would at least provide an opportunity to help the young people reflect on their attitudes and actions. Through a process of informal education, and a strong commitment to equality of opportunity, it would be hoped that the young people would begin to view their position from the perspective of others. It is often important to maintain some sort of working relationship with young people we find difficult to deal with, or who hold views we find uncomfortable – or objectionable. In this way, we may hope to see change, and an empowering environment is created. Of course, it would never be appropriate for a youth worker or minister to condone racist attitudes or actions.

> *To think about . . .*
>
> Is there anything you would not be prepared to support young people in? How do you work with young people who don't share your values or beliefs?

Power to the people

Politics is in trouble. Fewer people, it seems, are participating in the democratic purpose. Previous generations fought to secure the vote; today's generation appears more interested in who gets voted in or out of the *Big*

Brother 'reality TV' series. At a risk of declaring both my age and political bias it may interest you to know that 1997 was a political watershed for me. It was the first time, in Britain's 'first-past-the-post' system, that my vote had actually achieved anything. Previously, my voice had never been heard. I don't know who felt more empowered by that election, Tony Blair or me. The scale of the land-slide victory has now meant that people who hold similar views to New Labour don't bother to vote because they think that, once again, their vote doesn't count. I don't need to vote for them to be elected.

Of particular concern is the level of voter apathy among young people. However, things are not as bad as might first appear. First, as Furlong and Cartmel note, this is nothing new. Successive generations have always lamented young people's lack of involvement. Do you remember Labour's 'Red Wedge' campaign in the 1980s that used pop stars to drum up support for both demo-cracy and the Labour Party? Second, it is important to ask, why is that young people are not participating? Is it that young people are not interested in politics any more? The anti-capitalist and globalisation demonstrations, environmental campaigns and popularity of interactive media tell us otherwise. The increasing focus on single-interest campaigns through direct action bypasses the need for broader political debate. Why spend years campaigning through party politics when, like the young environmental campaigner 'Swampy', you can grab the nation's attention by simply living in a tunnel for a few weeks? Then there is the rejection of infantile party politics and apparent hypocrisy that is more evident through the televising of Parliament. All this serves to dissuade many young people from participating in democracy. Tragically, this serves to disempower them as their voice is further silenced. Perhaps it is time to

enfranchise young people as citizens in the democratic process. I would certainly favour lowering the voting age from 18 to 16 (if not 14) years.

Empowering Church

Ironically, a young person can join the army and be sent into combat but cannot vote for the politicians who are able to declare war. There are many young people who would be far more responsible with their vote than some of those going through the 'mid-life crisis'! Tut tut, we say, the Church is not like that. Yet there are times when the Church also disempowers young people. Many congregations are unclear when to baptise young people or admit them into church membership. Some will encourage children to believe in Christ but will not baptise them into his body until they are old enough to vote on the finer points of the congregation's Trust Deed. This seems absurd to me. The same question also vexes many concerning the minimum age for receiving communion. They forget that the body of Christ is made up of many parts, young and old, and that routinely denying children access to the 'Lord's Table' reduces the Church to a middle-aged institution.

Too many churches believe that empowerment simply involves asking young people to play their instruments in the worship band or perform a brief sketch in a guest service. Whilst this promotes a basic level of participation, it cannot be considered empowerment if the young people are expected to simply replicate the adult-controlled pattern. An empowering environment invites young people to bring their vision, energy, creativity and new technology to design new patterns of worship. Ironically, when young people have been given such opportunities

they have generally set a pattern for adults to follow in later years. For example, as we have previously seen, 1960s youth subcultures gave birth to the Beatles and the 'modern' chorus. Today our adult-controlled churches sing folk-based worship songs because young people in the 1960s took the opportunity to experiment with popular forms of music. It is in the Church's interest to create empowering environments for young people because, as Andy Hickford argues, this helps it remain contemporary in the present and prepare itself for the future.

> *To think about . . .*
>
> To what extent does your church create an empowering environment for young people? What barriers exist to their empowerment?

It is easy to be judgemental at times towards adult-controlled churches, but could the same be also true of our youth work? Youth work *and* ministry recognises that young people have much to contribute and, more than that, have a right to self-determination. It is vital that young people are not mere consumers of a youth programme but enabled to be active contributors. The aim must surely be for youth workers and ministers to lay down some of their power in order to see the young people empowered. Many of the youth workers and ministers I know are exceptionally gifted individuals. They are outgoing, funny, confident people who are the 'life and soul of the party'. Positively, they attract a crowd of young people and give the Church credibility. Negatively, there can be a danger of drawing too much

attention to themselves, and leaving young people feeling disempowered. When I first started out as a youth worker I was an ever-so-slightly more mature version of the young people I was working with. It was really important to me that the young people liked me. So I wore what they wore, listened to their music and generally tried to blend in. I was committed to an event-based programme, largely because I needed a stage on which to perform. Now, fifteen years later, my priorities have changed. I can honestly say I am more interested in seeing young people on a stage than being there myself. Having had more opportunity to reach a place of personal security, I see far greater value in enabling young people to develop. Youth work *and* ministry is now less about me and more about young people. Fortunately, not all youth workers and ministers take fifteen years to learn this lesson.

To think about . . .

To what extent does your youth programme create an empowering environment for young people? What barriers exist to their empowerment? How might they be removed or the young people empowered to overcome them?

Summary

Empowerment has become a 'buzz' word that is understood less than it is quoted. Rather than talk of

Empowerment – a response from Dr Nigel Wright

I am all for empowerment and I like the open and non-patronising approach to it outlined in this chapter. At the same time, constitutionally, when everybody else is picking up the latest buzz words and cliches, I find myself travelling in the opposite direction.

At the University of Essex, research has been done on the reasons behind the so-called 'democratic deficit' – the apparent reluctance, especially of young people, to vote. The major factor enabling people to predict whether a person or a household will vote is clear: it is the existence of a sense of duty.

Duty is definitely an un-sexy concept and you don't get brownie points for bringing attention to it. To describe a person as 'dutiful' would be regarded today pretty much as a slur on their character or on their actions. I am bound therefore to be on safely unpopular ground in extolling duty's virtues. Duty is regarded as doing something worthy because you have to rather than because you want to and for this reason has come to seem oppressive and restrictive rather than liberating and enabling.

But as important as possession of power is the use of power. It is characteristic of much contemporary political, social and religious thought that it is concerned with carving out for people the space and the dignity to operate

their God-given potential without undue hindrance. This is hardly wrong. But it does neglect the issue of what I do with the space or the 'agency' that is then given to me. This takes us into the realm of virtue and into a territory with which we are much less familiar. After all, who has the right to say to any of us what virtue looks like? And where do we derive our ideas from?

If economic or social empowerment means that power is squandered on self-gratification we are not collectively left better off except possibly in the marginal sense that consumption drives the economy. The use of power for collective well-being translates empowerment into enrichment for us all. Can this be done without teaching people a sense of duty? And how is this done in a climate of opinion which is more interested in empowerment than duty?

A sense of duty is created where there is a sense of obligation and responsibility to a moral demand that is greater than we are. This does not have to be explicitly religious and there are abundant examples of fine people who for basic humanitarian reasons use such power as they have for human betterment. A religious world-view, however, which believes there to be a basic story through which the universe can be interpreted and its underlying direction and purpose exposed, provides a compelling impetus for living according to that purpose and conforming to its demands. It encourages a sense of being obligated to live in a certain way and to do certain things.

Because we fear imparting to people feelings of guilt we shy away from this kind of talk, and not just with young people. We are afraid of being thought to lay the law down, of 'preaching' to people and so suggesting we are superior to others. Perhaps the best way to speak of duty is personally and by way of testimony, as that which we feel and which guides at least some of our actions.

The 'democratic deficit' might serve as an example. I feel a duty to vote because people have struggled and paid the price which enables me to do so. My empowerment was purchased at somebody else's cost. It is not a question to me whether or not I should vote. It is a duty – an obligation I owe to former generations, an act of respect for what they did, a way of keeping faith with them. It is also a duty performed for generations to come – to maintain a right that can be passed on to others and, I agree, extended to others who don't yet share it. Duty extends in several directions at once.

Yes, I'm prepared to vote for empowerment and to enjoy its benefits to me and mine. But I am concerned about the 'duty deficit' as well. I happen to believe that many of the people who have done the most good for future generations were like Moses in that they did not inherit themselves the good that they achieved for others. Such sacrifice is performed when people have come to see that their own small life is to be offered up to a greater movement which will outlast and outlive them even though its benefits to them personally may be minimal. This is heroic and heroes are needed.

Dr Nigel G. Wright
*Principal, Spurgeon's College and
President of the Baptist Union of Great Britain 2002–3*

Chapter 8

Equality of Opportunity

Working in London's Square Mile in the 1980s was an exhilarating experience. With the de-regulation of the London Stock Exchange and the privatisation of state-owned industries, vast quantities of stocks and shares were traded. Every fortnight on 'settlement day' I played a very small part in settling literally tens of millions of pounds worth of transactions. Every day the only question was; by how many points had the FTSE100 Index risen? It was a 'bull' market. But for winners to exist there must also be losers. When the bubble burst in 1987 jobs were lost, houses were repossessed and families placed under increasing strain. But even the new 'bear' market didn't reduce people's faith in capitalism. In contrast, the collapse of the Berlin Wall symbolised an end to communism as the antithesis social and economic system. Capitalism, with its inequalities, had triumphed over communism. Some said God had won the day.

This chapter is all about equality and, in particular, equality of opportunity as a value of youth work *and* ministry. Equality as a concept is both vague and contested. In economic terms, equality focuses on the differences in wealth between individuals or groups. Because some have more and others have less, taxation

and welfare are used to redistribute resources from the advantaged rich to the disadvantaged poor. Equality of economics is declared when all people enjoy the same material wealth. This may sound noble, but Bridger believes equality of economics has the following flaws:

- It is unrealistically utopian. The world doesn't work like this
- Human insecurity and greed always strives to restore wealth differentials, whether overtly or covertly. People use wealth to define their value
- Economic equality can only measure tangible forms of wealth; for example, it says nothing about power or physical attributes
- Personal freedom must be sacrificed to achieve economic equality. After all, who likes paying taxes?
- Removing economic incentives for wealth creation reduces the total wealth available for distribution. Why bother working hard to pay more taxes in order to secure the same standard of living as someone who does nothing?
- History shows that all attempts to impose equality have thus far failed.

In contrast, equality of opportunity refuses to define equality in economic terms. It strives to ensure individuals and groups have equal access to the common economic system and to be in a position to maximise their benefits from it. But what does equality of opportunity mean and how should it be incorporated into our practice with young people?

Definitions

Equality of opportunity has become another piece of modern language that is more readily used than understood. Some are quick to dismiss it as being a sop to political correctness. They bemoan the loss of tradition and identity, and demand that everyone else change to become like them. In so doing, they fail to recognise the uneven playing field that positively advantages some and disadvantages others. For example, how can someone whose first language is Tamil be expected to succeed in an environment where only English is spoken? Equality of opportunity is not about denying the very real differences that exist between individuals and groups. Instead, it strives to ensure all individuals and groups are given equal opportunity to succeed in life and, where necessary, are compensated for the unevenness of the playing field. For example, a Tamil-speaking young person may thrive in an English-speaking environment when given additional language support. Only then will they have the same equality of opportunity as English-speakers to succeed socially and educationally.

A number of terms are often used in the field of equality of opportunity and it is important these are recognised and understood. Though similar, they have important differences:

- *Multiculturalism* recognises and appreciates that society is made up of people from many diverse cultures. It respects the contributions made by each tradition and looks for educational opportunities to broaden people's awareness, placing great importance on tolerance. It sometimes appears to mould everyone into a uniform shape as differences are submerged in the name of diversity

- *Anti-racist and anti-sexist practice* strives to eradicate unequal treatment of individuals on the basis of ethnicity or gender. It tends to focus on the characteristics individuals are born with and therefore unable to control. Because no one can be held responsible for the ethnicity of their biological parents, the argument goes, why should they be treated differently from someone with a different inherited ethnicity?

- *Anti-discriminatory practice* is broader in scope. It incorporates and values all groups in society and is therefore anti-racist, anti-sexist and anti-ageist. But, as Millam recognises, it is concerned with gender, age, disability, sexual orientation, economic background, race, religion, culture and language. It sees people as individuals of equal value and strives to promote positive images, resources and attitudes. However, it also accepts that society is inherently unjust and that some individuals are treated differently than others

- *Anti-oppressive practice* goes further still. Phillipson argues that, whilst anti-discriminatory practice challenges unfairness, the more radical anti-oppressive practice positively seeks to empower and liberate the oppressed. It requires a fundamental rethink of values, institutions and relationships. It recognises that all people have the potential to oppress, and be oppressed by, others.

Think about it . . .

Which of these terms do you find most compatible with the gospel of Jesus? Which terms to you think present the most challenge to you and your practice?

Biblical equality

Many people talk the language of equality without embracing it as a value. However, for it to be authentic, equality of opportunity must fill not only the mouth but also the brain and heart. Christians are without excuse. Not only do they benefit from the considerable library of modern literature available to all, they also draw inspiration from the Bible. It is my contention that Jesus Christ provided the perfect demonstration of equality of opportunity at work. For this reason I am not ashamed to relate modern concepts of equality to the example of his life and ministry. Though the Bible does not use the sophisticated language developed during recent years, the principles leap out of the text. However, before grappling with the Bible it is important to recognise our own inadequacies.

As we have already observed, the Rt Rev Lesslie Newbigin understood that no one is capable of reading the Bible in isolation. He asserted that everyone has invisible lenses that filter their view of the world in the same way that sunglasses give an altered perception of reality. These invisible lenses are based on an individual's culture and history. This is why people from different cultures and ages can give different interpretations to the same biblical passages. It should therefore come as no surprise that those living in a sexist and racist society sometimes attach discriminatory interpretations to sections of the Bible. Though it is not possible to remove Newbigin's invisible lenses, through a process of reflection and education, it is possible to counter their effect.

The opening chapters of the Bible summarise the relationship Creator God sought to have with his creation. Unlike other species, humans were made in the image of

God (Gen. 1:26–28). This is true for all people and denotes significant worth. In creating males and females God does not appear to have intended a hierarchy. Both women and men were equally made in his image and given responsibility for exercising power over the rest of creation. God saw all that he had made and declared it to be *very* good. Therefore to consider one person as being lower, or higher, than another is a slur on what God declares to be good.

However, a quick glance at the news reveals that humans are capable of committing the most obscene crimes against one another and creation. This is the direct consequence of sin. Humanity now experiences enmity between itself, the environment and God. What God himself once declared good has now become distorted by manipulation, ill-treatment and abuse between individuals and groups. Creation can no longer be considered a place of equality. It is everyone for him or herself and the survival of the fittest. Despite this the Old Testament was not shy in calling people to live differently. For example, the Law commanded that, in addition to loving God (Deut. 6:5), people were to love their neighbours as themselves (Lev. 19:18), not more than or less than. Inevitably, selfish and wounded humanity found this to be impossible. Some Christians have become so preoccupied with the doctrine of 'original sin' that they forget this was preceded by 'original goodness'. For them the glass is half empty, not half full. Equality of opportunity reminds us, not only that all have equally sinned (Rom. 3:23) but also that all were originally declared good.

But there is good news. Because 'God is love', he immediately set in place a daring rescue mission involving the sacrificial death of his Son, Jesus Christ (Jn. 3:16). He put aside his own rights to equality with God in order that we might be reconciled to God and one another (Phil.

2:5–11). This offers humanity the one and only chance of true redemption. Consequently, for those who accept the benefit of Christ's saving work, 'There is neither Jew nor Greek, slave nor free, male nor female, for you are all one in Christ Jesus' (Gal. 3:28).

It is not that differences of appearance or temperament between the sexes cease to exist, but that they can no longer be considered grounds for unequal treatment. Christ restores humanity to its pre-fallen condition. This results in a direct ethical challenge: if this is how Christ treats us, how should we treat others? Those who have been reconciled to God must also be reconciled to one another. When we do this we prophetically point to the coming kingdom of God. Equality of opportunity then becomes not so much a trendy statement as a prophetic declaration that the kingdom of God is coming.

Think about it . . .

How are you influenced by discriminatory attitdes and how do they surface in your life? What do you have to do to counter them?

Race for justice

Almost all of the films made about Christ depict him as being of ethnically white European appearance but with one distinction: sandals. In contrast the incarnate Christ was probably of shorter stature, with darker skin tone, black hair and brown eyes. And whilst we're at it, yes, like any other healthy baby he would have cried. In the

West we have created a Christ-like figure that perfectly matches our likeness. It is time to accept that Christ was born into a different culture and ethnicity from our own. He was conceived out of wedlock, lived in temporary accommodation and then spent part of his early life as a refugee. He challenged the *status quo* and was eventually put to death as a common criminal. Ironically today's right-wing papers would have found much in his life to vilify. No amount of Christmas carols can alter this.

The Old Testament placed great importance on the receiving of strangers. 'Foreigners' were to be treated hospitably and with respect, as demonstrated by Abraham (Gen. 18:1–8). The writer to the Hebrews developed this further, warning

> Do not forget to entertain strangers, for by so doing some people have entertained angels without knowing it.
>
> Hebrews 13:2

To think about . . .

What does modern society's treatment of asylum seekers say about attitudes to ethnicity and equality of opportunity? How does your church respond to those from other cultures?

Some have claimed that God condones the unequal treatment of nations due to the privileged position afforded to Israel. This has been distorted to justify the vile treatment of whole people groups. This is wrong. God blessed Israel so that Israel might, in turn, bless the other

nations (Gen. 12:1–3). With the blessing came significant responsibility but, as history demonstrates, Israel preferred to selfishly withhold this. As a consequence, Israel lost its position as the custodian of God's plan.

It is wrong to talk of different races; there is only one race, the human race. Genesis demonstrates that we all share the same heritage. Likewise it is unhelpful to describe someone as being coloured. The same can be said of every person who has ever lived. We are all coloured. It is an arrogant and self-centred person who claims they are separate from those that are 'coloured'. This is not about being politically correct. It is about recognising the innate humanity in each other, appreciating what God declares to be good.

Theologically, all followers of Christ are declared to be aliens in a foreign land. Our true citizenship is in heaven. But this does not mean we cease to be interested in world affairs. Far from it! Our heavenly citizenship inspires us to act on behalf of the marginalised, oppressed and outcast. In Stourbridge, in England's West Midlands, the Christian churches united together to support a Muslim family's application for political asylum. Having fled ill-treatment in Afghanistan, they believed permission should have been granted for the family to remain in Britain. Christians stood alongside Muslims in the campaign for justice. This was not a question of Christianity versus Islam, but rather of right versus wrong.

The parable of the Good Samaritan (Lk. 10:25–37) provides a challenge to those with racist attitudes. An expert in the Law wanted to know what he could get away with before losing the promise of eternal life. Jesus responded with a story about a man who was attacked whilst on a journey. Both the Priest and Levite, as representatives of God's order, might have been expected to

assist the wounded man. But instead, being more concerned to protect their own standing and well-being, they ignored his cries for help. Then along came a Samaritan. Being from a different ethnic group, and one that was at odds with Jews, he was the one person who could be relied upon to reject the wounded traveller. Yet he overcame prejudice and fear to demonstrate the kingdom of God at work. Every day we are called upon to follow the Samaritan's example, standing with those from different traditions, cultures and nations to demonstrate Christ's offer of reconciliation.

From disabled to enabled

You may not be able to tell from my picture or writing style but I am disabled. Though I am relatively mobile for an unfit thirty-something there are certain situations that require me to use special equipment or rely upon others. Occasionally I wish it was different but I know this is something I have to accept. For example, I find it totally frustrating that I cannot climb a vertical wall without use of a harness and rope, or the support of others. Whilst able-bodied Spiderman scales those walls in seconds I am left completely disabled by them. I am left disabled by vertical walls. This may sound ridiculous and even slightly offensive and yet the popular understanding of 'able bodied' and 'disabled' can be equally nonsensical.

People are not disabled by the limits to their physical capabilities; we all have things we are incapable of doing. Rather, they are disabled by the barriers to their independence that exist in the environment. For example, young people who use wheelchairs are *dis*abled when they cannot gain access to churches that have copious

steps and no ramps or lifts. Those same young people are *en*abled when they enter church buildings that do have ramps and lifts. The issue is not the physical capability of wheelchair users, but the environmental barriers erected by the, so-called, able bodied. It does not take a genius to work out that, if wheelchair users designed these buildings, there would not be such reliance upon steps. I have heard it said, not providing appropriate ramps creates opportunities to demonstrate inter-dependence by forcing the disabled to rely upon the able bodied to carry them up and down stairs. Certainly youth work *and* ministry strives towards inter-dependence but this should never be used as an excuse to withhold equal access to facilities from those differently able from the majority. Such an attitude is thoughtless and unchristian.

Curiously, the able bodied are considered to be 'normal'. They use this to secure greater positions of power and then reinforce this by creating an environment that creates barriers that excludes others. Imagine what would happen if deafness was suddenly declared to be the 'norm'; all audio communication was withdrawn and only sign language used. I, for one, would suddenly be *dis*abled and would consider it a huge injustice when audio communication was not provided. This happens every day for those of partial or total hearing loss. Communicate in sign language, and they become *en*abled.

Unfortunately, there is nothing new about able bodied people disabling others. In Jerusalem there was a pool called Bethesda that was thought to contain healing water. People travelled from miles around to bathe in its waters in the hope it would cure them of their diseases. John records (Jn. 5:1–15) that many disabled people would gather outside and we are left to assume they would be reduced to begging for their survival. The term

'handicapped' is unhelpful because it stems from the phrase 'cap in hand ', implying that disabled people have nothing to contribute and must therefore beg for welfare. The truth became clearer when Jesus takes time to talk with one person who had been disabled for thirty-eight years. The man had not been able to get into the pool of Bethesda because, each time he had tried, those more able than he had beaten him to it. No one stopped to assist him. Jesus was stirred to act. On determining that the man did indeed want to walk, he said 'Get up! Pick up your mat and walk.' The man was cured instantly.

Tragically the only response that religious people made was to criticise the man for carrying his mat on the Sabbath. This reveals the small-minded, mean attitude that sometimes goes unchallenged in some of our churches. These religious people were the very ones who had day after day prevented the disabled man from reaching the healing waters. They had not given a moment's thought to the man's needs when he was disabled. Now they had the cheek to criticise him for carrying his mat on the Sabbath. It is the same attitude that causes some religious people to object to, or refuse to fund, alterations to their buildings that would turn them from *dis*abling to *en*abling environments. In the meantime, Jesus simply slipped away into the crowd so as not to distract attention from the healed man.

To think about . . .

What environmental barriers are present in your church premises? How do you overcome them?

Have you ever wondered why Jesus healed people? After all, every one of those he healed went on to die. Their death was merely delayed or, in the case of Lazarus (Jn. 11:1–6, 38–44), repeated. He didn't heal people because he believed their disability somehow made them any less human or complete. As well as being a demonstration of God's power, it seems Jesus used healing as a way of countering social exclusion. The temple system, with its substitutional sacrifices, placed considerable emphasis on perfection. Only those animals without defect could be used as sacrificial offerings. This pointed people to their need for a sinless offering that only God himself could provide. Yet, this was also used to discriminate against those who were not deemed 'normal'. These people were declared to be 'unclean', presumably by the majority who considered themselves to be 'clean'. Consequently many people were socially and economically excluded. Recognising this, Jesus powerfully demonstrated social inclusion by healing them. Those with infectious diseases and physical disabilities, as well as a woman suffering from constant bleeding, all benefited from this ministry. Nothing was perhaps more healing than Christ's use of touch extended freely to the outcasts of society. The gospel was truly available to all.

Religious equality

Until recently religion was not considered to be relevant to equality of opportunity. Humanist ideology preferred that people define their cultural identity by their first language, ethnicity or nationhood – anything but their religious beliefs. But, for many people groups, it is not possible to separate their cultural identity from their religion. It would be naïve, for example, to work with

Pakistani young people without considering how their Islamic beliefs, customs and culture shape their world-view. Religion must be considered alongside language, customs and ethnicity in determining cultural identity. This is gaining acceptance with the caring professions and, consequently, some local authority Youth Services now support work with Muslim young people that is mosque-based. I believe this helpfully acknowledges people's identity and demonstrates to Muslims a commitment to equality of opportunity.

This raises an important issue of equality of opportunity for different faith groups. For the principle to be true it must be applied consistently. I believe Christians have sometimes been denied the same equality of opportunity. Many social commentators consider Christianity to be oppressive. They cite the church's justification given through the years to apartheid and racial discrimination; the suppression of women as being less than men; and the imperialist exploitation of those the Church sought to convert in other countries. Before getting too defensive, it is important that past and present mistakes are acknowledged and put right. The Church did contribute to the imperialist ambitions of the British Empire with missionary zeal. Victorian values and Western diseases were bundled up with the gospel and literacy skills.

Yet, since its inception, the Church has also been a consistent force for good. When everyone else was fleeing from a deadly plague in North Africa, many Christians risked their lives to care for the sick and bury the dead. During the nineteenth century Christians campaigned successfully for the abolition of slavery and child labour, established schools and hospitals and reformed prisons. More recently, the Church has challenged consumerism, campaigned for the reduction of Third World debt and is, once again, a significant provider of youth work *and*

ministry. The Church cannot, therefore, be dismissed as a complete irrelevance, or worse still, an oppressor. Christianity is not alone in having shameful episodes in its history. Equality of opportunity requires that all religions be given equal access to resources and status.

The Faithworks Movement,[1] led by Oasis, has called on the British government to recognise the community benefit that churches provide. The Church is in every city, town and most villages, and employs tens of thousands of staff committed to serving the local community. It can only be hoped that the strong commitment to equality of opportunity demonstrated by those in both the statutory and voluntary sectors will be extended to those in the Church.

Summary

Equality of opportunity finds the perfect demonstration in the person and work of Christ. By the way he dealt with women, the disabled and socially excluded, he challenged the *status quo*. Youth work *and* ministry must demonstrate an equal commitment to equality of opportunity as a value.

---

[1] www.faithworks.info

Equality of Opportunity –
a response from Claire Leas

The words 'equal opportunities' often illicit no more than a grimace or a large sigh when mentioned within the church context. Just a quick look at local news reports on regional television will demonstrate the huge variety and diversity of humanity present in our communities and yet, how well is this reflected in our morning congregations? Whether you analyse the make up of our congregations by gender, age, disability, sexual orientation, economic background, race, religion, culture and language then largely it is a white, middle class and middle-aged picture. So this is the gospel, then, is it?

Danny quite rightly challenges us to examine this in this chapter on equality of opportunity. The gospel is for all, Jesus offers salvation to all and his life and ministry bear witness to this fact. Whether we like it or not, agree with it or not, we live in an unfair world, the playing field is not level. It is important to be clear that equal opportunities is not about us all being the same, it is about recognising that we are all very different.

And it is this difference which causes the problem as we feel more comfortable with people who are like us, who think like we do, who see the world the way we do. As Hauerwas says, 'We are creatures that fear difference. The fact that the other is not as we are, means that there

may be something wrong with us. The only solution is to make them as much like us as possible or to make them live apart.'[2]

The book of Genesis summarises the relationship that God sought to have with his creation; it tells us that humankind was made in the image of God (Gen. 1:26–28). What does it mean to be made in the image of God? Here our concept of a Trinitarian God is most helpful. Within the Trinity we have Father, Son and Holy Spirit, all different and yet of equal value. The concept of the Trinity is evidence of the vital importance of relationship and community within the nature of God. If we are made in the image of a Trinitarian God then we should reflect the relationality, mutuality and interdependence of the Trinity. Remaining separate from those who are different means we lose out on what it means to be made in the image of God. We need to be able to be mutually dependent upon each other, to value our differences and to be in relationship with each other – a community of the unlike. Our inability to cope with this very diversity is an outworking of the fallenness of humanity.

Through Christ and the work of the Holy Spirit we – and our relationships – are transformed into what it really means to be *imago Dei*. The reality of this transformation needs to be worked out in our relationships with each other, particularly those who are different from us in any way. This then becomes more evidence of the kingdom of God breaking in to our world.

This won't happen if we avoid those who are different from us, or continue to allow barriers to keep us apart. The gospel calls us to make the opportunities to experience

---

[2] S. Hauerwas, *Suffering Presence* (University of Notre Dame Press, 1986), 213.

God's love and compassion available to all. We must ensure that these opportunities are not lost because someone cannot hear this message because barriers relating to their race or language, gender or age has got in the way.

Although focusing on gender difference LaCugna's words provide the necessary challenge to the Church, 'To censure all structures/rituals, etc. which foster elitism, discrimination and competition and to look for inclusiveness, interdependence and co-operation'.[3] This will mean looking at how we organise church life as well as how we live out our faith. Are our buildings accessible to all? Do our services make sense for those for whom English is not their first language or who do not read as well? Do church meetings and activities make sufficient provision for childcare? Is it less 'Christian' to read the *Sun* or the *Daily Mirror*? Do we treat those who 'lead' worship with more value than those who 'participate' in worship? Is serving the coffee as valued as having a healing ministry?

And in our work with young people do we want to model the inclusive nature of the kingdom of God? Do we ensure that the programme enables the young people to experience and share in the diversity of humanity? Would we employ an Asian youthworker, a female minister or someone with a disability? As an employer would we be prepared to make the necessary changes so that they can explore with us what it means to be made in the image of God?

Youth work has always had an energy and enthusiasm, no doubt, because young people are involved! Christian youth workers have a role to play in helping young people harness that energy and enthusiasm to identify

---

[3] LaCugna, *God for us, The Trinity and the Christian Life* (Harper, 1991), 402.

Chapter 9

Incarnation

Another value

By now it should be clear that the values of voluntary participation, informal education, empowerment and equality of opportunity give definition to youth work *and* ministry. What's more, the life and work of Christ Jesus makes them biblically justified. Theology informs and is, in turn, informed by these four values. However, just because they find biblical support does not necessarily mean the Bible has nothing else to add. I have come to believe that the unique contribution of youth work *and* ministry is to add a fifth value; that being incarnation.

The doctrine of incarnation concerns the Christian belief that God the Son became fully human in Jesus so as to identify with, and atone for, humanity. John stated, 'The Word became flesh and made his dwelling among us' (Jn. 1:14). Paul masterfully wrote

> Your attitude should be the same as that of Christ Jesus: Who, being in very nature God, did not consider equality with God something to be grasped, but made himself nothing, taking the very nature of a servant, being made in human likeness. And being found in appearance as a man, he humbled himself and became obedient to death – even death on a cross!
>
> Philippians 2:5–8

All four Gospels depict Christ's humanity. Matthew and Luke describe at length the humble circumstances surrounding his birth. In addition, Matthew explained Jesus' genealogy (Mt. 1:1–17) in order to establish the Messiah's Jewish credentials. Closer inspection reveals that Jesus' family heritage comprised a mix of 'saints' and 'sinners'; adulterers, prostitutes, terrorists and spies mixed with Abraham, Jacob and Solomon. Even the incarnate Christ had to deal with a complex family history.

Though not much is known of his childhood and adolescence, Luke tells us that at the age of twelve, Jesus once went missing from his parents for five days (Lk. 2:41–50). The writer discreetly tells us that his parents were 'astonished' when they found him. It doesn't take too much imagination to suppose what might have been said. Could the God the Son have been grounded? But we are reassured that, 'Jesus grew in wisdom and stature, and in favour with God and men' (Lk. 2:52). Dr Luke was keen to describe his holistic physical, intellectual, spiritual and social development.

To think about . . .

If you had been Mary or Joseph how would you have dealt with Jesus' disappearance?

Jesus did not possess superhuman powers of strength and emotional intelligence. He experienced the normal physical and emotional limitations common to all people. He was susceptible to: thirst (Jn. 19:28); tiredness (Mt. 8:24; Jn. 4:6) and hunger; and ultimately death (Jn. 19:30). He

displayed: compassion (Mt. 9:36); love for friends (Jn. 11:35, 36); grief (Jn. 11:38); incomplete knowledge (Mk. 13:32); surprise (Mt. 8:10; Mk. 6:6); tears (Heb. 5:7) and pain (Lk. 22:44). God the Son truly became fully human. Yet the Gospel writers clearly felt he had qualities that marked him out as an extraordinary individual: he performed miracles (Mt. 8:23–27; 14:22–33); forgave people's sin (Mt. 9:2–8; Mk. 2:3–12); taught as one who had unique authority; and spoke of his intimate relationship with God the Father (Mt. 11:25–27; Jn. 5:19–23; 10:14–30). These claims were ultimately vindicated by his resurrection from the dead.

Incarnation and engagement

Through the incarnation God exhibited the full extent of his commitment to creation. It was undertaken at his initiative and without any obligation to anyone or anything. The mystery, as John put it, is not that we loved God, but that he loved us and sent his Son as an atoning sacrifice for our sins (1 Jn. 4:10). Without prejudicing the process of voluntary participation, God took the initiative to open a way for people to know *shalom*. Had he not, there would have been no choice for people to make. Put simply, God did not wait for people to look for him; he reached out to them. If the value of voluntary participation prevents us from over-zealous coercion, then incarnation saves us from indifferent passivity. Incarnate youth work *and* ministry takes the initiative to engage with young people. It reaches out to those who, as yet, are unaware of either their need or its merit.

The incarnation also reminds us that people matter. If anyone had the right to remain aloof, it was Jesus.

Being the Son of God he was liable to no one. Yet the Gospel writers portrayed Jesus as a people-person. He enjoyed conversations, thrived on debates, took great interest in people's stories and always maintained his approachability. He remained open to people even when emotionally and physically tired. At a time when today so much emphasis is placed on curriculum, target setting and performance systems, the incarnation reminds us that youth work *and* ministry is about engagement with real people.

The value of incarnation helps us to enter the world of young people with sensitivity and vulnerability. The incarnation required the God-man to become truly human, accepting the inherent discomforts and limitations for the sake of others. His was not a mission that could be completed from the safety of heaven. Jesus sent out his followers like 'lambs among wolves' (Lk. 10:3). They were not to seek positions of power or attempt to control their environment. Instead, they were to be guest in the community, accepting hospitality when it was offered. In the same way, those engaged in youth work *and* ministry enter the world of youth subcultures as guests of the young. Whereas inviting young people to participate in church-organised activities sometimes requires conformity to ecclesiastical expectations, youth work *and* ministry goes to where the young people are, respecting their rules and conventions.

To think about . . .

When do you feel most vulnerable in your practice? How does it make you feel?

Incarnation and culture

Any reading of Scripture must recognise that Jesus was born at a specific time into a specific culture that had specific values and traditions. God became incarnate as a first-century Jew and lived in Israel under Roman military occupation. He travelled to real places and met real people dealing with real issues. Consequently, Christ's teaching reflected the concerns of the day and drew upon culturally relevant symbols and metaphors. If Christ had been born in twenty-first-century Britain he would presumably have tailored his message and language to the different cultural context. Failure to recognise the cultural context of Christ's works results in poor theological interpretation and a culturally irrelevant message for today. Incarnate youth work *and* ministry helps young people to translate ancient truths into modern language. This leads to new patterns of worship, community life and mission.

The incarnation gives significance to sociology and anthropology, as well as theology. Effective youth work *and* ministry is aware of, and respects, the cultural symbols and metaphors of the day. Following Christ's example, practitioners should observe and engage with popular culture. Sometimes they will challenge – other times commend – the inherent values and cultural icons of the age. To do this, effective youth workers and ministers will be culturally aware. They should be encouraged to observe life, go to the cinema, and read newspapers and magazines. However, I have found conversations with young people are far more enlightening as they reveal their own perceptions of culture. Having highlighted the importance of cultural awareness, this should never be viewed as replacement for quality work with individuals and groups.

Incarnation and inclusion

The value of incarnation sometimes calls us to prefer identification with the socially and economically 'excluded' to the relative comfort of living among the 'included'. God the Son could have been born in any setting; that he chose such humble surroundings must serve as an example to us. The incarnate God was born as a helpless baby to a teenage mother, lived the life of a refugee as his parents fled from military occupiers and experienced the 'storm and stress' of adolescence, before working as a carpenter. Whereas youth ministry has traditionally benefited socially and economically 'included' young people in suburbia, youth work *and* ministry is well placed to serve the needs of the socially 'excluded' in urban and rural settings. Incarnate youth workers and ministers are sometimes required to make difficult decisions.

Many in the caring professions have been taught to remain emotionally detached from their work. Consequently, practitioners rarely live in the communities they serve. They instead commute in from the relative safety of suburbia to see their clients before leaving them behind as they return home. There are of course notable exceptions like Bob Holman. In contrast, the value of incarnation calls youth workers and ministers to leave positions of relative safety and comfort in order to live, as well as work, among those who have no means of escape. Only then will they truly identify with those they serve, gain their trust and, to some extent, feel their pain. The Church has often stood out as being the only organisation that requires its staff to live in the communities it serves. The evangelical and Anglo-Catholic wings have a particularly strong track record in urban settings. Maintaining this tradition, hundreds of

Christians have in recent years relocated to some of Manchester's most troublesome estates in order to live among those that have no choice but to live there. The Eden Project[1] has provided an inspirational example of incarnate youth work *and* ministry.

Incarnation and passion

Today there is greater recognition that Jesus and the Gospel writers did not live in a time of cultural vacuum. Jesus was a first-century Jew who was familiar with the religious, political and social customs and ideas of the day. Greek philosophy stressed divine impassibility, or *apatheia*, meaning that God was incapable of suffering or showing any form of passion or emotion. For the Greeks, anything or anyone could not affect God because, to be perfect, he must be absolutely self-sufficient, self-determining and independent. If God can suffer then it can only be because there is something or someone that is superior to him. Greek philosophy viewed suffering as a sign of weakness and always an involuntary response. By the same logic Hellenistic thinkers concluded that God was incapable of showing any emotion. Again, to be emotionally moved in any way is to be affected by something or someone and therefore less than self-sufficient. Along with impassibility, the Greeks also developed the notion of divine immutability, referring to God's unchangeable nature. They believed that any change would be an admission of imperfection.

The Church Fathers were influenced by Greek philosophy and therefore attached great significance to God's

---

[1] www.message.org.uk/eden

impassibility and immutability. They were convinced of God's love but did not view this in emotional terms. Certainly, there is biblical support for God's perfection and complete nature. The Church Fathers believed that those 'made in the image of God' should emulate God's impassibility, displaying maturation by an emotionless reliance upon logic. Many British people seem to have taken this to heart!

In recent years, the classic understanding of impassibility has been challenged. Greek philosophy offered just two alternatives: either the divinity was above and beyond suffering and emotional involvement or it was subservient to it. Jurgen Moltmann has suggested a third way; the voluntary laying oneself open to be affected by someone or something else. It is the suffering of passionate love. Abraham Heschel, the Jewish theologian, referred to divine *pathos* – in contrast to divine *apatheia* – to reveal the intimate and emotional involvement of God with his creation. He concluded that the central theme of the Hebrew Scriptures was God's concern, not his infinite wisdom or power. God is seen to grieve (Jer. 48:31; Hos. 11:8, 9) and even suffer when his people suffer (Is. 63:9). Before this is dismissed as being an attempt to form God in humanity's image, Heschel adapts Isaiah's declaration to affirm, '"For my *pathos* is not your *pathos*, neither are your ways my ways," declares the Lord. "As the heavens are higher than the earth, so are my ways higher than your ways and my *pathos* than your *pathos*"' (Is. 55:8, 9).

In contrast to the one-way relationship of *apatheia*, that has moved people but not God, new weight has been given to God's identification and involvement with his creation. This asserts that to love is to risk suffering. Far from being a sign of weakness, the ability and willingness to suffer shows strength of moral character. As well as positively experiencing the joy of love, this means that

God is also exposed to the full horror of humanity's sin and rejection, responding with both wrath and love. This means my actions can bring God joy or sorrow; it matters to God how I behave.

The traditional view, influenced by Greek philosophy, has rendered God one step removed from human passion and suffering. Yet the incarnation of Christ serves as a challenge to this. The Christ who suffered on the cross was God the Son, co-eternal member of the Trinity. Likewise, it was God the Father who experienced indescribable sorrow at seeing his beloved Son sacrificed for the sake of his wayward creation. Those who argue that God is unchanged throughout time must accept that the pain experienced by the triune God at the Cross was, and is, felt throughout all ages. It is the incarnation that enables God to express divine solidarity with those who suffer.

To think about . . .

What is there about your practice that you believe brings God joy? What have you seen that might have brought God sorrow?

The incarnation of Christ demonstrates vividly the level to which God identifies with his creation. In the same way, those engaged in youth work *and* ministry seek empathic ways to identify with individuals and groups. Effective youth workers and ministers are not emotionally detached from those they serve.

Incarnation and faith

The incarnate Christ's ultimate purpose was to bring reconciliation between God and his estranged creation. He gave up his own rights to life so that others, like the thief crucified at the same time as him, might know true peace. Without the incarnation of Christ there can be no youth work *and* ministry. It is only through Christ's example, teaching and authority that we have any concept of ethical ministry. It is the incarnate Christ who enables us to know the empowering of the Holy Spirit.

The incarnate Son of God invites people – young and old – to become followers of Christ. Maybe, as a result of reading this book, your own interest in spirituality has been rekindled. Maybe you find yourself attracted to the life and work of Jesus, seeing for the first time his radical and life-changing agenda. If so, I invite you to join me in seeking Christ wherever he may be found. You may be surprised where you find him. Jesus promised that 'those who seek will find' (Mt. 7:7–12).[2]

Summary

The incarnation of Christ inspires those engaged in youth work *and* ministry to enter the world of young people with sensitivity and vulnerability. Youth workers and ministers go as guests into young people's world, respecting their conventions and symbols. This some-times calls practitioners to make difficult choices about how they will live and work.

---

[2] To find out more about Christianity visit www.church.co.uk

Incarnation – a response from Dr Sally Nash

This chapter contains the seeds of a whole book or indeed many books! As the late Basil Hume wrote, 'None of us will ever be able to fathom completely the meaning of the incarnation.' Thus, reflecting on the implications of the incarnation for youth work *and* ministry should hopefully be a life-long process as youth workers learn more about who Jesus is, their own vocation and the situation and needs of the young people they work with.

This chapter helpfully brings theory and practice together, illustrating how applying the value of incarnation to youth work *and* ministry can inform and enhance work amongst young people. An inevitable question in reading a chapter like this is: what would I have chosen to write about? Hopefully, others reading this will be encouraged to think about other theological concepts that can inform and develop youth work *and* ministry such as grace, salvation, or the Trinity, which may have been their choice to add to the four core youth work values.

Danny begins his biblical exploration of incarnation by quoting John 1:14. The Message offers a helpful translation of this verse: 'The Word became flesh and blood, and moved into the neighbourhood.' It is interesting to reflect on what for young people today *is* their

neighbourhood? It will not always be easy to determine geographically. Exploring how incarnation as a value can be interpreted among groups of young people who do not share a geographic location is an area that needs to be considered more fully. Communities on the web, or based at a school with a city-wide catchment area don't facilitate the living among young people that Danny speaks of (although I support wholeheartedly his views about the benefits of doing so where it is possible). Youth workers need to be present everywhere young people are, and changing patterns of young people's relationships will lead to new approaches to youth work *and* ministry.

An area I would like to challenge Danny on is in interpreting the incarnation with too great a focus on the individual youth worker to the exclusion of the broader team/ community context they work in. One element of this is exploring a corporate approach to incarnation as together we seek to be the body of Christ. I think a constant challenge to those in ministry is John 13:35: 'By this everyone will know that you are my disciples, if you have love for one another' (NRSV). Part of understanding the incarnation in relation to youth work *and* youth ministry is expressing it in our relationships with colleagues and managers. Young people are often acute observers and will assess our work and message in the wider context of how we live our lives and relate to one another. My experience (of nearly twenty years of supporting youth workers) suggests that expressing the incarnation in relation to those we work alongside is often much harder than doing it with young people, but is equally vital. We need to live out the incarnation in a way that reflects rather than distorts the image of Christ.

When you do youth work among those who are poor and marginalised, as Danny talks about in his section on

'Incarnation and inclusion', it is hard to avoid confronting wider political and social issues. This structural as opposed to personal understanding of the incarnation is not fully spelt out. Sider describes the ministry of Jesus: 'Jesus modelled what he taught. He not only announced the arrival of the messianic time of justice and shalom for the poor and oppressed, he also fed the hungry and welcomed the socially ostracized into his new community. His diverse circle of men and women, rich and poor, crippled and well, was a visible demonstration of the kingdom that he announced.' It is important to see the full implications of inclusion beyond just economic inequalities.

I appreciated the encouragement at the end of the chapter to seek Christ. It should be difficult to engage in reflection on the incarnation without using the insights to critique one's own life and practice in the light of that of Christ. The acknowledgement that this can lead to difficult choices is also important. Jesus was often misunderstood, sometimes by the people closest to him. I like the way Ajith Fernando, a YFC leader from Sri Lanka, puts it: 'But the call of God is often like this. It takes us to places which others regard as impossible, to do work which looks like utter folly. Of course, with the call of God comes God's provision, but we don't always see that at the start'. Pursuing the sort of youth work *and* ministry that Danny is talking about may lead workers to share this experience of being misunderstood; not an easy option to take – but this book helps to provide some of the rationale for doing so.

DR SALLY NASH
Director of the Midlands Centre for Youth Ministry,
St Johns College, Nottingham

Part Three:

Practice of youth work *and* ministry

Chapter 10

Fellowship

Few words in the Christian language can be as over-used as fellowship. For some it conjures up images of unrelaxed 'fellowship group' meetings that bring together individuals whose only common feature is a pulse, albeit weak in some cases. For others it is the after-service 'time of fellowship' shared over a cup of fairly awful coffee, poured from a giant rusty teapot, into a chipped blue cup that has, against all odds, managed to outlive the sanatorium it was redeemed from. If it is a guest service there might even be a plate of rich tea biscuits to demonstrate that Christians know how to live! Worse still is the dreaded 'fellowship tea'; people seated at poorly covered tables, being careful to eat only what they have brought and staring at drab walls whilst being careful not to be seen looking at their watch. I'm sorry, but I have had one too many fish paste sandwiches to get over excited about fellowship teas. Surely there must be more to fellowship than fairly awful coffee and fish paste sandwiches?

Understanding fellowship

You don't need to be a Christian to have fellowship. Broadly speaking, fellowship involves the participation

in, and sharing of, a common interest with a select band
of people. For example, I enjoy fellowship with a tragically small number of fellow West Ham United Football
Club supporters. We find our love of soccer, shared optimism and frequent disappointments bring us together.
Likewise, Luke used the Greek term *koin noi* to describe
the business arrangement between Peter, James and John;
it had nothing to do with their Christian commitment (Lk.
5:10). They were in fellowship together as fishermen,
probably with a shared boat.

However, when Christians talk of fellowship they
usually mean more than simply a shared interest or common goal. The New Testament writers used the Greek
term *koin nia* to convey a new richness. For them, it was
a common participation in God's grace. The common
denominator then became, not the shared interests of
members, but their belonging to Christ. Paul's favoured
description was that of being 'in Christ'. Whilst astro-
physicists, such as Professor Stephen Hawking, continue to search for the 'unifying theory' of the cosmos,
Christians maintain it is revealed in the first four words
of the Bible, 'In the beginning, God . . .' (Gen. 1:1). Just as
the fatherhood of God is not modelled on our human
understanding of fathers but is rather the primary source
of all fatherhood (Eph. 3:15) that gives definition to our
human fathers, so too God is the source of fellowship.
True fellowship can only be realised with God's participation and is made available on a number of different
dimensions.

First, God maintains complete fellowship with himself.
The doctrine of the Trinity is foundational to a proper
understanding of God. This reveals that Father, Son and
Holy Spirit co-exist together as separate persons, enjoying
perfect fellowship with each another. There are no
squabbles for supremacy; not even the occasional tension.

They are social beings who are so united together in their fellowship that they are best described as being one entity (Deut. 6:4). Because God finds all that he requires within the Trinity, he has no need to seek anything from outside. This is profound mystery to us, partly because our qualitative experience of fellowship is so different. God enjoys perfect fellowship.

Second, though God is in no way deficient, he nevertheless creates others to give expression to his creativity, and to spread the benefits of fellowship. God seeks ways to enable those made in his image (Gen. 1:27) to enjoy fellowship with him. It is a two-way process. God enjoys having fellowship with us and we, in turn, are humbled by the invitation. The account of the Garden of Eden (Gen. 1; 2) presents in my mind a picture of Creator God and created humanity enjoying fellowship with one another. I long to experience the same level of intimacy with God.

However, humanity broke off fellowship with God with the introduction of self-interest, greed and deceit (Gen. 3:8–10). It is not called the 'Fall' for nothing. Yet generosity is part of God's character. Whereas I sometimes selfishly seek fellowship with just those who laugh at my jokes (an even more select band than West Ham supporters), God is open and inclusive. He actively seeks ways to draw people in. He is gracious to include those, like me, who are flawed. With immediate effect, God set in motion a bold and daring plan to restore fellowship with his creation that would require total sacrifice on his part. This was only achieved by letting go of the precious fellowship enjoyed within the Trinity. Who can know the pain that he must have felt as God the Son cried out, 'My God, my God, why have you forsaken me?' (Mk. 15:34). Surely he took up our infirmities and carried our sorrows (Is. 53:4) so as to restore our fellowship with him.

Consequently, young people, like adults and children, can enjoy fellowship with God.

Third, having fellowship with God enables us to enjoy fellowship with other people. The Fall represented not only a break in fellowship with God but also a complete collapse in relationship between fallen human beings. Divisions emerged between Adam and Eve and, within one chapter, the first murder had been committed (Gen. 4:8). Being in fellowship with God makes it possible to be in fellowship with fellow humanity. I find it easier to accept others when I reflect on God's acceptance of me.

Youth is a time of identity formation. Young people seek answers to some of the big questions in life: Who am I? Where am I going? What do I believe? Who are my people? What are our rules? Consequently young people can sometimes react aggressively to reject those they fear may damage their own reputation or standing within their peer group. Their developing sense of self is less able to accommodate those they perceive to be either a threat or a hindrance. It is a sign of maturity when an individual is able to accept those that are demanding or different from themselves. There is, of course, no guarantee that all people grow to achieve this.

Likewise, a characteristic of childhood is an inherent self-centredness. Swiss psychologist Jean Piaget (1896–1980) viewed children as inquiring scientists who conduct experiments on the world to see what happens. For example, what happens if I pour baked beans over daddy's new West Ham shirt? With the close of what Piaget called the sensorimotor stage (birth to two years) children are able to recognise they exist separately from the external world. But it is only by the close of the pre-operational stage (two to seven years) that they have any comprehension that the world, and all its inhabitants, may not rotate around them as they once assumed. It takes

many years of experimentation for young scientists to exchange an egocentric world-view for a sense of 'otherness'. This can become all too apparent when they are called upon to maintain fellowship with others. Because young people mature cognitively – as well as physiologically – at different rates, wide variations of maturation can often be observed between those of the same age. Some more common responses are: Why should I? What's it to you? I can't be bothered. Youth work *and* ministry provides a safe and encouraging environment in which young people can begin to take on the needs of others.

> **To think about . . .**
>
> When have you observed young people
> struggle to accept one another? How have you
> responded?

The early Church was characterised by the quality of its fellowship. Luke describes how the believers 'devoted themselves to the apostles' teaching and to the fellowship, to the breaking of bread and to prayer' (Acts 2:42). So strong were the bonds of fellowship that people were prepared to deny their own needs in order to secure the welfare of others. Life in the new community was no utopia; there were examples of dishonesty, jealousy, heated debates and disagreements (Acts 5:1–11; 6:1; 15:1–31, 36–40). Yet, the sense of fellowship never weakened. Their fellowship with God enabled them to maintain fellowship with each other. Seeing young people display this quality of fellowship must be the dream of all those engaged in youth work *and* ministry.

Inclusive or exclusive fellowship?

Taking a high view of fellowship, whilst at first sounding noble, presents us with some challenges. If true fellowship is only made available to those who are 'in Christ', what of those who might be considered 'without Christ'? The Lutheran mantra of *sola fides*, or faith alone, has been used over the centuries to separate the 'saved' from the 'unsaved'. The very concept of church membership defines whether people are 'in' or 'out'. In the hands of the self-righteous, this has been used destructively to deny some people the benefits of belonging to a faith community. This hardly seems consistent with the value of equality of opportunity and the inclusiveness displayed by Christ himself. Is this how it is meant to be, or is there another way?

Throughout history Christians have sought ways to recognise those who seek association with the Church whilst not being in a position to subscribe to all its beliefs and practices. Of particular interest have been the children of Christian parents. Typically they attend worship services, but their status within the fellowship of the church has not always been clear. William Strange is adamant that Paul counted the children as being *in* the community of faith, not out of it. How does he reconcile this? Perhaps the answer lies with the 'catechumenate'. Originally the term referred to a process of oral instruction but has come to represent those who are on the social periphery of faith. The catechumenate offers a way of belonging without all the requirements of belief. Though originally used to demonstrate the inclusion of children, it is equally applicable for young people and adults who are inquiring about the faith; for example, those attending a Youth Alpha Course. The value of voluntary participation allows them to decide

whether or not to belong to the catechumenate; they are not coerced or tricked. Of course, at any time they can end their participation or benefit from the authentic fellowship found 'in Christ'.

In return, the Church values the catechumenate and undertakes to offer them its full support and protection – as if they were full members of the Church. In doing so, it creates a safe space for people to grow into, and out of, the faith. I believe this concept provides a helpful way of valuing those young people who seek association with the churches without necessarily wanting, at this stage, to adopt its beliefs and practices. It ensures young people attending a Friday night youth club are valued as if they were fellow members of the Church without any need for others to make judgements about their Christian standing. As is often the case, there is method in the madness. Such an inclusive approach to fellowship often provides young people with a safe context in which to explore Christian belief.

To think about . . .

How does your practice enable those on the fringe to enjoy fellowship? What else could you do to promote this?

Believing or belonging?

Faith development theories seek to explain how individuals acquire a concept of faith and spirituality as they develop through different stages of life. In this

context faith is not limited to a creedal statement of beliefs – such as I believe in Jesus Christ – but is used in its broadest sense to include an appreciation of meaning and significance. Whilst this may not conform to the succinct definition of faith being 'sure of what we hope for and certain of what we do not see' (Heb. 11:1), it nevertheless provides a useful insight into the ways many people appropriate faith. All models of faith development present a pyramid of sequential and hierarchical stages that individuals must progress through as far as they are able, starting from birth. Though the direction of progress is fixed, the rate or inevitability of progress is left unspecified. John Westerhoff emphasises the social dimension in faith development. In doing so, he draws upon Erik Erikson's (1902–94) eight stages of psychosocial development. For Westerhoff, a key developmental stage is what he calls 'affiliative faith'. Most commonly found in late childhood and early adolescence, this shows how an individual's understanding of faith is influenced by their social environment. Faith is based more on belonging to a faith community than to a set of personally held religious convictions. Only later, with 'searching faith', do older adolescents or young adults begin to question presuppositions. Westerhoff's model helps us to recognise the benefit of involving young people in a faith community, or fellowship of believers. Though they will later question the beliefs and practices inherited from the community, it at least affords them an opportunity to acquire faith.

In recent years there has been growing recognition that religious belief does not necessarily result in people seeking to belong to a faith community. Many people with strongly held Christian convictions are choosing not to participate in church structures. Likewise,

in post-modernity, people are increasingly looking for ways to belong to something before deciding whether or not to subscribe to its values. They need to belong in order to believe. This has important implications for youth work *and* ministry. Providing an imaginative and fun social programme is hugely important for those on the fringe. Part of the success of the Alpha Course must surely be the emphasis placed on meals; attending an Alpha Course is great fun. Weekends away enable young people to gain new experiences and a deeper appreciation of fellowship with others in the group. Offering young people the chance to represent the group in a sports team communicates enormous value and respect. A social programme provides more than just entertainment; it creates a context in which youth work *and* ministry can take place. It brings young people together, offers them new experiences and allows them space to determine whether or not these are 'my people'. Above all, it communicates a sense of belonging to all, irrespective of their beliefs or practices. The decision then to devolve power from youth workers to young people, inviting those on the fringe to become members of the project, becomes a logical next step. Why should membership be open only to the 'owners' and not to the 'users'?

The fellowship meal

The ultimate symbol of Christian fellowship must surely be communion or the fellowship meal. It is hugely significant in my own faith. Perhaps it is somewhat ironic then that such a means of grace should sometimes bring out the most self-righteous attitudes in 'believers'. Picture the scene. During the last verse of the hymn a select group

of people, mainly men, make their way to the front of the church and sit in a row on uncomfortable-looking chairs behind a table covered with a lace cloth. Everything is done with military precision and no-one but the presiding officer dares utter a sound. After a reading and prayer, the detachment stands to attention and is handed silver plates containing laser-cut cubes of bread. In total silence they work their way down the assembled ranks of believers until their plates are emptied. One by one they make their way to the back to take their place in their assigned aisle. Looking straight ahead, they stand to attention. The Regimental Sergeant Major then looks left and right before giving the silent command – a nod of the head – and the detachment makes its way back to the front, managing to maintain perfect line with each other. The process is then repeated as the wine is dispensed. Oh, such sweet fellowship!

It is hard to imagine anything that could be further from the original event. Knowing the hour had almost come, Jesus gathered his twelve disciples in an upper room for a fellowship meal (Mt. 26:20–30; Mk. 14:17–26; Lk. 22:14–38). It was to be their last supper together. Whilst they ate and drank, the disciples discussed the most recent events, argued and boasted of their exploits. So far there was nothing unusual about this meal. Towards the end of the evening, Jesus took what was left over and visually began to prepare them for the coming days. They watched as he broke the bread and poured out the wine. They could even hear the wine being poured as its smell filled the air. Then they touched the brokenness of the bread before finally tasting it. This was the taste of forgiveness and acceptance. It was a profound moment, but no one would have said it was ceremonious. And not a lace cloth in sight.

However, I believe the greatest distortion comes when the presiding officer, having said it is an 'open table', reads the warning given by Paul (1 Cor. 11:27–34) without setting it in the right context. In a stern voice he warns the company of believers not to take communion in an 'unworthy manner'. On occasion, feeling remote from God, I have thought it better to abstain than face the divine judgement – dispensed through the presiding officer. But Paul's warning wasn't directed at those who, like me, sometimes feel unworthy or distant from God. After all, Jesus had served the bread and wine to Peter, knowing he would deny him, and to Judas, knowing he was about to betray him. The fellowship meal is for those who know they are unworthy. Perhaps the only people who should not take part are those that think they are worthy enough to receive it and who thus deny their need of Christ. Instead, Paul issued a severe warning to those who used the fellowship meal to gorge themselves on the bread and wine. If, just as the detachment stood to receive the silver plates, I ran forward and grabbed all the bread, stuffing the whole lot into my mouth before knocking back the contents of every shot of wine – so as to leave nothing for the assembled company of believers – I would be eating the bread and drinking the wine in an unworthy manner. Absurd as this might sound, this was the situation that Paul encountered in Corinth. People were getting 'hammered' – a feat not possible in most non-conformist churches – as they consumed the entire contents of the meal, leaving nothing for anyone else. The sin was not so much their gluttony as the destruction of the fellowship. They showed no consideration for their fellow 'brothers and sisters in Christ'. Communion is a powerful reminder, both of God's grace towards us and our fellowship with each other. We are not alone, we belong together.

> **To think about . . .**
>
> Take a few minutes to reflect on your church's
> pattern of sharing communion. What does this
> say about the availability of fellowship, grace
> and belonging? How are young people invited
> to participate?

The values of youth work *and* ministry that I have
sought to develop in this book are directly relevant to an
understanding of the fellowship meal. Let me explain:

- *Voluntary participation* ensures that we are invited to
  participate; no-one coerces us. Just to be sure, we
  are required to opt in and are respected if we choose
  to decline. However, if we do choose to opt in, we
  become participators in this simple act, not mere
  spectators

- *Informal education* helps us to understand the significance of the meal; the re-enactment of the breaking
  of bread and the pouring out of wine provide a
  powerful and sensory object lesson that communicates to us the sacrificial work of Christ

- *Empowerment* enables us to benefit from the grace
  that is offered to us. Though we recognised our
  inherent unworthiness (Rom. 3:23; Eph. 2:1–3), we
  hear the words of forgiveness and marvel that God's
  love for us should be so lavish (1 Jn. 4:10). Consequently, we are empowered to realise change in our
  lives (2 Cor. 5:17)

- *Equality of opportunity* ensures that no one is denied
  access to this means of grace. Young and old; rich

and poor; those who, like Peter, are inconsistent in their attitude towards Christ; as well those who appear as 'sorted' as Paul, are all equally invited to the fellowship meal

- *Incarnation* makes possible the knowledge of God. It turns religious ritual into communion with Christ.

Because communion is the ultimate symbol of Christian fellowship many of those who do not consider themselves to be 'in Christ' choose not to participate. That must be their choice. But I believe there is merit in creating new rituals that are accessible to those on the fringe. After a group discussion about faith and belief it may be as simple as offering young participants the opportunity to light a candle as a symbol of their quest for direction. Alternatively, towards the end of a beach barbecue, young people could each place a piece of wood in the fire as a symbol of their belonging to the fellowship. The significance is often not so much in the symbolic meaning of the act as the invitation to share in the group identity. This affords those on the fringe the opportunity to experience a taste of fellowship. Some will seek the source of true fellowship.

Summary

Fellowship may be an over-used word in the Christian language but, stripped back to its original meaning, it offers young people a totally unique sense of identity and belonging. Ultimately, youth work *and* ministry offers young people the chance of fellowship with God. Though it is inherently Christian and loaded with powerful theological concepts, fellowship can be tasted by those who do not consider themselves to be 'in Christ'. By

creating opportunities to intentionally promote fellowship we heighten the probability of young people choosing to seek the source of true fellowship. So maybe fellowship is powerful enough to withstand the onslaught of fairly awful coffee and fish paste sandwiches. Bring on the fellowship tea!

Chapter 11

Worship

For many years youth ministry has attached great significance to the place of worship. However, many have come to associate worship with singing. In this chapter we review the basis for worship and explore its role within youth work *and* ministry. Young people have consistently shaped the Church's approach to worship and therefore we look for the signs of change that youth work *and* ministry will inevitably bring.

Coming back to the heart of worship

The Anglo-Saxon root of worship is 'worth-ship'; to worship is therefore to attribute value to something. Christian worship occurs when young people recognise God's worth. It is more of an attitude than an activity. It does not end with a service's closing benediction but continues at all times in all places. The value of voluntary participation reminds us that we are invited to worship God and to do so wholeheartedly. Some believe God is vain enough to demand that others heap adoration upon him whilst he remains aloof. This overlooks the quality of relationship that exists between the members of the Trinity. Father, Son and Holy Spirit attribute continual

worth to one another. The triune God is a worshipper and he invites us to become the same.

Christian worship involves an encounter with God. As we approach in worship we find him waiting expectantly for us. It is as if, before we even recognise him, he runs out to greet us. It should therefore come as no surprise that authentic worship is experiential. True worshippers engage with God in spirit as well as truth (Jn. 4:23, 24). This means post-modernity's love affair with experience finds satisfaction in Christian worship. As we engage in worship we find ourselves temporarily transported into another world where multitudinous angels worship God night and day (Rev. 7:11). For some young people the prospect of spending eternity in worship is anything but attractive; ninety minutes a week seems challenging enough. Of course, if heaven is to be the state of perfection the focus must be on the quality, not the quantity, of existence. Youth work *and* ministry enables young people to become investigators, testing the authenticity of each experience. Without succumbing to destructive cynicism, it encourages critical inquiry.

Worship is primarily an act of submission. Just as citizens worship a monarch by submitting to their rule, so we worship God by submitting to his lordship. As King of kings and Lord or lords God deserves absolute, unreserved and unconditional worship. Ultimately we worship him, not because we agree with his values, but because he is all-powerful God. Therefore, whilst God's open and generous nature may be appealing to many, we would still be required to worship him even if he was a cruel and unjust despot. We might begrudge such worship but what choice would we have? This disturbing, yet important, principle prevents us from forming God in our own image.

Fortunately, God is not a cruel and unjust despot. He does not condone racist and sexist attitudes, or exploit the dispossessed. He is neither emotionally unmoved nor aloof from his creation. Instead, he is gracious and compassionate, slow to anger and quick to forgive. Because God is the sum of all perfection, worship is the natural response of an awe-struck creation. We submit willingly to his lordship because it is empowering to do so. Of course we worship God because of what he has done but principally we worship him because of who he is.

To think about . . .

If God was a cruel despot to what extent would you still be willing to worship him?

Many are the words we sing

Songs have always featured in Christian worship (Ex. 15:1–18, 20, 21; Ps. 96:1, 2; 150; Lk. 1:46–55; 1 Cor. 14:26). Whether it's been revivalist hymns, unaccompanied puritan or Gaelic psalms or the exuberant sound of massed choirs, Christians have always maintained a strong musical tradition. Many of the great hymn writers, like Charles Wesley, used hymns for educational purposes. As well as being lively and participative acts of worship, their songs enabled those unable to read to still learn about God. These hymns were rich in doctrine and aided the memorisation of Scripture. There remains a place for songs with strong lyrical content in modern Christian

worship. They can form an important element of young people's informal education. Yet, not all of today's songs lend themselves to such use.

Many of today's young people have come to equate worship with corporate singing. This can be quite unhelpful for those self-conscious about their developing voices and identity formation. Certainly as a teenager I hated singing. I could never be too sure what sound my croaky voice would make. And anyway, wasn't singing just for kids? The quality of young people's participation can be improved by inviting them to select from varied forms of worship. Youth work *and* ministry utilises a diverse portfolio, such as dance, audio-visuals, painting, poetry and creative writing. When all these are combined simultaneously the effect can be quite stunning. Whilst some sing songs about God the Creator, others may be painting a giant backdrop of mountains, fields and streams or reflecting on moving images of plant life interspersed with Bible readings. Such settings afford young people freedom to opt in or out and to construct their own pathway to Christian worship.

Youth work *and* ministry looks for creative ways to enable young people to express themselves in culturally appropriate ways. Pete Ward acknowledges that youth culture has its own subcultural expressions of celebration, lamentation and community life and that these can form the building blocks for new expressions of worship. Just as the Early Church discovered that Greek communities needed freedom to worship God in ways different from that of Jewish communities, so too young people must be free to find their own expressions of worship. Adults should not be surprised if and when they adopt different modes. Andy Hickford argues that history shows adults soon fall into line!

This means making full use of the God-given senses of sight, sound, touch, smell and taste. When youth worker at Altrincham Baptist Church[1] I used to take groups of young people to the local Anglican parish church to view their artefacts and stained glass windows. Many found a deep sense of mystery and awe in this peaceful building that they hadn't experienced in their non-conformist church. On other occasions, meditations on works of art were fused with sounds of flowing streams. I shall never forget making playdough for 300 people so that they could experience what it feels like to be like clay in the potter's hand (Jer. 18:1–10); I burnt my fingers on the bottom of the pan and had to lead the whole service concealing my fingers in a glass of water! The opportunities are restricted only by the limits to our own imagination.

> *To think about . . .*
>
> What would be the impact on you and the young people you served if all songs were removed from public worship? To what extent do you encourage other forms of worship?

The charismatic movement was born during the 1960s hippie revolution. Whilst Simon and Garfunkel sang of love and peace, the Jesus Revolution introduced greater informality to Christian worship. Mirroring elements of popular youth culture, it replaced church organs with guitars and drums and introduced the melodic folk

---

[1] www.altbapt.clara.net

songs that have become typical of mainstream evangelical worship today. Young people can be forgiven for not appreciating the struggle that many of their grandparent's generation went through to introduce choruses. Now there is need for another Jesus revolution and once again I suspect young people will lead the way.

When I became a Christian back in 1983 the first chorus I remember singing was 'Majesty'. I have been singing songs like it ever since. It seems there is only so much variation that can be achieved with the chords of G, C and D on a guitar. After twenty years of worship I can now listen to the first two lines of a new song and be able to sing the rest as if I had heard it many times before. The truth is, elements of evangelical worship have become a bit too predictable for me. Then, every so often I encounter something that requires me to switch out of 'automatic pilot' mode. Suddenly I don't know what is going to happen next and am disturbed by my own reticence. I find this both challenging and refreshing. Examples that spring to mind include: sitting cross-legged on a stone floor for three hours in south India listening to a translation from Telugu into English; repeating a chorus twenty times or more at the Oldbury New Testament Church of God in Birmingham, England; dancing to 'techno' music at Spring Harvest[2] as Back to Back Theatre Company led worship; encountering Kevin Prosche's world music for the first time at Soul Survivor;[3] and recently singing 'Give me oil in my lamp, keep me burning' with a group of young Christians in Holland.

Worship should at times be surprising if for no other reason than we are surprised by some of the places we

[2] www.springharvest.org
[3] www.soulsurvivor.com

encounter God. Youth work *and* ministry finds ways to maintain the elements of surprise and mystery. It does not necessarily offer explanation for every activity or make worship 'foolproof'. It challenges young people's traditions and fears and leaves them wrestling with the unusual and disturbing. Worship has to be a conscious response towards God with little need for 'autopilot' mode.

To think about ...

When was the last time you were surprised during worship?

This is the sound of a generation rising

In recent years there has been an increasing attempt to provide more youth-friendly expressions of worship. New services targeted specifically at young people have been established. Due to their unconventional use of dance music, post-modern liturgy and symbolic imagery, many of these were originally labelled as 'alternative worship'. Pete Ward rightly argues against this, affirming that they remain legitimate expression of orthodox Christian worship – albeit in a more contemporary form. Many of these youth services have encouraged young people to think for themselves and get the most out of worship. Peter Brierley's research indicates that areas with the highest concentration of youth worship services record higher levels of young people's church attendance. It has indeed been my experience that when young people

are given opportunity to engage with worship in safe settings they are more likely to participate in mainstream, intergenerational services.

Regrettably, the spectacular collapse of the Nine O'Clock Service in Sheffield, England, damaged the credibility of other projects untainted by manipulation and abuse. Without a credible alternative, youth worship has reverted to a more conventional form. Now it typically involves a band leading a young congregation in dynamic singing. Less emphasis is placed on the creative arts, youth participation or diversity. In some cases, there is little need for young people to think for themselves or to become part of the worship creation. Those leading the services do all the thinking and creating; young people's role is merely to respond. Despite their lack of creativity and youth participation, the emphasis on discipleship and personal example (1 Tim. 4:12–14) has found favour with many young people. They cannot therefore be dismissed.

Ego worship

A mantra for today's post-modern commercial world must surely be 'me, myself and I'. Far from indicating progress, this appears to signify regressive immaturity. We see this in human development. After a few months of experimentation, each baby concludes it is the centre of the universe. And it's not hard to see why. When you cry, people come running with food, milk and clean clothes. Gurgle and the whole world gurgles with you! If you howl, people will go to extraordinary lengths to pacify you! It is not long before babies can make their previously sane carers hop on one leg, moo like cows and bang their heads with feeding bowls; all whilst singing

'I'm a little teapot'. Believe me; I've been there, done that, spoilt the T-shirt! Babies must take great delight in testing their theory to the limits of parental tolerance. Developmental psychologists describe this immature understanding of self as being egocentric.

Then one fateful day the toddler cries but nothing happens. Even the best howl no longer brings people running. With time, the young child gradually begins to realise that they share the universe with others. They become aware that not everything revolves around them. This is a hard but necessary lesson to learn if maturity is to be realised. Of course, not everyone develops at the same rate. Some take longer than others to appropriate learning. Consequently some people in physiologically mature bodies can display immature attitudes to self and others. As any counsellor will tell you, this can hinder the formation of human attachments in later life. However, I believe egocentric attitudes can also impede people's ability to worship God. Let me explain.

In contrast to most traditional hymns, many of the new worship songs are written in the first person. A cursory glance at an alphabetical catalogue of songs reveals the greatest concentration is listed under 'I'. These songs describe the attitude and standing of the individual, with little cognisance of the corporate nature of faith. Consequently thousands of people can gather to worship, standing in close proximity to each other without entering into communion with each other. Some egocentric worship services appear reminiscent of aerobic exercise classes in that they comprise a hall full of individuals using the same beat to do their own thing. This misses the point. To be a Christian is to be a member of the body of Christ. There is a powerful communal dimension to Christianity. Youth work *and* ministry, with its commitment to inter-dependence, is well placed to

help young people appreciate the corporate nature of worship.

> ### To think about . . .
>
> What proportion of the worship songs you use are written in the first person?

In some circles, worship has become even more egocentric with the focus of song content diverted away from God onto the believer. Rather than describing God's attributes and actions, they affirm the attributes and actions of the individual. Through these songs, worshippers proclaim their devotion and loyalty to God using bold and emphatic language. Positively, these songs facilitate an emotionally intimate response that is quite proper in Christian worship. Negatively, however, they can be excluding and disempowering. There are times when I cannot claim total devotion to God. Some days I simply don't feel very Christian. I may not be putting God above all else, or able to say with absolute certainty I will love God until I die. Do not misunderstand me. It is not that I am uncertain of my faith; I simply have the odd 'off' day. On these occasions I am presented with a dilemma: do I sing the songs, knowing that I am proclaiming untruths and thus confirming my fraudulence; or do I abstain from singing, knowing there is no half-way measure and thus confirming my deficiency? With egocentric worship it is all or nothing.

True worship is God-centric not egocentric. It is about acknowledging that, despite all our God-given talents and attributes, there is One who is infinitely

more powerful, loving and wise than us. In worship we proclaim God's attributes, not our own. I believe it is unhealthy to go through life believing in one's own invincibility. We remain mere mortals. Youth work *and* ministry enables young people to become more fully human. This is achieved when young people begin to appreciate they are not the centre of the universe. For Christians this involves submitting to God's rule.

Some people on some days find egocentric worship songs empowering. I know I do. They provide a means to express devotion in personal and intimate ways. Yet, the same songs can also be quite disempowering at times. Participants unable to proclaim total devotion are left feeling emotionally distant from God. It is not that they are unable or unwilling to worship God; they just can't use such bold language. Youth work *and* ministry does not measure young people's worship by the songs they sing. Youth workers and ministers help young people to express themselves in meaningful and accessible ways. If this means using less emphatic language then so be it. Instead of relying upon the work of professional song-writers, youth workers and ministers should encourage young people to write their own material. This then creates a context for informal education concerning the nature and content of worship.

To think about . . .

How will you plan worship differently as a result of reading this chapter?

Summary

Worship is a lifestyle, not an event or a song. The apostle
Paul said, 'Therefore I urge you, brothers, in view of God's
mercy, to offer your bodies as living sacrifices, holy and
pleasing to God – this is your spiritual act of worship'
(Rom. 12:1). As Steve Chalke, founding director of Oasis
Trust, quips, 'It's not what you do when you fall down
but what you do when you get back up that counts.'
Youth work *and* ministry invites young people to
participate in Christian worship and to do so as critical
investigators.

Chapter 12

Mission

Great Commission

If fellowship and worship is one half of the Church's mandate, then mission is the other half. Jesus launched a renewed missionary movement when he instructed his followers to

> Go and make disciples of all nations, baptising them in the name of the Father and of the Son and of the Holy Spirit, and teaching them to obey everything I have commanded you.
>
> Matthew 28:19, 20

Jesus had not come to save just Israel; he was the Saviour of all humanity. Gentiles, as well as Israelites, were to have equal access to his saving grace. Though an outrageous claim at the time, Jesus was simply continuing what had been started generations earlier. God blessed Israel in order that she might channel his blessing to the whole of creation (Gen. 12:1–3). Instead of accepting the responsibility of widening participation, they maintained their own privileged position by excluding others. Consequently the nation was divided and lost the

blessing. Tragically, traits of this attitude can be found in the today's Church; God's blessing is sometimes restricted to those that attend its meetings and live by its conventions. The role of the Church must always be to demonstrate that faith works, enabling those beyond its boundary to know that 'God is love' (1 Jn. 4:16).

The Great Commission applies to Christian youth workers as much as to anyone else. Youth work *and* ministry provides a channel for God's blessing to those in and beyond the Church. Those who work in secular settings have an opportunity to extend God's blessing to those their church-based colleagues sometimes find hard to reach. In doing so, they enter into partnership with God and have the assurance that, as they go, Christ is with them always to the very end of the age (Mt. 28:20). This promise was given in the context of mission because God himself is actively engaged in mission.

We must consider the definitions of 'mission' and 'evangelism'; for some, they are interchangeable; for others they are quite distinct. The Lausanne Congress on World Evangelisation stated

> To evangelise is to spread the good news that Jesus Christ died for our sins and was raised from the dead according to the Scriptures, and that as the reigning Lord he now offers the forgiveness of sins and the liberating gift of the Spirit to all who repent and believe.
>
> Lausanne Covenant, para. 4

It is apparent from this that evangelism has a narrower focus than mission. Evangelism is primarily concerned with proclamation, or preaching, and enabling people to respond to the message of Christ. Mission, on the other hand, is much broader. Michael Green maintains that it embodies the total impact of the Church on the world: its

influence and involvement with the social, political and moral life of the community and nation. I prefer to think of it simply as being the continuance of Christ's ministry to the world. It involves following his example: preaching the good news, proclaiming freedom to prisoners, bringing healing to the sick, seeing the oppressed released and proclaiming God's favour (Lk. 4:18, 19). The kingdom of God was a major theme of Christ's ministry and teaching. Through actions, as much as words, he spoke of the kingdom as being both a future hope and a present reality. Each act of kindness and every healing provided a foretaste of what was – and still is – to be fulfilled at the end of the age. Mission is therefore concerned with realised eschatology; demonstrating the justice, peace and joy of God's kingdom here on earth. Its activity is spiritual, political and social. As such, mission is far broader than evangelism but can include it.

> *To think about . . .*
>
> Do you identify more with evangelism or mission? Which is more appropriate in your practice?

Works and wonders

In recent years there has been a growing recognition that mission is holistic. It is about politics as much as preaching. Evangelical Christians have often claimed that evangelism must take priority over social action. However, John Stott challenges this by asserting that social

responsibility and evangelism are 'two sides of the same coin'. Mission is replicating the holistic ministry of Christ and cannot therefore be reduced to matters of the soul alone. There is growing recognition of the Church's work in the community. I recently spoke at a conference organised by the London School of Economics[1] on the role of faith groups in crime reduction; a few years ago such a conference would be unheard of. Christian mission can make a difference in very practical ways.

A reoccurring theme of John's Gospel is his use of signs. From the mass of material available to him (Jn. 20:30, 31; 21:25), John selected just seven miracles to represent the ministry of Christ (Jn. 2:1–11; 4:46–54; 5:1–15; 6:1–14; 6:16–21; 9:1–7; 11:1–44). These he used to reveal to readers who Jesus was and what he had come to do. We appreciate road signs, not for their artistic value, but because they point us in the direction we want to travel. In the same way, John intended his readers to look beyond the signs to appreciate their meaning. The signs pointed to God. Miracles were not confined to John's Gospel. Lloyd-Jones stated

> Go through Acts and in every instance when we are told either that the Spirit came upon these men or that they were filled with the Spirit, you will find that it was in order to bear a witness and a testimony.

Mission relies on the supernatural as well as the natural. Ultimately it communicates that God is able to supernaturally transform individuals and groups. For John Wimber 'power evangelism is a spontaneous, Spirit inspired demonstration of God's power through signs and wonders'.

---

[1] www.lse.ac.uk

A few years ago I gathered together a select group of youth workers, academics and church leaders at Church House to discuss the direction of youth work *and* ministry in Britain. We began by asking what is the purpose of youth work. Maxine Green, who at the time was the Church of England's National Youth Officer, declared that it is to help young people die well. There followed a rare moment of silence from the assembled group! However, I have reflected on her words many times since and believe she is right. Let me explain. All those that Jesus healed died sometime later. Even those that he brought back to life died a second time. Paradoxically, death is a part of life. Jesus said, 'unless a grain of wheat falls to the ground and dies, it remains only a single seed. But if it dies, it produces many seeds. The man who loves his life will loose it, while the man who hates his life in this world will keep it' (Jn. 12:24, 25). Sometimes it takes greater faith to prepare someone for death than to believe in their healing. Death isn't something to be beaten; rather it is to be embraced as a gateway to a new and better life with God. Miracles make an important contribution to mission but should never become an end in themselves. As signs they should point people to the Miracle Maker.

Mission fields

When I was at Bible College, every Monday before lunch there was Missionary Hour which, curiously, lasted forty minutes. It was not long before it was dubbed Misery Hour as, week after week, those recently returned – or sent back – from foreign lands told of their escapades. Many hadn't so much lived by faith as almost died by it. Some of my fellow students took up the challenge, and the cycle is now being continued.

The stereotypical image of missionaries is of those who leave the safety of their own country for distant shores. Mission is, after all, what takes place in other countries, right? Certainly *'panta ta ethne'* is commonly translated as 'all nations' (Mt. 28:19). Yet it can equally be understood as 'all peoples'. This implies that the Great Commission is not just to go to all countries, reaching out to those defined by their geopolitical residency; it is to engage with people of all ethnic and cultural groups. It is 'all peoples', however they define themselves. Sociologists have helped us to understand the role played by peer groups and tribes in adolescent identity formation. Some young people identify themselves more by their taste in music than by their nationality. Fans of Marilyn Manson across the world unite to display their tribal affiliation through their shared taste in music, clothes and make-up. They stand out in contrast to fans of manufactured pop, with their different cultural symbols. Likewise those, mainly male, young people who inhabit Games Workshop stores in order to play strategic and fantasy-based board games form another tribe. And so the list goes on. For youth workers and ministers, the Great Commission often involves going as far as the high street to engage with a local youth subculture. For example, there is currently a significant missionary move among young skaters. Christians have built skate parks, organised competitions and established magazines to support the skate boarding subculture. This 'niche ministry' has given young people with little formal contact with the Church an opportunity to explore matters of faith and belief.

Towards the end of the nineteenth century there was a significant missionary movement, led by Britain, Germany and the United States of America. Many of the today's mission agencies were founded when the British Empire was at its most powerful. It is not always easy to

see where missionary endeavour ended and Western imperialism took over. Many of the missionaries struggled to separate Christian values from their own culture and exported Western traditions wrapped up in portions of the Bible. Over a century later, I have visited remote rural communities in India where the only stone buildings are still the vast churches, with their spires or bell towers, which missionaries from the West thought necessary to build. Naïvely, and with little respect for indigenous cultures, they communicated that to be Christian is to be Western. That said, mission agencies have learnt significant lessons from past mistakes, with anthropology now on the curriculum alongside theology. The point is that youth work *and* ministry must not make the same mistakes. Working with tribes of young people beyond the Church involves moving from the familiarity of religious subcultures to the unfamiliarity of youth subcultures. The challenge is to do this without being imperialist; this requires ethical consideration. Just as the early missionaries struggled with the issue of polygamy and, in particular, what to do with the numerous wives of polygamous men, the Church encounters many young people whose lifestyle may be considered anything but Christian. How should we respond? Perhaps more importantly, the Church must conduct its mission ethically. Here, once again, the values of youth work *and* ministry provide a useful framework.

Mission ethics

In the film *Leap of Faith* Steve Martin played the part of a bogus revival evangelist who tricked people into believing he could perform miracles. He took their money as well as their faith before being stopped in his tracks by

a genuine 'act of God'. Regrettably, a casual glance at some of today's religious satellite and cable channels reveals that truth is sometimes stranger than fiction. I recently attended a service at which young people were literally forced to receive prayer whilst the congregation watched in approval. Clearly no thought was given to the value of voluntary participation or the respect of the young people's humanity. The Church knew best. Like-wise, some churches adopt a form of personal evangelism that is anything but personal, with members trained in 'hard sell' doorstep tactics. Again, this shows no under-standing of the value of informal education.

Conversion has often been understood as something done to others. This egotistic view is challenged by the value of empowerment. People ultimately respond to the Holy Spirit (Jn. 14:26; 1 Thess. 4:9), not us. Yes, of course, others often play a part but the decision to believe rests ultimately with them. A key stage in my own journey towards faith in Christ was attending an evangelistic meeting held in a huge tent on a stormy night on London's Blackheath Common. Children's TV presenter, Tina Heath, the London Community Gospel Choir and evangelist Luis Palau all spoke of what their Christian faith meant to them. There is no doubt that it had a tremendous impact on me – and this despite not being brought up in a Christian family. I shall always be grate-fully to the Luis Palau Organisation and Nancy Blaby, the American girl I fancied and who invited me to go in the first place (so much for ethical evangelism?). How-ever, neither of them converted me. Instead, the event, together with the small group I attended afterwards, pre-sented me with an opportunity to explore the Christian faith. After asking lots of awkward questions (usually with the aim of catching people out), I chose to believe. The answers I had outweighed the questions I still had

remaining. In saying this I in no way wish to suggest the Spirit of God was not at work in me. I merely emphasise the part I was responsible for.

Ever since Campus Crusade for Christ managed to reduce the journey towards faith in Christ down to the 'four spiritual laws', evangelists have been calling people to say the 'sinners prayer'. Many give a highly polished presentation and – if results are measured by the number of prayers said – may be considered successful. So why is it that so few respondents stick with their initial decision? Either they find Christianity deficient or their action was in response to something different from what was being proposed by the evangelist. Often those who respond to the invitation are signalling their interest in the spiritual journey, not necessarily to adopt the beliefs of the evangelist. Failure to recognise the nature of people's response or the significance of spiritual journey leaves people with little choice but to pull out. Likewise, pressurising people to become Christians, as well as being unethical, is also counter-productive. Young people who are not, as yet, Christians rarely identify themselves as being *non*-Christians; only Christians call them that. They only become non-Christians when they are asked to decide. By forcing people to make a decision before they are ready we push them to become *non*-Christians. Having declared themselves to be non-Christians it becomes harder for them subsequently to change their minds and become Christians. I am not suggesting that a decision does not have to be made; I am simply advocating that young people be allowed space and freedom to make their decision at a time when they are ready. This enables evangelism to become an empowering process that helps young people fulfil their own wishes in connecting with God. Even evangelism can be person-centred.

The values of youth work *and* ministry that I have been developing here are relevant to an understanding of mission:

- *Voluntary participation* insists that young people are given adequate information about what it is they are being invited to attend. Only then will they be able to make informed decisions. Out of respect for the individual and to avoid the charge of cult-like practice, the Church should never resort to anything remotely resembling coercion or trickery. At every stage in the process, young people must decide how to respond; they must be free to opt in or out. As such, they are active participants in the process

- *Informal education* ensures that young people's questions, interests and individuality are respected during the process of spiritual inquiry. Conversation ensures this inquiry becomes a two-way process. We start where they are at, not where we want them to be

- *Empowerment* reminds us that faith in God enables young people to become more fully human. This should not be imposed by those who 'know best'

- *Equality of opportunity* ensures that all young people are given opportunity to experience authentic faith and freedom to follow their own conscience. Not everyone will choose to embrace faith

- *Incarnation* calls us to enter the world of young people with sensitivity and self-sacrifice.

Youth work *and* ministry calls for humility and a confidence in one's own beliefs. We engage in mission, not primarily because we know we are right, but because we understand our struggles. Henri Nouwen, albeit in masculine language, says that:

A deep understanding of his own pain makes it possible for him to convert his weakness into strength and to offer his own experience as a source of healing to those who are often lost in the darkness of their own misunderstood sufferings.

This requires youth workers and ministers to be vulnerable (Lk. 10:3), lay aside their power (Phil. 2:5–8) and have confidence in both the gospel (Rom. 1:16; 2 Tim. 1:12) and young people's ability to make informed decisions. It involves a willingness to embrace conversation, not preaching; questions, not answers. With this attitude it becomes quite appropriate for youth workers and ministers to share their own beliefs and values. Youth work *and* ministry is definitely mission activity. Yet young people are not only the recipients of mission, they can also be active participants. The rise in short-term mission gives young people new opportunities. But how useful are they?

Short-term mission

Operation Mobilisation,[2] Youth With A Mission[3] and Youth For Christ[4] have pioneered short-term evangelism programmes. Thousands of young Christians have spent a few days or weeks away from home gaining evangelistic experience. Many have discovered a new confidence in themselves and their beliefs as a result. They have also benefited from the social interaction of working with others in a different environment. Short-term evangelism

---

[2] www.om.org.uk
[3] www.ywam.org.uk
[4] www.yfc.co.uk

programmes can therefore be developmental opportunities. However, it is incumbent on youth workers and ministers to communicate that evangelism is only one aspect of Christian mission and that evangelistic methods should never eclipse the humanity of the people being reached.

In summer 2000, as part of its contribution to Message 2000 with the Message, Soul Survivor and YfC, Oasis ran the 'ground level' social action programme. Over 8,000 people worked on community projects across the city of Manchester, in England. Those that worked with my church spent days in the pouring rain installing security locks and spy holes in people's homes. The sight of young people drilling holes in doors will remain with me for years to come. You don't have to be a criminologist to work out that levels of recorded crime would fall when thousands of strangers turn up on an estate. Of greater surprise was the length of time the levels of recorded crime remained low after the programme. It seems faith worked!

Sometimes young people participate in short-term mission projects in the belief that they will transform whole neighbourhoods in a matter of days, bringing about total and lasting change. Community action and development can't be done in six days. It takes years of commitment and the active participation of local communities. Youth work *and* ministry strives to ensure that young people understand the nature of community action. Stephen Timms, British government Minister at the Department of Trade and Industry, recently told participants in an Oasis summer project[5] that he first committed himself to living and working in East London after

---

[5] www.oasistrust.org/passion

taking part in a similar short-term mission project. In six days it may not be possible to change a community but it is possible to change the outlook of a young person. Who knows what they will go on to do? This is changing the world, one life at a time.

Another benefit of short-term mission programmes stems from the opportunity to travel. Two years ago I spent a week in Hungary followed shortly afterwards by a week in Cuba. Both were work-related visits (honest!) and had a big impact on me. I walked with Gabor through a former Russian Army missile base, the tunnels now draped in weeds, as he described what it was like to live with the constant threat of the West. Later I listened to some of Cuba's finest doctors describe what it is like to live on the standard ration of $19 a week, with no prospect of additional income. Before these trips I could write an essay contrasting these two political and economic systems. Now, I understand that I live under capitalism and my outlook on life – and faith – is inherently capitalist. The collective impact of the trips was not so much what I saw in others as what I learnt about myself. People from England often appear to act far more 'English' when abroad than when at home. Just look at what happens to English football fans abroad. One of the benefits of short-term mission, be that at home or abroad, is the opportunity it presents for young people to discover more about themselves.

Summary

Mission is at the heart of the Christian faith. Youth work *and* ministry must continue to find creative and ethical ways to enable young people to experience the justice, joy and peace of the kingdom of God. This requires

practitioners to demonstrate love, sensitivity and deep respect for those they engage with. Mission is also something young people should become participants in. Short-term mission projects provide an opportunity to test the validity of their faith and discover more about themselves.

Chapter 13

Conclusion

In this book I have argued for an end to the destructive duel between secular youth work and sacred youth ministry. Each approach has strengths and weaknesses and therefore neither can claim sole desirability. Youth work has increasingly focused on socially excluded young people beyond the Church but has not always known how to offer young people the possibility of change. At the same time, youth ministry has generally sought to 'reach and keep' the minority of young people born into church-attending families. Its success has been measured by the number of 'church kids' attending its youth fellowships and has been open to the charge of indoctrination.

I believe the duel between youth work *and* youth ministry has been misguided. Drawing from both disciplines results in the 'joined up' approach that I have called youth work *and* ministry. This enables youth work to provide for young people's spiritual development and youth ministry to adopt more ethical methods. The values of voluntary participation, informal education, empowerment and equality of opportunity help give definition to youth work *and* ministry. Though they were first grouped together in the early 1960s by youth and community workers, they helpfully describe God's attitude towards creation. Theology shapes and is shaped by these values

and consequently youth work *and* ministry provides the Church with fresh theological understanding. However, a more complete picture is not possible without the value of incarnation by which God became fully human in Jesus Christ. Far from diluting effective ministry with the young, youth work *and* ministry helps to sharpen its effectiveness, enabling young people to make considered and sustainable decisions to follow Christ.

There is nothing new about youth work *and* ministry. A review of history reveals that Christians helped to lay the foundations of the modern-day Youth Service. Many of today's well-known youth organisations began as Christian responses to the needs of young people. Prior to 1945 the Church performed many of the tasks now undertaken by the Welfare State. Since then the Church has experienced gradual decline. The exile of young people from the Church has been almost biblical in scale. Many evangelical congregations have struggled to engage with the changing context and so retreated into holy separation. If youth work went east then youth ministry went west. This has led to further decline. Now the Church is beginning to learn the art of engagement and once again young people are leading the way.

I am more convinced than ever that the Church has a vital role to play in serving the young. The Church has emerged as the largest provider of volunteer and full-time paid youth workers in England and Wales. Its buildings are available for community use in every city and town, and most villages. Furthermore, it is able to support young people's spiritual quest without succumbing to indoctrination. The Church's work with the young must once again be taken seriously.

Youth work *and* ministry serves as a challenge to both Church and State. The Church is challenged to look beyond its ecclesial walls and to develop effective practice

modelled on Christ's open and generous example. This requires greater attention to theological and biblical inquiry. The State is challenged to drop its ideological objection to funding faith-based organisations that subscribe to the values of youth work *and* ministry. It is neither necessary nor acceptable to fund only those organisations that deny their faith-based foundations. It is time for a 'joined-up' approach to youth work *and* ministry.

References

Chapter 1

Aikin, N., *Working with teenagers* (London: Marshall Pickering, 1988)

Ashton, M. and P. Moon, *Christian youth work: a strategy for youth leaders* (Crowborough: Monarch, 1995), 27

Brierley, P., *The tide is running out: what the English Church Attendance Survey reveals* (London: Christian Research, 2000)

National Youth Agency, *England's local authority youth services – the basic facts 1999–2000* (Leicester: National Youth Agency, 2001), 6

——, *National Occupational Standards for Youth Work in the UK* (1999)

National Youth Bureau, *Towards a core curriculum – the next step: Report of the Second Ministerial Conference* (Leicester: NYB, 1991) 16; *England's local authority youth services – the basic facts 1999–2000* (Leicester: National Youth Agency)

Ward, P., *Youthwork and the mission of God* (London: SPCK, 1997) 2

Young, K., *The art of youth work* (Lyme Regis: Russell House Publishing, 1999) 2

Chapter 2

Baron, J., 'The emergence of counselling as a profession' in R. Bayne, *et al.*, eds, *New directions in counselling* (London: Routledge, 1996) 17

Fletcher, D., 'Professional ethics' in D. Atkinson and D. Field, eds, *New dictionary of Christian ethics and pastoral theology* (Leicester: InterVarsity Press, 1995) 692

George, T., *Theology of the Reformers* (Nashville US: Broadman Press, 1988) 79

Green, M. 'A religious perspective for youth work' in I. Ledgerwood and N. Kendra, eds, *The challenge of the future: towards the new millennium for the Youth Service* (Lyme Regis: Russell House Publishing, 1997) 73

Hull, J., 'Christian theology and educational theory: can there be connections?' in J. Astley and L. Francis, eds, *Critical perspectives on Christian education* (Leominster: Gracewing, 1994) 315–316

Moynagh, M., 'Vocation' in D. Atkinson and D. Field, eds, *New dictionary of Christian ethics and pastoral theology* (Leicester: InterVarsity Press, 1995) 882

Nicholls, D., 'Professionalism – a true reality' in I. Ledgerwood and N. Kendra, eds. *The challenge of the future: towards the new millennium for the Youth Service* (Lyme Regis: Russell House Publishing, 1997) 127

Richards, S., 'Christian youth work – a contradiction in terms or a paradigm for engagement?', Unpublished MTh dissertation (Kings College, London, 1997)

Ryken, L. *et al.*, eds, *Dictionary of Biblical imagery* (Leicester: InterVarsity Press, 1998) 134

Chapter 3

Bebbington, D., *Evangelicalism in modern Britain: a history from the 1730s to the 1980s* (Grand Rapids: Baker Book House, 1989) 225

Collingwood, J. and M. Collingwood, *Hannah More* (Oxford: Lion, 1990)

Davies, B., *From voluntaryism to Welfare State: a history of the Youth Service in England Volume 1 1939–1979* (Leicester: Youth Work Press, 1990) 9, 10

Dickey, B., 'Going about and doing good: evangelicals and poverty c.1815–1870' in J. Wolfe, ed. *Evangelical faith and public zeal* (London: SPCK, 1995) 53

Fabes, R. and A. Skinner, 'The Girls' Friendly Society and the development of rural youth work 1850–1900', in R. Gilchrist *et al.* eds. *Essays in the history of youth and community work* (Leicester: Youth Work Press, 2001) 66

Jones, B. and J. Rose, 'Early developments of the youth service in Wales 1830–1917' in R. Gilchrist *et al.* eds. *Essays in the history of youth and community work* (Leicester: Youth Work Press, 2001) 28, 34

Jones, M., *Hannah More* (New York, USA: Greenwood Press, 1968)

Oldfield, C., 'The worst girl has at least 5% good in her: the work of the Girl Guides and the YWCA with "difficult" girls during the inter-war period' in R. Gilchrist *et al.* eds. *Essays in the history of youth and community work* (Leicester: Youth Work Press, 2001) 135

Royle, E. 'Evangelicals and education' in *Evangelical and Public Zeals* (London: SPCK, 1995) 127

Spence, J., 'The impact of the First World War on the development of youth work; the case of the Sunderland Waifs Rescue Agency and Street Vendors' Club' in R. Gilchrist *et al.* eds. *Essays in the history of youth and community work* (Leicester: Youth Work Press, 2001) 119

Tidball, D., *Who are the Evangelicals: tracing the roots of today's movements* (London: Marshall Pickering, 1994) 62

Turner, S., *Nice and nasty* (London: Razor Books, 1980)

Ward, P., *Growing up Evangelical: youthwork and the making of a subculture* (London: SPCK, 1996) 30, 33

Young, K., *The art of youth work* (Lyme Regis: Russell House Publishing, 1999)

Chapter 4

Board of Education, *The service of youth* (London: Board of Education, 1939)

Brierley, P., *Reaching and keeping teenagers* (London: Monarch, 1993) 23

Davies, B., *From voluntaryism to Welfare State: a history of the Youth Service in England 1939–1979* (Leicester: Youth Work Press, 1999) 18, 45, 57, 48

Hastings, A., *A history of English Christianity 1920–1990* (London: SCM Press, 1991) 454

HMSO, *The Youth Service in England and Wales* (London: HMSO, 1960)

——, *Youth and community work in the 1990s* (London: HMSO, 1969) 1, 38

——, *Experience and participation* (London: HMSO, 1982)

Logan, N. ed. *The New Musical Express book of rock* (London: Star, 1975) 163

Martin, W., *The Billy Graham Story* (Hutchinson, 1991) 91

National Youth Bureau, *Towards a core curriculum – the next step. Report of the Second Ministerial Conference* (Leicester: NYB, 1991) 16

Osgerby, B., *Youth in Britain since 1945* (Oxford: Blackwell, 1988)

Senter, M., *The coming revolution in youth ministry* (Wheaton USA: Victor Books, 1992) 110

Ward, P., *Growing up Evangelical: youthwork and the making of a subculture* (London: SPCK, 1996) 62

Wilson, B., *Religion in sociological perspective* (Oxford: Oxford University Press, 1982) 138

Young, K., *The art of youth work* (Lyme Regis: Russell House Publishing, 1999)

Chapter 5

Baker, J., *The fourth partner: participant or consumer?* (Leicester: Youth Work Press, 1996) 1

Breen, M., *Outside in: reaching unchurched young people today* (Milton Keynes: Scripture Union, 1993) 37, 38

George, T., *Theology of the reformers* (Nashville: Broadman Press, 1988) 233

Gray, T. and C. Sinkinson, *Reconstructing theology: a critical assessment of the theology of Clark Pinnock* (Carlisle: Paternoster Press, 2000)

Nouwen, H., *The return of the prodigal son* (London: Darton, Longman & Todd, 1994) 95

Pinnock, C. *et al.*, *The openness of God* (Downers Grove, IL: InterVarsity Press, 1994) 41

Pinnock, C., 'An inclusivist view' in D. Okholm and T. Phillips, eds, *Four views on salvation in a pluralistic world* (Grand Rapids: Zondervan, 1995) 100

Stott, J., *The message of Ephesians* (Leicester: IVP, 1979) 134

Thompson Report, *The report of the Review Group on the Youth Service in England* (1982) 5.17

Whitehead, A., *Process and reality*, D. Griffin and D. Sherburne, eds. (New York: Free Press, 1929) 348

Young, K., 'Youth worker as guide, philosopher and friend: the realities of participation and empowerment' in S. Banks, ed., *Ethical issues in youth work* (London: Routledge, 1999) 85

Chapter 6

Boshers, B., *Student ministry for the 21st Century* (Grand Rapids: Zondervan, 1997) 227

Dewey, J., *How we think* (New York: D. C. Heath, 1933) 212.

Green, M., 'The youth worker as converter' in S. Banks, ed., *Ethical issues in youth work* (London: Routledge, 1999) 118

Green, M. and C. Christian, *Accompanying* (London: Church House, 1998) 2

Krallmann, G., *Mentoring for mission* (Hong Kong: Jensco, 1992) 32

Lewis, R. and G. Lewis, *Learning to preach like Jesus* (Wheaton: Crossway Books, 1989) 22

Mahoney, J., 'What is informal education?' in L. Deer Richards and M. Wolfe, eds, *Principles and practices of informal education* (London: Routledge Falmer, 2001) 31

Stott, J., *The message of the Sermon on the Mount* (Leicester: IVP, 1978) 15

Young, K., *The art of youth work* (Lyme Regis: Russell House, 1999) 43

Chapter 7

Green, M. and C. Christian, *Accompanying* (London: Church House, 1998) 13

Furlong, A. and F. Cartmel, *Young people and social change: individualization and risk in late modernity* (Buckingham: Open University Press, 1997) 97

Hickford, A., *Essential youth: why your Church needs young people* (Eastbourne: Kingsway, 1998)

Jeffs, T. and M. Smith, *Informal education: conversation, democracy and learning* (Derby: Education Now, 1996) 11

Chapter 8

Bridger, F., 'Equality' in D. Atkinson and D. Field, eds, *New dictionary of Christian ethics and pastoral theology* (Leicester: InterVarsity Press, 1995) 352

Millam, R., *Anti-discriminatory practice: a guide for workers in childcare and education* (London: Cassell, 1996) 196

Newbigin, L., *The Gospel in a pluralist society* (London: SPCK, 1989)

Phillipson, J., *Practicing equality* (CCETSW, 1992) 14, 15

Chapter 9

Edwards, R., 'The pagan doctrine of the absolute unchangeableness of God', *Religious studies 14* (1978) 305–13

Heschel, A., *The Prophets* (New York: Harper & Row, 1962) 241

Holman, B., *Kids at the door* (London: Basil Blackwell, 1981)

——, *Kids at the door revisited* (Lyme Regis: Russell House Publishing, 2000)

Moltmann, J., *The crucified God: The cross of Christ as the foundation and criticism of Christian theology* (London: SCM Press, 1973)

Ward, P., *Youthwork and the mission of God* (London: SPCK, 1997) 93

Chapter 10

Fowler, J. *et al.*, *Stages of faith and religious development* (London: SCM Press, 1992)

Hawking, S., *A brief history of time* (London: Bantam, 1988)

Stott, J., *The message of Ephesians* (Leicester: IVP, 1979) 133

Strange, W., *Children in the Early Church* (Carlisle: Paternoster, 1996) 71

Westerhoff, J., *Will our children find faith?* (New York: Seabury Press, 1976)

Chapter 11

Brierley, P., *The tide is running out: what the English Church Attendance Survey reveals* (London: Christian Research, 2000)

Hickford, A., *Essential youth: why your Church needs young people* (Eastbourne: Kingsway, 1998)

Howard, R., *The rise and fall of the Nine O' Clock Service* (London: Mowbray, 1996)

Ward, P., *Worship and youth culture* (London: HarperCollins, 1993)

——, *Youthwork and the mission of God* (London: SPCK, 1997) 127

Chapter 12

Allison, N., 'The contribution of cultural anthropology to missiology' in E. Rommen and G. Corwin, eds, *Missiology and the social sciences* (Pasadena: Evangelical Missiological Society, 1996) 30

Bosch, D., *Transforming mission: paradigm shifts in theology of mission* (New York: Orbis, 1991) 64

Green, M., *Evangelism through the local church* (London: Hodder & Stoughton, 1999) 9, 118

Langley, M., 'Morality of mission' in D. Atkinson and D. Field, eds, *New dictionary of pastoral theology and ethics* (Leicester: IVP, 1995) 596

Lloyd-Jones, M., *Joy unspeakable* (Eastbourne: Kingsway, 1984) 75

Nouwen, H., *The wounded healer* (London: Darton, Longman & Todd, 1979), 87

Tasker, R., *John* (Leicester: IVP, 1983) 27

Stott, J., *Christian mission in the modern world* (Leicester: IVP, 1975) 22

Wimber, J., *Power evangelism* (London: Hodder & Stoughton, 1985) 46

Wright, N., *The radical evangelical* (London: SPCK, 1996) 128

Youthwork – the Partnership

Oasis, the Salvation Army, Spring Harvest, Youth For Christ and Youthwork Magazine are working together to equip and resource the Church for effective youth work and ministry.

Youthwork – the Initiatives

1. *Youthwork – the Conference*
   - An annual training conference to inspire, network and equip – managed by Spring Harvest.
   www.youthworkconference.co.uk

2. *Youthwork – the Magazine*
   - A monthly magazine providing ideas, resources and guidance – managed by CCP.
   www.youthwork.co.uk

3. *Youthwork – the Foundation Course*
   - A nine-session/18-hour course for volunteer youth workers – managed by Oasis Youth Action, with support from the Salvation Army.
   www.oasistrust.org/youthworkcourse

4. *Youthwork – the Website*

- A gateway to online resources, community, information and learning – managed by Youthwork Magazine

  www.youthwork.co.uk

5. *Youthwork – the Resources*

- A range of books and materials edited by Danny Brierley and John Buckeridge – managed by Spring Harvest Publishing, an imprint of Authentic Media
  - Going Deeper
  - Developing Practice
  - Resourcing Ministry

Youthwork – the Partners

Oasis Youth Action, the youth division of Oasis Trust, empowers young people and equips youth workers.

Oasis Youth Inclusion tackles social exclusion among young people and children. It offers mentoring, group work and sexual health/relationship education.

Oasis Youth Participation empowers those aged 14 to 25 years

- *Passion* mobilises young people in social action.
- *Frontline Teams* is a UK-based gap year programme (18–25s).
- *Global Action Teams* enable young people to experience life in different countries.

Oasis Youth Work Training equips youth workers and ministers

- *Youthwork – the Foundation Course* is a nine-session/ 18-hour programme for volunteers.
- *Youth Work Degree* (BA Hons/DipHE) is a professional training programme in youth work and ministry.

To find out more Oasis Youth Action:

Visit: www.OasisTrust.org/YouthAction

Email: YouthAction@OasisTrust.org

Phone: (+44) 20 7450 9044.

Write to: Oasis Youth Action, 115 Southwark Bridge Road, London SE1 0AX, England.

Salvation Army Youth Ministry Unit

The Youth Ministry Unit exists to resource and develop youth work in 1,000 Salvation Army centres around the UK and the Republic of Ireland. It works with the Salvation Army's 18 divisional headquarters to implement local strategies for corps/churches, church plants, youth congregations, social centres and youth inclusion projects. In creating leadership development and mission training programmes for young people, young adults and

youth workers, the unit is constantly engaged in developing leaders and missionaries for a twenty-first century Church. In pioneering new projects and programmes, the unit is committed to developing new models of mission. In prioritising the marginalised and the excluded, the unit aims to extend The Salvation Army's rich heritage of social action and social justice. It provides young people with regular opportunities to experience, and engage in, evangelism, worship, discipleship and social action within youth culture. At present the unit is developing a new sub-brand of The Salvation Army focused on young people and young adults. In all this the unit aims to equip, empower and enable young people to reinvent The Salvation Army in their own community, context and culture.

To find out more about the Salvation Army Youth Ministry Unit:

Visit:	www.salvationarmy.org.uk
Email:	youth@salvationarmy.org.uk
Phone:	(+44) 20 8288 1202
Write to:	Salvation Army Youth Ministry Unit, 21 Crown Lane, Morden, Surrey SM4 5BY, England.

Spring Harvest

Spring Harvest is an inter-denominational Christian organisation whose vision is to 'equip the Church for

action'. Through a range of events, conferences, courses and resources they seek to enable Christians to impact their local communities and the wider world. Spring Harvest Holidays provide an opportunity in France for relaxation and refreshment of body, mind and spirit.

Their Main Event, held every Easter, attracts some 60,000 Christians of all ages, of which over 10,000 are young people. This event also includes specific streams which cater for over 2000 students. Alongside the teaching programme, Spring Harvest provide a range of resources for young people and those that work in youth ministry.

To find out more about Spring Harvest:

Visit: www.springharvest.org
Email: info@springharvest.org
Phone: (+44) 1825 769000
Write to: Spring Harvest, 14 Horsted Square,
Uckfield, East Sussex TN22 1QG,
England.

YFC

YFC, one of the most dynamic Christian organisations, are taking good news relevantly to every young person in Britain. They help tackle the big issues facing young people today. They're going out on the streets, into schools

and communities and have changed the lives of countless people throughout the UK.

Their staff, trainees and volunteers currently reach over 50,000 young people each week and have over 50 centres in locations throughout the UK. They also provide creative arts and sports mission teams, a network of registered groups and a strong emphasis on '3 story' evangelism. YFC International works in 120 nations.

To find out more about YFC:

Visit:	www.yfc.co.uk
Email:	yfc@yfc.co.uk <mailto:yfc@yfc.co.uk>
Phone:	(+44) 121 550 8055
Write to:	YFC, PO Box 5254, Halesowen, West Midlands B63 3DG, England.

YOUTHWORK
MAGAZINE

Youthwork Magazine

Youthwork Magazine is published monthly by CCP Limited. It is Britain's most-widely read magazine resource for equipping and informing Christian youth workers. It provides ideas, resources and guidance for youth ministry. CCP also publish Christianity+Renewal, Christian Marketplace and Enough magazines. CCP is part of the Premier Media Group.

To find out more about Youthwork Magazine:

Visit: www.youthwork.co.uk
Email: youthwork@premier.org.uk
Phone: (+44) 1892 652364
Write to: Youthwork Magazine, CCP Limited,
          Broadway House, The Broadway,
          Crowborough TN6 1HQ, England.